T0244569

PEACE AND FRIENDSHIP

PEACE AND FRIENDSHIP

AN ALTERNATIVE HISTORY OF THE AMERICAN WEST

STEPHEN ARON

OXFORD
UNIVERSITY PRESS

OXFORD
UNIVERSITY PRESS

Oxford University Press is a department of the University of Oxford. It furthers
the University's objective of excellence in research, scholarship, and education
by publishing worldwide. Oxford is a registered trade mark of Oxford University
Press in the UK and certain other countries.

Published in the United States of America by Oxford University Press
198 Madison Avenue, New York, NY 10016, United States of America.

Library of Congress Control Number: 2022905367
ISBN 978–0–19–762278–0

DOI: 10.1093/oso/9780197622780.001.0001

1 3 5 7 9 8 6 4 2

Printed by Lakeside Book Company, United States of America

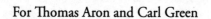
For Thomas Aron and Carl Green

CONTENTS

———❦———

ACKNOWLEDGMENTS

BEYOND THESE "ACKNOWLEDGMENTS," THE AUTRY Museum of the American West does not appear in the main text of this book. But for twenty years, the museum under various names has shaped how I think about connecting the past, present, and future of the American West. And it has decisively inspired the character and contents of this book.

As readers of the "Acknowledgments" of my first book, *How the West Was Lost*, will learn, my first visit in 1992 to what was then the Gene Autry Museum of Western Heritage ended badly. It led to an "anti-acknowledgment" in that book "to the thief who stole the notecards" from my rental car while I was inside the museum. I returned to Los Angeles four years later to join the History Department at UCLA, and, in 2002, I split my appointment between UCLA and the Autry. Among many awakenings, the next decade in which I divided my time between the academy and the museum brought the germination of this book. In its original incarnation, the core idea—how people in the American West got along and didn't—was not intended to be a book. Instead, it served as a framing question for an introductory space within an expanded and remodeled Autry National Center of the American West. Alas, that project did not happen (and for that, another "anti-acknowledgment," this one to José Huizar).

Upon coming back full-time to UCLA, I turned to writing this alternative history of the American West. I originally planned to take the book to the present. But I shrunk the chronology to the first century of the

American republic after I agreed to become the President and CEO of the Autry Museum of the American West. The deadline of a 2021 start date concentrated my mind and convinced me that I needed to get the book done before I took up the new appointment. I think of this as Volume 1.

This is not to suggest that my association with the Autry diminished this book's ambitions. To the contrary, my roles at the Autry prodded me toward a public-facing history that takes on questions that matter most. The roll of Autry staff, volunteers, trustees, and members who taught me valuable lessons about public history and helped me ponder whether, when, how, and why peoples found common ground is too long to acknowledge all the names here. Among so many who put the "we" in the Autry's West, I am particularly grateful to Carolyn Brucken, David Cartwright, John Gray, Michael Heumann, Brenda Levin, Gloria Mejia, Amy Scott, Jonathan Spaulding, John Sussman, and W. Richard West, Jr. I am also thankful for LA's frequent traffic jams (who has ever said that before!) as these gave me more time to think with Virginia Scharff. And a nod here, as well as a beer, to Josh Garrett-Davis for suggesting the painting by Kim Wiggins that adorns the cover of this book.

Although I have given pride of place to the Autry in these Acknowledgments, my debt to UCLA, where I have been privileged to be a member of the History Department for twenty-five years, is as great. Being chair of the department delayed the writing of this book, but funds from the Robert N. Burr Department Chair made finishing it easier, as did other generous research support from the university. More important, though, than UCLA's financing are its people. The roster of undergraduate and graduate students and faculty colleagues who sparked my thinking would fill several pages. Over the years, I've especially leaned on and learned from Verna Abe, Eric Avila, Ellen Dubois, Thomas Hines, Kelly Lytle-Hernandez, Ben Madley, Ann Major, Ron Mellor, David Myers, Thomas Rice, Teo Ruiz, and Joan Waugh. Brenda Stevenson belongs atop this list, the more so now for joining the Autry's Board of Trustees and joining me on the next stage of the journey. And I, like all who were fortunate to know and love them, continue to be inspired by Joyce Appleby and Gary Nash.

Beyond the Autry and UCLA, many institutions contributed to this book by providing me with forums to present and discuss the issues and ideas that play out in the pages that follow. In alphabetical order, they are Binghamton University, Brigham Young University, Claremont Graduate University, the Denver Art Museum, the Filson Historical Society, the Gilcrease Museum, the Huntington Library, the Kentucky Historical Society, the Kentucky

Society of the Daughters of the American Revolution, Louisiana State University, the Panhandle-Plains Historical Museum, Pomona College, St. John's University, Skidmore College, the Université de Paris 1, the University of Connecticut, the University of Missouri, St. Louis, the University of New Mexico, the University of North Dakota, the University of Oklahoma, West Texas A&M University, and Yale University. The Western History Association honored me with its presidency in 2016–2017, which prompted me to compose and publish a presidential address that rehearsed pieces of this book's Introduction and Chapter 3. Chapters 1, 2, and 4 update research that I initially did for my books *How the West Was Lost* and *American Confluence*, though put here to sometimes different purposes and sometimes differing interpretations.

I acknowledge the institutions that assisted me on the trail to this book; I cherish the individuals who have made the history of the American West such a welcoming home. The short list, of a much longer one, includes Katherine Benton-Cohen, Alfred Bush, William Deverell, John Mack Faragher, Andrew Graybill, Michele Hoffnung, Anne Hyde, David Igler, Maria Montoya, Elaine Nelson, Malcolm Rohrbough, Martha Sandweiss, Richard White, and my collaborators in the Western History Dissertation Workshop.

I had the privilege of working with Nancy Toff on *The American West: A Very Short Introduction*, a book in which I tried to distill the history of the American West into 35,000 words. It is fitting that she is the editor again for this book, which offers a longer history, an "alternative" one, and, thanks to her, a more readable one (with many fewer snippet quotes). Kudos as well to Don Fehr, for shepherding the deal that brought the book to Nancy, and Lena Rubin, who helped me get the notes and bibliography to the finish line. Finally, a shout out to Timothy DeWerff, who did an exceptional job as the proofreader for Oxford University Press. Alas, I have to take the blame for errors that Tim didn't catch.

Above all, I have gotten this book to its end and gotten along so well because of my family. The most immediate of whom are Amy Green, Carl Green, Daniel Aron, Jack Aron, Marilyn Aron, Nicole Aron, Paul Aron, Ruby Green, and Thomas Aron. My brother Paul gets here an added shout-out for bringing his superb editorial skills to the manuscript. Because of his pruning, my best lines are on the cutting room floor, and the book is better for that. Finally, my father Thomas Aron died when this book was first being conceived, though his imprint is on it, as it is on me. As a bookend, my father-in-law Carl Green died shortly before I finished the manuscript. I hope he would have found *Peace and Friendship*, as he did so many things in his life, "delightful."

WHAT'S IN A NAME AND WHY I USE THE TERMS I DO

—————⋙∘◦∘⋘—————

IN THE INTRODUCTION THAT FOLLOWS this Note on Terms, I devote a number of paragraphs to defining and distinguishing between "alternative history," "alternate history," and "wishtory." As the reader will discover, I maintain that the first two of these are improperly conflated, while the third I claim as my invention. Because "Alternative History" appears in the subtitle of the book and "alternate history" and "wishtory" play out through the chapters, it seemed appropriate to explain my usages within the "Introduction."

But there are many more terms and names that figure prominently in the pages that follow, including some of the most familiar ones, which turn out to be problematic for a variety of reasons and deserve explanations for why I choose to use them. For starters, consider the mistaken conflation of bison and buffalo, so common in my sources and perpetuated in this book. More controversial, I suspect, will be my frequent references to the "frontier." Not that long ago, a reference to the American frontier would be conventional in a book such as this one. Not so anymore. Back in the 1980s and 1990s, Patricia Nelson Limerick made "frontier" a controversial designation for that era's "new Western historians." The "f-word," she maintained, carried too much baggage, linked as it was to Frederick Jackson Turner's "frontier thesis" that had too long ruled the study of the American West. "Frontier," in her influential view, trapped Western history in a nostalgic and racist mythology and so needed to be banished from the lexicon of Western historians. Against Limerick's indictment, an assortment of historians, including me, sought to salvage at least some of Turner's insights and to save the frontier, which we claimed was too deeply embedded in the public's consciousness to be jettisoned. Rather than a drastic amputation, a more surgical revision could remove the racist taint of a "meeting point between savagery and civilization" and leave the frontier more simply as a "meeting point," a cultural contact zone in which no single polity had established political hegemony. It is in that sense and spirit that I employ "frontier" here.

Arguably more problematic, is the way in which the adjective (and noun) "American" is used. Typically, and usually without any commentary, "American" becomes synonymous with people from the United States, and, more specifically, with white people or even just white citizens of the United States. That is how "American" was often categorized in the nineteenth century, and how it appears in many of the sources on which this book is built. To avoid confusion, I allow the view of the sources to stand. But I certainly am aware of how misleading this restricted, racialized, and nationalized categorization is. Indeed, at the center of so many struggles in the history of the United States and across its frontiers is who got counted as American and got to enjoy the privileges of that status. What's more, an argument that figures in this book is that the interests of "Americans," especially those inhabiting frontiers, and the United States (as defined by the authority of its federal government) were hardly identical, and, in fact, were sometimes at odds.

Then, we come to the problem of naming people who preceded Americans, who were, in fact, the First Americans, and who later cohabited with Americans on American frontiers. Indians, Native Americans, Indigenous People all have come in and out of fashion and all come with some baggage. In this text, I use them all, again while recognizing what's wrong with the designations. More often, I try to attach more specific tribal labels, or even more local clan and band ones. What has become more common in recent scholarship is to reject English (mis)translations in favor of indigenous terms and names. In the interest of readability and because I also translate French and Spanish quotations, I have chosen not to refer to individual Indians by the names in their own languages. But I confess I'm not sure that is the right decision.

The text is full of references to "pioneers," "settlers," "colonists," and "settler colonists." Most of those references, including the ones in quotations from sources, are to Euro-Americans. But I do not reserve those designations for white people, recognizing that Indians and African Americans can lay equal claim to each of these titles.

Introduction

———✦———

IT RAINED THROUGH THE NIGHT and into the morning of December 12, 1805. That soaked the members of the Corps of Discovery, the exploring enterprise co-captained by Meriwether Lewis and William Clark, who were still building cabins for their winter quarters. Located near the mouth of the Columbia River, Lewis and Clark designated this encampment Fort Clatsop, naming it for the nearest neighboring Indians. On the evening of the twelfth, those neighbors paid their first visit to the construction site. The Clatsop party brought a sweet black root and a small sea otter skin, which the Americans purchased "for a few fishing hooks & some Snake Indian Tobacco." Deciding the Indians "appear well disposed," Lewis and Clark "made a chief of one" of the Indians. In his journal entry for that day, Clark, never much of a speller, recorded the leader's name as "Conyear" or "Con-ny-au" or "Com mo-wol." Historians more commonly refer to him as "Coboway." And to Coboway, Lewis and Clark presented a small medal.[1]

This exchange was the first at Fort Clatsop, but there was nothing unusual about the proceedings of December 12. It rained most days during the winter that the Corps of Discovery spent at the western terminus of the expedition. In the months that followed, Clatsops visited frequently, usually bartering food for assorted goods. That kind of trading was commonplace through the duration of the Lewis and Clark expedition.

So was the gifting of medals to selected Indian leaders. For almost a century from the founding of the republic until after the 1880s, a chronology that largely coincides with this book's, the presentation of medals figured in the diplomacy between the United States and American Indians. For their expedition, Lewis and Clark carried 89 medals in four sizes (4 inches in diameter, 3 inches, 2.25 inches, and 1.75 inches). The smallest were leftovers from the administration of George Washington. The other three sizes featured an image of Thomas Jefferson on one side. The flip side showed a scene of clasped hands, one an American officer, the other an Indian, and bore the inscription "Peace and Friendship." The American captains made the first gift of medals on August 3, 1804, some two and a half months into their journey up the Missouri River. On that date, the members of the Corps met with an assembly of Oto Indians, and Lewis and Clark conferred one large, two medium, and four small medals on seven different headmen. Over the next two years and across thousands of miles, the co-captains presented 88 medals, including the one to Coboway. They awarded the last one a few months after departing from Fort Clatsop on August 21, 1806, a few weeks before their return to St. Louis, with one medal still in stock.[2]

In their journals, Lewis and Clark did not specify which of the smaller-sized medals they gave to Coboway. But even if Coboway did not receive a medal with the words "peace and friendship" engraved on it, Lewis and Clark likely spoke to Coboway and the Clatsops of bringing both from the United States to Indian peoples. It was a promise they made in most of the speeches they delivered during the expedition.

It was not a promise the United States kept; neither peace nor friendship readily associates with either the history or the mythology of the American frontier. What would histories of the westward expansion of the United States be without their famous battles and infamous massacres? What would "Westerns" be without their clashes of "civilization" against "savagery" and their climactic gunfights? Even as popular culture and scholarship about the American frontier have shifted their views significantly in recent decades, violence has retained its centrality. A chief difference between older and newer Westerns and older and newer Western histories is what was once celebrated for manifesting America's destiny and making America great is now decried for enabling the expansion of the United States. Conquest, not concord, has become the watchword of Western American history.[3]

Recent scholarship has attributed much of the terror that accompanied the territorial expansion of the United States to the potency and logic of "settler colonialism." In the beginning, according to these histories, European colonialism in the Americas rested on the extraction of resources and the exploitation of labor. To varying extents in the different North

An example of the medals bearing the inscription "peace and friendship" that were gifted by Lewis and Clark and other American emissaries to Indian leaders. This one features an image of then President Thomas Jefferson on the opposite side. *Courtesy of the Autry Museum of the American West*

American colonies established by European empires, the getting of resources depended on Indigenous principals, and trading followed Indigenous principles. In the English, later British, mainland possessions, however, agriculture, peopled by European settlers and often powered by enslaved African labor, supplanted other forms of colonialism more directly reliant on the participation of Indians. Over the course of the seventeenth and eighteenth centuries, these "settler societies" increasingly drove Indian peoples out. As the successor state to the British colonies, the United States inherited and amplified the imperatives of its predecessors. Like other settler colonialists around the globe, "Americans" (here, used as a synonym for white citizens of the United States) desired only the lands of Indigenous peoples and determined to take it from them. In the oft-quoted words of historian Patrick

Wolfe, settler colonialism in the United States and in similar settler societies around the globe required "the elimination of the native." What followed in this scheme were a series of bloody ethnic cleansings and even genocides, which cleared lands for uncontested American occupation.[4]

Although the explanatory framework offered by settler colonialism (and by empire, ethnic cleansing, and genocide) can tell us much about the ends and endings of American expansion, this book detours from this now main-stream of Western American history. Dark and bloody as frontiers have often been, this book seeks out sites and situations in which colonialism wore a different face and relations between Indians, settlers, and states deviated (for a time) from the monolithic logic of elimination. The episodes pro-vide evidence of barriers breached and accords reached, of erstwhile enemies overcoming their differences, of would-be combatants standing down.

Peace and Friendship presents "an alternative history of the American West," a subtitle I expect may confuse some readers. Traversing American frontiers from the Appalachians to the Pacific and from the birth of the United States through its first century as a republic, each chapter focuses on a particular locale in which foes faced off. Nothing alternative about that. But in these cases, violence was contained. The book's contents ex-plore how amicable relations unexpectedly developed at these sites—and why they collapsed. That is an alternative history too often forgotten or misremembered, leaving for this book to recover the record of concord and to plumb its lessons.

Before proceeding further down this less traveled path, let me clarify what I mean by the book's subtitle. Googling the term "alternative history" automatically directs to its supposed synonym: "alternate history." Click on the link and you enter a world in which historical outcomes have been altered. The most numerous of these works have the South winning the Civil War and the Nazis the Second World War. But this genre does not ig-nore Western American history. In a similar vein to imagined Confederate and German victories, there is Martin Cruz Smith's *The Indians Won*. In Smith's book, Plains Indians band together in 1876 to defeat Custer and hold together to consolidate their power and establish their own nation in the center of the continent. Taking the same starting point but making a smaller tweak, Douglas Jones's *The Court-Martial of George Armstrong Custer* lets the title character survive the Battle of Little Big Horn and then stand trial for disobeying orders and negligence. The deeds and misdeeds of fa-mous outlaws have also been the stuff of alternate histories. Consider Peter Meech's *Billy the Kid: A Novel*, which finds the once young outlaw, having escaped death at the hands of Pat Garrett, living peacefully as a retired dentist in Colorado Springs in 1932—until a tangle with bootleggers brings him back to gunfighting.[5]

No historian reading these alternate histories would mistake them for histories. The examples cited in the previous paragraph have only a distant relationship to the historians' craft. Like a Quentin Tarantino film, alternate histories can elegantly (and elegiacally) evoke a "once upon a time" and place, but the alterations to what happened turn his films and scores of similarly shifted stories into fictions, science fictions, and fantasies.[6]

More respectable in academic circles are the counterfactual speculations that have occasionally engaged professional historians. In these "what if" exercises, scholars have sought to emphasize historical contingencies by focusing on pivotal moments and accenting how uncertain were the choices that produced particular outcomes. Plausible shifts in one factor or another then support conjectures about what could easily have been. Even more sophisticated are the elaborate counterfactual experiments authored by cliometricians, in which vast amounts of data are marshaled in the service of manipulating outcomes.[7]

Few historians, including those who study the American frontier, pursue counterfactual possibilities very far. "Counterfactuals," suggested Adam Gopnik in an article in the New Yorker, "belong . . . on lunch counters, where people can debate at meaningless leisure." That's generally where historians leave them, tending to raise rather than follow alternate pasts. Anything more, as E. H. Carr suggested, is just "a parlor game." Or, as E. P. Thompson bluntly put it: alternate history is "unhistorical shit."[8]

I am not interested in altering facts, or, for that matter, in "alternative facts." Although the search engine conflates "alternate history" and "alternative history," the adjectives have distinct meanings. Alternate means occurring in turns or serving in place of another. By contrast, alternative connotes a choice between two or more things or existing outside the mainstream. The second definition applies to my understanding of alternative history. The history in this alternative history *happened*. It requires no "what ifs" to set in motion.[9]

The peace and friendship that happened on American frontiers were often unstable. Local arrangements that curtailed violence gave way when balances of power and powerlessness tipped. The interventions and arsenals of empires and nation-states, though premised on enforcing law and creating order on Hobbesian frontiers, disturbed the peace and devastated border-crossing friendships. The situations featured in the book, then, demonstrate the fragility of conciliations and reconciliations and show how susceptible this alternative history is to being forgotten or misremembered. Still, the episodes lace together to allow us to better understand when, where, and how people pushed aside their enmities, why these moments occurred yet did not endure, and what we might take away from the legacies of broken concord.[10]

The contrast between the legacies of concord and conquest might seem to set my alternative history entirely apart from the mainstream of settler colonial history. The one emphasizes people dealing with one another; the other has them stealing from one another. The one features fortunate amalgamations; the other forced assimilations. The one glimpses better times; the other exposes trails of bitter tears.

Yet the currents of current scholarship and of mainstream history do not divide so cleanly from this alternative history. While alternate histories push into parallel dimensions (think Rod Serling's "Twilight Zone"), this alternative history does not exist on a separate plane. It runs alongside the mainstream, revealing a contiguous face of the American frontier. Indeed, it may be useful to see this alternative history as an adjacent history of the American frontier.[11]

Not then in worlds apart, histories of concord and conflict should instead be seen as playing out along a spectrum. At different moments on the same timeline, often quite proximate, we find examples of relations moving back and forth from one end to the other, of people trading with former foes in one instance and raiding supposed friends in the next, of convergences coalesced and conversions coerced, of truces between empires, nations, families, and communities brokered and broken. The shifts meant the common ground found was also lost. Accordingly, in the case studies that make up my alternative history's table of contents, accommodations were tenuous. Peace and friendship, while frequently heralded, rarely held.[12]

This recognition distinguishes my version of alternative history from the subset of alternate history that I refer to as "wishtory." I confess to some pride in the coinage of this term, which I use to refer to the history that people wish for. Or at least I did until I discovered that Sears had employed it in a 2008–2009 advertising campaign. Still, when Sears deployed actress/singer Vanessa Hudgens, fresh from starring in Disney's *High School Musical*, to peddle Christmas gifts in "an American wishtory," its usage was obviously not the same as mine. "Wishtory," as I see it, tells stories about the past, but fictionalizes them in ways that cater to contemporary yearnings. As with other alternate histories, "wishtories" are untethered from what actually happened. It's fitting, I suppose, that Sears chose a Disney star for its campaign, for Disney has long been a leading purveyor of "wishtories." Consider its *Pocahontas* (1995), which conjured a romance between the title character and John Smith, combined it with an eco-friendly message, and tapped into ascendant public longing for a kinder, gentler origin story for European expansion in North America. On such wishes (and hummable tunes) are blockbusters made. A decade later, similar sensibilities and yearnings for a "kumbaya" version of colonialism dominated many of the commemorations and cultural productions associated with the bicentennial of the Lewis and Clark expedition.[13]

Almost all "wishtories" project happily-ever-after illusions. In recent "wishtories," amicable relations, once established, are presumed to persevere. That's very much at odds with the episodes in *Peace and Friendship*. Nonetheless, "wishtories" do figure in my alternative history, for they are entangled with how the sites featured in this book are remembered and commemorated, and they, too, tell us much about shifting hopes and dreams.

Another qualifier is also necessary to insert here: the subtitle of *Peace and Friendship* is **An** *Alternative History of the American West*, not **The** *Alternative History of the American West*. The sites I have selected reflect some obvious choices and some more idiosyncratic ones. Some of the places in this alternative history appear in almost every history of the westward expansion of the United States; others show up in few such books. Ditto the individuals who figure prominently in these chapters. Several rank among the best known of frontier folk, others not so much. *An Alternative History* makes no claim to being definitive in its sampling of sites and its range of situations. It aspires not to be the last word, but to spark conversations about what it took for people to bond across presumed borders and to prompt searches for other times and places that fit within this alternative vein.

This alternative history starts at Chillicothe, a Shawnee Indian village in what is now the state of Ohio. Here Daniel Boone was adopted into the family of the Shawnee chief Blackfish, opening a path to peace and friendship between Americans and Indians. The story travels along with Indian and American pioneers from Chillicothe to Apple Creek in what is now Missouri. In their new refuge on the west bank of the Mississippi River, many of the people who a decade earlier in the Ohio Valley had been locked in a death struggle now lived harmoniously alongside one another.

The trail then moves across the continent to the edge of the Pacific Ocean, where the Corps of Discovery spent several months that did not quite live up to the "peace and friendship" stamped on the medals that Lewis and Clark gifted to Indian leaders. Nonetheless, the American emissaries avoided violent conflicts and traded for what they needed. That enabled them to proceed on with their explorations and succeed in getting back to the United States.

With the Corps, the trail returns east to examine changes around Apple Creek and the relations between Indians and Americans in the corner of the territory governed first by Lewis and later by Clark. Both men drew on the lessons of their expedition to promote a *Pax Americana*, though over time that translated into the removals of Indians through Missouri and from Missouri. Missouri then became a gateway for an assortment of traders and travelers heading farther west.

During the 1840s one of the signature landmarks along the principal road to Oregon and California was Chimney Rock, and the focus shifts there. In the imaginations of many then and later, Indians menacingly encircled covered wagons as they made their way past Chimney Rock and along the overland trail. The reality, though, more typically featured peaceful exchanges of goods and information, at least until this manifestation of peace and friendship began to give way in the 1850s.

This alternative history ends four hundred miles south of Chimney Rock at Dodge City, Kansas. Dodge has come to represent the West at its wildest, with rampant shootouts starring lawmen like Wyatt Earp. Yet, compared with many other parts of the American republic in the decades after the Civil War, Dodge City offered better possibilities for African Americans. It also boasted fewer gunfights than imagined and fewer homicides than other boomtowns in the American West.

It is fitting that Dodge City's most legendary lawman-gunfighter, Wyatt Earp, wandered to Los Angeles as early as the mid-1880s. There, Hollywood spun his story and other tales of the "Wild West" into movie epics and later into television serials. By the time Earp died in 1929 and through the next several decades, Westerns reigned. In the heyday of Westerns that stretched through the 1950s, the genre neatly sorted its good gunfighters from bad. The triumph of the former ennobled the violence that "won" the West.

These, we now understand, were "wishtories." Their plots and morality plays erased or forgave the messier ethnic and racial strife that shaped the history of the American frontier in the century after the American Revolution. Only in more recent decades have Western historians written in what the Westerns wrote out. Our "wishtories," too, have shifted. The preference for Disney's *Pocahontas* and the bicentennial Sacagawea speaks to our longing for a different kind of feel-good frontier tale.

That's not what readers will find in this book. But the alternative history tracked in the chapters that follow does push into view times and places where people unexpectedly got along. And perhaps, they prompt us to ponder anew how we might, too.

I

Chillicothe

Forget What Happened

TO GET TO CHILLICOTHE, THE Shawnee village that was the home of Daniel Boone for a few months in 1778, toss out your maps (which provide only the location of the current Chillicothe) and turn off your GPS (which directed me into a cornfield adjacent to Paint Creek State Park). Instead, head to Xenia, Ohio. From downtown Xenia, go north for about three miles on Route 68. On your left, look for the Tecumseh Motel, a place that has seen better days. In front of the motel sit several weathered historical markers that identify this as the ground on which a Shawnee village named Chillicothe once stood. Contrary to the name of the motel and one of the monuments which contends that Tecumseh was born "a few arrow flights south-east of Old Chillicothe," that nativity occurred at another Chillicothe, closer to present-day Chillicothe, some sixty miles (or far more than a few arrow flights) away.[1]

The signs and monuments in front of the Tecumseh Motel date from the early 1930s, when William Albert Galloway, the leader of the Greene County Historical Society, determined to bring a forgotten past to the attention of locals. A stone monument pays tribute to the "memory of Col. Daniel Boone and 27 salt makers, taken prisoners at Blue Licks, Ky. by the Shawnees, February 7, 1778, and brought to Old Chillicothe." The inscription elaborates that Boone and eleven of the captives were adopted by the Shawnees, while ten of the prisoners were held for ransom after being moved to Detroit. The fate of the remaining six, the marker concludes, is unknown. Another sign titled "Site of Old Chillicothe" notes that "the famous Shawnee Village" along the Little Miami River was "destroyed four times by pioneer forces." A second stone marker honors the ten Kentucky soldiers killed in an assault on the village in 1779; no mention is made of Indian casualties, including Boone's adopted father Blackfish, who was mortally wounded in the 1779 attack.[2]

Unrevised since their original erection, the monuments at the site venerate indomitable American pioneers sparring with and ultimately vanquishing Indians. They present a familiar history of the Revolutionary frontier in the Ohio Valley as a dark and bloody ground. And they celebrate the outcome of a generation of warfare that culminated with the United States wresting its first West from native peoples.[3]

In contrast to the on-site recitation of frontier conflict ushering in American success and succession, this alternative history begins by calling out what captors and captives had in common and how cultural borrowings

One of the historical markers erected in the early 1930s that marks the site of the Shawnee village of "Old Chillicothe" on the Little Miami River. This stone monument memorializes Daniel Boone and the salt-makers taken prisoner with him, who were brought to the site in 1778. *Photo by the author*

brought the worlds of Daniel Boone and Blackfish closer together. The Shawnees' adoption of Boone and several of his fellow salt-makers promised to close the gap even further and to open a path to peace between peoples by turning enemy into family. For Boone, the months in Chillicothe with his new Shawnee kin tested his allegiances. His decision to leave deprived him of a life that held undeniable attractions to him. It also significantly diminished the chances of peace or friendship between Americans and Indians in the Ohio Valley.

"We have always been the frontier." So claimed a Shawnee resident of Chillicothe not long after Daniel Boone's sojourn in the village along the Little Miami. The same could be said by and about Boone, who spent most of his life at the edge of European settlement and at its intersection with Indian countries. For the Shawnees, the observation called attention to movements over the previous 150 years that had taken them on a circuitous trail from the Ohio Valley southward to what are now Alabama and Georgia, then northeast to the colony of Pennsylvania, and then west back to the Ohio Valley. Their migrations and their adaptations to new countries, new neighbors, and new challenges made them pioneers par excellence. During their odyssey, Shawnees joined with other Indian groups and built new multiethnic communities. In Pennsylvania and then in the Ohio Valley, Shawnees encountered a heterogeneous assortment of European colonists and African slaves. Competition between Indians and Europeans for lands and resources bred conflict. But proximity also prompted appropriations that brought cultures together and created opportunities for individuals like Daniel Boone not just to live on the frontier, but to cross it.[4]

In addition to being the name of a village on the Little Miami (and several other Shawnee towns in various locations at various times), Chillicothe (or variations on that spelling) was one of five society clans that made up the Shawnee tribe (the others were Mekoches, Kishpokos, Pekowis, and Thawakilas). Connected by a common language, kinship ties, and shared rituals, the clans were assigned different roles within the tribe's cultural and political life. Traditionally, they inhabited separate villages, which were often named for the resident clan, where each maintained distinct sets of male and female leaders.[5]

In the early seventeenth century, Shawnee villages were dispersed across the Ohio Valley stretching east to west from present-day Ohio to Illinois and south into Kentucky. Like other woodland Indians, the Shawnees shuffled seasonally between summer farming villages, in which women took primary

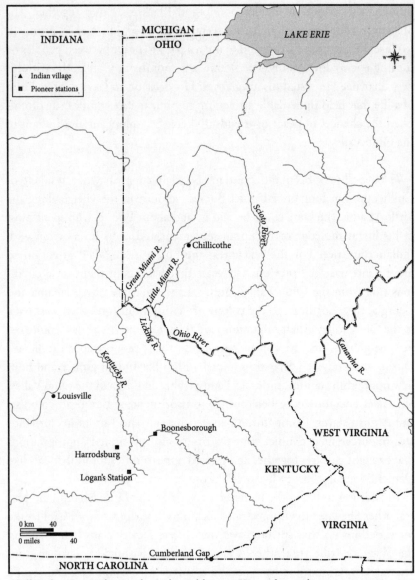

Chillicothe, Boonesborough, and neighboring Kentucky settlements in 1778

responsibility for growing crops, and winter hunting camps, from which men pursued game. When soils wore out and game thinned, the Shawnees relocated their settlements, typically to nearby areas.

The middle decades of the seventeenth century brought disruptions to the Shawnee traditions of local migrations and clan separations. The first wave of departures from the Ohio Valley occurred as early as the 1630s, apparently in the wake of devastating epidemics. Seeking refuge to the south, fleeing Shawnees established new towns in Alabama and Georgia. There, members from different clans mixed together to augment numbers. Shawnees who remained in the Ohio Valley, their ranks depleted by disease and outmigration, were then more vulnerable to attacks by Iroquois invaders. Those not killed or captured by the Iroquois hastened to join the Shawnees' exodus. By 1680, no Shawnee villages remained in the Ohio Valley.

Early in the eighteenth century, some Shawnees completed another long-distance move, this time to central Pennsylvania. This pioneering exploit put the Shawnees back into the orbit of the Iroquois. Based on their seventeenth-century conquests, the Iroquois asserted their dominion over the Shawnees in the eighteenth century. The Shawnees vigorously disputed such claims. In diplomatic councils with other Indians and with colonial officials, Shawnee leaders insisted on their independence from the Iroquois and on their freedom to deal with neighbors on their own terms.

In the first half of the eighteenth century, Pennsylvania presented the Shawnees with ample opportunities for interactions and exchanges with others. Numerous Indian peoples resided there, and the Shawnees developed particularly close associations with the Delawares, who, under pressure from an increasing colonial population, had moved westward into central Pennsylvania. An abundance of wildlife made for good hunting and good trading, as the Indians provided animal skins in return for a variety of English wares and weapons. Not all exchanges, especially those that involved alcohol, benefited the Shawnees. Nor were all contacts favorable to them. From the north, the Iroquois pressed their presumptions as conquerors. From the east, European colonists poured in.

European immigrants to Pennsylvania were a diverse lot. Some, like Squire Boone, who arrived in 1713, hailed from the south of England. Like the founders of the colony of Pennsylvania, the Boones belonged to the Society of Friends (Quakers). Other newcomers came from German-speaking principalities and professed a variety of faiths. Most numerous of all were Anglo-Irish (Scots-Irish) Presbyterians who had emigrated from Scotland, Ireland, and the north of England, countries where chaos and violence had long shaped cultures. Transporting those traditions with them to the interior or "backcountry" of Pennsylvania, the Anglo-Irish aggressively pushed their farmsteads onto lands held by Indians.[6]

By contrast, the Boones, following Quaker teachings, sought to avoid confrontations with neighboring Indians. Squire and his wife Sarah (who was of Welsh ancestry) instructed their eleven children to keep the peace.

Those teachings informed the upbringing of their sixth child, Daniel, who was born on November 2, 1734. Raised in Exeter Township (near present-day Reading), Daniel grew up in a home that welcomed visitors from a nearby Delaware village. As a boy, Daniel learned from those visitors, particularly skills in woodcraft, paramount among them how to hunt.[7]

The hunting that became central to Daniel Boone's being and part of the way of life of many Europeans in the Pennsylvania backcountry demonstrated how frontier cultures shaped one another. On the one hand, Europeans manufactured the tools used by hunters and trappers, especially as firearms supplanted bows and arrows among woodland Indians and metal traps replaced wooden ones. On the other, the techniques of hunting and trapping owed primarily to Indian practices. The first generation of settlers in the Pennsylvania backcountry lacked experience as hunters. In Europe, wealthy gentry reserved the privilege of hunting to themselves and criminalized the taking of game by commoners. Now freed from these restrictions, would-be hunters needed to be schooled in how to dress, how to track, how to decoy, and how to live off the land while they pursued their prey. Like Daniel Boone, they watched and learned from Indians. This emulation enabled increasing numbers of backcountry men to add wild meat to their family's diet; it permitted Daniel Boone to dream of making hunting and trapping his primary occupation.[8]

The copying remained more technical than cultural, which registered in the different ways backcountry and Indian hunters related to animals. This dissimilarity was not a stark and simple one between Christians and animists. Backcountry and Indian hunters each ascribed magical powers to the non-human world. But for white hunters, unlike their Indian counterparts, the charms they wore and the chants they uttered did not convey any sense of connection or equality with animals. For Boone and his compatriots, game was prey, not kin. Where Indian hunters paid respect to the game that sacrificed themselves, backcountry men had no concept of animal rights and performed no rites to honor the beasts that they consumed and profited from.[9]

The pioneering paths of the Shawnees and Daniel Boone diverged for a time after their times in Pennsylvania. In the middle decades of the eighteenth century, the Shawnees commenced another exodus. Looking to put space between their settlements and those of encroaching colonists, Shawnees, along with Delawares, headed west. For the Shawnees, their newest frontier returned them to the Ohio Valley, the country from which their diaspora had started a century before. The move put more distance between the Shawnee villages and the homelands of the Iroquois nations. It also put them closer to French trading posts, introducing competition for British traders and giving Shawnees more leverage in their exchanges with Europeans.[10]

Like the Shawnees, the Boones faced pressure from the fast-increasing population in the interior of Pennsylvania. For those with large numbers of children, which was the norm for backcountry families, the imperative of finding lands for the next generation sent them to new regions. Some moved farther west in Pennsylvania. Others, like Squire Boone, headed south through the Shenandoah Valley of Virginia. The search for cheap and fertile lands took the Boones in the early 1750s to the Yadkin Valley on the North Carolina Piedmont.[11]

Squire and Sarah Boone settled their family in North Carolina, but Daniel Boone never settled down there. As a young man, Daniel volunteered for the colony's militia during the Seven Years' War, service that brought him back to Pennsylvania as part of an ill-fated attack on French and Indian forces on the Monongahela River. After returning to the Yadkin, Daniel married Rebecca Bryan in 1756. As was customary, the couple soon started a family and a farm. The family grew quickly, eventually numbering ten children. The farm not so much, for Daniel preferred hunting to husbandry. While in the militia, he had seen the upper Ohio Valley and heard tales of the wildlife in the lands west of the Appalachian Mountains. During the 1760s, he made forays into the mountains. Initially, he confined these expeditions to the weeks and months after harvesting in the fall and winter. Over the course of the decade, however, the hunts got longer, both in their durations and their destinations. In 1767, Boone reached the eastern edge of Kentucky. In 1769, he led a group of seven, which included his brother Squire, on his longest hunt yet. Instead of waiting until after the harvest, the party set out in early May. Daniel left behind his wife and six children, with a seventh on the way.[12]

Forsaking their duties as farmers, the pursuit of pelts by "long hunters" pushed them across the mountains and deep into Kentucky. There, they came upon the remains of an abandoned Shawnee village and found a country teeming with deer and bison. The two were related: the emptying of Kentucky in the seventeenth century made it an unrivaled hunting ground in the eighteenth. By December 1769, the troupe had accumulated as many skins as their horses could carry and prepared to head home to sell their trove. But a group of Shawnees intercepted Boone and one of his companions, John Stewart (who was Boone's brother-in-law), near the

Kentucky River on December 22. One of the Shawnees, who had picked up some English from traders, introduced himself as Will Emery, or, as he referred to himself, "Captain Will." Interrogating the pair about what they were doing trespassing in a country claimed by the Shawnees, Emery ascertained the location of the camp at which Boone and Stewart had deposited their skins. He then impounded the pair's peltry and equipment, including their cherished Pennsylvania rifles.[13]

Poaching was a capital crime in England, but Shawnee justice was more merciful. Instead of executing the poachers as English magistrates might have ordered, Will Emery released them after a week-long captivity. He also presented Boone and Stewart with two pairs of moccasins, a doeskin, a little French gun, and a small amount of powder and shot. By this "trade," Emery afforded the released captives a means to survive on their return home. Captain Will likely hoped his leniency would be appreciated and his message that Kentucky was off limits to white hunters would be relayed across the backcountry.[14]

Years later, Boone allowed that Captain Will had treated him "in the most friendly manner"; at the time, he and Stewart raged at the theft of their property and, in violation of Emery's order, resumed their hunting and trapping for skins. When he was caught again, Stewart's recidivism cost him his life. Boone narrowly escaped and managed over the next year to pile a new stock of pelts. But having made his way back to the eastern side of the Appalachians in March 1771, Boone, now with his brother Squire, ran into another band of Indians. Once again, the Indians proposed to trade guns, an offer the Boones could not refuse, but did. The Indians then commandeered the animal skins of the Boones. Two months later, the brothers made it home, alive, yet fleeced of two years' work in the woods.[15]

Although Daniel Boone had no skins to sell, he did have tales to tell. Stories about Kentucky's abundant wildlife captivated kith and kin, and his reports about the condition of the country piqued the greatest interest. Information about trails, soils, and Indians was essential to backcountry settlers considering their next frontier. It was valuable as well to merchants, lawyers, planters, and government officials who hoped to engross vast tracts in the Ohio Valley. Some gentlemen, like George Washington, employed long hunters as land hunters. Boone may have been employed as a land scout during his excursions into Kentucky in the late 1760s. By the mid-1770s, he was working for a partnership of North Carolina gentlemen who styled their enterprise the Transylvania Company.[16]

William T. Ranney, *Boone's Party* (c. 1851–1852). The painter William Ranney is better known for his *Boone's First View of Kentucky* (1849), which depicted the scene when Daniel Boone and a party of long hunters first glimpsed the Bluegrass region of central Kentucky in the late 1760s. Here, Ranney puts on canvas a Boone story from 1773 when he made his first attempt to settle in Kentucky with his family, a scene that George Caleb Bingham simultaneously and similarly immortalized in his *Daniel Boone Escorting Settlers through Cumberland Gap* (c. 1851–1852). *Courtesy of the Kentucky Society of the Daughters of the American Revolution, Duncan Tavern Historic Center, Paris, KY*

Before throwing in with that enterprise, Boone determined to initiate his own settlement in Kentucky. In contrast with speculative ventures being launched by the wealthy and well-connected, Boone made no effort to curry favor with colonial authorities or strike a deal with Indians. Undeterred by the British crown's Proclamation of 1763 that prohibited settlement west of the Appalachian crest or by the warning from Captain Will and the losses he had suffered at the hands of Indians, Boone resolved to stake a preemptive claim to land in Kentucky.[17]

Boone's notions resonated with the aspirations of many in the backcountry. They shared his dismissal of the Proclamation Line as an unenforceable edict. "Not even a second Chinese wall," reported the *Virginia Gazette*, could hold back the tide of pioneers eager to breach the Appalachians. Many also embraced Boone's view that unclaimed lands should be granted to those brave enough to occupy them. In the summer of 1773, around fifty people, including his wife and children, joined Boone and headed toward Kentucky.[18]

They did not get very far before a contingent among them was ambushed by a group of Shawnees, Delawares, and Cherokees. Although none of these tribes then had villages in Kentucky, all hunted there. That backcountry men pursued pelts in Kentucky was a problem. Prospective settlers presented an even greater threat than poachers, one that could not be solved by sending them home without their rifles and their skins. A bloodier message was called for.

Among the ambushed was Boone's eldest child James. Shot through the hips and unable to move, James begged for his life. The attackers showed no mercy, pulling off James's fingernails and toenails. James then begged to be put out of his misery. His tormenters obliged. Later that day, his father found and buried James's mutilated body. Anticipating another attack, the remaining Kentucky-bound pioneers decided to turn back, for the time being.[19]

That was not for long in the case of Daniel Boone. To wait risked losing out on the best lands in Kentucky. In 1774, surveyors, representing a cadre of Virginia gentlemen and the colonial governor of Virginia, traveled down the Ohio River to mark lands. That year also saw Pennsylvanian James Harrod start a small settlement in central Kentucky. Boone made his move the following spring. In March 1775, he guided a party of thirty men through the Cumberland Gap and into Kentucky. Reaching the Kentucky River, they established a settlement that they named Boonesborough.[20]

Although Boone headed the pioneering group and the founding community carried his name, the enterprise was directed and financed by a partnership of North Carolina lawyers and merchants. Led by Richard Henderson, a judge on the North Carolina Superior Court, the partners imagined themselves as the proprietors of a new "Transylvania Colony." Like other speculators, the Transylvania group envisioned great profits from the sale of land and the collection of rent. First, though, the Transylvania proprietors had to create a plausible claim to Kentucky lands, which Henderson did by making a direct purchase from Cherokees. It was a daring scheme that bypassed colonial authorities and pretended that the Cherokees were the only Indian claimants to Kentucky.[21]

Negotiations between Henderson and the Cherokees opened in the fall of 1774. Prior to securing an agreement with the Cherokees, the Transylvania partners advertised terms for settlers in a Virginia newspaper. But Henderson's offer divided the approximately one thousand Cherokees who assembled for the negotiations. Younger men especially opposed any sale, as they were fearful of losing valuable hunting grounds. Even those who supported a deal were not prepared to give the Transylvania Company all the lands it wanted. In March 1775, with talks still going on, Henderson dispatched Boone to cut a road to Kentucky and establish a station as the headquarters of the new Transylvania Colony. A week after Boone set out, Henderson and the Cherokees struck a deal. For £10,000 worth of goods, the Cherokees deeded to Henderson and partners the territory between the Kentucky and Cumberland Rivers, as well as a 200,000-acre parcel east of the Cumberland Gap to serve as a pathway to the new colony.[22]

Land grants from the company for his services tied Boone's fortunes to the success of the Transylvania Colony, but those prospects faced challenges from many quarters. Most pioneers moving to Kentucky were skeptical about the validity of the Transylvania purchase and were disinclined to purchase on the terms offered by the proprietors. "The people in general," reported one pioneer John Floyd, "choose to settle" without payment, preferring to secure lands simply by building a cabin and cultivating a crop. These freeloading squatters exasperated Henderson. Meanwhile, rival speculators and their governing allies fretted about the precedent set by the Transylvania purchase and the ways in which it jeopardized their own designs on Kentucky lands—George Washington for one. "There is something in that affair which I neither understand, nor like, and wish I may not have cause to dislike it worse as the mystery unfolds," wrote Washington of the Transylvania Company's plans. Here, Washington received support from colonial governors in Virginia and North Carolina, against whose authority he was soon to be in rebellion. Their denunciations of the Transylvania purchase and rejection of the legality of lands bought from the company renewed the opportunities for Washington and fellow Revolutionaries to engross swaths of Kentucky.[23]

Indians presented a more immediate danger to Boone and fellow pioneers. On March 25, 1775, which was little more than a week after Henderson had concluded his agreement with the Cherokees, a pre-dawn raid awakened Boone's trail-blazing crew. Two of Boone's men were killed, another wounded, and the rest dispersed. Although the identities of the attackers were not certain, they were likely Cherokees, as one Cherokee leader apologized for the "accident," which he blamed on two "malicious" men.[24]

Sporadic attacks continued after the founding of Boonesborough. Some of the raiders, usually Cherokees, came from the south. Others came from the north, including Shawnees, Delawares, and a variety of Indians residing on the other side of the Ohio River. Sometimes, the raids combined Indians from south and north. Most followed a similar script. A small party surprised victims outside the relative security that pioneer forts (or "stations") afforded. The attackers then disappeared, taking with them a scalp or two, a captive or two, and some plundered horses. They left behind a frightened set of settlers. Hundreds were unsettled enough to retreat from Kentucky back across the mountains.[25]

A July 1776 raid fit this pattern. In this instance, the raiders numbered five. Three were Shawnees, two were Cherokees. Approaching Boonesborough on July 14, they spied three girls in a canoe on the Kentucky River. Seizing the girls, one of whom turned out to be Daniel Boone's thirteen-year-old daughter Jemima, the raiders started north toward the Ohio River with their captives. Jemima reported that her kidnappers were "really kind" to her and her peers during the two days they marched before stopping to rest at the Blue Licks salt spring. There, a posse led by Daniel Boone caught up with them and killed two of the Indians. By some recollections, it was Boone's shot that felled one of the Indians, who, according to some accounts, was the son of the Chillicothe Shawnee headman Blackfish. The surviving three Indians fled, and the rescued girls returned to Boonesborough, safe, if shaken.[26]

The rescue was exceptional; the raid was typical. So was the response to it. Some at Boonesborough wanted to retaliate against Indian villages to the north and south. Others hastened to retreat from Kentucky, seeking shelter to the east on the other side of the Appalachians. Indians also split in their responses. Among the Shawnees, the divisions between those who wanted to step up raiding and those who sought to contain conflicts partially adhered to traditional clan lines and the roles that each played within the tribe. But within villages, factions emerged as well. Often, older headmen attributed the violence to hotheaded younger men. These freelancing raids attested to a gap between generations. They also evidenced the limited control that "chiefs" exercised in Ohio Indian societies, where the ability to command rested on the capacity to convince; that is, headmen led by persuading others to follow, which they could not always do.[27]

Violence escalated in 1777, abetted by the intervention of outside forces. To win the Revolutionary War in the West, the British armed Indians in the Ohio Valley and Great Lakes and encouraged them to dislodge American colonists from Kentucky. With British supplies, Indians undertook larger and longer campaigns against Kentucky settlements. In March 1777, around two hundred Ohio Indians crossed the river into Kentucky. That April, a contingent approached Boonesborough. This time, it was Daniel Boone who was caught outside the fort. Shot in the ankle, he was carried to safety on the shoulders of Simon Kenton. Thanks to Kenton, Boone survived, but his shattered ankle caused him intermittent pain for the rest of his life. Ambushes around Boonesborough and at other stations in Kentucky kept pioneers penned in their forts, unable to tend their fields or protect their livestock. When that year's raids finally ended in the fall, seven stations in Kentucky had been abandoned; just four remained.[28]

To counter the British and validate its claim over Kentucky, the government of the state of Virginia increased its support for western colonists in their combat against Indians. That permitted Americans pioneers to go on the offensive, which they did without distinguishing much between Indians who were friends (or at least not hostile) and who were foes. Most egregious was the killing of the Shawnee leader Cornstalk in November 1777. Cornstalk had fought against Virginians in 1774. In 1775, he prophesized the dark future that the settler colonists' ethos held for his people. "We are often inclined to believe that there is no resting place for us and your intentions were to deprive us entirely of our whole Country," Cornstalk told a group of Virginians. Yet, even as Cornstalk worried that Americans intended to expropriate Indian lands and eliminate Indians, he sought to steer a neutral course in the civil war between the British and the Americans. Hoping to keep the Shawnees out of the fight, he joined a Shawnee delegation that traveled to Fort Randolph (in present-day West Virginia) to meet with American representatives in the fall of 1777. Instead of negotiating, the American commander, Matthew Arbuckle, took Cornstalk and his party hostage. A few days later, backcountry men broke into the prisoners' cell and murdered Cornstalk. "If we had anything to expect from" the Shawnees, wrote the American general Edward Hand when he learned of the incident, "it is now vanished."[29]

To make matters worse for Daniel Boone, Virginia's support meant that the lands he had gained from the Transylvania Company had also likely vanished. At the end of 1776, over the strenuous protests of Richard

Henderson, the government of Virginia created the County of Kentucky. The new county encompassed most of the Transylvania Colony's territory, over which Virginia now firmly asserted its sovereignty. His proprietorship undone and his property rights quashed, Henderson pressed the government of Virginia for compensation for the company's exertions and expenditures. But the Virginia assembly postponed taking actions through 1777, leaving Henderson and his partners, as well as confederates like Daniel Boone, with claims of doubtful and diminishing value.[30]

Bad as 1777 had been for Boone, 1778 began even more bleakly at Boonesborough. The previous year's raids left inhabitants nearly destitute of corn and livestock. Residents had to rely on hunting for sustenance, made more challenging because they had no salt to preserve meat. To get that precious item, twenty-eight men departed in early January 1778 for the nearest salt spring, which was at Blue Licks, approximately fifty miles north of Boonesborough. With Boone chosen to lead and acting as the hunter for the company, the rest of the men commenced their work, which involved boiling the briny water until only salt remained.[31]

All went well until the morning of February 7, 1778. While Boone was checking traps, four Indians surprised him. He tried to flee, but the Indians were younger and faster than the forty-three-year-old Boone and soon overtook him. Reckoning that discretion was the better part of valor, Boone halted, propped his rifle against a tree, and surrendered. Escorted to the Indians' main camp, Boone spotted Will Emery among the assemblage. It took Emery a moment to recall when and where the two had met. With some prompting from Boone, Captain Will remembered their prior encounter. Emery then exchanged hearty "howdydos" with his once and present captive.[32]

At the time of Boone's capture, the Indian force was on its way to Boonesborough. Although Ohio Indians did not usually make war during the dead of winter, the murder of Cornstalk had enraged and united the Shawnees. Seeking vengeance and supplied by the British, Blackfish led more than one hundred men across the Ohio River during the first week of February 1778.[33]

Learning the Indians' target, Boone sought to delay an assault on Boonesborough. He knew that the fort was undermanned without the salt-makers and its defenses were in a state of disrepair. The strategy Boone hit upon was to first arrange the peaceful capitulation of the salt-boilers, with the stipulation that his men would not be tortured or forced to run the gauntlet. After consulting with several of his men, Blackfish accepted Boone's proposal, with the proviso that if the salt-makers resisted, all would be killed. Boone then led the Indians to the boilers' encampment, where he appealed to his men to give themselves up without a fight. He assured them they would be well treated by the Indians and released to the British at Detroit. Yet a few hours later they heard Boone promise the Indians that the captives "will make you fine warriors and excellent hunters to kill game for your squaws and children." Still more dismaying, they listened to Boone pledge to conduct their captors to Boonesborough in the spring "when the weather will be warm, and the women and children can travel . . . to the Indian towns." Then, Boone declared, we will "all live with you as one people."[34]

Boone's declamation followed several hours of impassioned speeches by Indian men. The debate, as remembered by the salt-makers, was intense, though they understood only what Boone said. From the gestures of Indian orators, pioneer auditors could tell that the Shawnees were divided. Not thrilled by Boone's proposal or reconciled to the prospect of living as one people with the Shawnees, the salt-boilers preferred it to the alternative: their immediate execution as revenge for the killing of Cornstalk. Finally, a vote was taken, which again affirmed the democratic culture of Ohio Indian warfare. By a margin of sixty-one to fifty-nine, the Shawnees elected to spare the salt-makers and to wait until spring before absorbing the rest of the people at Boonesborough.[35]

The relief that Boone felt after the vote turned to distress the next evening as he watched Indians clear a long path in the snow and form two lines on the sides of it. To Boone, it looked like the Indians were preparing to make the captives run the gauntlet and had reneged on the agreement that his men not be harmed. Through an interpreter, Blackfish clarified that the gauntlet was not for Boone's men, but for Boone. Armed with sticks and clubs, the Indians rained blows upon Boone. Although Boone sought to minimize the damage by running as fast as he could and zigging and zagging as he went, several strikes staggered him. One opened a bloody wound on the top of his head. As he neared the end of the gauntlet, he saw one Indian setting up to wallop him with a "home lick." Boone bent his head and body forward and rammed directly into the last assailant, knocking the man over and winning cheers and backslaps from his assailants.[36]

Arriving at Chillicothe after a ten-day trek, the Shawnees began the process of incorporating the salt-makers into their ranks. The customs of the Shawnees (and other woodland Indian peoples) encouraged Blackfish to "cover the dead" by adopting a substitute for the son he had lost in July

1776. Fittingly, Blackfish chose Boone, headman adopting headman, though, in this instance, the father was only a few years older than the son he adopted. Boone and other salt-boilers selected for adoption then had their hair plucked in the style favored by the Shawnees, leaving only a scalplock. Next, Indian women stripped and scrubbed the adoptees. "I never was washed so clean before or since," remembered one captive of his scouring by Shawnee women. Symbolically purged of his past, Boone was renamed Sheltowee, meaning Big Turtle. A feast was then held to welcome Boone and other new adoptees into their families.[37]

That Boone led the rescue which resulted in the death of Blackfish's son was not lost on his adopters. According to one story, not long after Boone's capture, one of the Shawnees confronted Boone, asking him if he had been present when Blackfish's son was slain. Boone admitted that he was there and that he had fired upon the Indians. Whether his was a fatal shot could not be known. Besides, added Boone, "many things happen in war that were best forgotten in peace." Boone's response satisfied his interrogator, whose traditions of covering the dead depended on being able convert former enemies into family members. That Blackfish accepted the wisdom of Boone's words and embraced Boone as a son showed how far Shawnees could go in forgetting what happened in war, since it left open the possibility that the particular dead in this instance was being covered by his slayer.[38]

Boone was at Chillicothe for only a few weeks before Blackfish took him to Detroit. About ten of the salt-makers accompanied Blackfish and Boone, these men having been deemed unsuitable for adoption. The trip to Detroit afforded the Indians an opportunity to sell these captives to the British, and it allowed Blackfish to apprise the British commander, Henry Hamilton, of the results of the winter foray into Kentucky. It was widely rumored in Kentucky that Hamilton paid Indian allies for pioneer scalps, but, in this case, he ransomed the captives for £20 apiece and then imprisoned them. To his superior, Hamilton expressed frustration that the Indians could not be convinced to attack Boonesborough. What he only slowly grasped was that while Ohio Indian allies fought with British supplies against a mutual foe, they conducted their campaigns on their own schedule, by their own tactics, and for their own purposes.[39]

Hamilton was much happier with the intelligence he received from Boone. The situation in Kentucky, Boone told Hamilton, was desperate. Faced with starvation, expecting no support from the Continental Congress, and impressed by the benevolence of the Indians, the settlers at Boonesborough, said Boone, would gladly surrender when he returned with the Shawnees.

As Hamilton reported up the chain, "by Boone's account," the people at Boonesborough "will trust the Savages who have shewn so much humanity to their prisoners." So pleased was Hamilton with this information that he rewarded Boone with a horse, a saddle, and some silver trinkets. He also reportedly offered Blackfish £100 for Boone. To no avail: father would not part with son.[40]

From Detroit, it was back to Chillicothe. Blackfish and Boone arrived there on April 25, at which time Boone seemed to settle quickly into his new surroundings and to accommodate contentedly to his new situation. From all appearances, Boone was becoming Sheltowee, was becoming Shawnee.

The setting's familiarity smoothed Boone's transition. Chillicothe, in Boone's description, resembled "a Kentucke station," laid out in a long square. Its 12- to 15-foot square houses were "generally built of small logs and covered with bark, each one having a chimney and a door," very much in the style of backcountry cabins. The largest structure was the council house, which "extends the whole length of the town" and where villagers gathered to discuss "matters of importance." In this sketch, Boone failed to note that the Shawnee village was much larger, in size and population, than Boonesborough or any other settlement in Kentucky in 1778.[41]

The ethnic composition of the village was more varied than its designation as a Shawnee town or as Chillicothe, with its links to one group among the Shawnees, suggested. In the 1770s, the population of the town was predominantly Shawnee and leadership and traditions still followed Chillicothe lineages and practices. But within Chillicothe resided Mekoches, Kishpokos, Pekowis, and Thawakilas. A number of Delawares and other Pennsylvania Indians who had come west to escape Anglo-American encirclement joined the varied Shawnees. Indians from the Illinois Country who had moved east to position themselves between French and British trading orbits also congregated at Chillicothe. Within this and other multiethnic Ohio Indian towns, many residents spoke three or more languages. The prevalence of polyglots made it easier for newcomers like Boone to communicate.[42]

The influx of Euro-American traders, renegades, and captives brought foreign words into the local lexicon and foreign ways into Ohio Indian cultures, which also made Chillicothe seem more like home to Daniel Boone. A visitor to Chillicothe in the early 1770s counted around twenty "light skinned" people living in the town. As part of their incorporation into Indian communities, Europeans learned to live and think as Shawnees. But even as some Europeans embraced Indian life, they also introduced colonial foods, fashions, and furnishings.[43]

Among the transmitted traditions was livestock herding. Well into the eighteenth century, the absence of cattle, sheep, and hogs in Indian country marked a cultural divide between backcountry and Indian country. Ohio Indians occasionally likened wildlife to livestock. The analogy served a purpose. By maintaining that "the Elks are our horses, the Buffaloes are our cows, [and] the deer are our sheep," Ohio Indians justified their claim to game and their right to punish foreign poachers. These distinctions diminished, however, in the 1770s when Kentucky pioneers came to rely so heavily on hunting and Ohio Indians began to raise cattle in greater numbers. Already in the 1760s, European visitors to Ohio Indian villages remarked on the Indians' cattle and on their skill in making butter and cheese. By the time Boone became Sheltowee, the Indians' mix of hunting, herding, and agriculture largely mirrored the means of subsistence that prevailed at Boonesborough and other Kentucky settlements.[44]

Not that Daniel Boone cared much about stock raising or farming. His forte was hunting. Left to his own devices, hunting would be his primary, or, better yet, his exclusive, occupation. In Chillicothe, he found a gendered division of labor that assigned principal responsibility for growing crops to women. Once when Boone was helping out in the fields that surrounded the village, Blackfish reproached him for engaging in women's work. There was no need for Boone to worry about planting and tending corn, Blackfish told him, "for your mother can easily raise enough for my family, and yours also when they come from Kentucky." That was how Lyman Draper recorded the quotation. In a letter to Draper, a grandson of Boone put a different spin on the episode that heightened the racism of his grandfather's response. Daniel, according to his descendant's account, complained to Blackfish about being made to wield an axe to build a trough for feeding animals. "When I am at home[,] I dont do this kind of work[,]" Boone told Blackfish, for "I have Niggers to work for me, but here you make a Negroe of me." Supposedly, Blackfish replied, "well, well if you dont like to do it, dont work any more," just "go to the camp & stay with you[r] Mother."[45]

In both versions, Boone stopped working; in neither did he grasp the powers that his Shawnee mother and other Shawnee women held within their society. Kentuckians had no equivalent to the female peace and war chiefs of the Shawnees. These posts were customarily, though not always, held by the mother, sister, or another close relative of the corresponding male headmen. The female peace or village chief oversaw the everyday activities of women. She scheduled planting and arranged the feasts that coincided with various seasonal rituals. She was also responsible for conveying the consensus of village women to a male war chief. According to an early nineteenth-century ethnographer, when the wishes of women opposed those of a male war chief, the female chief "seldom fail[ed] to dissuade him."[46]

In his first weeks at Chillicothe, his father and mother restricted Boone's movements beyond the village; quickly, however, he won the respect of villagers and the affection of relatives. At home, he bonded with his new family. Although Boone later complained that his mother allowed chickens to roost in the same area that she cooked, he appreciated the cuisine she prepared and the kindness with which she treated him. Blackfish's affections were also obvious. Always referring to Boone as "my son," Blackfish would sometimes suck a lump of sugar, then pass it on to Boone to savor. Blackfish also engaged Boone in discussions about how Kentuckians and Indians could learn from one another when they lived as one people. According to Boone, Blackfish voiced enthusiasm for improving agriculture and adding to herds. In turn, Boone told Blackfish how much he enjoyed hunting and how much he appreciated the Shawnees' way of living. The ease with which Boone slipped into Shawnee ways and his easygoing manner soon gained him the trust of his family.[47]

So cheerful did Boone appear that doubts about his loyalties arose among less compliant adoptees. William Hancock, who had been adopted by Will Emery, wondered how Boone could be "whistling and contented among a parcel of dirty Indians." After escaping from Chillicothe, Hancock returned to Kentucky with news that Boone had turned against them. To the dismay of those at Boonesborough, Hancock related that while at Detroit, Boone had agreed to surrender Boonesborough and turn its people over to the British.[48]

This made for an awkward reception when Boone unexpectedly appeared at the gates of Boonesborough on June 20, 1778. Boone had trekked the 150 miles from Chillicothe to Boonesborough in just four days. Exhausted and famished, Boone was greeted with suspicion by people who had recently heard Johnson's allegations. With the exception of Jemima, who remained at Boonesborough, his wife and children were not around to welcome him, as they had returned to the Yadkin Valley, presuming Boone and the salt-makers dead. Vehemently disputing Johnson's account, Boone insisted that his surrender saved the salt-makers' lives and delayed the assault on Boonesborough. His dealings with Hamilton and his apparent serenity among the Shawnees were all clever ruses, which Boone employed to buy time, win the confidence of adversaries, and wait for the right moment to make his escape.[49]

Many at Boonesborough didn't know who or what to believe. First, they assumed that Boone and the salt-boilers had all been killed. Then, Johnson told them that Boone had consorted with the British and joined the Indians, aspersions subsequently corroborated by William Hancock after he made his escape. Now, Boone appealed for their trust on the basis of his deceptions.[50]

Possibly to regain his stature as a bold leader, Boone proposed to draw on his recently acquired knowledge of Ohio Indian country and mount a preemptive raid across the Ohio River. The target was not Chillicothe, but a smaller village that Boone had seen at the mouth of the Scioto River. The hit-and-run strike, argued Boone, would warn the Indians about the capacity of Kentuckians to attack them and would yield a trove of horses and pelts. The size and timing of Boone's expedition doomed it, however. With just twenty men, Boone's force posed little threat to Ohio Indian villages. Worse still, he launched it when the largest Ohio Indian force yet assembled, a mixed group including Shawnees, Wyandots, Miamis, Delawares, Mingoes, and a handful of British soldiers, was on the march. Securing none of their objectives, Boone's company beat a hasty retreat. They arrived back at Boonesborough on September 6, just one day ahead of the 350-man Indian force. Rather than restoring his reputation, Boone's action, which nearly deprived the fort of twenty defenders, damaged anew his standing among some of his peers.[51]

What happened next intensified the controversy about Boone's allegiances. Prior to launching any assault against outnumbered pioneers, Blackfish and other Indian leaders negotiated with Boone and other representatives from Boonesborough outside the station's walls. As a gesture of continuing affection for his peripatetic son, Blackfish presented Boone with seven buffalo tongues as a gift. At the conclave, he reiterated his offer of good treatment if the men submitted peaceably and death if they did not (the women would still be adopted). By good treatment, he meant a trip to Detroit or adoption by Indians. To ease the journey of women and children, he brought forty horses; to entice men, he conjured a country teeming with game.[52]

The gesture and the offer appealed to Boone, who restated to Blackfish his preference to surrender the fort. But Boone conceded that he no longer commanded. He also maintained that his was just one voice among many, a point Blackfish should have appreciated given the similar constraints on his own authority. Boone's assertions about his loss of leadership and the limits on leaders were true. He lied to Blackfish, however, when he claimed he had run away just to visit with his wife and children and when he denied participation in the previous days' raid.[53]

Still, Boone's desire to avert a bloody battle was sincere. In discussions inside Boonesborough, he urged fellow pioneers to trust the Indians. As Boone had already discovered, Ohio Indians preferred to incorporate, not eradicate, their backcountry counterparts. Boone was outvoted, but he continued to press for more talks.[54]

Among those suspicious of Boone's intentions, Richard Callaway was the most vocal, this despite the connections they shared. Back in 1776, Callaway's daughters had been kidnapped alongside Jemima Boone. Jemima stayed in Kentucky in 1778 when her mother and siblings departed because she was now married to Callaway's son, Flanders. Yet, Callaway vehemently opposed the raid across the Ohio, distrusted the faith that Daniel Boone placed in "savages," and balked at holding peace talks with Indians, especially outside the fort. In the council within the fort, he rebuked Boone and swore he would kill anyone who proposed surrender.[55]

Before any shooting started, Blackfish invited Boone for one more parley. What exactly transpired is hard to discern from conflicting accounts. In some versions, Blackfish first proposed to give settlers six weeks to clear out of Kentucky. When this was rejected, he modified the terms, promising peace in exchange for the acceptance of the Ohio River as a boundary between Kentucky settlements and Ohio Indian towns. These conditions represented a significant shift from the agreement in February, which had promulgated Boonesborough's inhabitants living with and as Indians. Now Blackfish suggested peaceful coexistence, based on a border that would restrict white settlements to the south side of the Ohio, but permit people on both sides to cross the river to hunt and trade. To appease his British backers, Blackfish may also have added that the Kentuckians would have to take an oath of allegiance to the crown. To these terms, the negotiators from Boonesborough agreed, though perhaps only to buy themselves time for reinforcements to arrive from Virginia.[56]

At that point, Blackfish suggested they seal the deal with handshakes. Boone and his comrades found themselves each clasped by two Indians. Clasps soon became grasps, which may have been a ritual of conciliation, but which skittish Americans interpreted as a plot to take their leaders hostage. According to eyewitness Daniel Trabue, Richard Callaway's skepticism of Indian intentions saved the day. At Callaway's insistence, the meeting was held close to the fort. Callaway had also warned the men in the fort that "they must be Redy with their guns" and instructed "the Women to put on hats and hunting shirts and to appear as men and git up on the top of the wall and as they might appear as a great many men."

At the first sign of what he considered trouble, Callaway jerked away from his would-be captors and shouted for the men in the fort to begin firing. In the ensuing melee, Boone, after throwing Blackfish to the ground, took a ball in his shoulder, but he and the other pioneers extricated themselves and hustled back inside the fort.[57]

The Indians declined to storm Boonesborough, which would have cost them many lives, and the battle settled into a siege. For ten days, Indians and pioneers exchanged shouted snipes and engaged in long-distance sniping. Owing to their more exposed positions, the Indians were more vulnerable. During the siege, they lost thirty-seven men, while only two people inside the fort died. Like frontal attacks, long sieges were not congruent with the Indians' way of war, and the pioneers were well-provisioned, having already harvested their corn. To increase the pressure on the population of the fort, Indians began to tunnel under the walls. When the shaft collapsed prematurely, the Indians had no immediate winning strategy left. With hunting season approaching, they withdrew.[58]

The siege lifted, but not the clouds over Boone. Richard Callaway saw to that. After the Indians departed, Callaway pressed for Boone to be punished. Callaway doubted Boone's loyalties. He considered Boone's leadership in military matters incompetent at best and treasonous at worst. How else to explain the series of damnable decisions and damaging actions taken by Boone from the beginning of 1778 to the end of the siege?

Callaway, with the backing of Benjamin Logan, who was the second highest ranking officer in Virginia's Kentucky County militia, leveled four charges against Boone. First, when captured at Blue Licks, Boone had given up the other salt-makers "against their consent," even though the Indians were "not going towards them." Second, with the British commander at Detroit, he had bargained to "give up all the people at Boonesborough." Third, after his return to Kentucky, he had imperiled the defenses at Boonesborough by causing men "to leave the fort to go away over the Ohio River" on a reckless excursion. And fourth, he had "take[n] all our officers to the Indean camp to make peace out of sight of the fort," resulting in their near destruction.[59]

A military tribunal convened in October 1778 at Logan's Station, which was about forty-five miles south of Boonesborough. The court-martial reviewed the evidence against Boone and heard his explanations. Although no transcript of the trial survives, we do know that the verdict vindicated Boone. With only circumstantial evidence and unverified suspicions against the accused, the court-martial judges accepted his version. More than just exonerating Boone, superiors in the Virginia militia promoted him from captain to major following the trial.[60]

To Boone's friends, this resolved the matter. Scoffing at those who accused Boone of being a Tory, a turncoat, or just a blundering commander, Simon Kenton insisted that "they may say what they please of Daniel Boone, he acted with wisdom." Callaway did not share Kenton's view, and he was not alone. Benjamin Logan, who founded the station at which the court-martial was held, also was reportedly displeased by the decision of the tribunal.[61]

Before the trial began, Boone composed a letter to Rebecca in which he recounted his trials from his captivity and his escape to the court-martial he now faced, which delayed his going back to see her. The letter has not survived, but Rebecca showed it to relatives who remembered how Boone, who rarely swore, profaned the British: "God damn them," he wrote, as "they had set the Indians on us."[62]

Once vindicated, Boone headed across the mountains, reaching the Yadkin Valley in early November. He did not return to Kentucky until the following year. When he did come back, it was not to Boonesborough. Enough ill will remained there for Boone to stay away. Instead, he founded a new settlement, Boone's Station, seven miles northeast of Boonesborough. A few years later, when Boone recounted his pioneering exploits in Kentucky to John Filson, he remained sufficiently indignant or embarrassed about the court-martial to cover it up. Filson's "autobiography" of Boone, which made Boone a legend in his own time, omitted the trying aftermath of the siege as "nothing worthy of a place in this account."[63]

The silence of Filson's Boone has left to the court of history to render judgment on Boone's intentions and deeds in 1778. The jury of biographers and historians has generally concurred with the original ruling. Lyman C. Draper, who during the nineteenth century collected and preserved many of the records on which we still depend to write biographies of Boone and broader histories of the Revolutionary era frontier, concluded that "not the least criminality attaches to Boone in all these various transactions." Working with Draper's evidence and additional sources, more recent Boone scholars have generally accepted the original verdict and Draper's, while seeking to account for the success of Boone's ploys. "Like a good hunter," John Mack Faragher's Boone "blend[ed] in with his surroundings." Echoing Faragher, Robert Morgan labeled Boone "a good actor," who "could assume almost any point of view." But more than just playing a role to charm adversaries, Morgan's Boone "genuinely appreciated others' perspectives and values," which made his ruses the more convincing.[64]

Yet, that ability to understand and sympathize with others' viewpoints also made his ruses more than mere deceptions. Boone's loyalties to nations and empires were malleable, and woodland Indian life held attractions for him. Although nineteenth-century descendants of Kentucky pioneers pretended that their ancestors were all devoted patriots, Boone had plenty of company in his uncertainties about where his interests and his sentiments lay. Likewise, while subsequent generations built a metaphorical wall between American "civilization" and Indian "savagery," Boone's worldview and the hunting ways he cherished bridged the eighteenth-century frontier.

The Revolutionary governments did little to secure the affection of Kentuckians. Repeated petitions to the Virginia Assembly and to the Continental Congress asking for troops and supplies failed to generate much of either. Frustration with nonresponsive governments combined with unceasing harassment by native "invaders" to create an opening for British loyalists.[65]

More than any other factor, the uncertainty of land titles confused the political allegiances of Kentucky pioneers. Those like Boone who had staked their claims under the authority of the now invalidated Transylvania Company had good reason to resent the hostile takeover of Kentucky by Virginia's Revolutionary government. For Boone, the land grab by the Tidewater and Piedmont planters who governed Virginia undercut his title to thousands of prime acres. The failure to enact legislation allowing settlers to preempt the lands that they occupied infuriated Kentuckians. "If some such thing is not done, and that very soon," warned John Floyd, "I really fear there will be a civil war among the people."[66]

Boone's grievances with Revolutionary governments did not turn him into a Tory, however. Far from opening Kentucky lands to pioneer occupants, the British government had tried to block settlement with the Proclamation of 1763, had aligned with moneyed speculators in plotting vast land grants in the Ohio Valley in the years before the Revolution, and had offered no promises to Boonesborough's inhabitants in 1778, other than that they would be removed to live among the Indians or taken to Detroit. And how could Boone side with the British when he damned them for "set[ting] the Indians on us"? In blaming the British for Indian attacks against Kentucky, Boone undervalued the agency of Indians in defending their own interests and fighting on their own terms. But he correctly identified how British support underwrote the change from what had been a conflict of raids and skirmishes into a war fought by larger armies in longer and bloodier campaigns.[67]

In 1778, Boone was neither ardent patriot nor committed Tory. That made him like most Kentuckians, the vast majority of whom cared less about nation or empire than about protecting land claims and promoting local interests.

What did distinguish Boone from most of his neighbors was the extent to which he could not only sympathize with Indians' perspectives, but also overcome past animosities. Thefts and wounds of the kind Boone had suffered at the hands of Indians permanently hardened the feelings of many of his compatriots, who had no equivalent to the belief and practice of covering the dead. Boone lost his brother-in-law to the Shawnees in 1769. Four years later, his eldest son perished. The sight of James Boone's mutilated body could not easily be forgotten or forgiven. But even after a second son was killed by Indians in 1782, Boone never succumbed to the blinding hatred of Indians that scorched the minds of men like Richard Callaway. Years later, reflecting on one of his many encounters with Indians, Boone told John J. Audubon of his desire "to lay open the skulls of the wretches." On this and other occasions, he resisted his murderous impulses. To his last days, Boone deeply resented the myth-makers who exaggerated his Indian-fighting exploits. The poetic liberties taken by his nephew Daniel Bryan incensed Boone. "The book [written by Bryan] represents me as a wonderful man who killed a host of Indians," he complained to Rebecca. "I don't believe the one has much to do with the other." Had the affronting author not been kin, Boone said he would have sued him for slander. While most frontiersmen of nineteenth-century lore boasted of their butchery, Boone in his reminiscences downplayed any deaths for which he bore responsibility.[68]

What explains Boone's exceptional qualities? Although he had long since stopped attending meetings of the Society of Friends, perhaps his Quaker upbringing imbued him with a more pardoning and pacific disposition. Or maybe, after experiencing the brutality of frontier war close up, he recoiled against such horrors. For whatever reason, Boone forgave, if not forgot, what happened in war, which enabled him to live in peace with Indians.

Adoption gave Boone the opportunity to live with the Shawnees, and as a Shawnee. It was a bridge that hundreds of other backcountry-born people successfully navigated. In towns like Chillicothe, many, who like Boone had been taken captive, embraced life on the other side of the frontier—so much so, that when peace came and treaties mandated the return of prisoners, they resisted their repatriation. William Smith, a soldier who witnessed the "liberation" of hundreds of white prisoners from the Shawnees after the Seven Years' War, described "the utmost reluctance" with which captives

Enrico Causici, *Conflict of Daniel Boone and the Indians, 1773* (1827). This sandstone relief adorns the Rotunda above the South Door of the United States Capitol in Washington, DC. Like others who shaped Boone's image in the nineteenth century, Causici's depiction emphasized the lethal struggle between Boone and Indians, a portrait that Boone had disclaimed. *Courtesy of the Architect of the Capitol*

parted from captors. Several quickly "found means to escape" and return to their Indian lives. Others "continued many days in bitter lamentations, even refusing sustenance." Their deliverance, Smith concluded, seemed instead a new captivity. The separation was equally painful for the Indians. Decades later, one Shawnee remembered how Shawnee women snuck into Kentucky to visit adopted children they had raised and lost.[69]

Shawnees drew a line at some repatriations. The treaty that concluded Dunmore's War in 1774 included a similar provision mandating the return of captives. Cornstalk agreed to abide by it, except in the case of a Black woman and her child by a Shawnee father. "We thought it very hard they shou'd be made Slaves of," Cornstalk explained.[70]

As William Smith noticed, women and children—some white, some Black, and some of mixed racial ancestry—accounted for almost all of the reluctantly repatriated captives. That kept with the adoption practices of Ohio Indians, which tilted heavily toward those groups. Children were more easily re-educated to Indian ways; women, too, were viewed as better candidates for adoption than adult men. In part, that followed from the belief in both backcountry and Ohio Indian country that warfare was the domain of men and that women, like children, would be more tractable. For adult men, execution rather than adoption was the more common fate of captives, one that Boone and the salt-makers narrowly escaped. The slight majority who voted to spare the salt-makers bucked that custom and invited Boone and his men to join them.[71]

A few of the salt-boilers adapted to varying extents to their adoption. Joseph Jackson stayed among the Indians until 1799 and fought with them against his former comrades. Jack Dunn escaped from Chillicothe in 1779 and joined the Kentucky militia. But then he had second thoughts and returned to the Shawnees. Richard Callaway's nephew, Micajiah Callaway, remained for five years among the Indians. During that time, he fought with them against Americans and then served as an interpreter for them in negotiations in Louisville in 1783. After being repatriated in 1783, he worked alongside Boone on survey teams. Yet, even as he fought against Ohio Indians in the 1790s, he continued to move back and forth between American and Indian worlds for the rest of his life, which for this last surviving salt-maker stretched until 1848.[72]

For the majority of salt-makers, however, their adoptions did not take or did not have time to set. Several fled, or at least tried to flee, when the chance presented itself. In addition to Boone, at least seven other adopted salt-boilers escaped from Chillicothe in 1778 and 1779, and like Boone, they did not go back. For Boone, too, despite his forgiving disposition and blended worldview, the invitation from the Shawnees was a bridge too far.[73]

Unlike several who bolted before and after him, Boone spoke only fondly of his time in Chillicothe. "All his life Boone had aspired to live like an Indian, to hunt with Indians, and during the months at Chillicothe that dream was realized," summarized biographer Robert Morgan. It could not have been easy for Boone to give up that dream.[74]

But give it up he did in 1778. By his flight from Chillicothe, by his subsequent leadership of the aborted raid against Ohio Indian towns, and, once outvoted, by his participation in the defense of Boonesborough, Boone proved his allegiances to the people of Boonesborough, if not to the broader cause of American nationhood. These actions demonstrated that despite his fondness for his Shawnee kin and Shawnee ways, he was not willing to leave what he had—and what he hoped for—in Kentucky behind. With some regret for the opportunity he was forsaking, he rode away from Chillicothe in June 1778. As he later admitted, at that moment, he "really felt sorry."[75]

Boone never apologized to Blackfish, who was struck down when Kentuckians struck back against Chillicothe in the spring of 1779. Unlike the small group from Boonesborough that Boone had assembled the previous summer, the 1779 foray marshaled nearly 300 militiamen drawn from settlements around Kentucky. After crossing the Ohio on May 28, the Kentuckians marched to Chillicothe and attacked early in the morning on May 30. Just as Blackfish would not (and could not) order Indians to storm the palisades at Boonesborough, so, too, John Bowman, who led the Kentucky force, determined with other leaders that it would be too costly to mount a direct assault against the council house. That fortress remained unbreached and unburned, but the invaders did plenty of damage. They torched cornfields, plundered and set fire to cabins, and shot at villagers who were unable to find shelter inside the council house. Blackfish took a ball in the leg. He survived the battle, thanks to three men who carried him to safety. But his wound did not heal, and he died about six weeks later.[76]

Over the next decade, residents of Chillicothe endured four more onslaughts. Just as British supplies enabled Ohio Indians to send larger forces into Kentucky, enhanced support from the state government of Virginia and later from the national government of the United States financed and armed bigger incursions against Indian towns north of the Ohio River. Consider these escalating numbers. In 1778, Boone brought just twenty men on his raid. In 1779, Bowman commanded a force of three hundred. In 1780,

George Rogers Clark invaded with nearly one thousand men. Larger armies multiplied casualties on both sides of the Ohio River, but especially so in Chillicothe, which invading armies targeted in 1780, 1782, 1786, and 1790.[77]

Ohio Indians often gave better than they got, but the numbers were increasingly stacked against them. During the Revolution, British support buttressed the Shawnees' military resistance. As late as September 1782, William Christian, a colonel in the Virginia militia, feared that with the Shawnees united against them, white settlers might soon be driven from Kentucky. Yet, Christian misunderstood the unity of the Shawnees and missed the outmigrations that reduced the bulk of their forces in the Ohio Country. Beginning around 1779 or 1780, more than one thousand Shawnees, principally from the Thawekila, Piqua, and Kispoki divisions, but also some among the Chillicothes, followed in the footsteps of their predecessors by looking to move out of harm's way. For many, this involved a relocation of a short distance to villages further north in Ohio or just west in what is now Indiana. In the tradition of earlier generations, Shawnees also undertook a longer-distance exodus. This migration took them several hundred miles to the west, across the Mississippi River to resettle outside the United States in the Spanish colony of Louisiana.[78]

Left behind at Chillicothe were those most committed to contesting American settlements in the Ohio Valley. Each time American invaders destroyed their village, inhabitants rebuilt, shifting the location to the north and west to provide greater security. Warfare, though, took a growing toll on those in the Ohio Country, and, with the end of the Revolution, Shawnee prospects dimmed further. In 1783, American horse thieves stole stock from Chillicothe, but when Shawnees appealed to British officials, they were informed that now "the World wants to be at Peace." Any retaliation, the British leader told his Shawnee children, "must be an affair of your own, as your Father can take no part in it." Or, as an American described the betrayal to the Shawnees, the British king treated his Indian children "like Bastards."[79]

Through the 1780s and into the early 1790s, Chillicothe (in shifting locations) remained at the center of a burgeoning movement that sought to build a pan-Indian confederation among Ohio Indians. No longer seeking to incorporate groups of Americans into their ranks, Shawnees at Chillicothe and neighboring villages turned their vengeance against captives. Even as they had more dead to cover, Shawnees eschewed adopting adult American men. A gruesome execution of the kind that Boone and the salt-makers escaped now awaited captured American men. No longer expecting to chase whites out of Kentucky, the leaders of the confederacy hoped that by joining forces, Ohio Indians would have sufficient numbers to revive and enforce Blackfish's proposal of the Ohio River as a boundary between American and Indian settlements. Although the British had refused to arm the Shawnees in 1783 and had that year ceded the lands south of the Great Lakes to the United States, they soon returned to supporting the Ohio Indian confederacy with goods and guns. By one contemporary estimate, Indians, with British backing, killed at least 1,500 settlers in or on their way to Kentucky between 1783 and 1790. In the early 1790s, the Ohio Indian confederation routed two armies of the United States sent north of the Ohio River.[80]

But newcomers still poured into Kentucky, whose population topped 70,000 by 1790. By then, American squatters were also spilling across the Ohio River and demanding that the United States government defend "their" lands by eliminating "savage" interlopers. In 1794, after the British again betrayed their allies by denying Ohio Indians supplies and security, the confederacy disbanded. The following year, Shawnees and other Ohio Indians signed the Treaty of Greenville, by which they formally surrendered much of what is now the state of Ohio to the United States.[81]

In light of the demise of Chillicothe on the Little Miami and of Ohio Indian claims, Boone's decision to leave the Shawnee town seemed to put him on the winning side of the long war. Certainly, Boone's military exploits during and after the American Revolution have figured prominently in the legends that grew up about him and that glorified him as one of the greatest heroes in the first chapter of the "winning of the West" for the United States. True, Boone, the man as opposed to the myth, wavered about his allegiances to a national cause and waived off claims about his Indian-killing tally. Boone did, though, contend that his captivity at Chillicothe had ushered the town's downfall and the broader defeat of Ohio Indians. "The worst act the Indians ever did," he told his son Nathan, "was showing the way to their towns." By Daniel's reasoning, that crucial intelligence about "the geography of Indian country" allowed Kentuckians to take the offensive and enabled Americans to take over the Ohio Valley.[82]

Yet the West that Boone won was not the West he wanted. Boone's passion was hunting. It is what initially brought him to Kentucky. There, he found a country teeming with animals, whose skins could earn him a living that might free him from farming. In the first years of Kentucky's colonization, Boone's calling became even more important, and his standing rose higher: pioneers needed men like Boone to feed them and turned to the ablest hunters to lead them. But if Boone emerged from the tumult of 1778 with his reputation mostly intact, leadership was passing in Kentucky to men better connected to Virginia's authorities, and the militia took on more of a military hierarchy. The need for hunters also receded as Kentuckians harvested more corn and added to their herds. The hunting, too, was not what it once was.

Take, for example, bison, the numbers of which in Kentucky in the 1760s astonished Boone and other backcountry hunters. From the mid-1770s, though, the new settlers went on a buffalo-killing spree. At Boonesborough, admitted one inhabitant, "some would kill three, four, five, or 1/2 a dozen buffaloes and not take half a horse load from the all." Already in 1775, Daniel Boone sought to curb the wanton destruction of buffalo and other wildlife. At the first (and only) convention of the House of Delegates of the Transylvania Colony, he proposed a bill for preserving game. The idea was buried, as were other schemes to restrain the slaughter. By the mid-1780s, hunters had exterminated all the bison in central Kentucky. The census of other animals, especially ones whose skins had commercial value, also fell precipitously, as Kentuckians exercised their religiously sanctioned dominion over lesser beasts.[83]

Although Boone wanted to hunt, not farm, he did wish to own land. Lots of it, in fact, for the wealth and status that ownership of land brought him and for the security it guaranteed his posterity. That was not so unusual. Lots of white men aspired to own lots of land—and leave the working of it to others, which in Virginia, North Carolina, and later in Kentucky meant to tenants or to enslaved African Americans. Boone owned slaves during much of his life, with his holdings of human property reaching seven in 1787. In these matters, his values clashed decisively with those of Shawnees, who had no wish to accumulate private landholdings. At Chillicothe, as at other Ohio Indian villages, families controlled the fields they worked, but only so long as they worked them. Individual title to land was not a concept that had yet translated into Shawnee.

Developments in Kentucky also dashed Boone's dreams of land ownership. He thought he had acquired vast land holdings from the Transylvania Company, only to see those claims invalidated by the state of Virginia. In 1779, Virginia enacted a new law to govern the distribution of lands in Kentucky, which contained a provision to reward pioneers who had earlier occupied and improved lands. Boone took advantage of that stipulation to obtain a certificate for the maximum 1,400 acres. As he had learned with his grant from the Transylvania Company, the certificate from Virginia did not readily translate into uncontested title. To the contrary, the uncertainty of boundaries and the proliferation of overlapping claims entangled almost every parcel in central Kentucky in costly and lengthy litigation, Boone's included. The problems were exacerbated, as were the inequities of land distribution, by other provisions in the 1779 law. These opened floodgates for speculators, often living far from the dangers of frontier Kentucky, to stake claims to holdings that dwarfed the 1,400-acre maximum allotted to "actual settlers."[84]

Not that Boone was innocent of engrossment or of contributing to the mess of overlapping claims. During the 1780s, hunting land for absentee purchasers and working as an official surveyor occupied Boone. These activities apparently enriched him. For locating lands, he customarily received half of the claim. Surveying brought additional rewards in the form of land bounties. At least on paper, his holdings in Kentucky topped 20,000 acres.[85]

For Boone and for thousands of Kentuckians, claims did not equate with clear titles. In Boone's case, having contracted to "forever Defend the land and premises" that he located, he soon was a party to countless lawsuits as more and more of his surveys came into conflict with other claims. In suit after suit extending through the 1790s, plaintiffs impugned Boone's honesty and accused him of making up instead of measuring boundaries. As damage awards piled up against him, Boone surrendered lands and sold off slaves to pay off judgments and legal fees. Increasingly acidic about the injustices done him by judges and lawyers, he stopped appealing adverse judgments. Frequently he did not appear in court to defend himself. In the fall of 1798, when Daniel failed to respond to a plaintiff's complaint over 6,000 acres of lost land, the judge ordered the sheriff of Mason County, where Boone resided, to take the missing defendant into custody. But the sheriff could not find Boone.[86]

Dispossessed and disillusioned, Daniel Boone had fled Kentucky, and this time he had no intention of returning. Considering how much had gone wrong for him in the two decades after his captivity at Chillicothe, it is no wonder that Boone, on reflection, "felt sorry" about having forsaken his Indian adopters. Seeking a fresh start, Boone accepted an invitation from Spanish officials to relocate to the colony of Louisiana. There, he reunited with some of the same Shawnees with whom he had lived at Chillicothe.

The sad fate of Boone and the sadder of Blackfish raise some obvious "what ifs." What if Boone had stayed with the Shawnees in 1778? What if others at Boonesborough had then joined him at Chillicothe? These "might have beens," however, are questions for an alternate history. For this alternative history, we are confined to what happened at Chillicothe (and Boonesborough), which turned out badly for Boone and worse for Blackfish—likewise, for the settler colonists of Boonesborough, most of whom lost their lands, and the inhabitants of Chillicothe, who lost far more.

In retrospect, Boone's regrets about leaving Chillicothe become understandable, but his actions at the time, which separated him from the Shawnees, spoke louder than any later words. By his deeds in 1778, Boone made clear that even for men with his affinities and empathies, the cultural distance between Boonesborough and Chillicothe remained significant. Although Boone could overcome past animosities, he could not shed his past, could not dump a lifetime of expectations and experiences to embrace the call of Chillicothe to him. He could not fully fit in there, for while exchanges brought greater commonalities to the way peoples lived at Boonesborough and Chillicothe, the similarities did not make them the same. In general, as Boone's actions attested, cross-cultural borrowings altered surfaces more than they changed underlying values.

Still, even as Ohio Indians and Kentuckians differed from one another, competed with one another, and killed one another, their capacity to go to war against one another depended on the encouragement and arms of outsiders. Prior to the interventions by nations and empires, the conflicts between cohabitants of the Ohio Valley were limited in scope and scale. The intrusion of the British Empire, the state of Virginia, and the national government of the United States weaponized the animosities between Ohio Indians and white Kentuckians. Had nations and empires stayed out of the conflict, violence could not have escalated as it did. If it had not, perhaps more combatants could have gotten past their earlier bloodshed and focused on what they had in common?

Here again, the "what ifs" stray into the realm of alternate history. Except that is what happened when these Ohio Valley enemies moved outside the United States and resettled on the west bank of the Mississippi River in Spanish Louisiana. Especially around Apple Creek in what is today southeastern Missouri, Shawnees and Americans made good on Daniel Boone's dictum: they forgot what had happened to them in war and found cross-cultural concord.

As for Chillicothe, the time has long since come to refresh the monuments in front of the Tecumseh Motel. Like the wearing markers and worn motel, the saga that William Galloway scripted ninety years ago is dated. A new sign would correct the misinformation on the existing ones, including the claim that Chillicothe on the Little Miami "remained Ohio's leading Indian town until 1807." More important, instead of just honoring the Americans killed in the attacks on the village, it would add information about the Shawnees and other Ohio Indians who lived in Chillicothe and who died defending it against invaders. Likewise, the stone monument, with its inscription to the "memory of Col. Daniel Boon and 27 salt makers" would benefit from addition. That would tell of Blackfish and the Shawnees who brought the prisoners to their village, adopted some into their families, and invited Americans to live in peace and friendship there.

2

Apple Creek
Rising

FINDING APPLE CREEK IS NOT the problem. Yes, one must distinguish between the creek and the unincorporated community along it that carries the same name. To add to the potential confusion, the village of Old Appleton, which is roughly four miles southeast of the unincorporated community, used to be called Apple Creek. But the waterway is marked on maps, its course meandering generally westward from its mouth on the west bank of the Mississippi River about twenty-five miles north of Cape Girardeau, Missouri.

More problematic is locating any of the six Indian villages that dotted the vicinity of Apple Creek in the late eighteenth and early nineteenth centuries. Home then to approximately two thousand Shawnees and Delawares, these communities emptied nearly two hundred years ago, and they have disappeared from our maps. Along Apple Creek today is a small hamlet named "Shawneetown," whose modern population is considerably smaller than the Shawnee village that was once in its vicinity. French colonists, who were the first European settlers in the area, referred to that original Shawnee town as "Le Grand Village Sauvage." Americans, who came a little later into the region, designated it "the Big Village" or "the Big Shawnee Village." The Shawnees, who were its principal inhabitants, at least sometimes called it Chillicothe.[1]

Present-day Shawneetown sits near the former Big Shawnee Village, but no plaque commemorates the community's bigger past. Nor are any of the other former Shawnee and Delaware towns in the vicinity of Apple Creek marked. In fact, the environs of Apple Creek merit not one of the more than 1,500 historical markers erected in and by the state of Missouri. The nearest official state historical site is at Trail of Tears State Park, about ten miles south of Apple Creek's mouth. There, in addition to picnicking, hiking, and fishing, visitors can, according to the park's website, "gain a better understanding of one of the saddest chapters in American history."[2]

The tragic saga of the Cherokees' forced relocation in 1838 surely deserves to be remembered, but so does the alternative history that earlier played out around Apple Creek. Given the prior troubles between Shawnees (and Delawares) and Americans in the Ohio Valley, harmonious relations between them seemed an unlikely possibility. Yet, that recent history did not repeat itself in the 1790s. Around Apple Creek, transplants from the Ohio Valley lived in the proximity of one another and with French colonists in a Spanish colony. For the most part, peoples got along and continued to do so into the first decade of the nineteenth century when the territory was transferred to the United States.

The surprisingly tranquil convergence of erstwhile enemies had its roots in the disasters suffered by Ohio Indians, the disappointments experienced by American pioneers in Kentucky, and the dilemmas faced by Spanish officials in the Louisiana colony—or, more specifically, that portion of the territory designated as "Upper Louisiana." Until the end of the Seven Years' War, the

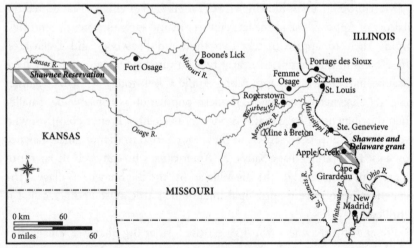

Apple Creek and the Missouri Country, 1780s–1830s

colony belonged to France. Anchored by New Orleans at the mouth of the Mississippi, the lower part of Louisiana offered climate and soil conducive to growing sugar, which attracted substantial investments in land and human property and brought thousands of African slaves to the southern end of the colony. Further up the Mississippi, colonization proceeded more slowly. Coming down from the Great Lakes, Catholic missionaries and fur traders established outposts in Upper Louisiana (which was sometimes designated as the Illinois Country and included territory on both sides of the Mississippi River). From there, the latter group, known as *coureurs de bois* (literally, runners of the woods), ventured up the Mississippi and its tributaries to engage Indians in commerce. By the mid-eighteenth century, a handful of French villages had also emerged on both sides of the Mississippi between its confluences with the Ohio and Missouri Rivers. In the fields around these villages, a few hundred French colonists, hailing primarily from Canada, grew wheat as the primary commercial crop, the local surpluses being shipped downriver to feed enslaved populations in Lower Louisiana and in the French Caribbean. In the early 1760s, French merchants from New Orleans founded a new settlement at the confluence of the Missouri and the Mississippi. The establishment of St. Louis coincided with the defeat of France in the Seven Years' War, which resulted in a remapping of the imperial cartography of North America. New France vanished from the North American mainland. French claims east of the Mississippi River (with the exception of New Orleans) went to victorious Britain, while France gifted the Louisiana colony west of the Mississippi (plus New Orleans) to its ally Spain.[3]

From the perspective of the colony's new Spanish rulers, the challenge was how to make Louisiana a gift that did not keep on taking from an already overstretched imperial treasury. Spain's officialdom particularly puzzled about Upper Louisiana. There, they confronted powerful Indian nations to the east and the west, with the Osages in the lower Missouri Valley being the most numerous and the most threatening to Spanish pretensions of dominion. To the east, Spanish administrators warily eyed the expansionist designs of Britain and later also of the United States. Meanwhile, Upper Louisiana's Francophone colonists were few in number, of uncertain loyalties to the Spanish crown, and engaged in fur trading and farming that did not produce enough revenue to offset the cost of administering and defending the province. No wonder Spanish negotiators balked when initially presented with the French offer of the western side of the Mississippi Valley and regarded the bequest from France as more of a problem than an opportunity.

Ruling on the cheap, Spain delayed sending a governor to Louisiana for several years. When Antonio de Ulloa finally arrived in New Orleans to assume the office, only ninety soldiers accompanied him. Not until 1769 did Spain dispatch a contingent of forty-five soldiers to Upper Louisiana, where they were charged with building and manning two forts on each side of the mouth of the Missouri River. These posts, Ulloa hoped, would keep "the savages in harmony with the Colony" and "prevent the British neighbors from intruding in the lands and dominions which belong to His [Spanish] Majesty." Ulloa was realistic about this show of force, or lack thereof, so he urged the expedition's commander to be polite in dealing with British neighbors, French colonists, and Indian inhabitants. Bowing to an imbalance of power that favored Upper Louisiana's Indians, especially the Osages, Ulloa advised his subordinates to be tactful, letting Indians "believe that we go into their lands without any claim of right, but because they want us to go." By following the French lead and distributing presents, the Indians, Ulloa hoped, would understand that the Spanish intended to preserve the status quo.[4]

Away from New Orleans, French holdovers remained in charge of local affairs and local militias. When residents of Upper Louisiana took the required oath to Spain's King Carlos III, they did so under the direction of officials who had until recently been in the service of his cousin Louis XV. Almost all government business continued to be conducted in French, because, as a lieutenant governor in Upper Louisiana conceded, "there is not at this post anyone who can write Spanish even moderately well."[5]

Although Spanish authorities in Louisiana pretended to preserve the status quo, they also set out to save money and solidify control—aims not easily reconciled. Ulloa pushed subordinates to cut back on presents to Indians. He explained that Indians "like to have lots of things given to them," but then they still "sell their friendship for anything that is offered." To weaken the threat posed by Indians, he also sought to curb their access to firearms. At the same time, Ulloa attempted to impose Spanish regulations on French fur traders by insisting that only those licensed by imperial officials could conduct commerce with Indians in their villages.[6]

These policies (sometimes just pronouncements) met immediate resistance, and Ulloa's successors, as well as lieutenant governors in Upper Louisiana, backed away from them. At the first meeting between Spanish emissaries and visiting Indian leaders in St. Louis, the assembled headmen let it be known that the British were more generous to them. More menacingly, the Osages had numbers on their side. In the early 1770s, the Little

Osages fielded approximately four hundred warriors, the Great Osages perhaps twice that number. By comparison, the contingent of Spanish soldiers
in Upper Louisiana had been reduced to twenty-three, split among three
posts. Angry about Spain's tight-fisted trading policies, groups of Little
Osage and Missouri Indians attacked traders traveling up the Missouri River.
In response, Spanish authorities ordered a halt to trade, which prompted
the Little Osages and Missouris to attack one of the Spanish forts along
the Missouri. The fort's small force quickly fled, leaving the Indians free to
plunder the post's munitions and provisions. Yielding to the Indians' show of
strength, Spanish officials dropped their efforts to discipline the Osages. For
the moment, they became more generous with gifts and stopped enforcing
prohibitions on unlicensed traders traveling to Indian villages.[7]

In the longer run, Spanish officials determined that the success of their
colony depended on attracting more loyal subjects to Upper Louisiana.
Efforts to entice Catholics from North America and Europe, however, lured
few new colonists to the Illinois Country in the 1760s and 1770s. In the
1780s, Spain turned to Indians as a source for settlers, which struck many
Spaniards as a strange choice. After all, some of those same officials had
warned of the dangers that Indians posed—until they decided that Indians
from the east might be enlisted as allies against the Osage threat from
the west.

Exploring this option, the lieutenant governor of Upper Louisiana
hosted four chiefs of the Shawnees, Delawares, Chickasaws, and Cherokees
in St. Louis in 1782. Afterward, he reported that these nations had de-
tached "completely from the affiliations they had previously had with the
English." That overstated the extent of any break and the authority of any
four headmen. Still, these talks laid the groundwork for future emigrations
of these people to Upper Louisiana. A trickle of Shawnees and Delawares
had already moved across the Mississippi in the late 1770s. The number of
Ohio Indians in Upper Louisiana leapt upward after the Revolution. In the
telling of Spanish officials, the independence of the United States was the
greatest blow to Ohio Indiana. With Americans extending "themselves like
a plague of locusts in the territories of the Ohio River we inhabit," Shawnees
and Delawares implored the Spanish lieutenant governor to shelter them
from their "cruelest enemies."[8]

In their dealings with Shawnees and Delawares, Spanish authorities
relied once more on a French mediator. In this instance, the intermediary,
Pierre-Louis de Lorimier, was also a refugee from the Ohio Valley. Born
near Montreal in 1748, Lorimier had moved to the Ohio Country to set

up a trading post in 1769. Through the 1770s and into the 1780s, he traded with and lived among Ohio Indians, gaining fluency in several Indian languages, and, like many *coureurs de bois*, marrying an Indian (in this case, half-Shawnee, half-French) woman. Lorimier developed particularly close ties with his wife's Shawnee relations. He accompanied them on the raid that captured Daniel Boone and the salt-makers in February 1778 (it is unknown if or how he voted on the question of adoption vs. execution) and on the siege of Boonesborough that September. His alignment with Ohio Indians and with the British made his storehouse a target for Kentuckians, who looted and torched it in 1782. Financially ruined, Lorimier joined Shawnees in relocating to the Wabash Valley (in present-day Indiana). He also began to look farther afield and traveled to St. Louis in 1786. There, he negotiated with the Spanish lieutenant governor for a land grant for Shawnee and Delaware Indians, small groups of whom continued to flee the United States and move to Spanish Louisiana during the late 1780s and early 1790s.[9]

In 1793, the Shawnees and Delawares received a formal grant of land from Spain. Totaling approximately 750 square miles, the grant's southern boundary was fixed on Flora Creek, just north of Cape Girardeau, its northern one on Cinq Hommes Creek. The grant ran along the Mississippi River for around thirty miles and extended inland between twenty and thirty miles to the Whitewater River. Apple Creek, running generally from west to east, bisected the grant's northern and southern halves. As a reward for his services and a signal of his influence with Indian and Spanish authorities, Lorimier was appointed as the commandant for the new Cape Girardeau district. He was also given a substantial tract of his own that bordered the south of the grant to the Indians. Over the next decade, he retained the charge of bringing as many Shawnees and Delawares as possible to this district.[10]

The grant, along with other spots in Spanish Louisiana, soon attracted substantial numbers of emigrant Indians from east of the Mississippi. By the mid-1790s, more than one thousand Shawnees and Delawares had moved to Upper Louisiana, clustering in three areas. The largest concentration settled on the grant obtained for them by Lorimier. Around 400 to 450 people inhabited the bigger of the two villages that had been established along Apple Creek, which was located around ten miles up the creek from its mouth on the Mississippi (though only a few miles from the river as the crow flies). The Big Shawnee Village (or Chillicothe) was unusually sizable for a Shawnee town and dwarfed the population of longer-settled French villages in the region between St. Louis and Cape Girardeau. A second cluster of Shawnees and Delawares located to the south and west of Apple Creek and Cape Girardeau along the St. Francis River. A third settlement area opened by the Shawnees was to the north near the Missouri River and around thirty miles west of St. Louis.[11]

If they were not the loyal Catholic subjects on whom colonial officials had initially pinned their plans, the Shawnees and Delawares were for Spanish officials the best immediate option. Along with several hundred Cherokees, who relocated farther south in present-day Arkansas, the Indians significantly expanded the population of the eastern edges of Upper Louisiana. The newcomers interacted amicably with nearby French colonists. Decidedly less peaceful were their interactions with Osages, who resented the incursion of large numbers of new settlers in what they considered not a Spanish colony, but their country. Soon after the Shawnees and Delawares had relocated in Upper Louisiana, the Osages began raiding the new settlements. A delegation of Ohio Indian transplants asked Spanish authorities to intervene and prevent the Osages from killing them and stealing their horses. And Louis Lorimier assured those officials that Shawnees and Delawares stood ready to help in a war against the Americans or the Osages.[12]

As the Spanish welcomed the emigrant Indians to Upper Louisiana, their imperial policy took a paradoxical turn. By the late 1780s, the Spanish authorities identified the expansion of the United States as a rising threat. Yet Spain decided to open its colony to American emigrants, and its minister to the United States made a sweetheart deal with the Pennsylvania merchant and land speculator George Morgan to encourage the settlement of Americans on a 15-million-acre parcel across from the mouth of the Ohio River and extending two degrees of longitude west from the Mississippi. Within this district, the agreement gave Morgan the right to appoint local officials, to have an assembly that enacted local laws, and to guarantee freedom of worship to Protestants. Without waiting for royal confirmation, Morgan circulated handbills promoting the new colony, which he called "New Madrid." The name may have gestured back toward Spain, but the special privileges granted Morgan appeared as if the enterprise were made in (and for) the United States of America.[13]

That is how Secretary of State Thomas Jefferson viewed it. "I wish a hundred thousand of our inhabitants would accept the invitation," wrote Jefferson to President George Washington. To Jefferson, the immigration of Americans into Louisiana promised to deliver "to us peaceably what may otherwise cost a war." The trick for American diplomats was to "complain of this seduction of our inhabitants just enough to make the [Spanish] believe it a very wise policy for them" to continue.[14]

Spanish officials in Louisiana were not fooled. Though a supporter in principle of American immigration, Governor Esteban Miró considered the grant excessive. "Great concessions to one single individual have never produced the desired effect of populating" lands, Miró advised his superiors. Worse, the special privileges granted Morgan would not turn newcomers into loyal, Catholic subjects. These would instead plant a "little republic" in the midst of a Spanish colony. To forestall that possibility, the governor significantly reduced the grant to Morgan, though he did offer the American an appointment as vice commandant of the district of New Madrid.[15]

Other Spanish authorities thought even this too generous and argued that the entire American initiative was misguided. Miró's successor, Governor Francisco Luis Hector, Baron de Carondelet, who took office in 1792, pushed for repeal of Spain's conciliatory overtures toward the United States and its citizens. This reversal involved tightening restrictions on American shipping on the Mississippi, removing Americans who had crossed into Spanish territory without official permission, and discouraging further immigration from the United States. Carondelet also negotiated alliances with Indians on the eastern side of the Mississippi, in hopes of stiffening their resistance to additional American expansion.[16]

Worried as Carondelet was, the American presence was not as yet too daunting. By 1790, fewer than 300 expatriates from the United States (including just over 100 slaves) had moved to Upper Louisiana. Morgan's colony, as Miró predicted, foundered. Most of the seventy colonists who had initially accompanied Morgan had, in the wake of flooding and sickness, departed New Madrid for points east. Morgan, too, returned to the United States.[17]

The greater immediate threat to Spanish rule and peace in Upper Louisiana came not from Americans, but from an escalating conflict with the Osages. In the late 1780s and early 1790s, the Osages intercepted more traders and launched more strikes against both recent immigrants and established villagers. In 1790, the Spanish tried again to put economic pressure on the Osages by preventing traders from traveling to Osage villages. And again, this punishment had limited impact on the Osages, who turned to American and British suppliers and plundered Spanish-licensed traders heading up the Missouri. Pulling back, Lieutenant Governor Zenon Trudeau reopened trade with the Osages, a decision that St. Louis fur traders welcomed. Emigrant Indians and French farmers, however, protested the reversal and demanded a declaration of war against the Osages. Trudeau wavered. His superior, Governor Carondelet, pushed for a test with the Osages. Because there were not enough European men in Upper Louisiana to protect their own settlements, much less successfully invade Osage villages, Trudeau concluded that the assistance of emigrant Indians was essential. If the newcomers "act in concert, they will be able to strike a terrible blow, which may drive the Osage Indians far away." Turning to Lorimier for assistance in recruiting Shawnees and Delawares, Trudeau promised the victors the fruits of conquest. To Shawnees, Delawares, and other Indians who defeated the Osages would come "a territory more abundant in animals than they have ever seen."[18]

In June 1793, Spain declared war against the Osages, but the Spanish lacked the forces to fight it. While French farmers who had suffered losses of property to Osage raiders celebrated the announcement of impending combat, they did not rush to enlist in a military campaign. Shawnees and Delawares also refused to launch an offensive until the Spanish bolstered their promises of lands with weapons, which Spanish authorities failed to provide. As Osage raiders continued to plunder colonial and emigrant Indian settlements in Upper Louisiana, Spanish officials shifted from escalation to accommodation. In part, this shift reflected a recognition of weakness vis-à-vis the Osages. It was also a response to renewed threats from the east. In early 1794, rumors reached Spanish officials that Edmond Genet, an emissary to the United States from revolutionary France, was conspiring with Americans to raise an army to invade Upper Louisiana. Worried that the Osages might combine with Franco-American invaders and fearing a two-front war, Governor Carondelet sent Lieutenant Governor Trudeau to make peace with the Osages. At a conference with Osage headmen in April 1794, Trudeau arranged a demonstration of force, in which "various exercises by the artillery and troops" were performed "to give [the Osages] a great idea of our strength." Yet he followed this ritualized display of war-making with a customary ceremony of conciliation, offering the Osage chiefs an assortment of presents.[19]

In May 1794, the Spanish put relations with the Osages in the seasoned hands of Auguste Chouteau and his family. Chouteau had been a founder of St. Louis. He and his family were the town's leading merchants and had deep ties with Upper Louisiana Indians. Like many French traders, Auguste and his brother Pierre had lived for a time among the Osages, marrying Indian women, fathering *métis* offspring, and earning the confidence of their extended trading families. The Chouteaus received from Governor

Carondelet a six-year monopoly on trade with the Osages. In exchange, Auguste promised to build a fort on the Osage River and to maintain a garrison of twenty men there under the supervision of his brother Pierre. Named Fort Carondelet, the stockade theoretically gave the Spanish a military presence in the heart of Osage Country; in fact, the fort was built more to be a store than a citadel. As operated by the Chouteaus, Fort Carondelet, which was completed in 1795, was principally a site at which to dispense gifts and goods and obtain pelts from the Osages.[20]

Having averted war with the Osages, Spanish authorities returned their attentions to the worrisome ambitions of Americans. Against these land-grabbing people, the Spanish hoped to make common cause with Indians who occupied the lands between Louisiana and American settlements. Yet by 1795, Spanish authorities conceded that support for strategically positioned Indian groups offered only a temporary shield. In a few years, these allies would be overwhelmed, and, at that point, the Americans would march into Louisiana. From there, nothing would keep them from turning south and toppling one Spanish colony after another. Nothing, that is, unless Spain employed "this precious time . . . in acquiring a population capable" of barring American advance across the Mississippi.[21]

It was therefore especially confounding when Spain lifted once more its ban on American immigration in 1795. The policy reversal came after colonial officials determined they had no realistic alternative. Other sources for increasing the dependable population of Upper Louisiana had not fulfilled expectations. The United States alone could supply the needed number of families, concluded Lieutenant Governor Trudeau. International developments contributed as well to the change in course. Rumors of France's interest in retaking Louisiana renewed anxieties about an invasion from that quarter or of an insurrection by French colonists. Also concerning were the persistent intrusions of British traders, particularly in light of Spain's break with England in what had been an alliance against revolutionary France. To this was added the alarming news of a new alignment between Britain and the United States. Looking to forge more cordial relations with the American republic, the Spanish Empire acceded to the 1795 Treaty of San Lorenzo, which resolved the disputed boundary between the United States and Spanish Florida and guaranteed Americans the right to navigate the Mississippi to its mouth. That same year, against the advice of Governor Carondelet, Spain reopened Louisiana to American immigration.[22]

With this policy shift, Spain resolved, for the moment, the problem of peopling Louisiana. Left unsettled was whether the opening to Americans would work. Would Americans come in the expected numbers? Could the defense of Louisiana against the United States be entrusted to people from the United States? Would American expatriates become Spanish patriots? Would these newcomers get along with their French neighbors in Upper Louisiana? And how would prior Indian emigrants from the United States respond to being thrown in again with those whose recent history had made them their "cruelest enemies"?

On all these questions, the policy more than fulfilled the wishes of Spanish officials. Numbers, but not overwhelming numbers, of Americans accepted the invitation to move to Upper Louisiana. The newest comers from the United States, most notably Daniel Boone, adjusted well to life as subjects of Spain. Their encounters with French colonists exposed cultural differences. Frictions between the groups, however, remained limited. Even more surprising were the relations between American emigrants and Shawnee and Delaware villagers. While exiles from the Ohio Valley did not live as one people in Upper Louisiana, they settled harmoniously alongside one another.

The Spanish surmised that with the right incentives Americans could be enticed to Upper Louisiana and away from their attachments to the United States. As Lieutenant Governor Trudeau gauged, many Americans in the Ohio Valley were "disgusted with their [federal] Government." The discontent had numerous causes, but the most important were the failures to protect settlers from Indians, to guarantee land claims, and to secure navigation rights for their commerce to the mouth of the Mississippi River. To win Americans over, Spain needed to promise that Indians would not cause trouble, that title to fertile lands would be certain, and that their produce would have an unimpeded water route to the ocean.[23]

The British undertook a similar program to lure disgruntled Americans to Upper Canada (now Ontario). With promises of peace, cheap land, lower taxes, and a navigable waterway to the Atlantic, the British wooed settlers from western New York across the Niagara River. What the British did not offer was republican governance. No colonial assembly was contemplated. No seats in Parliament were promised. But American immigrants to Upper Canada in the 1790s did not resurrect Revolutionary rhetoric. Low taxation without representation was fine, as long as the government lived up to the rest of the bargain about peace and land and did not interfere in the liberties that Americans expected.[24]

Spanish colonial authorities in Upper Louisiana largely followed the British model in Upper Canada. Spanish promoters touted the blessings of Upper Louisiana, while skillfully playing on the sources of western American discontent. Tracts circulated in Kentucky and Tennessee that boasted about how the soils were better and the climate more temperate on the western side of the Mississippi. According to one broadside, autumn in Upper Louisiana lasted until the fifteenth of January, a claim that proved Spanish boosters as extravagant as Americans when it came to promoting real estate. Even more attractive to Kentuckians and Tennesseans, whose lands were endlessly entangled in overlapping claims and costly litigation, was the assertion that Upper Louisiana had no place for lawyers. Instead, the few disputes that arose were supposedly settled amicably and inexpensively. A Spanish pamphlet also promised a respite for the war-weary; in Louisiana, the Indians were friendly to Spain and happy to assist colonists.[25]

Did Americans buy this hype? John Dodson headed west in the spring of 1798 after seeing an announcement in the *Kentucky Gazette*. That same year, William James, "in consequence of the encouragements, announced in Kentucky [that he was] determined . . . to come and settle" in Upper Louisiana. For many in Kentucky, the calculation was straightforward: stay in a place with high land prices and high taxes or go to one where land was cheaper and taxes lower.[26]

For Moses Austin, the move required little promotion, for a country that has "everything to make its settlers Rich and Happy" could hardly "remain Unnoticed by the American people." In Austin's case, the lure was particularly strong, thanks to a generous grant of more than 7,000 arpents (about 6,000 acres) from the Spanish government. Austin planned to make his fortune by setting up a lead-mining operation and then selling some of the lands to Americans whom he brought to his tract (precisely the system of colonization that Governor Miró had warned about, and essentially the one that Mexico later offered to Austin's son, Stephen, as a lure to bring him and American colonists to Texas).[27]

Other newcomers, like Daniel Boone and his sons Daniel Morgan and Nathan, together with their wives and children, came with less grandiose ambitions. Having lost most of his land claims in Kentucky and having tired of defending his surveys in one lawsuit after another, Daniel Boone sent his son Daniel Morgan to Upper Louisiana in 1797 to learn about prospects there. Father told son to find out how much land was granted to

new settlers, heads of families, and servants. Daniel also instructed Daniel
Morgan to ascertain if settlers were required to embrace Catholicism.
Daniel Morgan located lands he liked on Femme Osage Creek along
the Missouri River about fifty miles from St. Louis. He then met with
Lieutenant Governor Trudeau, who promised Daniel Boone 1,000 arpents
(about 850 acres) for himself and an additional 600 arpents for each
family that accompanied him. Trudeau further assured him that American
immigrants would be free to practice their religion so long as they did not
try to propagate their Protestantism. Enticed, Daniel and Rebecca, along
with sons Daniel Morgan and Nathan, daughters Susannah and Jemima,
their husbands and wives and seventeen grandchildren, set out for Upper
Louisiana in 1798.[28]

For Daniel Boone, land was not the only magnet. He relished as well the
esteem that Spanish officials bestowed upon him, reverence that had eluded
him in Kentucky as his lands were lost and his integrity was impugned.
On his arrival in St. Louis, the officialdom of Upper Louisiana came out to
greet Boone and staged a military parade in his honor. Trudeau's successor, a
Frenchman named Pierre Charles Dehault Delassus, met with Boone to re-
affirm his predecessor's land commitments and to appoint Boone as "syndic"
for the newly created Femme Osage district. In that position, which was
akin to Lorimier's in Cape Girardeau, Boone combined military, civil, and
judicial authority over the area in which he and his family settled.[29]

As syndic, Boone ruled as he wished had been the case in Kentucky. In
the administration of justice, Boone dispensed with the usual formalities.
Holding court beneath a big tree, Boone, the jurist, brooked no pettifog-
gery. He insisted that facts be presented quickly and clearly, and he rendered
judgments and punishments swiftly and surely.[30]

Abundant game also called Boone to Upper Louisiana. Although Boone
was in his mid-sixties when he moved to the Spanish colony, he remained a
man who loved to hunt. In his last years in the Ohio Valley, Boone struggled
to make much of a living, for the most valuable animals had been nearly
extinguished and thickening human populations had thinned the census of
other game. Upper Louisiana presented Boone with hunting opportunities
that rivaled those he encountered when he first came to Kentucky. The
Femme Osage was situated thirty miles west of St. Charles, which at the
time was the westernmost European village on the Missouri River. Far from
other population clusters, the local woods around Femme Osage Creek
teemed with wildlife. And Boone was surely enchanted by stories of the
game to be found further up the Missouri River.

Thomas Cole, *Daniel Boone Sitting at the Door of His Cabin on the Great Osage Lake* (1826). Painted six years after Boone's death, Cole's canvas portrayed the aging pioneer as an isolated hunter with only his dog for a companion. Cole, like many American artists who followed in his footsteps, erased the presence of Indians from the landscape. And, as in many nineteenth-century biographies of Boone, the painting erases the companionship he had with Shawnees in his later years. *Courtesy of Mead Art Museum, Amherst College*

The settlement nearest to the Boones was Rogerstown. Located along the Meramec River, it was about twenty miles south of Boone's home and was the northernmost of the Shawnee villages in Upper Louisiana. The town, which was home to around one hundred Shawnees, took its name from James Rogers, an adopted captive whose life story glimpsed what Boone's alternate history might have been had he remained in Chillicothe in 1778. Like Boone, Rogers had been captured and adopted by Shawnees, who renamed him Onothe. Although Rogers lived at a Shawnee village on the Scioto River, he had encountered Boone briefly in 1778, when Boone, hunting with Blackfish, had stopped in the village and repaired Rogers's rifle. Unlike

Boone, Rogers stayed with the Shawnees, (in one story) married a daughter of Blackfish, became a leader in his own right among his adopted kin, and a led a band of Shawnees to Upper Louisiana. Two decades after their first meeting, Boone and Rogers met again.[31]

The meeting between Boone and Rogers was one of many between Boones and Rogerstown Shawnees. In the years after the Boones had settled on the Femme Osage, Rogerstown Shawnees, a few of whom had been at Chillicothe on the Little Miami in 1778, occasionally stopped in to see Daniel at his home. Daniel reciprocated with visits to Rogerstown, and the aging pioneer sometimes went hunting with his Shawnee neighbors. A camaraderie developed between Boone and Rogerstown Shawnees, as they reminisced about times past and together ranged the lower Missouri Valley woods in pursuit of game. Among the Shawnees, one known as "Indian Philips" was a white man who had been taken captive as a boy and, like Rogers, had remained with the Shawnees. Remember, Philips told Boone, when you lived with us at Chillicothe and "we were all glad," a rose-colored recollection that erased the nastiness that had come between them in the years after 1778. But the sentiment certainly applied twenty-plus years later, when Boone and Shawnees, having come together once more, reveled in their reunion.[32]

How did Boone get along so well with Indians with whom he had been at war? His willingness to forget certainly helped. But there was more to it. While living on the Femme Osage, Boone revealed his secret to a traveler who had stopped by his home. When encountering unfamiliar Indians, Boone advised, "always meet them frankly and fearlessly, showing not the slightest sign of fear or trepidation." Then, "by kind acts and just treatment, keep on the friendly side of them." It helped too to give Indian women "small presents, however short you may be of them." The recipe generally worked for Daniel Boone, allowing him to get along with Indians, if not to live permanently with them.[33]

Would other emigrant Americans in Spanish Louisiana follow this prescription, or find another path to peace with Indians, as well as with French neighbors? Boone, after all, was different. He had set himself apart from his fellow expatriates, both in how he had acted toward Indians and where he had settled. Geographically, the vast majority of Americans in Upper Louisiana took up lands closer to the west bank of the Mississippi River. The choice of the Femme Osage reflected the premium Boone placed on hunting. Many of the other Americans who emigrated to Spanish Louisiana also pursued game as a core component of their livelihoods, though not as avidly as Boone. By 1800, American farmsteads could be found from New Madrid to St. Louis. One of the largest concentrations of Americans was in the vicinity of Cape Girardeau, where Louis Lorimier offered tracts to emigrants on the edges of the Shawnee and Delaware grant.

The pattern of American settlement contrasted with both those of emigrant Indians and of French *habitants*. American farmsteads dotted the landscape; emigrant Indians and French colonists clustered in villages. French colonists brought with them the system that had been in place along the St. Lawrence River in Canada. There and in Upper Louisiana, they lived in compact villages and farmed narrow strips of land. Their properties often fronted the rivers. By contrast, Americans dispersed their farmsteads across the countryside. The preference of Americans for upland areas away from the river's edge, which they believed to be healthier, put some distance—both cultural and physical—between them and French *habitants*. The benefits of American locations impressed at least one Frenchman, Nicholas de Finiels, who observed that the latest newcomers could be counted on "to pick an advantageous spot," while his countrymen, "who had occupied these shores for sixty years, never thought of building there."[34]

During the late 1790s (and for many decades after), the cultural differences between long-settled French and recently arrived Americans spurred considerable commentary. Sometimes, these were relatively neutral descriptions of French versus American ways, highlighting distinctions in architectural forms (French vertical log construction against American horizontal style) or agricultural and dietary preferences (French wheat as opposed to American corn). More often, though, cross-cultural commentaries came down in favor of one people's ways over the other. Typically, such comparisons set the traditionalism of creoles against the inventiveness of Americans. Even as he credited the industriousness of Americans, de Finiels paid homage to the easy ways and communal spirit of French residents. Yet in almost the next breath, de Finiels condemned the indolence of *habitants*. Some critics went further. The harshest insisted that French colonists must forsake their customs, especially their system of common-fenced open-field cultivation. So, too, the French connection with Indians came under fire from the advocates of American ways.[35]

This critique of the intimacy of French-Indian relations pointed to a difference bigger than what crops French and Americans planted and foods they preferred, which way they laid logs and fields, or how they clustered or dispersed homes across bottomlands or uplands. The French connection with Indians had its roots in the exigencies of the fur trade and in the imbalance between men and women in the French migrations to North American colonies. With French men greatly outnumbering French women across New France, marriages with Indians became common. People with Indian ancestry made up a substantial portion of the population of French villages in Upper Louisiana. These included the Indian wives of French men, their mixed offspring (*métis*), and enslaved Indians, the last group generally people who had been taken as captives by other Indians and then sold to French colonists. By contrast, most Americans who emigrated to Spanish Louisiana arrived, like the Boones, as families. Males and females came in much more equal numbers than among the French, which reduced the Americans' incentive to intermarry with Indians. Rather than enslave Indians, American emigrants preferred to stick with African American slaves, though many could not afford any, and those who could usually owned no more than one or two.[36]

All these differences could have created conflicts, but the French preference for bottomlands and American for uplands kept them mostly out of each other's way in the late 1790s. Only in a few places did cultural tensions get particularly heated. One flashpoint was around Moses Austin's lead mine. There, *habitants* spent a portion of each year skimming lead from the top three to four feet of soil. This custom, they held, was not trespassing. Appropriating unused lead from the surface, they insisted, was no different from collecting leftover crops after the harvest or to taking wood from forests that creoles considered common property. This assertion of customary common rights, however, flew in the face of Austin's more exclusive understanding of private property. French residents took a measure of revenge in 1802, when the Osages staged a raid against Austin's mine and store. Denied their common rights, they refused to assist Austin in the defense of his too private property.[37]

Although tensions between French and Americans ran high at times and in spots, their conflicts did not turn violent through the turn of the century. According to Lieutenant Governor Trudeau, the vast majority of Americans "behaved very well." They quietly acclimated to life in Spanish Louisiana and left their more disorderly ways behind them in the United States.[38]

More astounding was the absence of violence between American newcomers and the Indian peoples they had driven from the Ohio Valley. After a generation of incessant raiding and intermittent warfare between Americans and Ohio Indians, these people carried plenty of bloody baggage with them to Upper Louisiana. To the Shawnees, Americans were their "cruelest enemies," who had spread like "locusts" into their Ohio homelands and threatened now to do the same in their new country. To Americans, Ohio Indians were "savages," who had stolen their property, butchered their kin, and deserved no quarter, regardless of age or gender or protestations of being peaceful and friendly. While the French preference for bottomlands and the Americans for uplands kept them mostly out of each other's way, both emigrant Indians and emigrant Americans sought habitations away from alluvial floodplains. Both also mixed farming with herding and hunting, which meant each group claimed rights in the woods that extended beyond their fields. The ingredients for renewed conflicts appeared all in place. Daniel Boone and Rogerstown Shawnees overcame that history, but Boone was different from most of his fellow American migrants, living well away from them and distanced from them by his understanding that "many things happen in war that were best forgotten in peace." And yet, the relations between Boone and Shawnees were not so exceptional. In their first years together in Upper Louisiana, emigrant Indians and Americans lived near one another, traded with one another, and even socialized together.[39]

That was the case at Mine à Breton, where Moses Austin established his lead-mining operation. Austin's son Stephen remembered that scores of Shawnees and Delawares ventured from their villages on the St. Francis River to conduct business at his father's store. As a boy, Stephen recalled, he "often played with the Shawnee children." Adults played, too. Having traveled some distance to reach Austin's store, Indians then stayed to race horses, gamble, drink, and dance with French and Americans.[40]

Like Boone's place on the Femme Osage, Austin's operations at Mine à Breton were situated well west of the main belt of settlement in Upper Louisiana; the area between Cape Girardeau and Apple Creek closer to the Mississippi River presented a greater test to the rapport between emigrant Indians and emigrant Americans. In the Cape Girardeau district, Americans settled in larger numbers and the Shawnee and Delaware villages around Apple Creek were also much more populous than the ones on the St. Francis. Yet, at least in the first years after Americans arrived in the area, the peace between emigrants was not disturbed, and exchanges, both economic and social, created ties between them.

Several factors contributed to this amity. Certainly, size mattered. In the Cape Girardeau district, which saw the largest influx of emigrant Indians and Americans, the combined census of these newcomers numbered only a few thousand by 1800. With the nearest French village of any size in Ste. Genevieve to the north of the district, the density of population did not yet press on the availability of land. That allowed incoming Americans to settle close to, but not yet on top of, Shawnees and Delawares. Their fields did not overlap, and they shared the woods, where game was sufficient to meet the needs of locals. Within the district, the population of Shawnee and Delaware villages still surpassed the total on the more scattered American farmsteads, which checked more aggressive Americans from trespassing on Indian lands.

Spanish governance, particularly the appointment of Louis Lorimier as the local commandant, kept the peace between emigrants as well. Lorimier's long-standing ties to Ohio Indians, especially to his wife's Shawnee kin, reassured emigrant Indians of Spanish backing. At the same time, Lorimier cultivated links to incoming Americans. Here, he fused his military, civil, and judicial authority with his economic interests. Emigrant Americans buttressed the defense of Upper Louisiana and bolstered the bottom line of Lorimier's trading business.[41]

The relative absence of support from other imperial entities also contributed to the serenity of relations. In the Ohio Valley, backing by external governments—Britain for Ohio Indians, Virginia and then the United States for Kentuckians—underwrote the shift from small-scale raiding to larger-scale warfare. In Upper Louisiana, by contrast, the Spanish did not supply arms, even when they wanted to enlist emigrant Indians in a war against the Osages. British agents continued to siphon the fur trade in Upper Louisiana away from Spanish networks, but Britain did not seek to foment a broader revolt among emigrants against Spanish rule. So, too, individuals within the United States, secretly and not so secretly, coveted the territory west of the Mississippi River. But through the 1790s, expansionists within the federal government preferred, as Jefferson suggested, to take "peaceably what may otherwise cost a war." Moreover, the administrations of George Washington and John Adams did not share Jefferson's enthusiasm for territorial expansion. During their presidencies, the United States government made no move to encourage American immigration to Upper Louisiana or to lend support to Americans settled in Spanish territory. Finally, while France bid to reclaim its North American empire, Napoleon's men advanced no campaign to undermine Spanish rule in Louisiana by arming French colonists.

For their part, Shawnee leaders made clear they preferred being free of external meddling. In 1799, as rumors circulated of a new conflict involving the United States, Great Britain, and Spain, Shawnee emissaries conveyed their unwillingness to be pulled into a war among foreigners. As Joseph

Jackson, one of the salt-makers captured with Boone who had remained with the Shawnees and accompanied them to Upper Louisiana, reported, Ohio Indians had migrated to Upper Louisiana "for the purposes of living in peace & quietness & never intended to concern themselves again with the quarrels of White People."[42]

Emigrant Indians could not, however, avoid being entangled in conflicts with the Osages. Under the management of the Chouteaus, trading with the Osages resumed, but raiding by the Osages persisted, with settlements from Ste. Genevieve through the Cape Girardeau district bearing the brunt of these strikes. As one Shawnee headman complained, the Spanish "coddle[d]" the Osages when they should have killed them. Similar sentiments were expressed by another emigrant Indian leader, who asked why "the Osages when they steal, pillage, and kill, . . . get nothing but caresses, and are supplied with everything."[43]

These protests prompted no change in Spanish policy, but the movement of Americans did begin to shift the balance of numbers and power. For the moment, that most threatened the hegemony of the Osages. Americans in Upper Louisiana, having also suffered losses to Osage raids, found their interests aligned with Shawnees and Delawares. For emigrant Indians and emigrant Americans, a common enemy offered the best reason to make common cause.

In quick succession after 1800, the Louisiana colony passed from Spain to France to the United States. Transitions in colonial regimes initially brought limited changes on the ground. New flags flew. New officials appeared. Relations between the peoples of Upper Louisiana stayed mostly the same. Indeed, the borders between the cultures of emigrant Indians and emigrant Americans further blurred in the first years of the nineteenth century.

Signed on October 1, 1800, the Treaty of San Ildefonso transferred the Louisiana Territory from Spain to France. For Spain, the loss of Louisiana relieved its drained royal treasury of the expenses of administering an unprofitable colony. For France, the reacquisition brought it back to the North American mainland. Napoleon envisioned Louisiana as more than a partial restoration of the old New France; he saw it as the foundation for an enlarged North American empire, one that might regain Canada and appropriate part of the United States as well.

Not until the spring of 1803 did residents of Upper Louisiana's villages hear officially that they resided once more in a French colony. Yet, just as the cession from France to Spain in 1762 had resulted in no immediate change in governing personnel, so the retrocession left officials in place. Where four decades earlier Spain had assumed responsibility for the payment of French representatives, now France did the same for Spanish soldiers and administrators (many of whom were French).

Rumors about the deal between France and Spain and Napoleon's designs for an expansive North American empire—and they were just rumors, for Spain and France had struck their deal in secret—alarmed American officials, beginning with the newly elected president, Thomas Jefferson. "There is on the globe one single spot, the possessor of which is our natural and habitual enemy," wrote Jefferson in the spring of 1802 of the reported French take-over of New Orleans. French control over New Orleans, Jefferson fretted, would force the United States into a renewed dependence on Britain. To avoid that fate, he launched a diplomatic initiative to secure New Orleans for the United States. Talks between France and the United States took an unexpected twist; after Napoleon's dreams for a resurrected North American empire foundered in Haiti, his forces were depleted while putting down a slave revolt there. Now fearing that the Louisiana colony might fall into the hands of his enemy the British, Napoleon instructed his emissaries to offer the whole of the French territory on the North American mainland to the United States.[44]

In place of the reborn, though ultimately stillborn, French empire, Jefferson imagined the United States birthing an "empire of liberty" across the Louisiana Territory—the pursuit of which allowed him to overcome his misgivings about the constitutionality of the purchase and to revel in the peaceful acquisition of what he had earlier worried might have cost the United States a war. And, as almost every US history textbook informs students, for $15 million, the United States essentially doubled its territory, adding more than 500 million acres at the bargain price of three cents per acre.[45]

Not everyone shared Jefferson's enthusiasm, or that of subsequent textbooks. When word of the sale leaked, Spanish officials disputed its legitimacy, insisting that the terms of Spain's transfer of the colony back to France prohibited the territory's resale to a third party. Within the United States, opposition focused on the worthlessness of the lands acquired. As Federalist Fischer Ames archly observed, the United States had only "gained a great waste, a wilderness unpeopled with any being except wolves and wandering Indians." Yet even those like Ames who deemed the purchase far too expensive did not let the views of the territory's Indians enter their calculations about the costs and benefits of the acquisition.[46]

The dreams of the United States reached Upper Louisiana in November 1803 in the persons of Meriwether Lewis and William Clark and the Corps of Discovery they co-captained. Having made its way down the Ohio River, the expedition started up the Mississippi, stopping at Cape Girardeau on November 23. That day, Captain Lewis called on Commandant Lorimier. It was probably best that Lewis, not Clark, went to see Lorimier, for it was Clark's brother, George Rogers, who had commanded the force that sacked Lorimier's store in Ohio in 1782.

Upon arrival at Lorimier's house, Lewis discovered that the commandant had gone with his family to attend a horse race. Lewis tracked Lorimier to the course, though he missed the contest. He did witness its aftermath, when Lorimier was busy settling disputes about the wagering. The whole scene reminded Lewis of horse races "among the uncivilized backwoodsmen" of Kentucky and Tennessee, which was not surprising since most of the people at the races had come to Louisiana from those states. Worse, in Lewis's estimation, they were the most dissolute representatives of the American backwoods.[47]

Lewis assessed Lorimier more generously. In his journal entry, Lewis noted that Lorimier bore his wagering losses cheerfully. Lewis then reviewed Lorimier's personal history (including the financial losses that had driven him out of Ohio and the recovery of his fortune in Upper Louisiana). He also detailed Lorimier's appearance (with special attention to his long hair that almost reached the ground), and his wife (described as a Shawnee woman, though "from her complexion is half blooded only"). Lewis fastened on the ways in which her attire mirrored her mixed heritage: "She dresses after the Shawnee manner with a stroud leggings and mockinsons, differing however from them in her linin which seemed to be drawn beneath her girdle of her stroud, as also a short Jacket with . . . long sleeves more in the stile of the French Canadian women."[48]

After meeting Lorimier, the Corps of Discovery continued up the Mississippi and established a camp across the river from St. Louis. The winter months spent near St. Louis gave the co-captains time to prepare for their journey up the Missouri River, which was intended to explore the far reaches of the Louisiana Territory and, as Jefferson instructed, to discover the "most direct & practicable water communication across the continent, for the purpose of commerce." The most important instruction Lewis and Clark received in the winter of 1804 came from French merchants in St. Louis. In particular, the counsel of the Chouteaus provided essential information about the territory to the west and the diplomatic protocols for dealing with

Indians in the Missouri Valley. The Chouteaus and other French traders in St. Louis also supplied the Corps with a variety of goods—gunpowder, bullets, knives, awls, blankets, brass buttons, fishhooks, ivory combs, needles, textiles, tobacco, vermilion paint, and assorted other commodities—that experience taught were in demand in Indian villages upriver.[49]

Lewis and Clark's introduction to Upper Louisiana and their instructions from French merchants preceded the official transfer of the territory. Not until March 1804, a little more than three years after the territory had reverted to France and almost a year after its purchase by the United States, was the flag of the United States raised at St. Louis. At the formal ceremonies, Captain Amos Stoddard, appointed as the first American commandant of Upper Louisiana, represented the United States. Because France had no official in place, Stoddard also acted as the agent for Napoleon's regime. Stoddard wrote about the enthusiasm with which Upper Louisiana's inhabitants received news of the transfer to the United States. "I have not been able to discover any aversion to the new order of things; on the contrary, a cordial acquiescence seems to prevail among all ranks of people."[50]

Cordial acquiescence was far from universal. According to one resident, some French *habitants* believed that "the transfer of the Country by the FIRST CONSUL [Napoleon] is only a temporary thing & that he will ere long take them under his wing again." Stoddard also soon learned of discontent among the Osages, who, William Clark reported, had burned the letter notifying them that the United States had taken possession of the country.[51]

The fears of the French and the fury of the Osages would have flamed hotter had President Jefferson implemented the plan he floated for de-peopling and re-peopling Upper Louisiana. Rather than rapidly incorporating the territory and its colonists into the United States, as stipulated in Article Three of the treaty between France and the United States, Jefferson contemplated a radical alternative. Below the thirty-first parallel, the territory of Orleans would be established, and it would follow the usual path to statehood. North of that latitude, additional white settlement would be discouraged, with a constitutional amendment required to reopen lands for purchase. Taking this plan a step further, Jefferson suggested that French and American settlers in Upper Louisiana be relocated to lands east of the Mississippi. In turn, Indians living east of the Mississippi would move to Upper Louisiana. The separation of Indians and white Americans would end warfare between them, argued Jefferson, and it would allow future American settlement to occur in an orderly fashion. Only when lands east of the Mississippi were filled up, which Jefferson calculated would take fifty years, would American settlers recolonize Upper Louisiana. By that distant day, Jefferson hoped that Indians would be properly civilized and readily assimilated into American society. Eventual white settlement west of the Mississippi River would, however, still be carefully managed to assure that farmsteads were not strewn about in a haphazard manner and that litigation over land titles did not once more clog American courts.[52]

Political opposition in Washington scuttled Jefferson's population transfer plans, which was good for acquiescence to American rule in Upper Louisiana. Neither French nor American inhabitants wanted to uproot themselves to take up lands on the other side of the Mississippi. What they did want was to have their property claims in Upper Louisiana secured. News, or simply rumors, that the United States government was closing the territory to further American emigration, pushing for the unsettlement of existing colonists, or refusing to validate existing land claims agitated both French and American residents. So did word that Congress was debating bringing Upper Louisiana under the administrative aegis of the Indiana Territory. By Stoddard's estimate, 80 percent of Upper Louisiana's French and American settlers objected to this incorporation, which they feared would deprive them of local autonomy and leave them at the mercy of distant officials.[53]

For their part, the Osages vigorously and sometimes violently protested further transfers of Indians and Americans from east of the Mississippi, but they could not curb the flow. With or without the endorsement of the United States government, Indians continued to move from east to west, with many new groups joining Shawnees, Delawares, and Cherokees as emigrants in Upper Louisiana. Although some eastern Indians crossed the Mississippi only to hunt, many came to settle, and both hunters and settlers clashed with Osages. Americans, who came in even greater numbers, did too. Between 1800 and 1804, the American population in Upper Louisiana, which included both white American citizens and enslaved African Americans, jumped by more than 50 percent. By the time the United States assumed official control in Upper Louisiana, its non-Indian population topped 10,000, with white Americans and their African American slaves accounting for about 60 percent of that census.[54]

In response, Osages attacked European and Indian settlements near the Mississippi, as they had been doing for years, and assaulted interlopers who ventured closer to their villages. In the latter category fell Daniel Boone's son Nathan, who was punished by Osages while trapping on the Niango and Grand Rivers in the fall of 1803 and again in the winter of 1804. Each time,

Osage parties forced Nathan and his accomplices to surrender their store of skins, as well as their horses and other property. Nathan surely remembered his father telling of a similar expropriation in the late 1760s on one of his first hunts in Kentucky. Like his father, Nathan might have considered himself lucky to have escaped a bloodier punishment. Not everyone was so fortunate. Just as a number of the long hunters who accompanied the elder Boone into the Ohio Valley were killed when caught poaching, so the next generation of American pioneers found themselves the targets of the Osages of the Missouri Valley. For the most part in the first years of the nineteenth century, the Osages took property. They also occasionally killed people. But these punishments failed to deter new arrivals who continued to trespass in territory that the Osages considered theirs.[55]

In fact, the aggressions of the Osages backfired by bringing their adversaries closer together. Despite their misgivings about rule by the United States, French settlers valued the arms that emigrant Americans brought with them to Upper Louisiana and the armies that the United States could field. Ditto emigrant Indians: driven from their homes east of the Mississippi by encroaching Americans, they now joined with them for their mutual protection.

More than common defense underlay the collaboration between peoples around Apple Creek. Cooperation between cultures shaped the local economy in the Cape Girardeau district, to the benefit of both emigrant Indians and emigrant Americans. Some of the Americans who settled near Shawnee and Delaware villages performed useful services, acting as gunsmiths and blacksmiths, for neighboring Indians. In turn, Indians traded furs and farm produce to Americans in the area.[56]

In the early nineteenth century, the ways of emigrant Indians and emigrant Americans grew more alike. That process was now several generations in the making. Incubated in the eighteenth-century Pennsylvania backcountry and seasoned in the crucible of the Revolutionary Ohio Valley frontier, the convergence of cultures reached a new level in Upper Louisiana. The adoption by Americans of Indian modes of dress (the use of animal skins or the preference for moccasins as opposed to European footwear), Indian crops (especially corn, but also squash, pumpkins, and beans), and their increased reliance on hunting caught the attention of outside observers. But Euro-American pundits particularly fixed on the "progress" of emigrant Indians and how it made them more American. Although the Shawnees and Delawares resided in compact villages that more closely resembled French towns than American-style "open country neighborhoods," their mixed modes of subsistence and land-use patterns were difficult to differentiate from those of Americans nearby. Perhaps the most far-reaching of these adaptations was the Shawnees' embrace of stock raising that went beyond their activities in the Ohio Country. At their villages on Apple Creek, the Shawnees possessed large herds of horses, hogs, and cattle. Like European colonists in general, the Shawnees allowed their pigs to roam free in adjacent forests. But it was from Americans in particular that the Shawnees took their stock-raising ways. Their fields, according to Nicholas de Finiels, were "securely fenced in the American style in order to protect their harvests from animals." Adding to the similarities between Shawnee and American settlements was their shared practice of laying logs horizontally for their structures. Only on close inspection did observers notice a subtle difference in cabin architecture: Indians notched their logs on the top, while Americans did so on the bottom. But this small variation in material cultures was lost on many contemporaries, who emphasized instead the apparent confluence of cultures.[57]

In the 1980s, archaeologist Duncan Wilkie conducted extensive excavations in the Apple Creek region. His team focused its digs in places where historical sources and maps placed the Shawnee and Delaware villages. But Wilkie was unable to definitively determine the location of the Indian towns, because the similarities between the material cultures of emigrants in the late eighteenth and early nineteenth centuries blurred the distinctions between what were Shawnee and Delaware sites and what were American ones.[58]

Judging by contemporary accounts, the relative prosperity of emigrant Indian villages was one marker between their settlements and nearby American ones. After touring the Cape Girardeau district in 1804, Amos Stoddard pronounced the Shawnee and Delaware towns on Apple Creek "the most wealthy of any in the country." Their log houses, some of which had a second story, were well furnished, their storehouses held abundant supplies of surplus corn, and their barns sheltered a good supply of cattle and horses. To the new American commandant, the Indian settlements on Apple Creek were more American than neighboring American farmsteads, at least when rated by their material well-being.[59]

As had been the case in the Ohio Valley, the blending of subsistence systems and material cultures did not erase the disparities in underlying values. Although Boone and Rogerstown Shawnees occasionally hunted together, they continued to view their prey in oppositional ways. Shawnees and Delawares maintained the elaborate rites by which they expressed their gratitude to animal cousins. Neither Daniel Boone nor any of his American comrades adopted these rituals or accepted animals as their equals. Likewise, in taking up stock raising, emigrant Indians integrated domesticated animals into existing rituals; ceremonies once exclusively connected with hunting became means of paying respect to slaughtered cattle and pigs. Such ceremonies had no analog among Americans, whose religious views neither ascribed spiritual powers to animals nor assigned special rituals to the killing of animals. So, too, the powers and obligations of men and women marked a persistent divide between Indian and American newcomers. For Americans, farming remained the responsibility of men; for Indians, the fields stayed the domain of women. Control over this and other life-giving and life-sustaining activities gave Shawnee and Delaware women sway within their villages that still had no parallel among patriarchal American counterparts. Above all, divergent constructions of property rights in land impeded a deeper cultural confluence. The Americans' ideal of eternal, individuated ownership of a specific tract contradicted the understandings of Shawnees and Delawares, whose villagers held their land collectively, assigning only a temporary right to the farmers of smaller parcels.[60]

The cultural differences that kept Daniel Boone from being at home in Chillicothe on the Little Miami remained in the villages around Apple Creek, as well as at Rogerstown. What's more, if we accept Meriwether Lewis's estimation, the emigrant Americans in the Cape Girardeau district were no different from the "uncivilized backwoodsmen" of Kentucky and Tennessee. Alongside this unruly bunch resided Shawnees and Delawares, who had come to Upper Louisiana to get away from these same vicious nemeses.

But Lewis underestimated the ability of these Americans to live in peace with one another and with Shawnee and Delaware Indians. For their part, Shawnees and Delawares got past the cruelties that Americans had inflicted upon them in the recent past. Around Apple Creek, emigrant Indians and emigrant Americans generally got along while Spain administered the area. They continued to do so when France briefly reclaimed Louisiana. As the rule of the United States dawned, concord still prevailed.

How can we explain the unexpected turn in the relations between emigrant Indians and emigrant Americans? How did these groups overcome their differences? What factors figured in the escape from a recycling of recent history and the entry into this alternative history?

One critical takeaway is that relations between peoples did not develop in isolation. In a variety of locations over a couple of generations, the changing cast of surrounding players and the shifts in their relative powers shaped the character of contacts between emigrant Indians and emigrant Americans. In the Pennsylvania backcountry where Daniel Boone first met Delaware and possibly Shawnee Indians, the encounters occurred between peoples who were themselves relative newcomers to the area and in a colony whose demography was changing rapidly owing to the influx of large numbers of newer comers from the borders of Britain and German-speaking principalities. Looming over and trying to exert control over migrations and internal relations in Pennsylvania were leaders among the Iroquois, the colonial government of Pennsylvania, and the ministries of the British Empire. Decades later, Boone and Shawnees and Delawares reconnected in the Ohio Valley. These meetings took place against the backdrop of the clash of French and British empires and then between Britain and several of its North American colonies. When Ohio Indians first intercepted Boone, the imperial struggles lingered only in the background, and Indians merely stripped the poacher of his skins. By the time Shawnees captured Boone and the salt-makers in 1778, the Americans' War of Independence had inserted itself into the conflicts between Ohio Indians and Kentucky pioneers and enabled the combatants to shift from small-scale raiding to larger-scale warfare.

By contrast, in Upper Louisiana the reunions between Boone and Rogerstown Shawnees and between emigrant Indians and emigrant Americans around Apple Creek happened in a very different context. The Louisiana colony may have then belonged to Spain, but its colonial population was almost entirely French (insofar as French-speakers from Canada were customarily designated as French). These French men and (many fewer) French women provided examples of how to deal with and live in peace with local Indians, including through marriages to Indian women. The veneer of Spanish authority was especially weak in Upper Louisiana, which encouraged the policies that induced Indians and Americans to relocate from the United States. That weakness also discouraged Spain from escalating conflicts with Louisiana's Indians, particularly the Osages, who were the dominant power in the region to the beginning of the nineteenth century. Indeed, the weakness of the Spanish and the strength of the Osages abetted the alliance between emigrant Indians and emigrant Americans.

Another lesson is in how constricted and malleable were national and imperial attachments. How else to account for the ease with which French traders and *habitants* in Upper Louisiana accommodated to Spanish rule, adjustments made easier by the limited presence of Spaniards and the narrow changes they introduced? Or how Shawnees and Delawares, in the Ohio Valley and then in Upper Louisiana, proclaimed allegiances in turn to French, British, and Spanish "fathers," rhetorical pledges that held only as far as they aligned with the interests of their own villages? The same was true of the loyalties of Americans in the First West of the United States, who, with the right inducements, made themselves at home in Upper Canada and Upper Louisiana. The primacy of local concerns allows us to better understand how emigrant Indians and emigrant Americans could turn so quickly from cruelest enemies to newest friends.

Numbers also mattered in determining enmities and amities. Through most of the 1790s, emigrant Indians outnumbered emigrant Americans in Upper Louisiana, which further checked those Americans who tried to occupy lands claimed by others or to upend the peace with Shawnees and Delawares. A surge of immigration from the United States in the early years of the nineteenth century tipped the census toward Americans, even in the Cape Girardeau district where emigrant Indian populations were highest. The tilt, however, was not yet so great as to upset the general harmony around Apple Creek.

A final lesson here concerns the convergence and divergence of cultures. Generations of close contact instigated borrowings that heightened the resemblances between the material cultures and modes of subsistence of emigrant Indians and emigrant Americans in Upper Louisiana. Although growing similarities did not erase enduring differences, neither did cultural distinctions destine Indians and Americans to implacable hatred or doom them to unceasing conflict. To the contrary, under the right circumstances, which were in place in Upper Louisiana at the end of the eighteenth and opening of the nineteenth centuries, they could get along. And they did.

At the time of the territorial transfer to the United States, the remarkable rapprochement that had risen around Apple Creek did not attract the attention of officers of the United States. Amos Stoddard noted the prosperity of the Shawnees on Apple Creek; he did not comment on their peace with American neighbors. Meriwether Lewis had even less to report about emigrant Indians and their interactions with Americans. After visiting Lorimier on November 23, 1803, and commenting on the unruliness of Americans in the Cape Girardeau district, Lewis rejoined the Corps of Discovery and continued up the Mississippi. Two days later, his journal entry noted Shawnee huts and tents near the mouth of Apple River. Lewis added that about seven miles from the mouth of this stream, there was a settlement of Shawnees large enough to merit being called a village. Presumably, this information came from Lorimier, for Lewis did not visit any of the Shawnee settlements around Apple Creek.[61]

For the moment, the concerns of Lewis and Clark were with getting to the mouth of the Missouri River and readying themselves and their Corps for their journey west. Two years later, that venture brought the Lewis and Clark expedition to the shores of the Pacific Ocean. At the western end of the journey, as everywhere along their route, Lewis and Clark had the best reason to overcome their differences with Indians: their lives depended on it.

3

Fort Clatsop

A Pacific Coast

FINDING FORT CLATSOP IS NOT a problem. Located about five miles south-west of Astoria, Oregon, along a tributary of the Columbia River that Lewis and Clark named for themselves, the site has been designated a national monument. A reconstruction of the fort in which the Corps of Discovery spent the winter of 1805–1806 has been built there. But the location of Fort Clatsop—that is, on which side of the Columbia River the Corps wintered—has taken on more importance later than it did at the time. How the site was chosen and who helped choose it has become the stuff of "wishtories" that have recently developed about the Lewis and Clark expedition.

The Lewis and Clark expedition reached the Pacific Ocean in the middle of November 1805. On the 24th of that month, the co-captains decided the time had come to decide where to build their winter camp. They invited the members of the Corps to vote on the matter. Although they were then on the north shore of the Columbia, the majority supported crossing to the south bank. That side appeared to have a more temperate climate, to be better situated for contacting a passing "vestle [on the ocean] from whome we can procure goods," as Clark explained, and possessed more abundant game. The last factor figured prominently in the decision, for harvesting wild meat would be essential for surviving the winter. Even if Indians could supply enough food, exchanges over the last few weeks showed that their prices "are So high that it would take ten times as much to purchase their *roots & Dried fish* as we have in our possession." Fortunately, from Indian

The reconstruction of Fort Clatsop was based on the drawing of its plan by William Clark in his journal. But while the reconstructed fort stands on the site of the original, its entrance faces south. The original was likely entered from the east. *Photo by the author*

informants, the Corps ascertained that elk were plentiful on the south shore of the river. That animal was especially valuable, as it was larger than deer, easily killed, and its skins better for clothing.[1]

What has taken on heightened significance two hundred years later are the ballots cast by two members of the Corps. As Clark recorded, York, his African American slave, sided with the majority to examine the south side for a suitable site. The other ballot of exceptional note was attributed to "Janey," Clark's sometime name for Sacagawea, an Indian woman who had joined the expedition the previous spring. He recorded that she was "in favour of a place where there is plenty of Potas," likely meaning a plant local Indians called "wapato."[2]

The vote about which side of the Columbia River should be the site of winter quarters became a centerpiece of bicentennial commemorations of the expedition. It is easy to see why: as reimagined at age two hundred and encapsulated in the siting of Fort Clatsop, the Lewis and Clark expedition delivered a kinder, gentler origin story of US westward expansion. In museum exhibitions, historical re-enactments, theatrical performances, television documentaries, toys, biographies, and even cookbooks, bicentennial productions typically featured a multiethnic cast that got along with one another and with the Indians they encountered. And in the votes by York and Sacagawea, the expedition glimpsed the democratic promise of the American West.[3]

In truth, these were "wishtories." The one-time enfranchisement of Sacagawea and York presaged no new birth of freedom for either of them, and the soggy winter that the Corps of Discovery spent at Fort Clatsop created neither fast friendships nor lasting bonds between the representatives of the United States and local Indians. Beyond the vote on the fort's location, the Corps of Discovery's season at the western end of the expedition's trail offered few actual moments from which to construct stories about racial and gender uplift or enhanced cross-cultural understandings. Interactions between the Corps and their natives near the mouth of the Columbia River were strained from the start and did not much improve as neighbors got to know one another. And the actions of the explorers on their March 1806 exit from Fort Clatsop nearly shattered the cold peace that had prevailed over the previous months.[4]

There were no breakthroughs in intercultural relations at Fort Clatsop; the best that could be said is that the Corps coasted through its sojourn there. In their management of Indian affairs at Fort Clatsop, Lewis and Clark did just enough to get what they needed and to get away without any blood spilled. A low bar? Perhaps. But the absence of violence was no small accomplishment, especially compared with the abundance of bloodshed on the Ohio Valley frontier where Lewis and Clark (and many in the Corps) had come of age.

From that perspective, Fort Clatsop offers a vantage point from which to assess how far Lewis and Clark had come. In most histories of the expedition, that is logged in miles, which the co-captains carefully calculated and daily entered into their journals. Measured in those terms, Fort Clatsop marked the westernmost point of their expedition and its literal turning point. But of greater significance is the figurative distance Lewis and Clark had traveled.

For many years prior to the Louisiana Purchase, Thomas Jefferson dreamed of a grand expedition to explore the territory beyond the Mississippi and find the best route to the Pacific Ocean. Even before the deal with France was finalized, now President Jefferson appointed his secretary, Meriwether Lewis, to command the "Corps of Discovery." Lewis, in turn, brought in his friend, William Clark, as co-captain. Jefferson did not know Clark, but he knew his older brother George Rogers Clark, who had commanded the

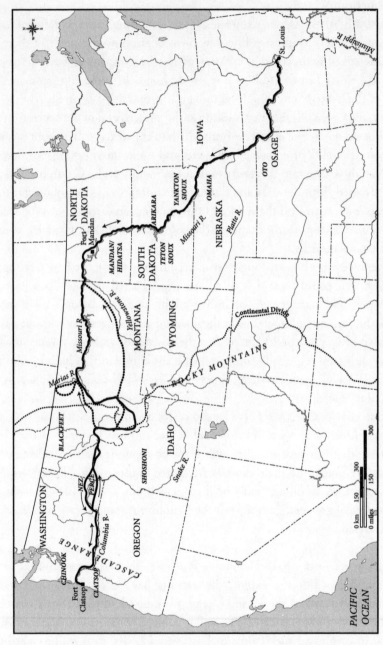

Lewis and Clark expedition route from St. Louis to Fort Clatsop and return, 1804–1806

invading army that sacked Chillicothe in 1782. Immediately following the War of Independence, Jefferson first proposed an exploration of the continent and approached George Rogers Clark about leading it. That expedition remained on Jefferson's drawing board, but twenty years later, William Clark and Meriwether Lewis prepared themselves for a journey to the Pacific. In May 1804, the co-captains led the Corps up the Missouri River. Their way west turned out not as Jefferson or they anticipated, but the captains and their troops adapted well enough to the unforeseen to reach their Pacific destination eighteen months after departing from St. Louis.

To ensure that the expedition fulfilled his designs for it, Jefferson issued an extensive set of directives to Lewis. The president instructed the explorers to chart the course of rivers and range of mountains, to catalog information about plants, animals, and peoples, and to establish the sovereignty of the United States over it all. In dealing with Indians, Jefferson charged Lewis to make a "friendly impression" while making clear that the United States had supplanted other European powers. "You should inform [the Indians] through whose country you pass, or whom you may meet, that their late fathers the Spaniards have agreed to withdraw all their troops, from all the waters of the Mississippi and the Missouri, that they have surrendered to us all their subjects Spanish and French settled there, and all their posts and lands." Still, just as Spanish authorities had several decades earlier sought to win over Indians grown accustomed to the French, so Jefferson reminded Lewis to reassure natives that they need not worry about the change in regimes. The United States stood ready to "become their fathers and friends" and to furnish in trade an array of valuable goods to accommodating Indian children.[5]

In addition to providing written instructions, Jefferson concerned himself with the explorers' training. That preparation began with his own tutoring of Lewis, including giving his secretary access to the expansive library at Monticello. It continued by sending Lewis to Philadelphia, where he received a crash course in the natural and human sciences from the nation's leading experts, most notably Dr. Benjamin Rush. Although Jefferson claimed to have selected his secretary to command the expedition because of his "familiarity with the Indian character," Lewis had far less experience than the man he brought on as his co-captain. As an officer in the United States Army, Lewis had traveled through Ohio Indian countries, but his duties involved few face-to-face dealings with Indians. Clark's military service provided him with more direct acquaintance. Clark's experiences, however, hardly prepared him for the diplomacy the expedition required; he had previously fought against Indians in battles and been present at treaty-making councils in which American officers dictated to, as opposed to negotiated with, Ohio Indian leaders.[6]

Much of what Lewis and Clark learned in the East turned out to be wrong about the West. Consider their miseducation about North American geography. Schooled in Enlightenment theory, Lewis and Clark were taught that the continent possessed a rational, symmetrical design, in which its West paralleled its East. The Missouri River, in this cartographic blueprint, resembled the Ohio, the Rocky Mountains replicated the Appalachians. Thus, the easiest route to the Pacific seemed a matter of following the Missouri to its source, locating a western equivalent of the "Cumberland Gap" through the Rockies, which the maps carried by Lewis and Clark optimistically depicted as a single ridge, then navigating down the Columbia River to the ocean. Based on these assumptions, William Clark plotted out in January 1804 how long each of the legs of the upcoming journey would take. Laying out distances and travel times, while factoring in variables about the size of the expedition and the potential of being slowed by encounters with hostile Indians, Clark concluded the Corps would make it to the Pacific and back to St. Louis by September 1805. That prediction underestimated the duration of the journey by a full year. The western half of North America, Lewis and Clark learned, was no mirror of the East.[7]

Fortunately for Lewis and Clark, they acquired better guides and more informed guidance as they proceeded west. The core of the Corps was composed of soldiers in the United States Army, who, like the captains, had cut their martial teeth wresting the Ohio Valley from Indians. Clark also enlisted several civilians from around his home in Louisville. The ideal candidates, according to Lewis, were backwoodsmen in the profile of a young Daniel Boone, expert in hunting and inured to the hardships of frontier life. To these ranks, Lewis and Clark added several Frenchmen (often of mixed European and Indian heritage) once they reached the Mississippi River. Many of the French additions were employed solely as boatmen, prized for their knowledge of the Missouri River and for the muscles needed to pole and pull the expedition's heavy boats upstream. While most of these *engagés* (engaged men) signed on only for the first leg of the Missouri River journey, others, like François Labiche and Pierre Cruzatte, ended up employed for the entire expedition and brought to it their experiences as traders with Indians in the Missouri Valley. The Corps was especially well served by the hiring of George Drouillard in November 1803. Born to a French-Canadian father and Shawnee mother, Drouillard had migrated to the Cape Girardeau district of Upper Louisiana as a youth. Around Cape Girardeau, his family associated with the similarly lineaged relations of Louis Lorimier, and Drouillard honed his proficiencies as a hunter, tracker, scout, and interpreter, particularly of Indian sign languages. On the way west (and the way back), Drouillard's skills in each of these realms proved of critical importance.[8]

During their final preparations for the voyage up the Missouri, the Corps of Discovery camped across the Mississippi River from St. Louis, which afforded the co-captains opportunities to make useful contacts and gather valuable intelligence. Through the winter, the captains crossed the Mississippi several times to attend events in St. Louis, including the official ceremony transferring the Louisiana Territory to the United States in March 1804. Lewis and Clark also parlayed with St. Louis's creole merchants and enjoyed the hospitality of Auguste and Pierre Chouteau. From the Chouteaus and other French traders in St. Louis, the captains gained more knowledge about the Indians of the Missouri Valley and about the protocols that governed diplomacy and commerce with native peoples.[9]

Chief among these insights was the importance of presents to the construction of peaceful and friendly relations. Like French, Spanish, and British authorities, Thomas Jefferson and other American officials disliked the expense of gifts. They preferred to decree terms of intercourse to Indian supplicants. But bowing to the reality of Indian power in a region beyond the control of the United States and the need to compete for Indian affections, the government of the United States supplied Lewis and Clark with eighty-nine medals to bestow upon Indian headmen. Although Lewis and Clark expected to make the presentation of the peace medals a signature of the bid for friendship with Indians, their discussions with traders in Upper Louisiana convinced them to augment the expedition's store of gifts and goods.[10]

The Corps embarked up the Missouri River on May 14, 1804, but the captains had to wait eleven weeks before first testing their diplomatic skills. Frustrated by their inability to meet with Indians in the lower Missouri Valley, Lewis and Clark finally got their desired gathering in early August. At a site the captains designated Council Bluff, six chiefs and their warriors of the Oto and Missouri tribes, along with a French trader who resided with them, came to the camp of the Corps of Discovery. After initial greetings on the evening of August 2, a more formal council commenced the next day. The conclave afforded Lewis and Clark their initial opportunity to display the military power, technological prowess, and material wealth of the

United States and to assert their charges from Jefferson. The exhibition, which was intended to shock and awe, featured a parading of the Corps, a rapid, repeated firing of the expedition's booming air gun, and a flaunting of the store of goods carried by the expedition. In keeping with Indian expectations about which Lewis and Clark had been tutored in St. Louis, the rites also included the passing and smoking of a ceremonial pipe and an exchange of gifts. For their first council, with their stock full, Lewis and Clark were generous with presents, awarding Oto and Missouri headmen whiskey, printed commissions acknowledging the authority of chiefs, and several peace medals. Finally, this and future councils involved lengthy speeches, made longer by the need for translations (which were often problematic). On this occasion, Lewis spoke first, announcing the change of regimes in the Louisiana Territory, promising Indians an abundance of trade goods from their new "great father," pleading for peace among his Indian "children," and inviting native emissaries to visit the nation's capital. Indians then responded. According to Clark, the Otos and Missouris expressed great satisfaction with what they had heard and pledged to heed the counsel offered by the captains of the Corps of Discovery.[11]

The responses pleased Lewis and Clark. The proceedings, in their view, offered a model for establishing good relations between the United States and Indians in its newly acquired Louisiana Territory and for enabling the Corps of Discovery to get along with and get what they needed from the peoples they met as the expedition went west. But while Lewis and Clark hoped to emulate their initial success by following the format of the first council and speaking from the same script, changing circumstances and changing Indians precluded that.

The challenges of dealing with different Indians became obvious seven weeks later when the Corps of Discovery encountered the Teton Sioux (Lakotas), or more specifically, the Brulé band of the Tetons. Before the expedition began and again from informants in St. Louis, Lewis and Clark heard tales of Sioux hostility that painted their aggressions against other Indians and their extortions of traders traveling along the Missouri River with a broad and undifferentiated brush. Lewis and Clark witnessed one manifestation of this generic threat during their meeting with Oto and Missouri chiefs, whose nations had coalesced in part to defend themselves against attacks by the Sioux. In late September 1804, when the Corps of Discovery moved into the stretch of the Missouri peopled by the Tetons, the American party got a firsthand look at the pride and power of the Lakotas and some sense of the divisions and distinctions among those labeled (by their enemies) as Sioux. In councils with Teton chiefs, Lewis and Clark paraded their men, displayed their technology, demonstrated their weapons, delivered their speeches, participated in smoking rituals, and offered what they considered a generous assortment of presents. Lakota leaders were neither shocked nor awed. To the contrary, at the conclusion of a meeting on the expedition's keelboat on September 25, one of the Teton headmen, known to Lewis and Clark as the Partisan, demanded more gifts and hurled insults at the Americans. In response, Clark drew his sword. Lewis ordered the Corps to ready for combat. Indians on shore brandished their weapons. Only the intervention of another Lakota chief, Black Buffalo, de-escalated the tensions. Black Buffalo's conciliatory gestures kept the peace, but he rejected Clark's subsequent bid to shake hands.[12]

The following day, Lewis and Clark accepted an invitation to visit a nearby Teton village. There, they were generously feted, watched Indians dance, and received a gift of 400 pounds of buffalo meat. The good feelings the event engendered were tempered, however, by the co-captains' refusal of Black Buffalo's offer of female companionship, which the Lakota headman intended as a means to make these outsiders into insiders, into fictive kin. In addition, the Lakotas' conspicuous display of Omaha Indian captives, as well as Omaha Indian scalps, flew in the face of Lewis and Clark's command that Indians be made to get along with one another under a *Pax Americana*. Clark also noticed that the flag of the United States that captains had presented the previous day was set alongside Spanish banners, an indication to the Americans that these Indians did not accept the claims of a new sovereign. In fact, the Lakotas recognized neither the Spanish, nor the Americans, nor any Indian or European power as their superiors.[13]

The next day mixed another set of visits and ceremonies that ended badly. Once more, Clark rejected the opportunity to consort with a young Lakota woman, despite being asked by his negotiating counterpart "to take her & not Dispise them." Further misunderstandings led 200 armed Tetons to gather menacingly in sight of the Corps. And when the Corps of Discovery sought to take leave of the Brulés on September 28, several warriors, again following the Partisan's lead, grabbed the keelboat's rope, demanding that they be given another flag and additional tobacco. The first impulse of Lewis and Clark was to resist this shakedown. But Clark reluctantly tossed some tobacco to Black Buffalo, who used it to again defuse the tensions. Momentarily mollified, the warriors released the rope and ended the attempt to further detain the Corps.[14]

Ill will from the various altercations lingered. Reflecting on the behavior of the Lakotas several months later, Clark declared them the "vilest miscreants of the savage race" and "the pirates of the Missouri." Viewing American traders with contempt, Clark reasoned that the Sioux believed the worse they treated merchants from the United States, the better terms they would get. Only coercion would make them dependent on the goods and then the goodwill of the United States, bringing peace and prosperity under American rule to the Missouri Valley.[15]

Although Clark did not spell out what coercive measures he had in mind, he and Lewis knew Jefferson's preferred strategy. East of the Mississippi River, Jefferson argued, controlling trade, rather than fielding large armies or fighting costly wars, was the best and least expensive means to get along with Indians while subordinating them. As eastern Indians became ever more reliant on American traders for their supply of merchandise, especially agricultural implements, Jefferson hoped Indian men would give up hunting in favor of farming. That transition would ease their assimilation into the American republic, while also leaving Indians with "surplus" lands to sell to the United States. Or, in a less hopeful version of Jefferson's scheme, commercial dependence would ensnare Indians in debts that forced them to cede their lands.[16]

As protégés of Jefferson, Lewis and Clark embraced this long-term vision for the peaceful subordination and incorporation of Indians, but their immediate situation required different practices and postures. In the First American West, before the Louisiana Purchase gave the United States a new West, the fast-growing population of American settlers tilted the balance of power ever more against Indians. There, by the beginning of the nineteenth century, American emissaries like Lewis and Clark could dictate to Indians and resort to armed force when needed. But out where Lewis and Clark were on the Missouri, the Corps of Discovery had only its crew, guns, and goods to buttress the captains' assertions about the wealth and power of the United States and the "empire of liberty" that Jefferson projected the Louisiana Territory to become. The fact that the Partisan and his followers did not prostrate themselves to American pretentions insulted Lewis and Clark and the nation they represented. Having been raised with the honor code of the Virginia (and by extension Kentucky) gentry, the captains were conditioned to answer such offenses with lethal force. They recognized, however, that the time was not right to fight. For the moment, they confined their full fury to the pages of their journals.

For all the blood pressures raised, the confrontations between the Lakotas and the Corps of Discovery resulted in no bloodshed. Most of the credit for calming the waters belonged to Black Buffalo, not Lewis or Clark. The American captains expressed only grudging appreciation for Black Buffalo's interventions, and they developed little understanding for the internal politics of the Lakotas, evident in the rivalry between Black Buffalo and the Partisan. They showed even less awareness of the ambitions and anxieties that drove the external relations of the Lakotas. Lewis and Clark did grasp that their mission did not depend on securing the dependence of the Sioux; the Corps of Discovery alone could not accomplish that. Nor did it require that Lewis and Clark and their men get along with the Tetons or any other band of Sioux; they did not accomplish that either. It did hinge on getting on with their journey. That they did.[17]

The volatile, yet not violent, encounter with the Lakotas set the Lewis and Clark expedition up for its successful passage to the Pacific Coast. Imagine an alternate history in which Lewis and Clark had manfully defended their honor and their nation's honor. Had the Corps of Discovery battled the Partisan's people, it seems almost certain the combat would have ended the expedition's westward journey. If some of the Corps had survived a skirmish, the party's ranks and supplies would have been too depleted to continue up the Missouri. But instead of demonstrating the undaunted courage befitting men of the upbringing of Lewis and Clark, the captains opted for wiser caution. In their initial confrontation with the Lakotas, they let their pride fall so the expedition could go forward. That dexterity was critical in late September 1804, and this trait became more and more important as the Corps of Discovery ventured farther west.

The first sign of new flexibility came less than two weeks later, when the expedition arrived at the villages of the Arikaras. In their formal councils with the Arikaras in mid-October 1804, Lewis and Clark stuck to their familiar speeches and to the same exhibitions of American prowess, prestige, and presents they had employed downriver. Their journal entries about the Arikaras evinced no greater understanding of that people's domestic politics or foreign policies than had been the case with the Lakotas. But relations between the United States and the Arikaras also advanced outside these official channels, as men in the Corps accepted the invitations to engage in sexual intercourse with Arikara women. With the Arikaras, the captains again refused, but they bowed to local custom by allowing the men in the Corps to indulge.

Not that Lewis or Clark were proud of their bending or of the ensuing intimate associations. Of the dalliances between their men and Arikara women, the captains wrote sparingly and obliquely. "Their womin verry fond of carressing our men. &.," relayed Clark in his journal entry of October 15, 1804, the ampersand alluding to the activities that followed the caresses. Subsequent references to sexual intercourse stayed in the same bowdlerized lane, though repeated references to administering treatments for venereal diseases to the men of the Corps spoke more directly to the prevalence of such relations.[18]

In the captains' eyes, sexual relations, which commenced with the Arikaras and continued through the journey, reflected the depravity of Indians. To Lewis and Clark, the Indian men who offered them women were pimps. Indian women who allowed themselves to be offered, or who solicited members of the Corps on their own, were prostitutes, selling their bodies in exchange for gifts and goods. The sexual relations with Arikaras and later with other Indian women reinforced the instructions that Lewis and Clark had received about gender relations in Indian societies, which had taught them that native females were essentially enslaved by their fathers and polygynous husbands.[19]

What Lewis and Clark did not learn back east and did not pick up on their way west was the status and powers that Indian women held in many of their societies. This was particularly true of groups like the Arikaras, where women's roles as the principal agriculturalists gave them exalted roles as protectors of their people's material and spiritual well-being. Likewise, while native women saw sexual relations as an avenue to acquire material goods, they also envisioned them as a means to obtain spiritual powers from the men with whom they copulated. In turn, these powers could be transmitted to their Indian partners.[20]

This explained the allure of York to the Arikaras (and several other tribes). As historian James Ronda discerned, "in the Arikaras' eyes, York was the central attraction of the Lewis and Clark expedition." To the Arikaras, York's blackness was viewed as a sign of his special spiritual power. For Indian women, then, sexual intercourse with York created a conduit to awesome supernatural forces.[21]

The buffalo-calling rite of the Mandans, which Lewis and Clark witnessed in January 1805, depended on such transmissions from man to woman and then to another man. One aim of the ceremony was to lure bison toward Mandan hunters. Another was to pass the powers of older hunters to younger men. To facilitate the transfer, young men offered their wives to their elders.

As with many of the sexual practices and religious beliefs of Indians, much of the meaning behind this rite eluded Lewis and Clark. Not that lack of understanding precluded the men in the Corps from participating. In the words of a French trader who was also present during the 1805 buffalo-calling rite, the members of the expedition were "untiringly zealous in attracting the cow."[22]

Abetting their understanding of these Indians' ways, Lewis and Clark spent more time near the Mandans and neighboring Hidatsas than they did with any other Indian group. After their meetings with Arikaras in mid-October, the explorers headed upriver and reached the five villages of the Mandans and Hidatsas in what is today central North Dakota later that same month. They stayed there until the following spring, building a fort, which they named Fort Mandan in honor of their nearest neighbors. Because they interacted with the Mandans and Hidatsas over a period of months, as opposed to just a few days, Lewis and Clark and their men got to know more about these Indians than those they had encountered earlier in their travels. They also got along better with them.[23]

As had become the pattern, after arriving in the vicinity of Mandan and Hidatsa villages, Lewis and Clark moved quickly to initiate the formal councils through which the captains introduced American technologies and goods and their vision of a new Plains order. Like tribes downstream, the Mandans and Hidatsas were impressed by the Corps of Discovery's weapons and wares—not so impressed, however, for while the message of the American emissaries was new, the trade items they carried were not. The Mandan villages were a grand emporium to which Indians from across the northern Plains came to barter, as did European traders peddling an array of commodities that eclipsed in quality, variety, and price the items presented by the Corps of Discovery. Unwilling to disrupt existing arrangements, the Mandans and Hidatsas, like the Lakotas and Arikaras, resisted the imposition of a *Pax Americana* in which raiding ended and trading with non-Indians was exclusively routed through St. Louis (and the United States).[24]

Although the inability to instantly rearrange relations on the Plains frustrated the diplomatic objectives that Thomas Jefferson had assigned to Lewis and Clark, the American cause was once again served by informal contacts. During the five months that the Corps lived close to the Mandans and Hidatsas, the Americans' triangular-shaped fort welcomed scores of Indian guests through its generally open gates. Many stayed for hours. Some remained overnight. Indians reciprocated by hosting explorers in their circular lodges. Often trade motivated visitations. The Corps, like many of the more nomadic tribes on the Plains, traveled to the Mandan and Hidatsa villages to obtain beans, squash, and especially corn. Indian trading partners offered hides and meat, and the Corps had metal goods to exchange. Over the course of the winter, the expedition's smiths did a brisk business repairing guns, mending hoes, and sharpening and fabricating knives and axes for Mandan and Hidatsa customers.

Beyond commerce, the visits back and forth afforded time for the members of the expedition and their Indian neighbors to learn more about one another and from one another. From the Hidatsas, who regularly ventured west to hunt buffalo and take captives, Lewis and Clark received new and much-needed information about the country and people that lay ahead of them. With the Mandans, the Corps developed especially amiable relations. Days and nights in the company of one another offered opportunities for Indians and Corps members to socialize: to swap stories, play music, sing, dance, and sleep together. "They are the most friendly, well disposed Indians inhabiting the Missouri . . . brave, humane, and hospitable," wrote Clark of his native neighbors at Fort Mandan.[25]

The period of close and congenial contact ended in early April 1805 when a downsized Corps, now numbering thirty-three, departed from Fort Mandan. The captains had earlier discharged the expedition's *engagés* since the keelboat they manned was not suitable for the upper stretches of the Missouri River. At the same time, during the winter at Fort Mandan, the Corps added four newcomers to its ranks: Jean Baptiste Lepage, Toussaint Charbonneau, Sacagawea, and Sacagawea's newborn son. Lepage and Charbonneau, having traded with Indians further up the Missouri River, brought some knowledge about the territory and people that awaited the Corps. Sacagawea possessed greater familiarity with them, having been born and grown up in the mountains to the west as a member of the Lemhi band of Shoshone Indians. Taken captive by Hidatsa raiders around 1800, when she was about thirteen years old, Sacagawea was one of two Shoshone wives of Charbonneau. The other wife was left behind and has been largely forgotten. Sacagawea accompanied the American party to the Pacific and back to the Mandan and Hidatsa villages and has become the most famous member of the expedition, apart from the co-captains.

For all the acclaim she has gained posthumously, the basics of her biography remain uncertain. We have no idea what she looked like. The journals of the Lewis and Clark expedition are silent on her physical appearance, and no other firsthand account has been discovered. The questions about when and where she was born and when and where she died continue to provoke debate, as does the meaning and pronunciation of her name (or, as some claim, her names). In the expedition's journals, she is mentioned more than one hundred times, but only eleven of these use her name—ten times by some spelling of Sacagawea and once by Clark, in his record of the vote on the location of Fort Clatsop, as "Janey." The vast majority of the references to Sacagawea designate her as "the Indian woman" or as an appendage of her husband, as in "Charbonneau's woman" or "Charbonneau's wife."[26]

The ways in which the expedition's journalists referred to Sacagawea exposed large blind spots about their view of her, of other Indian women, and of gender relations in their society and Indian societies. The degradation of Indian women was a topic to which Lewis and Clark repeatedly returned. Indian women, according to the captains, were loose, lascivious, and lewd, either willingly prostituting themselves or doing so under the command of tyrannical fathers and husbands. Sacagawea generally escaped such censuring, though Lewis found her imperturbable demeanor as she related the story of her capture and her lack of emotion upon returning to her native country a sign of how simple her wants were. "If she has enough to eat and a few trinkets to wear," Lewis contemptuously suggested, "I believe she would be perfectly content anywhere." But neither Lewis nor Clark, who was far more kindly disposed toward Sacagawea, ever vilified her as they did other Indian females. Ironically, Sacagawea better fit the profile of a slave than did many of the Indian women Lewis and Clark so disparaged. Hidatsa raiders had abducted Sacagawea and forcibly relocated her. Then, Charbonneau had purchased her, along with another Shoshone woman, and made both his wives. To the expedition's journalists, being the wife of a European man raised Sacagawea above other Indian women. But the appellation "Charbonneau's woman," in fact, denominated the freedoms Sacagawea had lost as a captive of the Hidatsas and the consort of a European man.[27]

The gaps in the historical records about Sacagawea have left ample room for "wishtorical" exaggerations of her role in the expedition and about her personal life. Sculptures, paintings, plays, poems, novels, and movies make her the pathfinder for the expedition. Fictional representations imagine that she and William Clark got along *really* well. The sources that exist offer no evidence of a romance, though they do reveal that Clark sought to protect her when Charbonneau beat her and oversaw the education of her son after the expedition ended. For her part, Sacagawea did not guide the Corps of Discovery through the mountains and to the sea; she did provide helpful

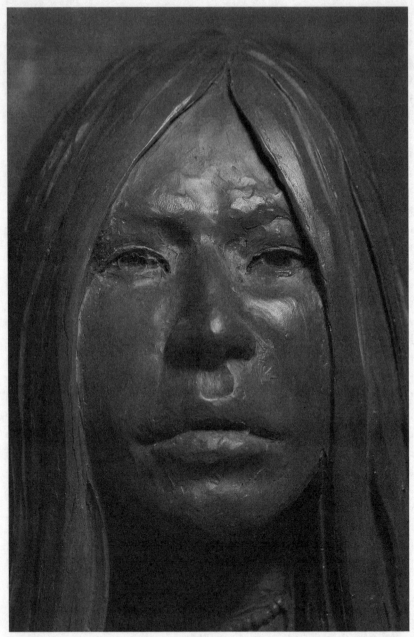

Richard V. Greeves, *Bird Woman* (2001). For the bicentennial commemorations, Richard Greeves completed a series of sculptures of the Lewis and Clark expedition, including of individual Indians the Corps of Discovery encountered. For his lifesize rendering of Sacagawea, designated here by one of her other names, "Bird Woman," Greeves, like so many other artists, had to invent what Sacagawea looked like, since there are no descriptions of her on which to base her likeness. *Courtesy of the Autry Museum of the American West*

recollections about routes when the explorers reached the lands in which she had spent her childhood.

In the country of the Shoshones and through her time with the expedition, Sacagawea's mere presence mattered. Meeting Shoshones proved a challenge for the Corps of Discovery. For several days in August 1805, the explorers searched for Shoshones, from whom they needed to obtain horses to transport them and their supplies across the mountains. Day by day, the necessity increased as it became apparent that the "Stony Mountains" were much more than the single ridge their maps and their miseducation had told them to expect. After a number of near misses, they finally found a band of Shoshones, and a council commenced. The appearance of Sacagawea, who turned out to be the sister (or perhaps just a close relative) of the Shoshone chief Cameahwait, made for what Lewis described as a "really affecting" encounter and undoubtedly assisted the captains in their negotiations. In other instances, too, the presence of Sacagawea and her baby persuaded Indians that the Corps of Discovery was not a war party, as an all-male company might have been taken. "The Wife of Shabano our interpretr We find reconsiles all the Indians, as to our friendly intentions," determined Clark, for "a woman with a party of men is a token of peace."[28]

Clark's reference to Charbonneau as "our interpreter" and other entries in which Sacagawea is the Corps' "interpretess to the Snake Indians" speak to the principal role for which the two were hired. Although not the stuff of "wishtories," able translation was of vital import to the peaceful passage of the Corps of Discovery through the countries of scores of Indians. From the start of the expedition, the problem of accurately translating from one language to another and often through several languages plagued the expedition. At times, the captains had to rely on sign language, at which George Drouillard was particularly skilled, to "converse" with Indians. At best, the resort to signing and the reliance on interpreters of uneven abilities made for cumbersome communications. At worst, mistranslations and misinterpretations created potentially dangerous misunderstandings. At the very least, it should remind us that when the journalists of the Lewis and Clark expedition recorded what Indians said, it was what they understood once the words came through a long and less than perfect chain of translations.[29]

What Indians said to the Corps of Discovery is hard for us to know; what they thought about the Lewis and Clark expedition is even more elusive. We do know that many of the groups that Lewis and Clark encountered were not particularly impressed by these travelers or their wares, not impressed enough at any rate to take note of the expedition's passage in their people's "winter counts" and oral histories. For many, this was just one more trading party, and not a very well-stocked one. Especially as their store of goods depleted, the Corps of Discovery seemed like an impoverished band of traveling salesmen. Their bold pronouncements about American wealth and power stood in sharp contrast to their limited resources and their growing dependence on Indians to guide and supply them. We also know that some recipients of peace medals did not always welcome the gifts. One Cheyenne chief tried to return his medal, fearing it or any present from white people would contaminate him and bring ill to his people. Taking the belief that the medals transmitted "bad medicine" a step further, the Hidatsas passed theirs on to their enemies.[30]

And yet, Lewis and Clark made it to the Pacific Ocean. Considering what went wrong and what could have gone wrong, that alone was a significant feat. More remarkable given the moments of confrontation with Indians and the weeks of desperation while crossing the mountains, only one member of the Corps died on the way west. And this casualty occurred early in the journey, not at the hands of Indians, animals, or the elements, but likely from a ruptured appendix. Although the travel took much longer than the captains anticipated, the Corps surmounted one geographic hurdle after another, not so much proceeding ahead directly, as straggling across the mountains and then struggling along the Columbia River watershed. The same could be said of the expedition's diplomacy with Indians, which did not go as desired, but did not blow up in the face of American emissaries either. And the intercourse of all kinds with Indians enabled the explorers to get the supplies and the directions they needed.

Years later, Clark distilled the diplomatic lessons he had learned: "It requires time and a little smoking with the Indians, if you wish to have peace with them." The deceptively simple formulation, however, masked the re-education Lewis and Clark had received and the adaptations they had made on their way west. From one end of the continent to the other, the captains clung to rhetoric that proclaimed the dependence of Indians on the United States; the reality of the Corps of Discovery's condition, especially as the explorers moved away from the relatively familiar territory east of Fort Mandan, manifested the contrary. Upon reaching the Pacific, the necessity for adjustments continued, as did the contradictions between the words and needs of the explorers.[31]

"*Ocian in view!* O! the joy," recorded William Clark on November 7, 1805. Clark's rapture was premature. The sighting that day was only the wide estuary of the Columbia River, which Clark in the rain and fog mistook for the Pacific Ocean. Soon enough, the actual ocean came into sight, and the members of the Corps cast their ballots to decide the side of the river on which build their fort. But the months at Fort Clatsop, named for its nearest Indian neighbors, brought little joy to its inhabitants. While the temperatures there were not nearly as cold as the previous year at Fort Mandan, complaints about the wet and windy weather recurred in page after page of the journals of the explorers. Making matters worse, relations with the Clatsops and other Indians in the vicinity were considerably cooler than those that had prevailed the previous winter. The soggy season spent at Fort Clatsop showed how far the explorers had come and how much ground still separated them from their Indian neighbors.[32]

From St. Louis to the Pacific, Lewis and Clark logged the miles the Corps had covered, 4,118 in total by their estimate; the captains did not try to quantify the cultural distance they had traveled. For that tally, the attire of the Corps offered one measure of the material cultural changes that had occurred. In the beginning, the captains and the soldiers in the Corps dressed in uniforms that the army issued to them. The clothes of soldiers and civilians were spun from cotton, woolen, and linen fibers. But the long and difficult way west took its toll on coats, vests, shirts, and pants. Leather shoes wore out first, and those that lasted through the muck of the Missouri proved insufficiently insulated for the extreme cold that the explorers endured at Fort Mandan. By the time the Corps arrived at the Pacific coast in November 1805, robes and blankets made from buffalo, deer, and elk hides had almost completely replaced clothing of eastern origin. The Corps had obtained these new garments from Indians or had crafted them by methods they learned from Indians. When the expedition departed Fort Clatsop in March 1806, Clark counted "358 pair of Mockersons," some Indian made, some manufactured by the members of the Corps, as the footwear of the Corps for the return trip.[33]

What the Corps ate revealed similar alterations. The food and drink the explorers consumed on the lower Missouri generally conformed with the standard rations (including alcohol) allotted soldiers in the United States Army. These supplies quickly ran short, and freshly killed meat soon went from supplement to staple. Enormous quantities were needed to feed hard-traveling men. "We eat an emensity of meat," acknowledged Lewis in the summer of 1805. "It requires 4 deer, an Elk and a deer, or one buffaloe, to supply us plentifully for 24 hours." Under these conditions, the best hunters, like George Drouillard, gained an elevated status. Keeping ravenous men sated became more difficult when the Corps traversed the mountains, where big game was scarce. There, the Corps sometimes went hungry or eked scanty meals from gathered bulbs, roots, tubers, and berries, leaning on Sacagawea's knowledge of the botany of Shoshone country. The travelers also became more reliant on Indians to trade food, including dog meat, which famished explorers overcame their cultural biases to eat. They learned as well to prepare dishes as Indians did. For example, the eulachon (which Lewis referred to as anchovies) was one of many fish first added to their diets when the explorers reached the Columbia River. According to Lewis, it was "best when cooked in Indian stile," which entailed "roasting a number of them together on a wooden spit." So prepared, he declared the eulachon superior to any fish he had ever tasted. Less enthusiastic were the reviews of Columbia River cuisine by members of the Corps. During their time in the Columbia watershed, including their season at Fort Clatsop, the visitors carped frequently about the monotony of meals of dried, pounded fish (if not as much as they did about the "disagreeable" weather near the Pacific coast). Fish, especially salmon, was the great staple of Columbia River Indians, who augmented that fare with a variety of foods, including mammals, wild fowl, and wapato. This last item, an aquatic plant, Clark likened to an Irish potato and judged it "a tolerable Substitute for bread."[34]

Concerns about food drove the decision about the location of Fort Clatsop. The south side of the river, the vast majority of the Corps agreed, offered better access to elk and to sources for making salt to preserve animal flesh, if not to the wapato growing grounds upriver that informed Sacagawea's dissenting vote. Democracy did not extend to the selection of the particular site of the fort, which the captains made on their own. Their choice was in a thick growth of trees about two hundred yards from the river. That put it close, but not too close, to the water and with ready access to trees from which to construct a stockade and shelters and collect firewood. It also offered a route to the ocean, where salt could be boiled and where passing ships might be spotted, yet was far enough away (the captains hoped) to buffer them from the worst of the Pacific gusts. It was, the captains announced on December 7, 1805, "the most eligible Situation for our purposes of any in its neighbourhood."[35]

Topping those purposes was the effort to reduce purchases of food from Indians. While crossing the mountains in the summer and fall of 1805, an ongoing trial for the Corps of Discovery was finding enough to eat. The

Indians they met often had little to spare, though Shoshones and Nez Perces earned the praise of Lewis and Clark for their generosity in the face of scarcity. Venturing down the Columbia River in the fall of 1805, the travelers confronted a different state of affairs. The explorers' difficulties in obtaining the provisions they needed was more a matter of affordability than availability. Lower Columbia River Indians, the members of the Lewis and Clark expedition repeatedly complained, asked too much in exchange for the dried fish, wapato, and other edibles they proffered. Worse, when they did not get what they wanted from trading and were not carefully watched, they stole from the Corps. "All the Indians from the Rocky Mountains to the falls of Columbia, are an honest, ingenious and well disposed people," wrote Corps member Patrick Gass, "but from the falls to the seacoast, and along it, they are a rascally, thieving set." Although the captains and the corpsmen blamed the greed and bad character of lower Columbia Indians for souring relations, their own circumstances exacerbated the problems. The longer-than-anticipated journey west and the greater-than-expected reliance on Indians on the way from Fort Mandan to the Pacific had severely depleted the store of goods the Corps had to trade. The items most coveted by Indians (at least to the east) were gone by the time the explorers descended the Columbia. All they had left were some fishhooks, beads of various colors, a hodgepodge of metal goods, and several peace medals. Not nearly enough, the captains realized, to buy food from Indians, especially given the high prices Indians along the Columbia had demanded. Fort Clatsop's favorable location, it was hoped, would free the Corps from dependency on Indian purveyors and allow them to save some of their stock for trading on the trip back to St. Louis.[36]

From December 1805 through March 1806, Drouillard and other hunters killed an impressive number of animals. Nearing the end of their stay at Fort Clatsop, the count totaled 131 (or, in a higher estimate, 155) elk, 20 deer, "plus a few smaller quadrupeds" for the 110-day period from December 1, 1805, to March 20, 1806. For elk alone, that tally amounted to 1.2 to 1.4 per day, which, with other game taken, exceeded the dietary requirements calculated by Lewis. Unfortunately for the Corps, the fortunes of hunters were not evenly distributed. Some days and weeks yielded plentiful prey; on others, hunters returned with nothing for their efforts. Profligate practices wasted surpluses that more careful consumption could have stored. Despite some success in making salt, much meat spoiled in the damp climate. Nor did salt-makers spy any vessels on the ocean, depriving the Corps of an alternative source of trade for food and other supplies, as well as a possible alternate means of transporting their records and maybe themselves back east. All these failings, combined with the desire for a more varied diet, forced the captains to continue to engage with Indians to secure food.[37]

Fortunately for the subsistence of the Corps, there was no shortage of Indians with whom to trade and no shortage of foods being offered. Almost immediately after Lewis and Clark settled on the site for Fort Clatsop, natives arrived bearing dried fish, wapato, and other regional delicacies. Prospective trading partners, it became clear, were also eager to barter a wider range of goods and services. They had been doing so for years with other travelers from afar, though prior voyagers from Europe and eastern North America had come by sea, not by land.

Relations between the Corps and their nearest neighbors appeared to get off to a promising start. While searching for a route from the site of their planned fort to the ocean on December 9, 1805, William Clark and five corpsmen ran into three Clatsop Indians and accepted an invitation to visit their village. This Clatsop settlement was located about seven miles southwest of the Corps of Discovery's new winter encampment and was populated by about twelve families. Upon arrival, Cuscalar, who Clark thought was the chief of the village, heartily welcomed the visitors. That evening "all the Men of the other houses Came and Smoked with" Clark. Together, they enjoyed a fine meal, after which Cuscalar gave the visitors new mats and invited Clark to sleep in his home at a coveted spot by the fire. "Those people," reported Clark, "treated me with extrodeanary friendship." In his journal entry, Clark also commended the cleanliness of the Clatsops, who, he claimed, washed their faces and hands more frequently than other Indians. What weighed even more in their favor, according to Clark, was the Clatsops' honesty. Compared to the Indians with whom the Corps had contended along the Columbia, the Clatsops were less prone to "Stealing, which we have not Cought them at as yet."[38]

The next morning, however, showed that gracious hospitality did not translate into a new deal when it came to trading. For a few wapato roots, Clark offered red beads. Like other Indians in the area, the Clatsops "would give Scarcely any thing for Beeds of that Colour." They made clear that only white and, better still, blue, would do. Rebuffed, Clark then offered small fishhooks, with which he was able to close the deal.[39]

Over the following days and weeks, the Clatsops tried to school the Corps in the art of their deals, which resembled that of other Indians in the lower Columbia Valley. The next instruction came on the evening of December 12, when ten Clatsops dropped in on the construction site of the Corps of

Discovery's fort. Determining that one of these Clatsops, Coboway, was a "principal chief," the captains bestowed on him a peace medal. Getting down to business, Coboway's party offered wapato and a sea otter skin, which they knew was highly valued by seaborne traders. In exchange, the Indians rejected any beads but blue ones and eventually settled for a few fishing hooks and some tobacco. The challenge of coming to an agreement taught Lewis and Clark that the Clatsops struck hard bargains. A week later, on December 20, three visiting Clatsops buttressed that lesson. On this occasion, no deal was made, which Clark claimed owed to the Clatsops' asking double and triple the value of everything.[40]

The divide between the Clatsops and the American captains expanded after Cuscalar paid a call on the nearly completed fort on Christmas Eve. Cuscalar, who Clark acknowledged had treated him very politely at the Clatsops' village, arrived in the company of his younger brother and two women. The visit began cordially enough, with Cuscalar presenting Lewis and Clark several mats and a parcel of roots. But sometime that evening, Cuscalar demanded several metal files in exchange. Unwilling to part with these items, the captains returned the gifts they had received. Seeking to salvage a deal, Cuscalar then offered a woman to each of the men. The captains declined, and reported that the women "appeared to be highly disgusted at our refuseing to axcept of their favours &c."[41]

For Lewis and Clark, these incidents reinforced their convictions about the avarice of lower Columbia River Indians, which the captains compounded with their familiar criticisms of the sexual relations (and, more broadly, all gender relations) among native peoples. "They do not hold the virtue of their women in high estimation and will even prostitute their wives and daughters for a fishinghook or stran[d] of beads," was Lewis's conclusion about coastal Indian men. That coastal Indian women seemed eager participants in this sexual commerce, the captains ascribed again to the lewd and lascivious nature of native females. Such unflattering appraisals were not new for Lewis and Clark, but the captains' critiques of the coastal Indians' trading in sex carried more censure than similar diatribes earlier in their journeys (and in their journals).[42]

The alienation of the Corps of Discovery from coastal Indians added a physical barrier with the opening of Fort Clatsop and its closing to Indians at night. This inhospitality contrasted with the prior winter, when Indians and members of the Corps came and went from Fort Mandan without strictly supervised curfews. But Lewis ruled out a repeat of such unregulated interactions, for the people in the environs of Fort Clatsop possessed "an avaricious all grasping disposition." Thus, the Indians must now be removed from the fort each evening lest their "hope of plunder . . . induce them to be treacherous." The edict was not well received by the Indians who were at the fort, and who, Clark wrote, left reluctantly.[43]

The captains began the new year by detailing to the Corps how the fort would be maintained, including when Indians were to be allowed inside it and who would be responsible for enforcing the restrictions on their entries and exits. These instructions directed the garrison to "treat the natives in a friendly manner," ordering them "not to abuse, assault, or strike" any Indians unless attacked first. But the orders allowed sentinels to refuse admission to any Indian, as well as remove from the fort any native who caused trouble. In the event an Indian refused to leave or entered after being prohibited, the captains charged the sergeant on duty to employ whatever measures seemed necessary, short of killing them. The new year's orders also reiterated the ban on any Indians spending the night inside the fort.[44]

These rules stayed in place through the Corps of Discovery's time at Fort Clatsop and worked as intended. For the next two and a half months, Indians gained only limited admission into the post and almost always departed by sunset. A few incidents in which sentinels caught Indians pilfering sparked tensions, though not ones that provoked violence. Sergeants at the fort never had to resort to coercive measures to eject troublesome Indians.

But the cold peace that prevailed through the Corps' winter on the Pacific coast fostered no warm bonds. The rules succeeded in keeping a distance between coastal Indians and the inhabitants of Fort Clatsop. Even the few occasions in which the captains permitted Indians to spend the night inside the fort did little to break down the gap between peoples. One of these overnight stays followed a visit by Coboway, accompanied by twelve to fourteen Clatsop men, women, and children, on February 24, 1806. Coboway's party came to sell a sea otter skin, some hats, and fish, and a deal was reached for all the goods. Since the trade was made, the Clatsop contingent included women and children, and the weather was particularly harsh, the captains relented on their "no Indians after dark" decree. They hardly rolled out the welcome mat, however. "We *suffered* them to remain all night," was how the captains described their hosting of Indian guests on two other dates.[45]

If not whole nights, the men at Fort Clatsop did spend time in the company of Indian women. Through the winter, a stream of coastal Indian men and women came to the fort to trade. As part of these deals, Indian men offered Indian women, and Indian women offered themselves. There was nothing private about the bartering of sexual favors. As Clark put it, the "womin are lude and Carry on Sport publickly."[46]

Although the captains did not record how often sexual deals were consummated and they kept salacious details out of their journals, their entries obliquely referenced the prevalence of trysts and explicitly mentioned their efforts to restrict this intercourse. The former was evidenced in notes about women carrying venereal diseases and the treatment of men for those diseases. The latter emerged in pleadings for celibacy and warnings to steer clear of certain women. In making the case for restraint, the captains appealed to propriety, to protecting the health of their men, and to conserving the wealth of the Corps.[47]

How much these entreaties to the hearts and minds (and other body parts) of their men curbed the sex trade is not clear. In one case near the end of the time at Fort Clatsop, Lewis claimed his pleas had the desired effect. That episode involved a visit on March 15, 1806, by Delashelwilt, a Chinook chief, his wife, and six women, which "his wife had brought for market." As these were the same women who had transmitted venereal diseases to his men the previous November, Lewis ordered his men to steer clear. Over the next two days, Delashelwilt's party camped near the fort and continued to entreat the members of the Corps. But corpsmen preserved their vow of celibacy—or so Lewis believed.[48]

Propriety had its place, and health mattered too, but economics especially imposed restraints. Just as having to barter for provisions depleted the Corps' store of tradable goods, so did purchasing sex sometimes cost too much. Even before Fort Clatsop opened for habitation and business, the captains implemented a plan to save knives and more valuable items by dividing some ribbons among their men to bestow on Indian women. The women appreciated these ribbons, but they, no less than Indian men, communicated their strong preference for blue beads and metal objects.[49]

The most pressing problem facing the Corps as they neared the end of their season at Fort Clatsop was how to obtain additional canoes for the journey back up the Columbia River. Lewis and Clark had admired the canoes of Chinookan peoples from the first time they had sighted one easily crossing the rough waters of the Columbia estuary, something that the Corps' boats could not do. Seeking several of these canoes for the first leg of their return voyage, the captains and other Corps members entered negotiations with neighboring Indians. These soon encountered the hitch that had plagued their haggling through their entire time on the lower Columbia. Canoes were available, but not affordable. On March 17, 1806,

Drouillard managed to acquire a canoe, but only after he gave away a laced coat and some tobacco. As Lewis chronicled, "nothing excep[t] this coat would induce them to dispose of a canoe which in their mode of traffic is an article of the greatest val[u]e except a wife, with whom it is equal, and is generally given in exchange to the father for his daughter." For this purchase, Lewis noted that the "U. States" owed him a new coat, for the one of his that Drouillard had bartered away. Of more immediate concern than settling his accounts with the United States was the failure of the negotiations that Lewis had undertaken with a visiting party of Clatsops. After the talks in which he had been engaged broke off on the 17th, Lewis concluded that the Clatsops would not sell a canoe at an affordable price.[50]

The captains could have continued to negotiate with the Clatsop party or found another group among the Clatsops or some other Indians in the vicinity with a canoe to sell. Time should have been on the Corps' side. The captains had originally planned to stay at Fort Clatsop until April 1, 1806. But as the winter at the western terminus of their expedition wore on, Lewis and Clark chose to move the departure up by ten days. For this decision, no vote was taken. It is unlikely that any dissent would have been registered. Eagerness to start home and leave their wet, flea-infested Pacific quarters behind was a universal sentiment among the members of the Corps. Having made the decision to depart in the next few days, the captains reckoned that they had no more time for dickering. That left Lewis and Clark with one option for getting a canoe from the Clatsops: "we will take one from them."[51]

The captains justified this action as payback for the many thefts that coastal Indians had perpetrated. In particular, Lewis excused the taking of a canoe as being in return for six elk the Clatsops had stolen back in February. What Lewis's account omitted was that the Indians had already made restitution. After the captains complained to Coboway about this theft, the Clatsop chief dispatched one of his kinsmen to Fort Clatsop on February 12 with three dogs as payment for the elk. Although the dogs bolted before the Corps could take possession that day, George Drouillard soon retrieved the animals from the Clatsops' village to which they had returned. That closed the matter from the Clatsops' point of view; it might have for Lewis and Clark as well had the Corps not so badly needed a canoe or had enough merchandise left to buy one.[52]

The expropriation occurred on March 18. While Coboway was visiting Fort Clatsop, four men from the Corps snuck away from the fort and traveled to Coboway's village. There, they secretly commandeered a canoe. The vessel, John Ordway conceded, belonged to the Clatsops, offering only the rationale that "we are in want of it." Upon returning with the canoe to Fort Clatsop, the men hid it nearby, since they knew Clatsops were also in the vicinity.[53]

Coboway departed the following day, unaware of the theft of the canoe. Before he left, the captains presented him with "a Certificate of his good conduct," crediting him for the friendly intercourse during "our residence at this place." We do not know how he and the Clatsops in his village reacted when they learned of the robbery, because Lewis and Clark were not around to record it. Although bad weather delayed the Corps' departure for a couple of days, at midday on March 23, 1806, the explorers left their winter home. They had not gone more than a mile when the travelers met Delashelwilt and a party of twenty Chinook men and women. Having learned that the Corps needed a canoe, Delashelwilt had intercepted the party to bring one for sale. Without further comment, Clark noted that they did not purchase it, since they no longer needed one.[54]

What if the Clatsops had caught the Corps in the act or had caught up with the explorers before they had ventured far? Would the captains have offered restitution as Coboway had done? Probably not. Would blood have been shed? Possibly. Since this is not an alternate history, those are not questions for here. As luck had it, fortune favored the bold bandits. The Corps made a clean getaway. That kept the peace and kept the Fort Clatsop chapter of the Lewis and Clark expedition in this alternative history, albeit in a version that little resembles bicentennial "wishtories."

Summing up that chapter, Lewis glossed over the negatives of the Corps' Pacific passage. "Altho' we have not fared sumptuously this winter . . . at Fort Clatsop, we have lived quite as comfortably as we had any reason to expect we should." His upbeat appraisal made no mention of the frequent complaints about the coastal weather and the coastal Indians. Instead, it was mission accomplished. The only missed opportunity, he acknowledged, was not having met any seafaring traders.[55]

Neither Lewis nor Clark (nor any of the men in the Corps) reflected on missed opportunities with coastal Indians, or if they did, they kept those reflections out of their journals. They did not question why relations that had started so promisingly with Clark's stay in Cuscalar's village had devolved so quickly and had led the captains to treat Indian visitors to Fort Clatsop so inhospitably. Miscommunications certainly played a part in creating misunderstandings. Although coastal Indians had picked up some English words during their dealings with mariners, their knowledge of sailors' profanities did not give them a broad vocabulary. Likewise, no one in the Corps of Discovery was conversant in any of the Chinookan languages spoken in the region of the fort. "We cannot understand them Sufficiently to make any enquiries relitive to their religious opinions," the captains grumbled, and that lack of comprehension extended to economic matters. Struggling to make sense of one another's words, would-be trading partners resorted to gestures and signs that left room for misinterpretations.[56]

Suspicions and tensions also arose from differing perceptions. Consider personal appearance. Throughout the journey, journalists among the Corps of Discovery included derogatory comments about how Indians looked and dressed. But coastal Indians around Fort Clatsop were on the receiving end of some particularly harsh barbs, especially for the practice of flattening heads. A sign of elite status for Chinookans, the flattened heads of coastal Indians were a target of the Corps' derision. Yet from the perspective of coastal Indians, the round heads of the explorers gave them the appearance of lower-status people, for Chinookans prohibited their slaves from flattening the heads of their children.[57]

From the perspective of Lewis and Clark, it was not language or looks that caused problems; it was the "avaricious all grasping disposition" of coastal Indians. That phrase appeared more than once in the journals, which were laced with disapproval of the greed and dishonesty of natives about Fort Clatsop. Because of these imputed traits, negotiations often fell apart or took much longer than necessary. On more than half of the days that Indians came to Fort Clatsop, no deal or only a partial purchase was made. "If they conceive you anxious to purchase," wrote Lewis, it "will be a whole day bargaining for a handfull of roots." As a rule, the Indians with whom he dealt at Fort Clatsop "invariably refuse the price first offered them," even if "afterwards [they] very frequently accept a smaller quantity of the same article."[58]

Based on the entries in their journals, Lewis and Clark recognized no irony in their critiques of the commercial culture of coastal Indians. In emphasizing the distance between themselves and their Indian neighbors at Fort Clatsop, the captains did not acknowledge that Indians to the east accused Americans of the same practices for which Lewis and Clark now assailed Pacific coast Indians. East of the Mississippi in particular, Indians confronted American emissaries who sought to dispense with costly gift-giving rituals and impose strictly commercial rules on the exchange of goods and services. There, the Americans' all-grasping hunger for land had led Daniel Boone away from Chillicothe and led to wars between Indians and the United States.

By contrast, what made the estrangement between the Corps and coastal Indians so strange was how similar their dispositions were when it came to trading. Prior to the start of the journey and again from French traders in St. Louis, Lewis and Clark had learned the importance of gift-giving to their diplomacy with Indians. Across the continent, the captains had catered to Indian customs and Indian customers, even as they resented the time and expense of giving (and receiving) presents and the rituals of establishing peace. At Fort Clatsop, the American emissaries still cultivated chiefs by giving out medals and engaged in a little smoking with Indians, but they were able to forgo the elaborate ceremonies and lengthy speech-making that had characterized councils on their westward journey. Beyond the western boundaries of the Louisiana Purchase, the captains were less certain about the sovereignty of the United States, or, at any rate, less in-sistent on proclaiming it. Nor did they try to present the Corps as the ad-vance guard for future American possession of Columbia River lands. For their purposes, meetings with Indians at Fort Clatsop were commercial, not colonial, encounters.

This suited their native counterparts, who approached the dealings with similarly commercial ends. Coastal Indians were not seeking long-term relations with the temporary inhabitants of Fort Clatsop. These im-mediate calculations extended to their sexual relations with the visitors as well. Coastal Indians viewed copulation with men in the Corps as busi-ness transactions (unlike Plains Indians, who imbued intercourse with the transmission of spiritual powers). Whether bartering goods or services at Fort Clatsop, coastal Indian women and men put a premium on the ac-quisition of exotic items that could not be procured from local networks. They also shared with Americans a materialistic mindset, though coastal Indians assigned individuals' status not simply for their skillful trading and for accumulating things, but also by then redistributing these goods to fellow villagers. Already attuned by local markets to precepts of supply and demand, coastal Indians used their dealings with sea captains to sharpen their knowledge of global markets, of what travelers from afar wanted and what they would pay for it. Some adjustments were necessary in bargaining with the Corps of Discovery, whose captains were less in-terested in obtaining the skins of animals than they were in getting stuff to eat. Like the merchants with whom Lewis and Clark were acquainted in the United States, coastal Indians adapted to this shift in demand and started bringing ample supplies of dried fish and wapato to Fort Clatsop.[59]

Rather than appreciating their commonalities with coastal Indians, Lewis and Clark fixed on their differences and endeavored, not always successfully, to keep their neighbors at Fort Clatsop at a distance. In the case of wapato, Lewis and Clark evinced some understanding for the high prices that Indians asked, knowing that it could only be obtained through trading with people upriver where it grew. For the most part, however, the captains contended that coastal Indians were trying to extort goods from them. When not condemning Indians as gougers, Lewis and Clark denounced natives as beggars and thieves. Lewis reminded his men to be ever vigilant "and never place our selves at the mercy of any savages." Yet, this reminder served also as a rebuke, for the captains feared that the members of the Corps had let go of their suspicions about Indians and were coasting through their time at Fort Clatsop. As Lewis confessed, "so long have our men been accustomed to a friendly intercourse with the natives, that we find it difficult to impress on their minds the necessity of always being on their guard with rispect to them."[60]

In their way, the captains were coasting as well at Fort Clatsop. Lewis and Clark had learned a lot from and about Indians on their way across the continent. Those lessons informed essential adjustments in how they looked to, looked at, and approached Indians. At Fort Clatsop, they did not forget what they had learned, but they did not grasp what their trading with coastal Indians might have taught them. So long had the captains been accustomed to intercourse based on transcending differences between Americans and Indians that they found it difficult to get their minds around their similarities to coastal Indian traders.

Loath though Lewis and Clark were to admit it, their journey placed them continuously at the mercy of Indians. Raised as conquerors of the First American West, the co-captains began the expedition expecting to awe Indians into accepting the supremacy of the United States. For the first few months on the Missouri River, Lewis and Clark sought to sway native allegiances with performances of power and talk about American greatness. In their speeches in councils in 1804, Lewis and Clark pretended that Indians were now dependent on the United States. They attributed their successful procession up the Missouri to the American prowess they projected and the American commerce they promised. But peaceful relations with the peoples whose countries they passed through depended less on the explorers' guns, gifts, and goods than on the goodwill of the natives. Rather than peace through strength, the amity that mostly prevailed between the Corps and

Indians along the Missouri rested on how unthreatening the explorers were in the eyes of their Indian hosts.

As the expedition ventured west of Fort Mandan in 1805, the addition of Sacagawea made the Corps even less threatening, which was important because the survival of the Pacific-bound party required further bowings to Indian ways and requests for Indian help. During their trek across the mountains and through their stay at Fort Clatsop, trade in food and, more broadly, the Indianization of attire and diets saved the Corps of Discovery. Absent the assistance of Indians and the adjustments that explorers made in what they wore and what they ate, the Corps would have frozen to death or starved to death.

Blendings and bendings enabled the explorers to proceed on their journey and to get along with Indians on the way to the Pacific; we should be careful, however, not to inflate expedient and temporary adaptations into deeper and enduring transformations. Dressing like Indians and eating like Indians did not make its members (other than Sacagawea) into Indians. For the Lewis and Clark expedition, the switch in garments and the shift in diets demonstrated that clothes did not (re)make the men, who were not what they ate.

Nor did more similar outlooks foster better relations between the Corps and Indians. Had that been true, interactions around Fort Clatsop would have been much warmer. Instead, when Lewis and Clark dealt with Indians who shared many of their assumptions about commerce, cordiality was as rare as dry days on the Pacific coast during the winter of 1805–1806. Sex, like food, could be purchased, but these sales offered only short-term sustenance. Lasting bonds were more elusive, since one party believed it was always being ripped off.

Which raises the question, Why Fort Clatsop? The site's featured role in bicentennial "wishtories" is not matched by its history. Certainly, other places along the Lewis and Clark Trail offer better examples for an alternative history of peoples getting along. Around Fort Mandan, far more than around Fort Clatsop, hospitalities were more generous and affection more genuine.

Still, for all that did not go right at Fort Clatsop, what did not go wrong there holds important lessons for this alternative history. The explorers got the food they needed and got along peacefully, if not cordially, with Indian trading partners. Despite the captains' misgivings about the dispositions of coastal Indians, they did not let their suspicions overcome them, did not revert to their pre-expedition ways of dealing with Indians. And they got away without their stolen canoe being discovered, the luck of which preserved the peace and the place of Fort Clatsop in this alternative history.

As they headed away from Fort Clatsop and up the Columbia River, it remained to be seen if Lewis and Clark would revert to past practices once they left the farthest west. To be determined was whether the captains would leave the lessons of the trail behind when they got back to St. Louis. Once there, Lewis and Clark received promotions that placed them in governing roles over the Louisiana Territory, which made them responsible, among other matters, for overseeing the relations between Indians and Americans around Apple Creek.

4

Apple Creek

Falling

SIX MONTHS TO THE DAY after leaving Fort Clatsop, Meriwether Lewis and William Clark led the Corps of Discovery back into St. Louis. The return trip, though not without significant tests, took much less time than the outbound one. When the explorers arrived in St. Louis around noon on September 23, 1806, residents gave them an enthusiastic greeting, some having earlier given up the overdue travelers for dead. That evening Auguste Chouteau hosted a dinner for Lewis and Clark. Guests toasted the captains in French and English, while the explorers regaled the gathering with tales of their adventures. Celebrations spread across the nation with news of the explorers' safe return. President Thomas Jefferson, who had authorized the expedition and provided the explorers with their instructions, exulted that "never did a similar event excite more joy through the United States" than did the homecoming of Lewis and Clark.[1]

Soon enough, it was back to business for the co-captains, with new jobs to keep them occupied. In early 1807, Jefferson named Lewis governor of the Louisiana Territory. Around the same time, Clark received a commission as a brigadier general in Louisiana's territorial militia. He also was appointed as the United States agent for all Indians in the territory (with the exception of the Osages, the responsibility for whom remained with Pierre Chouteau). Lewis's gubernatorial tenure turned out to be short. After journeying to Washington to brief Jefferson about the expedition, Lewis remained back east and governed in absentia through his first year in office. He returned to

Thomas Mickell Burnham, *The Lewis and Clark Expedition* (c. 1850). Burnham's painting, executed around a half-century after the return of the expedition, isolates the two co-captains from the members of the Corps of Discovery. One points to the dark forest ahead, to the discoveries to be made and the destiny that awaits the explorers and the American nation. *Courtesy of the Autry Museum of the American West*

St. Louis in 1808, but his time there was politically and personally tumultuous. Clark had a much longer run as a territorial official. In addition to his command of the militia and as chief Indian agent, it included a stint as governor, which was followed by a return to a posting as superintendent of Indian affairs, an office he held until his death in 1838.

These positions gave Lewis and Clark broad authority over an expansive geography with a diverse population, a small slice of which was around Apple Creek, where emigrant Indians and emigrant Americans had earlier congregated. The Corps of Discovery has passed by the area in the fall of 1803. At Cape Girardeau, Lewis made the acquaintance of Louis Lorimier, and the captains entered some information about Indian villages near Apple Creek into their journals. The explorers did not then visit the towns, and their journal entries contained no reflections on the state of relations between residents. After the expedition, Governor Lewis and Agent (later Governor) Clark learned more about the situation of Shawnees and Delawares and their American neighbors. In office, they applied Jeffersonian precepts and the education they had received in dealings with Indians to the west to their governance of peoples across the Louisiana Territory and around Apple Creek. But the balances of power and numbers that had shaped relations between Indians and the Corps of Discovery and between inhabitants around Apple Creek were changing rapidly in the Cape Girardeau district. The shift in demography and the rise of democracy—or more specifically, white man's democracy—made the lessons of the Lewis and Clark expedition anachronistic and doomed the once harmonious cohabitation of Indians and Americans around Apple Creek.

Although their return trip was considerably shorter than the journey to the Pacific, the Lewis and Clark expedition hardly coasted back to St. Louis. The eagerness to get away (and make a clean getaway) from Fort Clatsop put the Corps on the Columbia River in the early spring, when the water was running much higher and faster than on the downstream journey the previous fall. It also put the homeward-bound explorers on the river before the first salmon run of the season, which meant the staple on which Columbia Indians depended was in shorter supply than later in the year. Just two and a half weeks after bidding adieu to Fort Clatsop, having already struggled against the current and having been alerted that food was in short supply upriver, the Corps confronted a nearly two-mile portage around the cascades of the Columbia. Compounding the trials of hauling canoes and supplies past the rapids, the explorers had a series of fraught encounters with Indians, whom they again accused of gouging and stealing. The theft of Lewis's dog Seaman provoked his owner to authorize violence to retrieve his pet. Before any shooting started, the dog thieves released Seaman and fled the scene. Following Seaman's rescue, Lewis and Clark put Indians on notice and kept the Corps on alert. As at Fort Clatsop, the captains ordered guards to prevent Indians from entering the explorers' camp; unlike at Fort Clatsop, Lewis and Clark now empowered sentries to kill natives caught stealing. For Lewis, the heightened state vindicated his earlier warnings about "the necessity of always being on guard" against Indians. It also reinforced his conviction about the need to project strength. As he wrote in his journal on April 11, 1806, "I am convinced that no other consideration but our number at this moment protects us."[2]

At that moment, Lewis may have been right, but through most of the twenty-nine months that the Corps of Discovery was away from St. Louis, numbers were against the explorers. What protected them was not their ability to project strength, though the captains often tried to do that. It was instead their agility in adjusting to circumstances in which the balance of power tilted against them and in making the adaptations that were necessary to their progress.

Mistranslations were as much a problem on the way home as they had been on the journey to the Pacific and at Fort Clatsop. Still, the difficulties that beset the Lewis and Clark expedition after leaving Fort Clatsop were not simply a matter of misunderstanding what was said. While Lewis and Clark continued to talk to Indians, they did not always listen to them. In May 1806, Nez Perce informants cautioned the captains not to start across the mountains until more snow had melted. Clark cursed the "icy barrier which seperates me from my friends and Country." By mid-June, the captains' impatience overruled the Indians' intelligence. Setting out against Indian guidance and without Indian guides, the Corps and their horses slipped and slid and nearly perished in deep snow before turning back and waiting for Indians to lead them.[3]

Crossing over the Continental Divide in July 1806, the Corps had put the hardest part of the trail behind them. But Lewis and Clark were hardly out of the woods when it came to dealing with Indians, or, from their perspective, complaining about the dealings of Indians. The most lethal confrontation occurred late in July. As with so many prior incidents, this one, which involved Blackfeet Indians, started with miscommunications and accusations of thefts. It culminated in the death of two Blackfeet, including one shot by Lewis. Before dying, the mortally wounded Indian fired back at Lewis, the bullet whistling past the captain's bare head. A few inches spared Lewis's life.[4]

Good fortune continued to smile on Lewis, Clark, and the people they commanded for the next two months. On August 11, Lewis was accidentally shot by one of his own men. The wound, while painful, soon healed. A few days later, John Colter left the Corps to join a trapping and trading enterprise heading back into the mountains. When the Corps departed from a Hidatsa village on August 17, Charbonneau, Sacagawea, and their toddler stayed, despite Clark's plea that they continue to St. Louis. Lewis, Clark, and the remainder of the Corps then hastened downriver. They had another tense meeting with Black Buffalo's Brulé band during which Clark rebuked the Lakotas for their treatment of the explorers two years earlier and of white people in general. He warned that the "white people" would "Come Sufficiently Strong to whip any vilenous party who dare to oppose them." To the Lakotas, Clark's were fighting words. Fortunately for the Corps, which was outnumbered at that moment, the Indians chose not to fight. The luck of Lewis and Clark held for the next three weeks, and the explorers returned triumphantly to St. Louis without additional casualties.[5]

More than luck delivered the Corps safely home and made the death of two Blackfeet the exception and not the rule of encounters between Indians and explorers. Any accounting should begin with the actions and inactions of Indians, who permitted the Lewis and Clark expedition to traverse their countries unharmed. In general, the Indians who met the captains treated the explorers more as a curiosity than a threat, more as the representatives of an added trading partner than as those of an exclusive sovereign. The captains deserve credit, too. Although they had been raised to view Indians as threats, they did not let that overwhelm their curiosity about native peoples and cultures. During their travels, Lewis and Clark did not shed all their pre-expedition biases. But they learned much about Indians and from Indians. Those lessons and the adaptations they encouraged saved the lives of the Corps during the journey and prepared the captains for the diplomatic and administrative duties they assumed upon the expedition's completion.

One lesson their travels imparted was the magnitude of challenges they faced as governor and general/agent. First was the vastness of the territory and the difficulties of getting across it, much less establishing meaningful American authority over its diverse and dispersed peoples. Upon their return to St. Louis, the captains proclaimed the success of their venture. They insisted that they had fulfilled Jefferson's instruction and had found the best route across the continent. But the duration of their journey and their struggles navigating rivers and surmounting mountains dashed hopes of an easy northwest passage and of a symmetrical continental geography. Lewis and Clark did not admit it, but their trail was not a practical one for extending American commerce and securing US sovereignty across the Louisiana Territory and beyond to the Pacific. In fact, the farther Lewis and Clark ventured from St. Louis, the less their declarations about the enlarged map of the United States mattered on the ground.[6]

By contrast, in and around St. Louis the signs of US sovereignty had taken on more substance during the travels of Lewis and Clark. When the captains headed up the Missouri in May 1804, the flag of the United States had been flying over St. Louis for only two months, and a lone official, Amos Stoddard, had represented both the United States and France at the transfer ceremony. Over the next three years, the United States shifted the administrative structure and personnel responsible for governing St. Louis and Upper Louisiana several times, first separating it from the Territory of Orleans, which was formed out of Lower Louisiana, then attaching Upper

Louisiana to the Indiana Territory. By the time Lewis was appointed in March 1807, the United States had abandoned that alignment with Indiana, making St. Louis the seat of governance for the (Upper) Louisiana Territory and beefing up its administrative presence there. From his new perch, Lewis prophesized a great future for the Louisiana Territory and particularly for the district of St. Louis. The town and surrounding lands, he prophesized, offered "more advantages than any other portion of the U[nited] States to the farmer, the mechanic, [the] inland merchant or the honest adventurer who can command money or negroes."[7]

Ultimately, the future of US control over St. Louis and its environs rested less on the small coterie of appointed officials who joined Lewis than on the area's attractions to American farmers, mechanics, merchants, and adventurers (honest and otherwise), who moved there along with their slaves. Already in 1800, Americans (white and Black) outnumbered French settlers in Upper Louisiana. With the continuing additions of new American migrants in the wake of the Louisiana Purchase, the balance of numbers tilted further in their favor by 1806.[8]

As in other western territories that had witnessed an influx of settler colonists from the United States, the national loyalties of the newcomers remained in flux. Contrary to Jefferson's earlier assertion that the movement of Americans into Spanish Louisiana would by itself bring about the peaceful transfer of the territory to the United States, migrants like Daniel Boone adjusted easily to life as Spanish subjects. After the Louisiana Purchase, the reconciliation of American expatriates and other earlier colonists to the rule of the United States required as a start that their Spanish (and French) land claims be validated. The allegiance of newer migrants from the United States also began with land. Arriving after the United States acquired the territory, these settlers wanted as much land and the best lands to be available, affordable, and secure, and wanted a government to make that happen.

This tasked the territory's administrators with a complicated and contradictory assignment. Satisfying one set of claimants, those with grants dating to French and Spanish regimes, often ran against the interests of newer residents. To sort out the tangled state of affairs, the United States appointed a three-person commission in 1805. But the findings of the commissioners angered more recent American migrants. Two of the three commissioners consistently voted to uphold claims dating back before 1800, including ones with vague locations and ones that had never been certified by Spanish authorities. The majority even endorsed many claims made by Spanish officials after October 1, 1800, despite explicit instructions to nullify grants made after Spain had retroceded the territory to France. Instead of quieting controversies, the commission's rulings inflamed tensions between older and newer colonists, which often, though not always, pitted French against Americans. As Frederick Bates, the territorial secretary (and acting governor in Lewis's absence), reported in 1807, "Slander, Detraction and Violence stalk thro our *forests*, as well as our *villages*."[9]

Through 1807 and into 1808, Lewis took in this turmoil from afar. After his return to St. Louis in September 1806, he had journeyed to Washington to meet with Jefferson. From there, he went to Philadelphia to debrief with scientists and ready the expedition's journals for publication. Next, Lewis headed to Virginia to visit with family and friends. The alarming updates he received from Bates did not prompt him to hurry back to St. Louis. Only in November 1807 did he again head west, arriving in St. Louis a year after his appointment as governor had begun.[10]

Contemplating the challenges awaiting him, Lewis composed a lengthy treatise that focused on the governance of the Indians in the territory and the trade with them. He began what he titled "Observations and Reflections" by reviewing the Spanish system, in which, he complained, officials made a mess of the commerce with Indian nations. The rewards collected by Spanish officials came at the expense of the profits of traders, though that was the least of the system's evils. Worse was the impact on Indians, who were compelled to pay ever more exorbitant prices even as game became scarcer. Aggrieved, Indians became more aggressive. When traders responded by accommodating them, Indians observed "*that the white man are like dogs; the more you beat them and plunder them, the more goods they will bring you, and the cheaper they will sell them.*" In the end, merchants operating from (British) Canada reaped the benefits, for they trespassed into Spanish Louisiana bringing goods at prices that undercut those of traders licensed by Spain.[11]

Another basis of discord identified by Lewis was "the uncontrolled liberty which our citizens take of hunting on Indian lands." Such trespassing, Lewis noted, had created problems everywhere on the frontier. History showed it to be a frequent cause of war and, Lewis predicted, it seemed destined to become that in Upper Louisiana.[12]

Written around the middle of 1807, Lewis's "Observations and Reflections" contained numerous recommendations for how the United States should revise these arrangements. Echoing the reprimand that captains Lewis and Clark had given to the Lakotas the previous summer, now Governor Lewis contended that the key to correcting misbehaving

Indians lay in withholding goods. As a good disciple of Jefferson, Lewis maintained that a trade embargo was more effective and less expensive than a military campaign. For it to work, however, merchants in St. Louis had to abide by temporary prohibitions, and traders from outside the United States had to be barred from bartering with Indians west of the Mississippi and along the Missouri. "If we permit the British merchants to supply the Indians in Louisiana as formerly," warned Lewis, "the influence of our government over those Indians is lost." Restraints were also required to prevent whites from hunting on Indian lands.[13]

Lewis's observations, reflections, and recommendations almost entirely concerned how to deal with Indians at a distance from St. Louis. His experiences as an explorer gave him unique insights about Indians to the northwest. But Lewis's far-sighted view was blind to the disputes flaming closer to the seat of territorial governance.[14]

Prior to and then upon his arrival in St. Louis in March 1808, Lewis set about making it his home. Seeking leads on a residence in St. Louis, Lewis had reached out to Auguste Chouteau. The dwelling Lewis ultimately rented was in the style favored by the town's creoles, its logs standing vertically in the French style. He proposed that his best friend, expedition co-captain, and now fellow territorial officer William Clark join him there (along with Clark's new bride and two of Clark's nieces). Lewis also bought from Pierre Chouteau (Auguste's brother and business partner) a tract of land lying on the Missouri adjoining that of Auguste Chouteau.[15]

From Lewis's perspective, the invitation to Clark and the connection with the Chouteaus made sense. Superiors in Washington constantly badgered territorial officials to reduce expenses. Sharing a house seemed a good start, and it would make the bachelor Lewis's residence into more of a home. In St. Louis, French-style dwellings dominated and in them resided the town's leading merchants. The Chouteaus stood atop that business elite. Who better to consult with on local real estate matters than the town's oldest-established merchants? The Chouteaus, after all, had previously proved themselves to Lewis and Clark by providing valuable intelligence and goods to them back in 1804.[16]

This seemed obvious to Lewis, but it showed he was oblivious to the sources of local discord. A growing proportion of Lewis's constituents, recent American migrants to the Louisiana Territory, resented the sway that the Chouteaus and other French merchants held over territorial affairs. In their view, Lewis's predecessor, James Wilkinson, had aligned politically with St. Louis's creole elites, because they had entangled his economic interests with theirs. The majority of the land commissioners had also sided with the French. That the new governor appeared to cozy up to the Chouteaus and his French-style home symbolized the persistence of the old order.[17]

Governor Lewis had no time to recover his bearings before a confrontation with the Osages consumed his attention. In March 1808, around the time Lewis was returning to St. Louis, Osage raiders struck settlements to the south and west of St. Louis. Moving from farm to farm, the Osages plundered all sorts of property, splitting furniture to pieces, ripping open featherbeds, and rendering useless anything they could not carry away. As Lewis alerted Henry Dearborn, the secretary of war for the United States, the Osages also took several prisoners, and, after holding them for several days, freed them without any provisions and barely clothed.[18]

The Osages' depredations did not surprise Lewis. Back in 1803, Jefferson had advised him that the Osages were the most powerful Indian nation south of the Missouri—just as the Sioux were north of that river. Compared to these two nations, Jefferson conceded, the United States was "miserably weak." During the expedition, the Osages, unlike the Sioux, had not disturbed the explorers, but they continued to make trouble for French, American, and emigrant Indian settlements in Upper Louisiana. After 1804, American authorities, like Spanish officials a decade earlier, contemplated going to war against the Osages.[19]

When weighing options for how to retaliate against the Osages, Lewis occupied a different office and the United States was in a different position than when Jefferson had offered advice five years earlier. The United States, Governor Lewis recognized, was now much stronger in the portion of the Missouri Valley claimed by the Osages. In addition to several thousand new American migrants in Upper Louisiana, the years immediately after the Louisiana Purchase saw a stream of Indians relocating from east of the Mississippi. Increasing numbers of Indian and white hunters poached on lands that the Osages considered theirs. With the balance of power appearing to tilt against the Osages, an emboldened group of Shawnees, who had suffered from Osage raids since their initial settlement west of the Mississippi, urged a combined offensive against the Osages.[20]

Despite the differences between the situations in 1803 and 1808, Lewis did not embrace the Shawnees' appeal for a joint military campaign, or, for that matter, any large attack against the Osages. Having identified trespassing hunters as the main culprit in inciting wars with Indians, the governor sympathized with the Osages' complaints about poachers. Although the latest raid had resulted in the loss of substantial property, Lewis also took into account that the Osages had released their prisoners and had avoided killing people. The governor considered as well a plea from White Hair, a chief of the Osages, who had traveled to St. Louis in the spring of 1808. At a meeting with Lewis, White Hair maintained that the perpetrators were young men who operated in defiance of his wishes and whose rogue banditry should not be held against his entire nation. Still, in opting to cut off trade rather than go to war, the governor insisted he was not going soft on the Osages. As he had advocated in his journal entries during the Lewis and Clark expedition, reaffirmed in his "Observations and Reflections," and now implemented against the Osages, Lewis remained steadfast in his belief that denying goods worked better than deploying guns.[21]

Lewis's faith in the efficacy of what we would call "soft power" paid off when several Osage leaders signaled their desire to make peace and regain trade. Lewis entrusted the negotiations to William Clark (even though Pierre Chouteau was technically in charge of relations with the Osages). Traveling up the Missouri in the summer of 1808, Clark was accompanied by a squadron of eighty mounted militiamen. At Fire Prairie, some eighty miles from the Osage villages, Clark ordered his company to build a fort (to be named Fort Osage) that was intended to firm up American control over the lower Missouri River. As a further signal of American hard power in the region, Clark did not himself go to the Osage villages. Instead, he sent his subordinate, Daniel Boone's son Nathan, to warn Osage leaders of the consequences awaiting those who failed to accept the summons to convene at the site of Fort Osage. Although the Osages took offense at Boone's uninvited arrival and his threatening tone, a number, including White Hair of the Big Osages and Walk-in-the Rain of the Little Osages, agreed to meet with Clark at Fire Prairie.[22]

The talks resulted in a treaty in which the Osages surrendered all claims east of a line from Fort Osage south to the Arkansas River, as well as their rights to hunt north of the Missouri River. Clark justified this vast cession as compensation for stolen and destroyed property and for the costs of the troops and fort that supposedly safeguarded the Osages. The protection of the United States, Clark claimed, was not from the United States and its encroaching settlers. Rather, it shielded the Osages from the "continual dread of all the eastern Tribes whom they knew wished to destroy them & possess their Country." Plus, the treaty restored the Osages' access to American trade goods. After the treaty was set, Clark further sweetened its terms by distributing an assortment of gifts to the signers.[23]

Word of the treaty divided the Osages and infuriated a substantial portion of them. Arriving in St. Louis shortly after attending the treaty conference, a delegation of Osages protested that they had been deceived about the treaty's provisions. At issue was not so much land north of the Missouri River, which the Osages had earlier lost to Sauk, Meswaki, and Iowa Indians. The Osage delegation, however, vigorously disputed the fixing of a hard boundary south of the Missouri from which they were to be excluded. The treaty, they insisted, merely created a shared hunting territory. Even angrier were Osages who had not attended the meeting at Fire Prairie and who insisted that the signers had no right to dispose of land without first obtaining the consent of the entire nation.[24]

Publicly, Clark upheld the fairness of the treaty-making process and insisted that the agreement profited the Osages; privately, he confessed his doubts. Perhaps because Clark shared his reservations with Lewis, the governor reopened talks with an Osage delegation in the fall of 1808. The revised treaty added a few new articles intended to mollify the Osages. But the basic terms of the dispossession were not altered.[25]

For Lewis, the agreement completely validated his (and Jefferson's) approach to Indian affairs. "In consequence of the measures . . . taken last spring in relation to the Osage nations," Lewis informed Jefferson, "they were reduced in the course of a few months to a state of perfect submission without bloodshed"; this happy result proved "the superiority which the policy of withholding merchandise has over the chastisement of the sword."[26]

Lewis saw benefits beyond chastising the Osages in the treaty. The lands the Osages vacated, he hoped, would now serve as a refuge for "such Indian Nations as have long been on terms of intimate friendship with us." By this, Lewis meant the Shawnees and Delawares principally in the Cape Girardeau District. This was not a new idea; captains Lewis and Clark had plotted along these lines in their journals after passing through Osage territory in the spring of 1804. Clark suggested that two villages on the Osage River might be prevailed on to move to the Arkansas, leaving enough land to relocate to the Shawnees, Delawares, and other emigrant Indians. Four years later, Clark did prevail on the Osages. With the Shawnee and Delaware settlements around Apple Creek increasingly coveted by new settlers from the United States, the time seemed right to move ahead with the second phase of the scheme.[27]

Yet, as Lewis affirmed, these Indians had a recent history of living in peace and friendship with territorial officials and with their non-native neighbors.

Such amity surely surprised Lewis and Clark too, since their prior military service had acquainted them with a deeper history of hostilities between Shawnees and Delawares and Americans in the Ohio Valley. Also a welcome surprise to Lewis and Clark was the progress of these emigrant Indians. From a variety of observers, the governor and principal Indian agent received accounts of flourishing fields and large herds of livestock, which served for them as evidence that the Indians around Apple Creek were attaining a higher stage of civilization. From the perspective of Lewis and Clark, the improvement of farms and the adoption of herding fulfilled Jeffersonian hopes that Indians were on the road to assimilation into the American republic.[28]

By 1808, the civilizing path and the secure possession of land by emigrant Indians faced a fresh challenge. Shawnees and Delawares near Cape Girardeau and in various other settlements south of the Missouri River felt themselves increasingly beset by a new set of American settlers. These newer comers had no respect for the tracts granted by the Spanish to the Indians and had no attachment to the recent history of friendly relations between Indians and Americans around Apple Creek. All too aware of the troubled times they had left behind, emigrant Indians also knew how American squatters in the Ohio Valley had obtained preemption rights based on occupation and improvement. They worried that history would repeat. To prevent that outcome, they turned to Louis Lorimier to plead their case to US territorial officials. In 1807, Lorimier appealed on behalf of the Apple Creek Shawnees and Delawares to Louisiana's acting governor. Through Lorimier, the emigrant Indians called for the territorial government to act against intruders, lest the inaction be someday construed as consent by the Indians and the government to the presence of the squatters and then lead to the validation of occupant land claims.[29]

It fell to Lewis to respond to the pleas and resolve the building conflicts. As a long-term ideal, Lewis floated to Jefferson the idea of emigrant Indians trading their Spanish grant near Cape Girardeau for tracts the United States would provide them in the country relinquished by the Osages. There were already plenty of precedents for similar land swaps and accompanying Indian removals. At the time of the Louisiana Purchase, Jefferson had put forward a grand blueprint for a mass transfer of populations and land holdings. In this scheme, Indians would give up their residences east of the Mississippi in exchange for lands in the newly acquired Louisiana Territory, while colonists in the Louisiana Territory would shift their residences to the eastern side of the Mississippi. Jefferson soon abandoned this proposal in the face of widespread opposition from all involved parties. Shortly after returning to St. Louis in 1808, Lewis revived Jefferson's plan for separating whites and Indians, though the governor's draft drew the northern boundary on the Missouri River and a western line set approximately thirty miles west of the Mississippi. Whites who had settled beyond the border were to "remove" themselves. In fact, few Americans had yet moved across this boundary. Even so, Lewis's proposed proclamation line met objections from Americans, who wanted no limits on their spread. The governor retreated. With the Osage cession sealed, Lewis turned instead to a one-sided version to separate whites and Indians, in which only the latter exchanged lands and relocated.[30]

Lewis's pitch to Jefferson in the fall of 1808 conformed with the one-sided demands that US officials had grown accustomed to dictating to Indians in the Ohio Valley, but the eviction of Shawnees and Delawares was not the policy the governor unveiled for the Louisiana Territory in the spring of 1809. Rather than calling for emigrant Indians to trade away their current holdings, Lewis issued another proclamation on April 6, 1809. This one ordered all intruders within five miles of the Shawnee and Delaware towns to depart. As Lewis argued, if these squatters were allowed to settle near the Shawnee and Delaware villages, "discontents and disturbances will most probably arise." To prevent costly conflicts, Lewis's edict required sheriffs to prosecute any squatters who defied his directive.[31]

The governor's 1809 proclamation did not reverse his earlier views so much as it extended the time frame for their realization. Lewis hoped the Shawnees and Delawares would eventually be persuaded to exchange their current holdings for new tracts in the country ceded by the Osages. He insisted, though, that such transfers be voluntary and contractual. Until the Shawnees and Delawares acquiesced to another relocation, their property rights should be respected. In 1809, Lewis also slightly amended the explanation for conflicts that he had put forward in his earlier "Observations and Reflections." Then, he had blamed whites hunting on Indian lands for causing conflicts. No doubt, poaching had precipitated conflicts between Indians and Americans on prior frontiers, and Lewis was right to be concerned about its potential to provoke violence in the United States' new Louisiana Territory. Still, the experiences of Daniel Boone and long hunters in his generation showed that the fallout from whites hunting on Indian lands tended to be contained. Only the interventions of nations and empires brought in the resources to unleash wars on larger scales and of longer durations. What's more, Lewis now grasped that the greater problems ensued not from Americans hunting *on* Indian lands, but from Americans hunting *for* Indian lands. Hence, his edict ordered squatters removed from the property of emigrant Indians.

The political fallout from Lewis's shielding of Shawnee and Delaware holdings around Apple Creek overshadowed the proclamation's practical impact. During Governor Lewis's tenure, squatters did evacuate settlements on the Missouri River below its junction with the Osage River. It was, however, fear of an Indian attack rather than of a crackdown by territorial officers that induced a temporary flight. In the eyes of squatters, as well as other men seeking to usurp Indian holdings, the proclamation stamped Lewis as an enemy of their cause. According to Bates, who opposed the protections Lewis offered emigrant Indians, the governor had by July 1809 "fallen from Public esteem & almost into the public contempt."[32]

The fall from favor was swift and steep. True, Bates and Lewis had contempt for one another, so the secretary's estimation of public opinion carried biases. But by the summer of 1809, Lewis was clearly a troubled man. Besieged by controversies over Indian affairs and land matters, mistrustful of subordinates, at odds with his superiors, including Jefferson's successor James Madison, Lewis despaired about his political future. That he also found himself accused of financial improprieties for various unauthorized expenditures added concerns about his personal fortune to his woes. Deciding to plead his case in person in Washington, Lewis set off from St. Louis on September 4, 1809. Just short of three years since his triumphant return with the Corps of Discovery, no crowds cheered him on his way. He never reached his destination. On October 10, 1809, Lewis met his end at Grinder's Stand, an inn along the Natchez Trail in central Tennessee.[33]

For more than two centuries, the mysterious circumstances surrounding Lewis's death have stirred contention. At the time, most of Lewis's acquaintances, including his dearest friend William Clark, accepted that Lewis took his own life. Most historians and biographers have agreed with that judgment, supplementing the original conclusions with new insights about Lewis's bouts with severe depression and the diminished state he was in because of the recurrence of malarial fever and heavy drinking. Some contemporaries, however, questioned the evidence for Lewis's supposed suicide, and those doubts have been the kindling for ongoing debates about what happened on the last night of Lewis's life. Uncertainties have invited speculations that Lewis was murdered, accusations about who committed the crime, and theories about what nefarious purposes motivated the perpetrators.[34]

For this alternative history, the question of how Lewis died matters much less than what his death meant for intercultural relations across Upper Louisiana and around Apple Creek in particular. During his brief reign as chief executive of the Louisiana Territory, Lewis, with Clark's assistance, had moved away from some of the conventions that had governed diplomacy with Indians during the Lewis and Clark Expedition. Then, gifts often initiated parleys, and did not, as at Fire Prairie, close them. Then, too, the co-captains had not coupled commercial considerations with demands for land, as they had done in their negotiations with the Osages. Still, Governor Lewis, like Captain Lewis, retained greater respect for Indian rights than did many of his contemporaries. First warning against the dangers of Americans poaching on Indian lands, Governor Lewis subsequently stood up against his fellow Americans when they squatted on the holdings of the Shawnees and Delawares. His death left in greater jeopardy the people and property about Apple Creek.

Less than three years later, the Apple Creek Indians suffered another loss with the death of Louis Lorimier. His passing in June 1812 deprived the Shawnees and Delawares of a long-trusted intermediary. It came in the same month that the United States declared war on Great Britain, a conflict that Americans in the Louisiana Territory came to view primarily as a war against all Indians.

Within a few years of Lewis's death, William Clark became a territorial governor. After initially turning down the chance to succeed Lewis, Clark accepted the appointment in 1813 as chief executive of the portion of the Louisiana Purchase newly designated as the Territory of Missouri. Clark brought to the post a familiarity with Indians in the territory that had no equal among American officials. More than his co-captain and predecessor as a territorial governor, Clark established close ties with individual Indians and exhibited a deeper interest in native cultures. In matters of policy, though, there was little distance between Clark and Lewis, which had allowed them to work so well together. As explorers and as territorial officials, both shared core Jeffersonian precepts. Individually and collaboratively, Lewis and Clark acted as agents of an American imperium, albeit of an empire that extended inconsistent protections to the liberty and lands of Indians. The critical distinction between the post-expedition careers of the two was that Lewis died shortly after Jefferson's presidency ended; Clark lived and served for another thirty years. Over that time, the power that Clark helped to project came to rest less on the practice of Jeffersonian principles than on the force of Jacksonian Democracy, as illustrated by the removals of the Shawnees and Delawares from around Apple Creek.

Inseparable as Lewis and Clark were (and have become in the public mind two centuries after their expedition), their personal relations with Indians displayed important differences. During the expedition and in his brief time after it, Lewis was more stand-offish and mistrustful than Clark. That extended to the most intimate relations with Indians. Although their journal entries cite only the captains' rejections of sexual favors, testimony from Indian sources suggest that Clark was less adamant in his refusals. That evidence, never corroborated by Clark or maybe unknown to him, was two children supposedly sired by Captain Clark. One, who came forward as an old man decades later, was a redhead, his hair bolstering his unproven claim about his paternity. Undeniable is the warmth Clark displayed toward Sacagawea and her son. If not the romance concocted in latter-day "wishtories," Clark clearly liked "Janey" in a way that went beyond any feelings that Lewis evinced for "the Indian woman." Clark's concerns for Sacagawea's infant child, Jean Baptiste, or "Pomp" as Clark nicknamed him, led the captain to offer to raise the boy. In a letter to Charbonneau written shortly after the interpreters and their child had left the Corps of Discovery, Clark extolled Sacagawea's contributions to the Corps' mission, which "deserved a greater reward for her attention and services . . . than we had in our power to give her." To make up for the inadequate compensation and because of his fondness for Pomp, Clark proposed that Charbonneau let him educate the child. A few years later, Charbonneau agreed, and Clark fulfilled his promise to raise the *métis* boy as if he were his own offspring.[35]

Clark's personal relations had professional implications. Clark cared for and about individual Indians, and Indians reciprocated. Many native leaders placed greater faith in "the Red Headed Chief" than they did any of his contemporaries. Their trust accounted in part for Clark's success in reaching agreements with them. During more than thirty years as a governor and a superintendent of Indian affairs, Clark negotiated thirty-seven treaties with Indians that received congressional approval, more than any other American emissary. His tally represented one-tenth of the pacts made between Indian nations and the United States. Add in agreements concluded by agents under his supervision and Clark's count jumps to more than one-fifth of all Indian treaties ratified by the United States.[36]

Charlton Heston as William Clark and Donna Reed as Sacagawea in the 1955 film *The Far Horizons*, which came out during the sesquicentennial of the Lewis and Clark expedition and concocted a romance between Clark and Sacagawea. *Courtesy of Paramount Pictures Corporation*

Building trust with emigrant Indians in Missouri, Clark endorsed an 1811 petition of Rogerstown Shawnees, who sought the right to mine lead on lands near the village. In a letter to President James Madison, Clark, who was then still serving as the territory's principal Indian agent, esteemed the Shawnees in Missouri as "a peaceable and well disposed people." In an acknowledgment of their loyalty to the United States and their history of amicable relations with American neighbors, Clark cited their "great service to our frontier settlements." Clark's backing convinced his superiors to approve the bid for lead-mining rights. At Clark's behest, the secretary of war further instructed territorial officials to take measures to expel white squatters from the lands of the Rogerstown Shawnees, a recognition that recent arrivals from the United States were violating Indian rights and destabilizing harmonious relations.[37]

When Clark became governor of the Missouri Territory in 1813, the United States was at war with Great Britain, and Clark's constituents in St. Louis and to the city's south and west expected an attack by a combined British and Indian army. That sense of impending doom persisted into 1814. "God only knows what our fate is to be," wrote William's wife Julia Hancock Clark on New Year's Day 1814. During the War of 1812, smaller Indian forces struck settlements in the territory, particularly along the Missouri River west of St. Louis. But the big invasion did not materialize, and fears about Indians in their midst proved without foundation.[38]

In fact, Missouri's Shawnees and Delawares remained friendly to the United States, and some fought alongside Americans in the territory. For the Shawnees in the Missouri Territory, that allegiance meant breaking with their tribal kin still living in the Ohio Valley. There, the calls by the Shawnee leader Tecumseh for a pan-Indian alliance against the United States (and with the British) rallied many Shawnees. By contrast, Tecumseh's message moved few Shawnees in the villages around Apple Creek, at Rogerstown, and along the St. Francis River. Instead, Missouri's Shawnees (and Delawares) signaled their willingness to join with Americans in defending settlements west of the Mississippi River. As governor, Clark worried about arming Indians, but he concluded that the "Missouri Tribes must either be engaged for us, or they will be opposed to us without doubt." Clark dispatched a contingent of Shawnees and Delawares to guard against incursions by British-allied Indians along the Missouri River.[39]

Unfortunately for Missouri Shawnees and Delawares, their allegiances and actions earned them little credit. During the War of 1812, many Americans in the Missouri Territory made no distinction between one set of Shawnees and another. They tarred all as Tecumseh's people and as enemies of Americans. Amid wartime hysteria, Americans also treated rumors and sensationalized tales of Indian barbarism as facts, which spurred demands for indiscriminate retaliations. After reporting on various Indian atrocities, some exaggerated, some fabricated, the St. Louis newspaper *Missouri Gazette* asserted in May 1814 that "the BLOOD of our citizens cry aloud for VENGEANCE." The time had come for all Indians to be "JACKSONIZED," meaning adopting Andrew Jackson's take-no-prisoners approach to warfare with natives.[40]

As the clamor for a military blow against any and all Indians rose, Governor Clark stuck to his guns, which for him meant not resorting first to arms. Sticking to his Jeffersonian penchants, Clark proposed to negotiate treaties and purchase territories. Before any talks commenced, he singled out the Boone's Lick Country (in what is today central Missouri) as a particularly desirable acquisition. Named for the salt works that Nathan Boone established in 1804 at a salt spring on the north side of the Missouri River, Boone's Lick and adjacent lands fell within the domain ceded by the Osages in 1808, though Clark conceded that the country north of the Missouri River was still claimed by the Sauks and Iowas.[41]

In the summer of 1815, Clark convened a council at Portage des Sioux, a site just north of St. Louis. Approximately two thousand Indians from nineteen tribes gathered at Portage des Sioux. Among the assemblage were leaders from the Sauks, Iowas, and Meswakis, the tribes whose claims to the Boone's Lick Country had often been recognized by Clark and other American officials. For the council at Portage des Sioux, Clark was joined by Ninian Edwards (governor of the Illinois Territory) and Auguste Chouteau. Following protocols he had practiced on the expedition to the Pacific, only on a much larger scale, Clark and his fellow "peace commissioners" dispensed more than twenty thousand dollars' worth of gifts, spoke and listened to multiple speeches, and joined in ceremonies intended to consecrate good relations. A great success in Clark's view, the meeting resulted in thirteen treaties, each promising "perpetual peace and friendship" and restoring commerce.[42]

The territory's citizenry was far less pleased than Clark by the Portage des Sioux treaties. Colonists welcomed the promise of peace, but they did not trust Indians to keep it and wished for more punitive terms. The presents that Clark distributed rankled many Americans who wanted Indians slayed, not paid. More troubling for land-seeking American migrants, the treaties left Indians in their prewar places, containing no provisions for further cessions or removals.

At least as far as the Boone's Lick Country, Clark did aim to unseat Indian landholdings. Contradicting his own pronouncements about the validity of Sauk, Meswaki, and Iowa claims, he issued a proclamation in March 1815 that used the 1808 treaty with the Osages as the basis for sweeping aside all Indian rights to the lands immediately north of the Missouri River. The "pretensions of other nations of Indians," Clark declared, were "of very recent date" and thus not valid. With that dismissal of Sauk, Meswaki, and Iowa rights, Clark's proclamation opened the floodgates to American settlement. An unprecedented rush to the Boone's Lick Country commenced after the War of 1812. By 1820, close to twenty thousand free and enslaved Americans had taken up lands there.[43]

Not that American squatters waited on treaties and proclamations to plant themselves on Indian lands and plunder Indian property. That was happening around Apple Creek. "We are very much crowded by the whites," complained a group of Shawnees in 1815. In addition to coveting the fertile fields that surrounded the Indian villages, many of the American intruders found the livestock and household possessions of the Shawnees and Delawares tempting targets. Between 1811 and 1814, Apple Creek Shawnees claimed to have lost 65 hogs, 49 cattle, and

48 horses to thieves. In 1815, Wabepelathy, the headman of one of the Shawnee villages, returned from a winter hunt to find that his house "had been broken open, and what I had left in it was all gone." More than just robbing valuable property, the Apple Creek Shawnees understood that thieves intended to intimidate. Wabepelathy got the message; later in 1815, he led members of his community away from Apple Creek, resettling with them along the Castor River a few miles west in what was still part of the Shawnees' Spanish grant, but on what he hoped would be lands less desirable to white interlopers.[44]

Alerted to the trespassing and banditry around Apple Creek, Governor Clark issued a proclamation in December 1815 that stood up for Shawnees and Delawares against the incursions of American squatters. Reversing his dismissal of the more recent Sauk, Meswaki, and Iowa claims in the Boone's Lick Country, Clark now reverted to his and Lewis's previous affirmations of Shawnee and Delaware holdings north of Cape Girardeau. These, too, were only a few decades old. But unlike Sauk, Meswaki, and Iowa claims in the Boone's Lick Country, which rested on Indian rights of conquest, the lands occupied by Shawnees and Delawares around Apple Creek traced to a Spanish grant. That distinction was enough for Clark. Nine months after inviting American squatters into the Boone's Lick Country, he ordered them out of Apple Creek. "All white persons who have intruded and are settled upon the lands of the Indians within this territory," Clark declared, must "depart therefrom without delay." To add more bite to the decree's bark, Clark warned he would call on military power to enforce the proclamation.[45]

Not that Governor Clark presumed his proclamation a final resolution. He hoped that the Shawnees and Delawares might yet be persuaded to exchange land on the Mississippi above Cape Girardeau for acreage to the south and west in the Ozarks that had been ceded by the Osages. These mountainous lands, Clark claimed, would not attract many whites, but they were "rich, well watered, and covered with cane," and thus "well calculated for the convenience of the Indians." But like Lewis before him, Clark refused to force the expulsion of Shawnees and Delawares and threatened to use military power against white trespassers. In a January 1816 letter to President Madison, Clark recapitulated the history of the Spanish grant to the Shawnees and Delawares and reiterated his defense of the Indians' holdings, which he certified as extending from a few miles north of Cape Girardeau for nearly forty miles along the Mississippi and reaching inland in places for twenty miles.[46]

The governor's proclamation and his expansive conception of the Shawnee and Delaware holdings were at odds with the position he had taken eight months before about Sauk, Meswaki, and Iowa claims, and it sparked an immediate protest from the Missouri Territorial Assembly. The resolution from the legislature disputed Clark's reasoning, casting doubt on the extent of the emigrant Indians' real estate and emphasizing the inconvenience to white inhabitants. According to the assembly's resolution, the Spanish government never expected the Indians to hold much land, if any. As proof, the resolution cited the grants subsequently made by the Spanish to individuals within the emigrant Indians' supposed domain. Further, because the American land commission had confirmed most of these claims, recent emigrants assumed that the United States considered only the Shawnee and Delaware villages and surrounding fields to be off limits, with the rest temporarily returned to the public domain. Led by this evidence to occupy these lands and to make substantial improvements to them, the settlers should be spared from the execution of the governors' proclamation. The assembly asked Congress to reduce the Indians' tract to a reasonable size and then to persuade the Shawnees and Delawares to exchange this claim for lands to the west. In a follow-up resolution in 1817, the Territorial Assembly repeated its request that the Shawnees and Delawares be relocated to "some more remote part . . . better suited to Indian pursuits."[47]

Shawnee and Delaware leaders countered the assembly's contentions. Not the meandering hunters they were portrayed to be, emigrant Indians positioned themselves as true settlers, pointing to their flourishing fields, burgeoning herds, and well-built homes. During the War of 1812, they had demonstrated their loyalty to the United States and had always been on good terms with American neighbors, at least before the recent onslaught of squatters. Some now spoke English, and Shawnee and Delaware parents had indicated a willingness to have their children taught to read. By these measures, they had fulfilled (or were well along the way to fulfilling) the prerequisites that Thomas Jefferson had stipulated for the incorporation of Indians into the American republic. So why deprive them now of their improved lands and prod their removal to a distant and undeveloped country?[48]

Governor Clark sympathized with the Shawnees and Delawares; territorial legislators did not, and their views better represented the majority of the territory's white American population. After Clark's Portage des Sioux treaties and proclamation in defense of Shawnees and Delawares, a friend of Bates (and, thus, an adversary of Clark) claimed that 90 percent of the territory's citizens no longer wanted him as governor. That overstated Clark's unpopularity, but it should not be dismissed as mere political axe-grinding. Under the territorial system of the United States, the president appointed the governor. The territory's voters elected the members of the assembly, which made them more directly accountable to the will of enfranchised citizens.[49]

As the territory's non-Indian population swelled in the aftermath of the War of 1812, the tide of public opinion turned increasingly against Clark's stance about Apple Creek. Before the War, the 1810 territorial census registered a little over 20,000 non-Indian inhabitants between the Missouri and Arkansas Rivers; the combined Indian population in that area was approximately the same, with the Osages accounting for about 30 percent of this total, and emigrant Indians from the east (principally Shawnees, Delawares, Cherokees, and Choctaws) comprising most of the rest. But the rough balance of numbers gave way when white Americans, often accompanied by African American slaves, flooded into the Missouri Territory after the war. To the Baptist minister John Mason Peck, who likened the rush of Americans in the immediate postwar period to "an avalanche, it seemed as though Kentucky and Tennessee were breaking up and moving" across the Mississippi. Echoing Peck, the land speculator Justus Post claimed in the fall of 1816 that "it does appear as if all Kentucky are on the road for the country in the fork of the Mississippi & Missouri." This torrent from Kentucky, Tennessee, and neighboring states more than tripled the non-Indian population of the Missouri Territory between 1810 and 1820, with most of the newcomers arriving in the second half of the decade. Along the western side of the Mississippi from St. Louis south to Cape Girardeau and along the lower Missouri, the migrants pushed onto Indian holdings, then demanded that elected representatives clear the tracts for them.[50]

Despite widespread defiance from squatters and popular backing for them, Clark did not retreat, but he found himself impotent to enforce his proclamation. In January 1817, in an ominous sign for Clark's command, Alexander McNair reported that members of the militia would not march against squatters on Indian lands. As a colonel in the militia and the register of the St. Louis Land Office, McNair was in a good position to judge local sentiments. Without federal troops to enforce his order and with the militia resistant to doing so, Clark conceded in March 1817 that removing the illegal occupants had proved more difficult than he had imagined.[51]

Just how out of step Clark was with the majority of Missouri voters became clear in 1820 when the territory moved toward statehood and the governorship became an elected office. On a national level, Missouri's bid to become a state exploded into a conflict about slavery that split politicians into northern and southern camps. For Jefferson, in retirement at Monticello, the intrusion of slavery into national politics rang like a "fire bell" in the night, awakening him in terror for the future of the union. Within Missouri, however, the campaign for governor, which pitted William Clark against Alexander McNair, did not turn on disagreements about slavery. Both candidates owned slaves and supported Missouri's right to be a slave state.[52]

Adhering to an older tradition, Clark did not run for office; he stood it on the basis of his position as the territory's governor, its best-known person, and his friendship with other well-known persons. In support of his candidacy, he wrote a letter to a St. Louis newspaper in which he touted his extended residence in the territory and the various appointments he had held. The letter referred any inquiries about his character to his wealthy and well-connected friends. But other than that statement, Clark, who was mourning the death of his wife and was back in Kentucky and Virginia during the months leading up to the election, left any campaigning on his behalf to surrogates.[53]

In conducting his campaign in this old-fashioned manner, Clark demonstrated his unfamiliarity with how much the political climate had shifted since the War of 1812. He seemed not to appreciate that boasting of his friendship with the "old inhabitants and early settlers" would be a political liability with the majority of voters, who had arrived in Missouri after the war and who chafed at the control of territorial governance still exercised by the coterie of French merchants, lawyers, and land speculators in St. Louis who were styled "the little junto." As a public official, Clark had partnered in the Missouri Fur Company, a private concern whose business rested on trade with Indians. That further tied him to the old order and not to the new wave of migrants who wanted their government to remove Indians. By contrast, McNair and his supporters sensed and effectively exploited the rising sentiment for more democratic governance. Although McNair had been a friend of Clark's and had also been aligned with the little junto, he broke with that faction, positioned himself a defender of farmers against fur traders, and championed the cause of squatters. Sounding a populist note, McNair's surrogates also blasted the governor for being too close to the wealthy and too distant from "the people." More ruinous to Clark were accusations that he was "too good to the Indians" and that he had fathered children by Indian women, then educated his mixed-race offspring at public expense. The damage of the negative campaign became apparent when the election results were tallied. McNair received 6,576 votes, Clark just 2,656.[54]

Clark's defeat ended his pursuit of elected office, but not his career as a government official. Staying on in St. Louis, he soon returned to his post as superintendent of Indian Affairs, which he held until his death in 1838. During the 1820s and 1830s, he and his sub-agents negotiated dozens of new treaties with numerous Indian nations in the Mississippi and Missouri Valleys and across the Great Plains. The treaties he directly handled, and even ones he just had a hand in, reflected the faith that many Indian leaders vested in Clark. They trusted Clark more than other American officials.

Yet Clark was a defender of Indian rights only by comparison to others. That was already evidenced by the treaty he forced on the Osages in 1808 and the claims of the Sauks, Meswakis, and Iowas that he casually dismissed in 1815. And after 1820, his defense of Indian rights was not what it once was. Before 1820, as on the Lewis and Clark expedition, his diplomacy with Indians focused on avoiding wars and expanding commerce. With notable exceptions, Clark did not engineer major dispossessions, particularly from Indians at peace with the United States. That changed during the 1820s and 1830s, when land cessions and deportations became the order of the day. Although Clark still argued that the United States had a duty of protect Indian rights and fulfill its treaty obligations, his work in later years made him an agent of Jacksonian Democracy. As superintendent, he arranged pacts that cleared Indian titles and made lands safe for white claimants by expelling Indian peoples.

Consider the fate of Missouri's Shawnees. In 1820, the Reverend Jedidiah Morse counted nearly 1,400 Shawnees living in Missouri, most in villages around Apple Creek, with smaller numbers residing on the St. Francis and Meramec Rivers. Four years later, the Department of War of the United States government enumerated similar totals for the Shawnees. At that point, the Shawnee population in Missouri was probably slightly larger than it had been a decade earlier. In the wake of the War of 1812, many of the remaining Shawnees in the Ohio Valley withdrew, and some rejoined tribal brethren in Missouri settlements.[55]

But within Missouri, voters wanted the United States government to halt any further relocations by eastern Indians into the state and to compel Indians residing in the state to relinquish their holdings in exchange for tracts to the west. Not waiting for government action, trespassers took matters into their own hands by taking up Indian lands. North of Cape Girardeau, a swarm of squatters occupied ever larger portions of the Shawnees' domain. As a result, wrote Missouri Senator Thomas Hart Benton in 1824, the Shawnees and other Indians in the state were "surrounded, or pressed upon, by the white population."[56]

Because the superintendent of Indian Affairs in St. Louis was appointed by the president, Clark felt freer to ignore popular opinion. In the spring of 1824, in response to the latest incursions on Indian lands north of Cape Girardeau, he determined that whites "settled on lands designed for the Delawares and Shawnees will be required to remove." Those words sounded very much like the proclamation he had issued in 1815, suggesting that Clark's views had not changed. Clark's determination, though, had no force behind it. As governor, he lacked support from the militia, thus dooming efforts to carry out his edict; in 1824, elected state officials had no intention of doing so either.[57]

To the contrary, they lobbied for the removal of Indians and provided a variety of justifications for such a policy. Some asserted that it was in everyone's interest, including Indians. Benton, who had been an ally of Clark's and a friend of French merchants during the territorial era, shifted with the political winds and championed the will of the white American majority. Benton argued that Missouri's Indians, aware that they would eventually have to move, would welcome the opportunity to occupy "a fixed and permanent home" beyond the state's boundaries. Others cited violence by Indians as the preferred rationale. Missouri's citizens, intoned Governor McNair in his annual message in 1822, "suffer much from Indian" attacks. McNair's successor, John Miller, issued similarly dire updates in his yearly messages. Missourians, he claimed, were surrounded by warlike tribes and at "all times liable to Indian depredations." Such rhetoric was not new, but its persistence was curious, since Indian raiding was far less of a problem in the 1820s than it had been in the previous decade.[58]

That hatred was endemic and violence unavoidable became a frequent, if historically amnesiac, refrain. As Timothy Flint, a Christian minister who came to Missouri after the War of 1812 and went on to write one of the most popular nineteenth-century biographies of Daniel Boone, related, while French and Indians had gotten along, the hatred between Americans and Indians was "fixed and unalterable." Flint's view that divisions between Americans and Indians were insurmountable ignored the history of harmonious relations at Apple Creek. He should have known better. Flint had met Daniel Boone, whose reconciliation with Rogerstown Shawnees rebuked his soon-to-be biographer's myopia. Boone, however, had died on September

26, 1820, six years before Flint published his recollections about his time in Missouri. Nor was Boone around to challenge the Indian-fighting hero that Flint's 1833 biography turned him into. Many of Boone's contemporaries, who had emigrated to Spanish Louisiana in the 1790s and knew better about Shawnee-American relations, had also passed away. The few who were left were so overwhelmingly outnumbered by newer arrivals that the voices that spoke for an alternative history were drowned out by the blare of intemperate Indian haters.[59]

Occasionally, voices did rise that cut through the rationalizations for removal, even as they still endorsed the eviction of Indians. John Scott, who held a variety of territorial offices before being elected to Congress, allowed that conflicts between Shawnees and Americans in Missouri were not the result of the stark cultural divide between savagery and civilization imagined by Flint. Instead, the advances made by Shawnees caused disturbances, such as when the Indians' livestock intermingled with animals belonging to neighboring Americans. Under these circumstances, Scott concluded that Shawnees must go—for their own protection. But the safety of Indians was a secondary concern. The bottom line, acknowledged Scott, was that the tracts held by the Shawnees were too valuable to remain the property of Indians, and the lands to which they would be removed were much inferior. Similarly candid was Thomas Hart Benton's assessment: "to remove the Indians would make room for the spread of slaves."[60]

More tortured, as he came around to supporting and overseeing removals, was William Clark. As territorial governor, Clark's defense of Indian landholdings had hardly been absolute. In 1808, he had negotiated the Osages' first vast cession; ten years later, he helped impose another land forfeiture on the Osages. The Osages' loss, he envisioned, would be the Shawnees' (and Delawares') gain. Yet as late as 1824, he contended that squatters, not Shawnees, must be removed from lands around Apple Creek. By then, however, Clark had accepted the inevitability of Indian removal from Missouri. "The Government will sooner or later have to do this," he wrote, and "the sooner it was done the better." Waiting would only increase difficulties of buying Indian lands and deepen the dissatisfactions among those forced to abandon their improvements. Putting the best face on his shift, Clark wrote Jefferson in 1825 that his goal was to "meliorate the condition of those unfortunate people placed under my charge, knowing as I do their [w]retchedness and their rapid decline." Clark insisted that he remained committed to the eventual incorporation of Indians into the American republic. For now, though, their survival depended on being transplanted to a country "where they could rest in peace." By that, he did not mean, as many other Americans wished, where they would go to die. Instead, the United States had an obligation to educate Indians so that they might live like Americans.[61]

These were long-term obligations. The immediate task confronting Clark was securing treaties that eliminated Indian land holdings in Missouri, and here he and his sub-agents worked quickly. Accords in 1824 with the Sauks, Meswakis, and Iowas fully cleared Indian claims from that portion of Missouri lying north of the Missouri River. In 1825, treaties extinguished the Kansa Indians' claims in the western part of the state and expunged the Osages' last holdings within Missouri.[62]

That year, Clark was also negotiating with Indians in the Cape Girardeau district. Knowing the fate of other Indians in the state, Shawnee leaders sought the best deal in their talks with Clark. In return for the 25-square-mile tract they still held title to around Apple Creek, Shawnee delegates asked for 100 square miles to the west of Missouri. They also insisted on the right to first examine the new lands to assess their suitability. Ever the economizer, Clark countered by offering a 25-square-mile parcel, while sweetening the package with six to eight thousand dollars to pay off the Shawnees' debts and to facilitate their move. After some back and forth, Clark came to terms with the Apple Creek Shawnees in November 1825. In exchange for giving up the remainder of their Spanish grant, the Shawnees received a 50-square-mile tract near the junction of the Kansas and Missouri Rivers, just beyond the western border of Missouri (on lands the United States had purchased from the Osages the same year). To cover "the losses and inconveniences" and enable the Shawnees to obtain supplies for their new settlements, the United States committed to pay $14,000. The federal government also agreed to provide $11,000 to settle claims by Shawnees against citizens of the United States for "spoliations of various kinds."[63]

Although the treaty was signed in November 1825, it took several years to organize the removal. Under Clark, the St. Louis superintendency made treaties quickly in the mid-1820s; the United States government was much slower to marshal the resources to manage the deportations. The Shawnees also had the right to look over the lands before finalizing their move to them, which added to the delay. Not until 1830 did the official exodus of the Shawnees from Apple Creek take place. Even then, the government's failure to provide promised supplies increased the hardships of the journey and made the first seasons in new homes along the Kansas River tougher.

Not all Shawnees went as stipulated. Numbers "continue[d] to loiter in and occupy the country," complained Governor Miller in November 1830. Months after the supposed removal of the last Shawnees, Miller claimed the greater portion of the tribe still remained within the boundaries of his jurisdiction.[64]

One option that some Apple Creek Shawnees of mixed Indian-white ancestry availed themselves was to claim that their heritage exempted them from expulsion and might even entitle them to an individual land grant. In the 1825 treaty with the Osages, the United States affirmed this differentiation by awarding 640-acre grants to forty-two *métis* who had worked as traders and interpreters while living among their Indian kin. That the government did not mandate removal and instead set aside nearly 27,000 acres for individuals with European fathers and Indian mothers suggested that *métis* were placed in a separate category from Indians.[65]

Unfortunately for Shawnees of mixed ancestry, their 1825 treaty contained no article exempting such individuals from removal or awarding them additional lands. Even if it had, it might not have mattered. The Osage treaty's distinction did not alter the changing social climate, which drew racial lines in such a way that *métis* were made as unwelcome in Missouri as their "full-blooded" kin. Rather than battle the prejudices of American neighbors, most children of French, as well as of British and American, fathers opted to move west with their Indian kin. Especially for the offspring of Americans, staying within Missouri often brought rejection from fathers for whom sons and daughters born to Indian mothers were now viewed as an embarrassment. Or worse. In Flint's words, those of mixed race were "monstrous" mongrels.[66]

Another option available to all Shawnees was to leave Apple Creek, but to stay in the state. They could do so by resettling at or near Shawnee villages along the St. Francis River or at Rogerstown on the Meramec. The St. Francis settlements south and west of Apple Creek in the foothills of the Ozarks offered less desirable farmlands, which made them less attractive to squatters. With whites fewer, older traditions of amicable and compatible associations between Indians and Americans persisted. Along the St. Francis River, the presence of Shawnees (and Delawares) was still welcome, maintained trader Samuel Goode Hopkins. Responding to a rumor that these Indians were also to be evicted, Hopkins wrote Indian Agent Richard Graham asking him to prevent that removal. The country in which the Shawnee and Delaware villages were located had little appeal to whites, and the Americans who did live there benefited from the trade with Shawnees and Delawares. What's more, added Hopkins, the presence of these Indians saved the area from "worse [white] neighbors."[67]

Also beckoning were lands farther west in the Ozarks in the southwestern corner of the state. This was country ceded by the Osages, which Lewis and Clark had long proposed as a permanent homeland for Apple Creek Shawnees. Knowing the lands in the Ozarks were inferior in quality to the ones they held at Apple Creek, most rebuffed the offer of a swap. But the sanctuary promised in the Ozarks looked more attractive by the 1820s. As early as 1823, Graham reported 2,500 Shawnees had settled in the Ozarks, principally along the White River on Missouri's southern border with Arkansas. Some of the Shawnees had come from within Missouri; others had relocated there from the Ohio Valley. Few white Americans joined them on the White River, and the ones who did seemed at ease with Indians. Into the 1820s, white pioneers in that portion of the Ozarks recalled days spent hunting and long nights passed gambling and dancing with emigrant Indians. Pioneers John Tabor and Allen Trimble remembered neighboring Shawnees laughing at the awkwardness of white dancers. But the mocking was in good humor, and afterward all smoked tobacco together.[68]

While the move to the Ozarks brought some immediate relief from the pressures of land-grabbing Americans, life in the mountains was not as bountiful as in the fertile country they left behind. Because the Shawnees were joined by other Indians in taking refuge in the Ozarks, the crowding of people depleted resources and made sustenance more challenging for all. Game rapidly thinned; the hilly, stony soil yielded insufficient crops. Already in 1825, three of the Shawnees' White River headmen complained that their people had been reduced from "rich and happy" to "poor, indebted, and Miserable."[69]

In the end, and the end came quickly, the remaining older holdings and the newer ones up in the Ozarks offered Missouri Shawnees only a brief asylum. Encircled and harassed, Rogerstown Shawnees abandoned their homes and lands and moved to Kansas in 1828. Pressure also built against Indians in the Ozarks from the St. Francis River to the far southwestern boundary of Missouri. Knowing elected officials would back them, squatters seated themselves across the Ozarks. For his part, in 1829, Clark once more decried the encroachment of Americans onto remaining Shawnee lands on White River. By then, however, Clark's regret was not the trespassing. What upset him was that the incursions interfered with the efficient execution of the Indians' removal, which would otherwise have been completed in the next year.[70]

In fact, it took a few years, but in October 1832, William Clark reached an agreement with the "Warriors and Counsellors of the Shawnoes and Delawares, late of Cape Girardeau." The new treaty stipulated that the Shawnees and Delawares relinquish all their lands within the State of Missouri, and also all claims which they might have against the United States. In exchange and to enable the Shawnees to remove immediately to a tract west of the state of Missouri on the Kansas River, the United States paid eight hundred dollars in cash and four hundred dollars in clothing and horses, with an additional five hundred dollars allocated to cover the expenses of the relocation. With this treaty, Clark's dealings with Shawnees *in* Missouri ended. By the time William Clark died on September 1, 1838, the removal of Shawnees from Missouri was also done.[71]

The year of Clark's death also witnessed the removal of Cherokee Indians through Missouri. Unlike earlier emigrant Indians from the east, these Cherokees were not settling in Missouri. They were traveling across the state, escorted by the United States military, on what became known as "the Trail of Tears."[72]

It took until 1957 for the government of Missouri to consecrate the Cherokees' tragic passage. That year, the state established the Trail of Tears State Park. Sited just north of Cape Girardeau, the park marks the spot where Cherokee Indians entered Missouri on their forced migration to "Indian Territory." Dedicated to commemorating Indian removal *through* the area, it provides no information about Indian removal *from* the area. The Shawnee and Delaware towns to the north of the park remain unmarked. Vanished from view are the villages near Apple Creek in which these emigrant Indians resided and where for a time they flourished, living comfortably and compatibly with French and Americans nearby. Lost, at least from public commemoration, is their history in Missouri and the alternative history that rose and fell at Apple Creek.

For the Shawnees, the fall from concord played out over several decades, though, in retrospect, it appears predictable. The differing rationales put forward for removing the Shawnees and other Indians all had in common the inevitability of the eviction. How could it be otherwise when Americans and Indians could not live alongside one another in peace, when there were so many more whites and their enslaved Blacks waiting to improve the land than there were Indians wasting its bounty, when democracy (for white men) made demography destiny? All of these justifications ignored how Shawnees had developed their lands and themselves. They missed how emigrant Indians and emigrant Americans had lived alongside one another in peace. They dismissed the compatibility of people around Apple Creek as an aberration, or worse, as an abomination.

Daniel Boone and William Clark knew better. Boone's reconciliation with Rogerstown Shawnees showed the way to forgetting what happened in war in order to live in peace. Clark also imagined it possible for Indians and Americans to coexist without descending into violence. Like Boone, Clark overcame earlier wartime experiences in the Ohio Valley. As an explorer, he learned to negotiate rather than dictate to Indians, a skill that was vital when outnumbered and outgunned. In his post-expedition dealings, he continued to favor goods over guns as the means to keep frontiers in order.

But Boone died in 1820, the year Clark overwhelmingly lost Missouri's gubernatorial election. Statehood further tipped governing scales away from the inclusive relations that fur trading fostered to the exclusive occupation that white farmers favored. That left Indian policy answerable to white male voters, the majority of whom forgot or never knew and never could imagine the peace and friendship that happened between Americans and Shawnees in Missouri. William Clark did not forget what he had learned about living alongside Indians during his expedition to the Pacific. True to Jefferson's ideals, he continued to envision a day when Indians might be incorporated into the American republic. Yet former Governor Clark's latter years as a superintendent saw him accommodating to a Jacksonian world. The protections he promised Indians amounted to limited compensation for the "improvements" Indians made and the "spoliations" they suffered. His treaties, like the ones he made with Apple Creek Shawnees in 1825 and those "late of Cape Girardeau" in 1832, ushered their exile from Missouri and erased their alternative history from view.

One path to truth and reconciliation requires restitution, but there is little chance the Apple Creek Shawnees will regain the lands they lost. A more modest proposal prods the State of Missouri to erect historical markers on the sites of the Shawnee and Delaware towns near Cape Girardeau. The Missouri Humanities Council has made a start in this direction, sponsoring a new project combining aerial surveillance and excavations that has located the site of the Big Shawnee Village on Apple Creek. Once that work is completed, the next step should be to officially memorialize the location. The inscriptions on new historical markers offer an opportunity to properly remember the Indian communities that prospered on Apple Creek and, as important, to call attention to the peace between former foes that had its day before numbers shifted and white man's democracy had its way.

5

Chimney Rock
Uncircle the Wagons

LOCATED ABOUT FOUR MILES SOUTH of Bayard, Nebraska, on the southern edge of the North Platte River Valley, Chimney Rock is hard to miss. Named by fur traders for its 300-plus-foot spire that looked like a chimney, and composed of volcanic ash, clay, and sandstone, Chimney Rock looms above the horizon. In the middle decades of the nineteenth century, it certainly stood out to hundreds of thousands of travelers who passed by it while making their way west along the principal overland trails that ran beside the North Platte River. Many claimed it was visible from thirty to forty miles away and remained in their sights through several days of travel. Some exaggerated its height; one diarist contended the rock's chimney reached up 700 feet. Others maintained that it was once twice as tall and twice as wide but was wearing away because of winds and rains. In addition to a chimney, observers thought it resembled a haystack, a furnace, a watchtower, and an obelisk. Almost all agreed that getting to Chimney Rock was a signal accomplishment; they had ventured beyond the boundaries of "civilization" and had withstood the rigors of the Platte River Road, the first segment of their great overland journey.[1]

Chimney Rock's prominence among mid-nineteenth-century travelers was quantitatively confirmed by historian Merrill Mattes, who tabulated the frequency with which the eight most noted landmarks along the Great Platte River Road appeared in a sample of overland journals and guidebooks.

Chimney Rock merited a mention or description in 97 percent of the sources. Its nearest rival, Scott's Bluff, came in at 77 percent.

For travelers today, most of whom roll by in automobiles at considerably faster speeds, Chimney Rock still catches the eye (even if wind and erosion over the last 150 years may have further diminished the spire's height). Those who drive by can follow the overland trails, which are well-marked along the whole route from the Missouri River to Pacific destinations. Those who stop at Chimney Rock can get a closer view of the landmark and a broader view of the history of the overland trails at a small Visitor Center. As at Fort Clatsop, Chimney Rock is managed by the National Park Service, which designated it an official National Historic Site in 1956.[2]

Many millions more now know Chimney Rock virtually, as it is one of the featured places in *The Oregon Trail* computer game. First developed in 1971, the game has sold over 65 million copies through its multiple editions and introduced generations of players to some of the challenges and choices that confronted overland travelers in the late 1840s. Who's coming? What to bring? What to buy? What to leave behind? When to start? How fast to

William Henry Jackson, *Approaching Chimney Rock* (1931). Jackson joined a wagon train in 1866 and traveled overland to the Salt Lake Valley. Jackson is best known for his work as a photographer on several expeditions for what became the US Geological Survey, where he worked closely with the artist Thomas Moran. Late in his life, Jackson returned to painting and completed this scene of a caravan in the foreground and Chimney Rock in the background. *Courtesy Scott's Bluff National Monument*

travel? What to do when oxen wear out, when wagons break down, when supplies run low? To trade or not to trade? Chimney Rock is among the first milestones along the journey. Many players (or members of their party) do not get that far, however, having suffered misfortunes or succumbed to diseases on the initial leg of their westward treks.

The original version of *The Oregon Trail* presented Indians as among the misfortunes players might encounter. That was in keeping with decades of movie and television Westerns in which Indians menaced wagon trains. Teachers, however, alerted the game's creators to the impact that negative portrayals might have on students of American Indian ancestry. One of the developers at first felt that altering the role of Indians amounted to denying history. After further consideration, the creators relented. The revised version removed Indians, in some cases, replacing warnings about "Indians ahead" with "riders ahead" and attributing killings to knives rather than tomahawks.[3]

Subsequent editions of the game assigned Indians more benevolent roles. Like a good historian, creator Don Rawitsch dug into primary sources. Reading trail diaries, he "admit[ted] to being surprised by how often people wrote about the help they received from Native Americans who helped them understand where the trail was, where it went, what kind of food along the way was edible and which would make you ill." In later editions of the game, Rawitsch allowed struggling overland travelers to gain assistance from Indians, who shared food and offered guidance about routes. For the 2021 update, the creative team engaged Indigenous consultants to root out stereotypes and anachronisms, while also foregrounding Indian perspectives about the Oregon Trail.[4]

As in computer simulations, so in this alternative history. The reconsideration of the trail in general and the passage by Chimney Rock in particular highlights how Indians and emigrants, as the overland travelers in the mid-nineteenth century were called, traded with one another and how peace, if not friendship, generally prevailed during the 1840s. Emigrants and Indians, however, faced decisions and divisions not yet introduced into *The Oregon Trail*. Nor have the computer versions ever grappled with changes over time. In the earlier periods of this alternative history, concord did not stand that test. The 1850s brought a similar trial, when numbers again shifted and the United States government made its presence felt.

Some mid-nineteenth-century overland travelers were inspired by Lewis and Clark, but none followed the earlier explorers' trail to Oregon. In

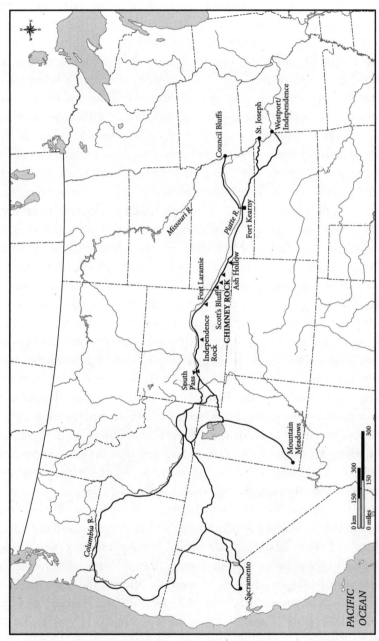

Principal overland trails to Oregon, California, and Utah following the Platte River, 1840s–1860s

1804, the captains chose the Missouri River as the Corps of Discovery's passageway to the Pacific. Upon their return, Lewis and Clark insisted that they had fulfilled Jefferson's instructions of finding "the most practicable water route across the continent." In their wake, as they had done before Lewis and Clark, fur traders continued to follow the Missouri River. During the 1820s and 1830s, "mountaineers," as they called themselves (or mountain men, as they came to be called), also used the river as a conduit to beaver-rich trapping grounds in the Rockies and even to the Pacific slope. But the Lewis and Clark expedition's difficulties crossing the mountains between the headwaters of the Missouri and those of the Columbia River system made its trail impractical for mass migration to the western edge of the continent. "My father's reading of Lewis and Clark's journals was the cause of our crossing the plains," wrote emigrant Andrew Jackson Chambers. J. A. Cornwall similarly ascribed his family's trek to Oregon in 1846 to "the thrilling narrative of the expedition of Colonels Lewis and Clark." Fortunately, for the Chambers and Cornwall families and for other mid-century migrants, they did not allow inspiration to become imitation. The captains' (not colonels') route was unsuitable for heavy wagons pulled by less than nimble oxen. An alternative to the south ran west across the Plains along the Arkansas River, a route that saw increasing traffic in the 1820s and 1830s as traders caravanned goods between Missouri and Santa Fe. For emigrants bound for the Pacific slope in the 1840s, though, the principal pathway lay between the Arkansas and the Missouri along the Platte River. Not on the river, but alongside it, wagon trains traversed present-day Nebraska. Where the Platte split, most took its north fork, which led them by Chimney Rock. From there, the main trails ran through "South Pass," which provided the gentlest crossing of the Rockies and which its boosters touted as less challenging than the Cumberland Gap through the Appalachians.[5]

Although Captain William Clark did not show emigrants the way west, Superintendent Clark did pave the way for mid-century migrations. During the 1820s and 1830s, Clark's agency cleared Indians from the eastern sides of the Mississippi and then from the lower Missouri Valley, while managing relations with Indians to the west of those waterways. The removals from the lower Missouri opened lands for white families (and African American slaves), including the "Platte Purchase" in 1836. Not to be confused with the Platte River, the Platte Purchase involved a triangle-shaped territory of approximately three thousand square miles between the original western boundary of the state of Missouri and the Missouri River (the Platte River flowed on the opposite side of the river, and its mouth was more than forty miles above the northern boundary of the Platte Purchase).[6]

The lead-up to the Platte Purchase reprised what had happened at Apple Creek and elsewhere in Missouri. Because the Platte Country, as the territory came to be known, lay west of the state's original boundaries, Clark and his agents, as well as their superiors in Washington, viewed it as a district to which eastern Indians and Indians from Missouri could be relocated. Treaties in 1830 and 1833 with the Potawatomis designated the Platte Country as the place for their resettlement. National plans, however, conflicted (again) with the designs of land-hungry Americans and the officials they elected. Lured by descriptions of the region's fertility, squatters entered the area, then, sticking to a familiar refrain, complained when Indians defended their holdings. In response to the outcry of squatters, Missouri's governor, John Miller, called for pushing the western boundary of the state to the Missouri River. The removal of Indians, he maintained, was necessary to protect white settlers from hostile savages. In Washington, Missouri's senators, Lewis Linn and Thomas Hart Benton, lobbied to delete the Platte Country from the Potawatomi treaties. From St. Louis, Superintendent William Clark (again) tried to uphold the rights of resident Indians. A September 1835 proclamation ordered all trespassers out of the Platte Country. In February 1836, a United States Army squadron burned the cabins of two white families living illegally in the area. No sooner had the troops departed than the squatters returned, confident their perseverance would soon be rewarded.[7]

It was. In May 1836, the efforts of Senators Linn and Benton paid off with the passage of bill that attached the Platte Country to the state of Missouri once remaining Indian claims were extinguished. Doing his duty, Clark negotiated the necessary agreements, which were ratified in early 1837. The Potawatomis then exited, removed to lands north and west of the newly expanded boundaries of the state of Missouri. Little more than a year later, Clark died, the Platte Purchase capping his career as superintendent and encapsulating its contradictions.[8]

Even as Clark engineered one last Indian eviction, the Platte Purchase erupted in violence *between* American pioneers. The new conflict pitted Mormons against those whom they referred to as "Gentiles." During the early 1830s, thousands of members of the recently formed Church of Latter-day Saints, most of whom traced their roots back to New York and New England, moved into western Missouri. Inspired by founding prophet Joseph Smith's vision of the New Jerusalem located in Missouri "on the borders by the Lamanites" (Indians), these pioneers settled initially around the town of Independence, along the Missouri River just south of the Platte Purchase. The Mormons' growing numbers, theology, communal practices, anti-slavery sympathies, and too-friendly dealings with Indians made them objects of suspicion among non-Mormon neighbors, most of whom had roots in the Upper South. Animosities first boiled over in the summer and fall of 1833 when Gentile mobs attacked Mormon residents, damaging property and killing several Mormons.

Mormons fled the area around Independence, eventually resettling in the Platte Country. Their respite there from persecution was brief. Threatened by the arrival of thousands of Mormons in 1838, western Missouri's non-Mormons fomented violence. Extremists among the Mormons answered by creating vigilante groups of their own. Acts of intimidation quickly escalated. On October 30, what came to be called the "Mormon War" witnessed its deadliest battle. More accurately, it saw a brutal massacre, in which upwards of two hundred Missouri militiamen attacked a Mormon settlement at Haun's Mill and murdered seventeen people. The dead included a nine-year-old boy, shot in the head at point-blank range despite pleas to spare an innocent child.[9]

Governor Lilburn Boggs (who was married to a granddaughter of Daniel Boone) heightened the conflict by adopting the state's favored policy toward Indians. With Executive Order 44, Boggs commanded the Missouri militia to expel the Mormon populace from the state and, if they resisted, to bring about their "extermination." With the force of the state now against them, the Mormons withdrew from Missouri. As with Indian removals, the evicted were denied due process, and compensation fell well short of the value of their lost property.[10]

In the wake of the Mormons' expulsion, more American migrants arrived in what was emerging as a gateway to the West. By 1840, the federal census of the Platte Country recorded more than 15,000 inhabitants. Most came to farm, but a substantial number opened mercantile enterprises. Already in the 1820s, the town of Independence had emerged as a gathering place for traders sending and receiving goods from across the Plains along the Santa Fe Trail. During the late 1830s and 1840s, more establishments popped up in Independence and in new towns to its north along the eastern bank of the Missouri. These entrepôts served the fast-growing local population and profited too by supplying army garrisons and Indian settlements across the river. Where once the "Indian trade" had been synonymous with animal skins, merchants in northwestern Missouri in the late 1830s and early 1840s more often exchanged goods for government payments. Although illegal, much of the trade with Indians involved alcohol, which was amply available thanks to the presence of five distilleries located near the state's new line. The early 1840s brought a further expansion of the scope of operations as Independence and the newer towns to its north became the principal gathering points for overland travelers setting out in increasing numbers for Oregon and California.[11]

In 1846, Boston-born historian Francis Parkman described these places, his prejudices about the assortment of people clustered there leaping off the pages of a book entitled *The Oregon Trail*. Approaching Independence, which was "the common rendezvous," Parkman first encountered "parties of emigrants, with their tents and wagons, . . . encamped on open spots near the bank" of the Missouri. So far so good. Upon arriving in Independence, however, he spotted "some thirty or forty dark slavish-looking Spaniards, gazing stupidly out from beneath their broad hats." Nearby were "one or two French hunters from the mountains, with their long hair and buckskin dresses." Neighboring Westport "was full of Indians[,] . . . Sacs and Foxes, with shaved heads and painted faces, Shawanoes and Delawares, fluttering in calico frocks and turbans, Wyandots dressed like white men, and a few wretched Kanszas wrapped in old blankets." This heterogeneous assemblage, strolling in the streets and lounging in the shops, disturbed the Boston Brahmin's sense of order. Adding to what Parkman saw as a combustible mix of benighted people was the abundance of whiskey, which "circulates more freely in Westport than is altogether safe in a place where every man carries a loaded pistol in his pocket."[12]

One of those Westport establishments belonged to Daniel Boone's grandson, Albert Gallatin Boone. The grandson shared his grandfather's wanderlust. When still a teen, Albert ventured up the Missouri River and into the Rockies. There, he worked as a mountain man, trapping beaver pelts, trading with Indians, and accumulating adventures. After a few years, he returned to Missouri and opened a store on the state's western edge. An international clientele of American, French, and Mexican colonists from St. Louis to Santa Fe frequented Boone's establishment. So did more than a dozen Indian groups, including the Shawnees and Delawares who had been removed from eastern Missouri to eastern Kansas, just across the border from Westport. Again, as with his grandfather, warm feelings prevailed. A nephew remembered how Delawares and Shawnees would sit for hours with Albert, sharing their memories of Daniel Boone.[13]

In Westport, Albert's relations with Indians went beyond business. Although mountain men often married Indian women, there is no evidence of Albert having done so (just as tales of Daniel Boone having wed a Shawnee woman during his 1778 captivity also remain in the realm of uncorroborated lore). But in 1853, Albert opened his Westport home to three children of a trapper-trader companion, William Bent, and his Cheyenne wife. Albert promised to oversee the education of Bent's mixed-race offspring, which he did at a time when his fellow Missourians were demonizing and banishing people with any Indian blood.[14]

Albert Boone's familial ties did not stand in the way of his plying Indians with liquor to increase his profits. In 1846, Parkman observed a number of inebriated Indians about Albert Boone's shop. Because Boone's store in Westport was not on Indian land, liquor sales were legal there. That may not have always been true of Boone's dealings. In 1852, a rival merchant accused Albert and his partners of illegally selling brandy and whiskey out of their trading post within the Indian country.[15]

In the 1840s and the 1850s, much of Albert Boone's profits derived from supplying emigrants headed west to Oregon and California. Although Boone kept a hand in the fur trade and in commerce to New Mexico via the Santa Fe Trail, the depletion of beavers and changes in European fashions ended the brief era of mountain men and depressed the fur trade. For Boone and other merchants in Westport and similar towns along the Missouri River, there was now more money to be made selling goods to emigrants headed west to Oregon and California.

Until almost the end of the 1840s, these emigrants resembled those of previous generations of westering Americans. Their goal was familiar, as were the families in which they traveled. The Oregon-bound, like pioneers before them, sought fertile land—to own, to farm, to keep families with large numbers of children intact, and ultimately to pass real estate on to sons so that they could do the same. What Elijah Bristow, an Illinois native who trekked to Oregon, wrote about the Willamette Valley (the principal destination for overland travelers to Oregon) echoed the Edenic claims that Daniel Boone's contemporaries had made about Kentucky and the Ohio Valley. The Willamette, exulted Bristow, boasted very rich soil and the healthiest climate in the world. These natural attributes made it ideal for "any man disposed to be industrious," though the Oregon Country also beckoned as a place where "people can live . . . with half the labor as they can in Illinois."[16]

The motives of emigrants to Oregon matched pioneering predecessors; what was different were the lengths the Pacific-bound were willing to go to get to that land. In the early 1840s, Oregon still lay outside the established boundaries of the United States, as it had been when Lewis and Clark wintered at Fort Clatsop four decades earlier. In that sense, "emigrant" was a fit description for the Oregon (and California) bound. There was, of course, precedent for Americans moving beyond the borders of their nation and adjusting, to varying degrees, to life outside the United States. Examples included those like Daniel Boone who had gone to Spanish Louisiana in the 1790s, the "Late Loyalists" who had moved to British Upper Canada around the same time, or the much larger flow into Mexican Texas during the 1820s and early 1830s. The distance to Oregon, however, was much greater than any previous overland relocation.[17]

From the Platte Country, the next "West" lay just across the Missouri, but in the early 1840s Americans looked (well beyond) the adjacent lands on the Great Plains. Indians, including Shawnees and Delawares, some earlier relocated from the Ohio Valley, others more recently removed from the state of Missouri, resided on the lands immediately across the river from the Platte Purchase. Three score and seven years (or so) of the history of the United States demonstrated that the presence of Indian occupants and the guarantees of treaties would not deter American squatters from taking up lands they coveted. The grasslands of the Great Plains, however, held limited allure. Although Lewis and Clark had praised the quality of the lands through the entire Missouri Valley, subsequent explorers disputed that assessment. Stephen Long's 1819 description of the Plains as a "Great American Desert" stuck and dampened enthusiasm for American settlement beyond the eastern fringe of the Louisiana Purchase. Better to leave the inhospitable terrain as a reserve for Indians, especially since reports like Bristow's lured Americans to the Pacific slope. The challenge was getting there, which for overland travelers in the early 1840s entailed a journey of five to six months and a crossing of the forbidding Great American Desert.

Traffic on the overland trails to the Pacific slope started at a trickle and built slowly over the course of the 1840s. Only 13 people went overland to Oregon in 1840. The following year saw 24 arrive in Oregon and 34 in California. From there, the combined annual tally ticked upward to 125, 913, 1,528, and 2,760. Over the period from 1840 to 1845, Oregon was the destination for more than 90 percent of overland travelers to the Pacific. That balance shifted in 1846, when the California-bound slightly outnumbered the Oregon-goers. In 1847, Oregon again witnessed a surge; four thousand arrived by land that year, compared with only 450 going to California. That year, the first segment of the overland trail was also crowded with Mormon migrants, more than 2,000 of whom traveled to the Salt Lake Valley, where they hoped to find a safe refuge. Another 2,000 Latter-day Saints hit the trail in 1848, joined, though on separate sides of the Platte River, by 1,700 people headed to the Pacific slope (three-quarters of these to Oregon).[18]

Conditions on the trail changed as the volume of traffic grew, but emigrants shared many expectations across the opening years of their wagoning across the Plains. Most brought deep biases against Indians with them. Unlike Daniel Boone, Meriwether Lewis, William Clark, and the vast majority of American pioneers who joined them in Revolutionary Kentucky, in the Louisiana Territory, and in the Corps of Discovery, the animus toward Indians was rarely based on previous interactions. Most of the overland emigrants in the 1840s had had little, if any, direct contact with Indians before venturing onto the Plains. Many had never even seen an Indian before their journey, native peoples having been largely removed from most of the lands east of the Mississippi. By the 1840s, they had also been banished from Missouri, the state from which the largest contingent of emigrants on the overland trail hailed. But American culture was saturated with stories and images that instilled dread of "savages," and emigrants brought this heavy baggage with them. Opponents of such long-distance migration ramped up fears with warnings that the Pacific-bound would be in constant jeopardy from Indians poised to attack at any point between Missouri and Oregon. Stay put, contended the *Daily Missouri Republican*, a state that the boosterish local newspaper insisted was superior to Oregon and California. And if a man determined to go, he should leave his wife and children behind. Guidebooks, which became more widely disseminated by the middle of the decade and which were more positive about the benefits awaiting overland travelers, nonetheless cautioned trail-goers to be always on guard against Indian treachery and thievery.[19]

Negative associations with the Great American Desert similarly pervaded American culture and shaped the assumptions of emigrants. Americans had long judged the fertility of land based on the number and type of trees that it supported; from that vantage point, grasslands made poor farmlands. Reports about the scarcity of water added to emigrants' fears.[20]

No wood and no water were a common refrain in emigrant diaries, especially once they reached the split in the Platte River and followed its north fork toward Chimney Rock. For Francis Parkman, the dreary sameness of the entire Plains was the trail's most striking feature. "One day we rode on for hours, without seeing a tree or a bush, . . . the unbroken carpet" of grass stretching "as far as the eye could reach." The skulls and bleached bones of buffalo, which Parkman described as scattered everywhere, exemplified the deadliness of these lands. With alternative water sources hard to find and unreliable, emigrants clung to the Platte. But the river too disappointed and frightened trail-goers. Parkman estimated the water to be a half mile wide but barely two feet deep. Others downgraded that measurement. "A mile wide and an inch deep," went the joke repeated by emigrants. "Too thick to drink, too thin to plow, too pale to paint," was another piece of caustic humor. Yet even that shallow held its dangers. As emigrant Clarence Bagley discovered in 1852, the Platte's wide, shifting bottom was "quite often quicksand" in which wagons and stock got stuck and sometimes sank. Sudden storms added to the menace, the usually placid stream flooding its banks.[21]

Preexisting notions about Indians also weighed heavily on the minds of emigrants as they made their initial progress across the Plains. The first Indians that Francis Parkman encountered on the other side of the Missouri were Shawnees and Delawares living along the Kansas River. The Shawnees, he allowed, were "tolerable farmers . . . in a prosperous condition." The Delawares, by contrast, "dwindle every year," which he attributed not to their repeated dislocations, but to men lost in intertribal warfare. For most emigrants on the trail, it was the Pawnees who first set off alarms. Unlike the Shawnees and Delawares, whose roots were in the East and who had a history of dealings with Euro-Americans, the Pawnees were "wild" Indians. To Parkman, they were "treacherous cowardly banditti." Reaching the part of the lower Platte River where Pawnee bands roamed, he deemed it likely that the Pawnees would attempt to steal from him.[22]

As bothered as emigrants were by what Indians stole, the travelers were more infuriated by what Indians charged. At a number of places, Indians had established ferries or constructed bridges, which they demanded emigrants pay to use. "Crossing in any way but the bridge would be a hard job," wrote emigrant John Hawkins Clark about one of these points on the Wolf River. The crude bridge, Clark estimated, cost perhaps $150 to construct; the Indians who manned its toll booth charged $1 per wagon. That made for exorbitant profits, and it convinced Clark that white men must be behind the enterprise. The Indians, he presumed, were mere employees, who would blow their wages on whiskey. Emigrants like Clark despised what they considered extortions and resented even more the tribute that Indians exacted for crossing their territories.[23]

The trepidation of emigrants intensified as rumors circulated of murders and massacres perpetrated by Indians. One 1847 story, which made its way back into a Missouri newspaper, reported on the decimation of 100 emigrants on the Oregon Trail. The rumor quickened the pulses of many then on the trail, who only later heard that those supposedly killed had, in fact, arrived alive and well in Oregon.[24]

To some extent, attitudes toward Indians softened as emigrants moved further onto the Plains and up the Platte River. Some let go of the presumption of guilt when, for example, they saw Indians dressed in manufactured clothing. Whites learned that Indians did not steal clothes but bartered for them, or sometimes picked up garb and other goods from the items discarded by emigrants needing to lighten wagon loads. Many on the trail came to understand, too, that Indians were not always to blame for the crimes of which they were accused. Two weeks after paying the toll at Wolf River, John Hawkins Clark recorded that his party, making its way along the Platte, was on a stretch of the trail where cattle had recently been stolen. He soon ascertained that the perpetrators were not Indians, but white men. "We are continually hearing of the depredations of the Indians," observed emigrant Caroline Richardson, "but we have not seen one [case] yet."[25]

Deadly violence was also much less prevalent than fearmongers had asserted it would be. Only one of the many rumored massacres during the 1840s proved true, an 1847 incident that claimed the lives of at least twenty-three emigrants near the end of their journey in Oregon. For their safety, guidebooks and wagon train leaders had warned emigrants to travel in large companies and to stay close to the caravans. With those strictures in mind, diarists fretted whenever a family member wandered away from camps, certain that Indians lurked, waiting to pick off isolated emigrants. But these fears, too, proved overblown. In fact, several historians who have scrutinized the records reached the same conclusion: lethal violence between Indians and emigrants was rare in the 1840s. The most careful and comprehensive tabulation by John Unruh found no emigrants killed by Indians from 1840 to 1844. Unruh counted 4 such deaths in both 1845 and 1846. The annual tally spiked to 24 in 1847, when the one massacre occurred. The following year, the number of homicides fell back to just 2. Over the same period, emigrants killed few Indians: a total of only 2 between 1840 and 1845, then a jump to 20 in 1846, but again dropping to just 2 each in 1847 and 1848. A further breakdown of these numbers reveals that Indians and emigrants had the least to fear from one another in the Platte Valley portion of the overland route. Almost all the killings that occurred during these years, including the one massacre, happened west of the Continental Divide, after emigrants had passed Chimney Rock and left the Platte behind.[26]

Judging by mortality statistics (incomplete as they are), emigrants had as much to fear from one another (and from themselves) as from Indians. Accidental shootings accounted for as many fatalities as did killings by Indians. In some instances, anxieties about Indians triggered friendly fire episodes. While camped on the North Platte, Alonzo Delano related how a "young scamp" of about fourteen or fifteen wanted to pay a joke on the caravan's sentry by sneaking up on him and giving the guard a good scare. Because the young man stayed silent when hailed by the guard, "the Sentinel naturally supposed him, in the darkness of the night, to be an Indian, whose object was plunder," and fired his gun at the shadowy figure. The jester survived this shooting, and, according to Delano, learned his lesson. Others were not so lucky, including those who shot themselves while rushing to gather loaded weapons in anticipation of an impending Indian attack. In general, the vast majority of friendly fire and self-inflicted shootings occurred early in the overland passage, when emigrants were most on edge about Indians and least seasoned about the proper handling of firearms.[27]

By the numbers, emigrants had the most to fear from the elements, water in particular. Emigrants complained frequently about the challenges of finding water, especially those who headed to California across the most arid portions of the Great American Desert—which makes it difficult to fathom how drowning deaths outnumbered killings by Indians. Even the Platte, whose depth was often mocked, swallowed up emigrants and their livestock in its occasional floods. More dangerous than drowning in the water was drinking it. Contaminated water caused dysentery, an affliction familiar to many a player of *The Oregon Trail* and dreaded by their real-life predecessors. Cholera, also a frequent game-ender of *The Oregon Trail*, was deadliest of all on the Oregon Trail, taking the lives of more emigrants than any other disease.[28]

The Mormons have never been a part of the computer game, but their presence on the trail generated animosities from American emigrants with whom they had a history of conflict. After being chased out of Missouri, Latter-day Saints re-congregated in Illinois. Persecution followed them there. After a mob murdered Joseph Smith in 1844, his successor as president of the church, Brigham Young, decided that Mormons should seek a permanent sanctuary distant from American oppressors. With the Great Salt Lake and surrounding Wasatch Valley as the chosen location, Young, like a modern Moses, prepared to lead an exodus across the desert to the new promised land. In 1846, rumors spread that 2,300 Mormons had assembled at St. Joseph, Missouri, a major jumping-off point for the overland trail. "A great alarm was excited" by these reports among the emigrants waiting then to depart from nearby Independence, according to Francis Parkman. "The people of Illinois and Missouri, who composed by far the greater part of the emigrants, have never been on the best terms with the 'Latter Day Saints,'" wrote Parkman, in what was for him a rare understatement. Parkman expected the worst when "large armed bodies of these fanatics" ran into "the most impetuous and reckless of their old enemies on the broad prairies, far beyond the reach of law." For the moment, the prospect of a mass Mormon migration and their sharing of the overland trail with Gentile tormenters turned out to be a false alarm: the group of suspected Latter-day Saints turned out to be "good Christians," as zealous in their hatred of Mormons as many other Americans.[29]

The rumors were not entirely baseless. In 1846, the Mormons were massing for a move. But where emigrants to Oregon and California usually crossed the Missouri River in April or May, the Salt Lake–bound had a shorter journey ahead of them. They could afford to depart later in the year without worrying about getting trapped in mountain snows (the tragic fate that year of the "Donner party"). To avoid conflicts with Gentiles, the initial exodus of Mormons, very few that first year, waited until most of the emigrants were already well ahead of them on the way west.[30]

Their numbers grew much larger in 1847, when Mormon and non-Mormon parties traveled alongside one another in the Platte Valley, their mutual fear and loathing barely concealed. Near the crossing points of the Missouri River, west-bound Missourians taunted Mormons by reminding them of their expulsion from the state a decade earlier. Latter-day Saints returned the verbal fire, contemptuously referring to Missourians as "Pukes." But contrary to Parkman's prediction, the foes did not renew their physical assaults against one another once they traveled beyond the reach of state authority. It helped that antagonists kept a little distance from one another. Mormons stuck to the north side of the Platte, leaving the opposite bank to Gentile wagon trains. Still, the wide and shallow stream hardly presented an impermeable barrier. Crossings occurred. So did contacts, yet these remained peaceful. In part, fear of a common foe again tempered the historical animosities between Mormons and Gentiles. Wary of Indians, the dual streams of emigrants avoided duels with one another. Still, as had been the case at Apple Creek, relations between recent combatants went beyond preserving an uneasy truce. In 1847, along the Platte River portion of the overland trail, a small trade also developed between Mormon and non-Mormon emigrés.[31]

Even more unexpected was the peace on the Platte between emigrants and Indians. For emigrants, that meant letting go of at least a little bit of their pre-judgments about native peoples. Such deeply held biases and enmities were not easily overcome, and they were by no means wholly cast aside. But repeated, peaceful meetings allayed suspicions, and exchanges of goods allowed mutually beneficial relations to develop.

Consider the evolution of John Hawkins Clark's views. His first encounter with Indians at the Wolf River Bridge, which occurred on May 9, 1852, left a bad taste. Subsequent thefts would have reinforced his prejudices, had he not realized that white men were the perpetrators. By the end of May, after a couple of weeks journeying along the Platte, Clark and his company were comfortable enough to admit several Sioux into their camp and to provide them with something to eat. There may also have been some intimidation involved in the invitation. The reputation of the Sioux as fierce warriors, and, as William Clark described them, "vile miscreants," could have been a factor in the gift of food; John Hawkins Clark pronounced these Indians "imposing." Yet, greater familiarity with Indians further softened Clark's views. On June 14, the caravan, having just passed Chimney Rock, was visited by another party of Indians. This time, Clark sensed no threat, and his company extended a warm welcome and another summons to dine together. The Indians' presence, wrote Clark, offered a break from routine and added to the pleasures of their encampment. By the fire, "passing the pipe from mouth to mouth, from white man to Indian, a stranger would have sworn we were all of the same tribe as we smoked together." Except "for the slight difference in our looks," suggested Clark, "we were brothers of the same mould."[32]

The extent and speed of Clark's transformation made his evolution unusual. Very few emigrants welcomed Indians as warmly as Clark's party did; fewer recognized any brotherhood (or sisterhood) with Plains Indians. Emigrants occasionally shared meals with Indians, smoked with them, and engaged them in sporting competitions. But guards, like long-held views, were not often dropped. Besides, the mission of overland travelers was not to study Indian cultures or take time befriending people, it was to proceed on as quickly as possible.

Typically, what brought Indians and emigrants together was trade, not friendship. Like Lewis and Clark before them, overland travelers often needed horses to replace animals that broke down. Trading with Indians sometimes involved a straightforward bartering of animals. On the Plains in 1847, a cow could be had for a horse. Again, like Lewis and Clark, emigrants turned to Indians for food and garments. Buffalo robes and dressed deerskins remained much desired by emigrants, as they had been by the earlier explorers. Moccasins were in especially high demand. "Everybody's shoes gave out," remembered Harriet Scott Palmer, "and we bartered with Indians for moccasins." In exchange, overland travelers offered Indians many of the same goods that the Corps of Discovery and generations of traders had supplied: clothing, blankets, buttons, beads, mirrors, and metal tools—metals, but unlike Lewis and Clark and other official emissaries of the United States, no medals. Often, according to several emigrants, Indians asked for alcohol. As emigrant James Abbey related of an encounter with a dozen Indians along the Platte in 1850, their initial greeting was "how-do-whiske[y]."[33]

The presence of women in most emigrant companies prior to the Gold Rush facilitated trading with Indians. Just as Sacagawea's company with the Corps of Discovery signaled to Indians that the Lewis and Clark expedition was not a war party, so, too, did families on the overland trail

Z. S. Liang, *Trading for Moccasins, Chimney Rock, Oregon Trail, 1853* (2012). Trained in China, the emigré artist Z. S. Liang painted a scene that defied so many caricatures about the Oregon Trail. Instead of circled wagons surrounded by Indian warriors on horseback, Liang's painting highlights the trade in moccasins and features women, both Indian and white, in the foreground, with men and Chimney Rock in the background. *Courtesy of Z. S. Liang*

make the caravans less threatening. In some cases, women took the lead in the bartering. In their otherwise spare reminiscence about their journey to Oregon in 1847, husband and wife James and Nancy Coon detailed how, while camped at a Sioux Indian town not far beyond Chimney Rock, "quite a trade was got up between the women and Squaws." They recalled a lively scene in which white women offered beads and various trinkets in exchange for the bread and meat bartered by Indian women.[34]

The presence of women and the particular roles they played on the overland trails is the most significant omission in every version of *The Oregon Trail* game. True, players do assign names to people in their party and are free to mix male and female ones. But the gender of these personas makes no difference in the game. It certainly did in the mid-nineteenth century. The difference began with the decision to emigrate. In keeping with the patriarchal customs of mid-nineteenth-century American families, husbands and fathers made the choice to move. The input of wives was not always solicited. Their consent was not required.

Men's and women's accounts of the journeys were notably different. For both, there was plenty of toil and plenty of tedium in what was a very long walk across half the continent. For men, though, the trail brought a break from the routines of farm life and often a breaking away from fathers in pursuit of their own independence. "Hunting Buffalow is the greatest sport that can be conceived," raved Samuel Crockett in 1844. Crockett's account, like those of many of his brethren, brimmed with excitement about adventures on the trail and prospects at journey's end. Wives, mothers, sisters, and daughters were generally far less exuberant about "seeing the elephant," the phrase that emigrants attached to the passage across the continent. While men waxed enthusiastically with one another about hunting bison and even meeting Indians, women, in the company of other women and in the privacy of their journals, voiced their doubts. Not a break or a breaking away, for women the trail brought long days of walking and unending chores under challenging conditions. "We have no time for sociability," complained Helen Carpenter in her diary. "From the time we get up in the morning, . . . it is hurry-scurry" until "it is time to go to bed." Women's routines were often further complicated by pregnancies that meant going into labor and delivering babies while on the move. Much less certain about the destinies that awaited them at their destinations, some women confided in their diaries their reluctance about leaving homes and friends behind and questioned the decisions made for them by husbands and fathers. But what choice did they have other than to go along? Staying behind meant abandonment by husbands, separation from children, and likely a stigmatized, impoverished life.[35]

Most wives made their peace with the move in order to keep the peace within their wagons. And through the opening years of the great overland migrations across the western half of the continent, peace generally prevailed outside the wagons. In 1847, the emigration of more than two thousand Mormons put them alongside old adversaries on the Platte River portion of the overland route. But the mob violence that had erupted in northwestern Missouri in the 1830s and in Illinois in 1844 did not flair anew on the adjacent trails that Mormons and Gentiles followed. In 1847, a massacre on the western portion of the Oregon Trail spiked the death toll of emigrants at Indian hands. But retaliations and escalations did not immediately ensue. In 1848, the overland trail was again peaceful, between Mormons and non-Mormons and between emigrants and Indians. That year, Indians killed only two emigrants, and emigrants killed only two Indians.[36]

Around four thousand emigrants made their way to Oregon, California, and Utah in 1848, and almost all of them passed by Chimney Rock. Like the approximately fifteen thousand emigrants who had proceeded them on the overland trail during the 1840s, most of the "class of '48" jumped off sometime in May. Chimney Rock came into view about a month after the crossing of the Missouri. Emigrants welcomed the sight of Chimney Rock and other sandstone formations along the North Platte, which represented a break from what they considered the monotony of rolling grasslands. Some memorialized their passage by inscribing their names on the rock's base, others by describing or sketching it in their journals. Reaching Chimney Rock meant they had completed the first leg of their great journey. Few noted that the harder part of the trail lay ahead, with steeper ascents, drier lands, and more dangerous relations with Indians. None knew that much harder years lay ahead for Plains Indians, who through 1848 had generally abetted the flow of people across their countries.

Beginning in 1849 and continuing through the next decade, the pursuit of California gold multiplied the number, changed the composition, shifted the destinations, and altered the destinies of overland emigrants. Historian Malcolm Rohrbough likened the discovery of gold in 1848 to a "stone dropped into a deep pool," the rush of people to California rippling outward "to touch the lives of families and communities everywhere in the Republic." Rohrbough could justifiably have extended the reach of the metaphor: the "ever-widening circles" that emanated from California upended lives far beyond the United States. Its impact certainly reverberated on the overland trails to California.[37]

Technically, those on the trails were no longer emigrants, at least from the point of view of nation-states. A war with Mexico and an 1848 peace treaty, together with an 1846 agreement with Britain, had brought the route and the destinations entirely within the United States. Indians, as usual, were not part of these negotiations and rejected remappings that wrote their territories out. On the Plains adjacent to the Platte River trail, they continued to battle one another for control of lands and resources, while also increasingly coming into conflict with overland travelers and the United States Army. Among overlanders, more serious divisions emerged as well, reflecting the deepening rifts among Americans back in "the states." Yet when it came to Indians, trail-goers and the agents and armies of the United States that assisted them found unity. They increasingly viewed Indians along the way as in the way.

The numbers on the trail in 1849 and the following years dwarfed those seen earlier in the 1840s and in any prior American emigration. Around 4,000 people passed by Chimney Rock in 1848. Close to 60 percent of that year's total were Mormons headed for the Salt Lake Valley. More than three-quarters of the 1,700 Pacific-bound travelers were on their way to Oregon. In 1849, almost seven times as many people took to the overland trail. More than nine in ten of these '49ers were California gold-seekers. The next year witnessed an even greater flow. More than 50,000 people ventured across the Plains, approximately 44,000 of whom were argonauts. From 1849 through 1860, overland emigration to California topped 200,000, nearly four times the count of those moving to its neighbor to the north.[38]

Traffic on the trails left emigrants literally gasping. Near the jumping off points, teams sometimes traveled ten or twelve abreast. Further along the Platte, wagons extended on the horizon as far as the eye could see. "I believe there are wagons stretched in sight of one another for 500 miles," contended one '49er. That was an exaggeration, but one caravan that year included an unbroken line of wagons and pack animals that spread across six miles. It required two hours for those at the rear to reach a point passed earlier by the front of the train. In 1849 and 1850, during the peak times of the year, which at Chimney Rock lasted from late May through late June, several hundred vehicles rolled by the landmark each day. Emigrants gasped not only at the unprecedented volume, but also from all of the dust churned up by so much traffic.[39]

They gasped, too, because of the speed with which emigrants now hastened to California. Between 1841 and 1848, it took on average 157.7 days for an emigrant to amble overland to California. Hurrying to California to start prospecting, '49ers shaved an average of twenty-six days off the journey. Speed was even more of the essence in 1850, when gold-seekers worried that the best sites might already be claimed or tapped out. That year, argonauts truly rushed to California, completing the trip from jumping-off point on the Missouri to destination in an average of only 107.9 days.[40]

Motivations mattered, but lighter loads really shortened the trips. Argonauts began with considerably less baggage than would-be farmers. They did not need to load wagons with a variety of agricultural implements and household items to start and stock a family farm. At least in the early phase of the Gold Rush, miners presumed that the primary tools of their trade, picks, pans, and shovels, could be bought in California. In addition, most of the California-bound did not intend to settle there. Hence, they sometimes dispensed with wagons entirely, piling supplies for the journey onto pack horses and mules. After a year or two in California, they expected to return home, their fortunes and futures secured. Or so men, and gold-seekers were almost always men, promised the parents, wives, and children they left behind. Still, because speed was of the essence for those rushing to California, they jettisoned possessions that weighed down mules, horses, and wagons. Scattered from the Missouri to the Sierras, discarded objects littered overland trails.[41]

The absence of women gave men a taste of the work that wives, sisters, and daughters did; it did not give them a taste for it. Unencumbered by families and by the supplies needed to establish a family farm, parties of men could move more quickly. But they could not escape many of the chores that men had depended on women to do. Who would do women's work became a source of contention on the trail, as it would later be in the gold fields.[42]

The volume of traffic also created conflicts. Congestion, as any modern driver knows, is rarely conducive to concord. The same was true on the trails. In addition to dealing with the frustrations brought on by dust and heat, emigrants in 1849 and the early 1850s had to contend with heightened competition for scarcer resources. Timber, always in short supply, became harder to find. Overgrazing depleted grasses. Game disappeared from the immediate environs of the trail. Securing suitable campsites proved much more challenging than it had been.[43]

For Indians, the traffic presented greater dilemmas. On the one hand, the opportunities that many had seized in the 1840s multiplied with the number of travelers in the 1850s. Instead of hundreds of people passing through annually, there were now thousands (and even tens of thousands in peak Gold Rush years). For Plains Indians along the Platte portions of the route, which carried the combined traffic headed to California, Oregon, and Utah, the increases meant more people to ferry, to guide, to assist in locating wandering animals, from whom to steal stock, and with whom to trade. On the other hand, there were also far more opportunities for misunderstandings. Mutual suspicions bred misinterpretations, as, for example, when a large group of Lakotas came into the camp of an 1853 emigrant party not far from Chimney Rock. Upon entry, the Indians laid down their blankets, a gesture that signaled their readiness to barter. The jumpy campers, however, viewed it otherwise and scurried to their guns. Fortunately, on this occasion, cooler heads prevailed. Not that Indians were always eager to lay down their blankets, as an 1850 emigrant party discovered when visiting a Lakota encampment in the same part of the trail. On that occasion, the Indians, reported a puzzled overland traveler, retired to their lodges rather than engage in bartering. What the travelers interpreted as a lack of hospitality more likely reflected the Indians' exhaustion from having already entertained so many visitors that year. They may also have had nothing left to trade.[44]

If the Lakotas and other Plains Indians in the vicinity of the Platte River had viewed emigrants as both a blessing and a curse, the scales tipped toward the latter during the 1850s. While the depletion of timber, grass, and game and the competition for camping sites inconvenienced emigrants, the damages so many travelers and their moving stock did to local environments posed an existential threat to inhabitants. Consider the decline in bison, the animal so central to Plains Indian cultures. In 1843, Nathan Boone estimated that one hundred thousand bison were slaughtered on the Great Plains that year. In a few years, he predicted, the "buffalo will only be known as a rare species." Boone was prophetic, though the systematic extermination of the buffalo by Americans awaited the 1860s and 1870s. Nonetheless, mass emigration across the Plains contributed to a decline in the bison population in the 1840s and especially the 1850s. Around the Platte in particular, bison herds thinned as emigration thickened. Hunting by emigrants and Indians accounted for some of the drop. More of the local reductions in the bison population owed to the depletion of the grass on which they fed and for which they now competed with the emigrants' livestock. Overgrazing also took a toll on the horse herds that Plains Indians prized.[45]

To these grievances were added the grieving for loved ones lost to cholera and smallpox epidemics that overland emigrants brought with them. The first wave of cholera in 1849 coincided with the tidal wave of gold-seekers, who poisoned the waters of the Platte with their defecations. The disease took a considerable toll on overland travelers, but their losses paled next to what Plains Indians suffered. A Lakota winter count for 1849 depicted a kneeling, twisting man dying of dysentery, a year in which one-seventh of their people perished. "The odor from the dead bodies could be scented for miles," remembered one who lived through the terrible year. More terror followed in the early 1850s, as cholera returned and smallpox too swept through Plains Indian communities.[46]

This left Indians around the Platte to grapple with how to stop or at least stem the stream of people and animals that trampled their lands and brought diseases that decimated their ranks. One option was to step up violence to try to intimidate emigrants and curtail the flow. While the tactic appealed to some men, especially younger ones looking to gain status through martial exploits, it seemed to others a diversion from the intertribal conflicts. These had long pitted Indian nations against one another, with the Lakotas' westward expansion in the first half of the nineteenth century putting pressure on other Plains peoples. Moreover, numbers (and weaponry) made war against whites a bloodier and less promising proposition. Already in 1843, Matthew Field, reporting his experiences on the trail for a New Orleans newspaper, had claimed that the Sioux, after watching the many wagons heading west along the Platte, pondered a return to homelands east of the Plains. Those lands must now be empty, for they had "seen, they supposed, *the whole white village* move beyond the mountains." A joke, to be sure, but one that seemed even truer in the early 1850s when the waves of emigrants crested ever higher.[47]

In lieu of open and ongoing warfare, Plains Indians pursued other means to protect vital resources and obtain compensation for their losses. Covert raids offered one avenue of redress. Stealing animals, particularly horses, which brought both wealth and honor to raiders, was not new for Plains Indians. But the justification and the imperative for taking stock from emigrants grew with each passing caravan and with the losses to their own herds with each passing year. Another avenue for redress was to demand that emigrants pay for the resources they consumed and for the right to travel through Indian lands. This could be done, as in the 1840s, by enforcing tolls at bridges, ferries, and fording points, or at other places along the Platte River road. Emigrants in the 1850s, no less than in their predecessors in the 1840s, resented and often resisted the orders of Indians. Seeking external support, some Plains Indian leaders turned to the government of the United States for protection and compensation.[48]

Overland travelers sought the same from Washington, DC. In looking to the federal government for assistance, the latest set of westering pioneers drew on an old tradition, one that predated the establishment of Washington, DC. Back in the late 1780s and the early 1790s, Daniel Boone's contemporaries called on the newly established government of the United States to defend Kentucky settlements and then to extend American landholdings by displacing Ohio Indians from Chillicothe and other villages north of the Ohio River. A generation later, overseeing the removal of Indians became a paramount concern of William Clark's superintendency. From the moment that emigration commenced across the Plains, travelers appealed for federal protection. They had already received words of support from President John Tyler, who in 1841, in his first annual message to Congress, requested funding to build a string of forts from Council Bluffs on the Missouri River (just north of its confluence with the Platte) to the Pacific. With only a handful of emigrants then making their way to Oregon and with the claims of the United States to the Pacific as yet unclear, Tyler justified the military posts as a way to protect trade and cultivate friendly relations with Indians. Anticipating an enlarged American presence in Oregon, Tyler also deemed the forts essential to "safe intercourse with the American settlements at the mouth of the Columbia River." As the volume of overland traffic swelled, emigrants and their advocates repeated Tyler's request. Only the prompt construction of a chain of posts and a steady show of American military force could forestall Indians from menacing overland travelers. That notion failed to explain why peace generally prevailed in the absence of any forts along the trail.[49]

Through most of the 1840s, the United States did not construct any new forts along the overland trails, much less a series of them. Given spare budgets, military authorities believed permanent posts too expensive to maintain. Instead, Colonel Stephen Kearny proposed "a military expedition . . . every two or three years." He was confident that would suffice to remind Indians "of the facility and rapidity with which our dragoons can march through any part of their country." Kearny led one such expedition in the summer of 1845 that followed the overland trail as far as South Pass. During the march, he reported meetings with Pawnees, Sioux, Cheyenne, and Arapahos. He warned each of these groups not to disturb white travelers. The following year, Congress authorized a beefed up and more permanent military presence on the trail, appropriating what at the time was a considerable sum ($76,500) to pay for the construction and manning of several posts and to compensate Indians whose territories would be impacted by the chosen sites. Left to be determined were how many forts would actually be built. Nor was any work immediately initiated. Only in 1848 did the United States establish a military post along the Platte in central Nebraska, which was christened Fort Kearny (despite its namesake's objections to such fixed installations). In the last year of the decade, in keeping with Kearny's preferred policy, another army unit was sent out on the trail. From Fort Kearny, it went all the way to Oregon, providing a military escort for at least some emigrants. That the overwhelming majority of overland travelers were headed to California in 1849 did not alter the dragoons' route. In that year, the federal government also purchased Fort John, from its fur-trading owners. The post, located seventy-five miles up the trail from Chimney Rock, was officially renamed Fort Laramie and turned over to the United States Army.[50]

Near Fort Laramie, officials from the United States met with representatives from numerous Plains Indian nations in September 1851. First to arrive and the largest delegation were Lakotas, which was fitting given the dominant position they had gained among Indian peoples in the Platte Valley and across the northern Plains. The Lakota emissaries carried an American flag given them by William Clark more than forty years earlier, harkening back to a moment when both Lakotas and Americans first spread themselves westward across the Plains. American agents presented themselves, as they often had, as peacemakers. In the rhetoric so many times deployed since the beginning of the republic, "peace commissioners" from the United States acted on behalf of the "great father" to halt the wars between his "red children." To that end, the treaty that was signed on September 17, 1851, established territorial boundaries, which American authorities claimed would keep Indians from different tribes away from one another and would result in a lasting peace. But it was not intertribal conflicts that upset Plains Indians along the overland trails. It was the continuing rush of gold seekers through their countries. In response to Indian complaints, the agreement promised annuities of $50,000 per year from the United States for fifty years as compensation for the damages wrought by emigrants. It also bound the United States to protect the Indian nations against all depredations committed by Americans. In exchange for this protection by the United States,

Indian signatories agreed to the right of the United States to build roads and forts within their territories and to let Americans pass peacefully through their lands.[51]

Thomas Fitzpatrick, one of the two commissioners who negotiated the 1851 treaty, discerned the choice facing the United States government. In dealings with Plains Indians, he advised, "the policy must be either an army or an annuity." The treaty pushed the latter course. By "an inducement . . . greater than the gains of plunder," the United States could make peace between Indians and keep it with them. The alternative, contended Fitzpatrick, was "a force . . . at hand able to restrain and check" the Indians. "Any compromise between the two systems," he warned, "will only be productive of mischief."[52]

Because American policy was immediately compromised, the 1851 Fort Laramie Treaty did not bring about peace or build goodwill. With the United States unprepared to intervene militarily to enforce treaty provisions about territorial boundaries, intertribal conflicts continued as before. Far worse from the perspective of the Indians who signed the pact, the United States Senate amended Article 7 before ratifying the treaty. Rather than paying annuities for fifty years as the original agreement had stipulated, the Senate unilaterally reduced the duration to ten years. Protests by Indians about the changed terms fell on newly deaf American ears.[53]

During the 1850s, the policy of the United States tilted toward the army, which significantly expanded its footprint (and hoofprints) across the trans-Missouri West and along the overland trails. Between forts Kearny and Laramie, the army erected a new post at Ash Hollow in 1855. From these posts, more frequent mounted patrols extended the army's presence on the Platte portion of the overland trails. The mission remained to protect both emigrants and Indians and avert discord between them. Peacekeeping, however, was an enterprise for which the army was poorly suited. The enlarged presence was not enough for soldiers to be present for most encounters between emigrants and Indians and to prevent misdeeds that provoked violence. Soldiers, too, produced mischief of their own, with harmful consequences for relations with Indians.[54]

Scattered confrontations and minor skirmishes, which killed and wounded a few soldiers and Indians, kept relations on edge in the early 1850s; an incident along the North Platte River near Fort Laramie in August 1854 pushed matters over the ledge. Like many prior episodes, this one began with a seemingly trivial misunderstanding. A lame cow had wandered off from a Mormon encampment and into a nearby Lakota one. There, an Indian named High Forehead slaughtered it. The cow's owner went to the fort to seek justice. The leader of the Lakota band, Conquering Bear, offered a horse as restitution. That should have settled things, just as similar disputes had been handled on the trail. But the commander at Fort Laramie, angry about other recent livestock thefts around the post, charged Lt. John L. Grattan with exacting a stiffer punishment and teaching Indians a lesson. Fresh out of West Point and looking to prove himself, Grattan was eager to crack down on the Lakotas. Rejecting the proposed recompense, the lieutenant demanded the arrest of the cow's killer. When the Lakotas refused to turn over High Forehead, Grattan ordered soldiers to fire on them. Even after one of the Lakotas had been wounded, the Indians did not return fire. Another volley from the soldiers killed Conquering Bear. At that point, the Indians, who vastly outnumbered the contingent sent out from the fort, abandoned their restraint and killed twenty-one soldiers, including Grattan. They then mutilated and desecrated the bodies of the dead Americans. Despite all the vitriol that had been exchanged between Lakotas and American army officers, going back to Lewis and Clark castigating the Sioux as "vile miscreants," this incident in August 1854 was the first to result in significant casualties. It would not be the last.[55]

Word of what was soon dubbed the "Grattan Massacre" incited cries for vengeance that circulated in eastern newspapers and western forts. A few government officials sought to dampen these sentiments. The superintendent of Indian Affairs ruled that Grattan had no authority to arrest or try the Indian who killed the cow. Also weighing against retribution, the Lakotas who had perpetrated the "massacre" had dispersed, and emigrants went unmolested as they made their way along the Platte in the spring and summer of 1855. But an avenging army, six hundred strong, under the command of General William Harney, had already assembled at Fort Leavenworth, and the outfit set out that summer to chastise whatever Sioux they might find. On September 3, Harney's force came upon a contingent of approximately 250 of them on the north side of the Platte about seventy-five miles east of Chimney Rock. Revenge ensued. At least eighty-six Indians died in the massacre on Blue Water Creek against only six of Harney's men. Harney also captured seventy Indian women and children, whom he took with him as his army continued west to Fort Laramie. Along the way, he held councils in which he admonished Lakotas not "to lurk in the vicinity of roads travelled by the whites."[56]

By the mid-1850s, the contest between army and annuity had clearly skewed to the former. The choice of army ensured that force, not friendship, would govern any peace along the trail. It was also clear that Indians had much more to fear from emigrants than vice versa. With numbers and soldiers on their side, some emigrants struck a more belligerent tone in their encounters with Indians. One Lakota woman remembered that in the aftermath of the Grattan and Blue Creek massacres, her people "felt uneasy—no matter where they camped, . . . it seemed as though the white people wanted to fight" them.[57]

Emigrants remembered it otherwise, and their recollections carried their day—and long after. Although Indian attacks on wagon trains remained an infrequent occurrence through the 1850s, emigrants often told stories that exaggerated their confrontations with Indians. Such tales tended to get embellished over time. In retrospect especially, the dangers emigrants faced from Indians escalated, the better to align with popular imagery of circled wagons and marauding savages. Obscured was the continuing occurrence of more cordial encounters and mutually beneficial exchanges.[58]

Tales about Indian attacks on wagon trains and calls for the United States Army to protect emigrants appeared to win the day in 1857. That year, a force many times the size of any previous US outfit on the Plains gathered at Fort Leavenworth. William Harney was again in command, this time with 2,500

This still from the 1914 film *The Indian Wars*, starring William F. (Buffalo Bill) Cody, is one of the first cinematic depictions of an attack on a wagon train. The "circling the wagons" scene, though, was already familiar to many filmgoers, having been featured in scores of nineteenth-century dime novels and illustrations, as well as through reenactments in Buffalo Bill's and other Wild West Shows. *Courtesy of the Autry Museum of the American West*

men (approximately one-sixth of the entire United States Army), preparing for another foray across the Plains. Late that summer, the legion made its way along the Platte River road. No doubt, the massive display of force sent a chilling message to Indians who watched the procession of soldiers, horses, wagons, and cannons. But unlike his mission in 1855, Harney's orders were not to assail and terrify Indians; instead, he was to march his troops to the Utah Territory, where he was to compel the Mormons to submit to the authority of the United States government.[59]

In Salt Lake City, Brigham Young, president of the Church of Latter-day Saints and the appointed governor of the Utah Territory, readied his followers to resist. He declared martial law, directed that weapons be stockpiled and the mountain pass into Salt Lake City fortified, forged alliances with Indians, and sent a corps out to harass the American force. The hope was that raids by Indians and Mormon militiamen might delay the army's progress; plans included scorching the earth to deny provisions to the soldiers and their animals. Should the army reach Salt Lake, the inhabitants would set fire to the town, flee, and fight on.[60]

Meanwhile, in early September, a California-bound caravan camped at Mountain Meadows, about 320 miles south of Salt Lake City. This was a large group, numbering more than 150 men, women, and children and hailing mostly from northwestern Arkansas, with a smattering from neighboring Missouri among them. While passing through Salt Lake City and making their way south through Utah, these emigrants were consistently rebuffed by local Mormons when they attempted to buy food and other essential supplies. Wary of resident Mormons and Indians, the travelers circled their wagons and posted sentries. But they were unprepared for the gunfire that rained down from the hills above at daylight on September 7. The initial attack killed several in the party. Although the circled wagons offered some protection, the emigrants found themselves cut off from their livestock and the nearby spring. Without food or water, the situation of the besieged party grew increasingly desperate. When a Mormon emissary came to them under a flag of truce on the morning of September 11, they welcomed his promise to escort them safely away from the Paiute Indians who had supposedly ambushed them. Lured into the open, well over one hundred men and women met their end, their slaughter perpetrated not by Paiutes, but by Mormon militiamen. Only children under the age of eight were spared and sent to live among local Mormons.[61]

The terrifying episode, which came to be known as the Mountain Meadows Massacre and which one book titled "America's First 9/11," eclipsed the bloodshed in any prior "battle" on the overland trails. When word seeped out, Mormon authorities blamed the Paiutes for the carnage. The truth soon leaked. It was no coincidence that the massacred hailed primarily from Arkansas and Missouri. The latter state was the place from which Latter-day Saints had been expelled nineteen years earlier, a history about which the emigrants reportedly taunted the locals as they made their way past Mormon settlements. At Mountain Meadows, Latter-day Saints avenged the massacre at Haun's Mill and their expulsion from Missouri during the Mormon War of 1838.[62]

The massing and marching of an army, the defiance of defenders, the settling of scores, and the shedding of blood augured bigger battles to come. A civil war, shading into a holy war, loomed. If not secession from the United States, Brigham Young was determined to protect the Mormon Church's autonomy (and freedom of religion) in the Utah Territory (and in what he hoped would become the enlarged state of Deseret). By sending an army, the administration of President James Buchanan asserted the dominance of the United States over Mormons, often derided as "fanatics" by other Americans, many of whom adhered to their own militant Christianity. Some critics of Buchanan's show of force contended that the president was trying to unite states against the Mormons to resolve the growing division between Northerners and Southerners over slavery (or just distract attention from the fractures between Northern and Southern states).[63]

But a repeat of Missouri's Mormon War, this time in Utah and involving larger numbers and the armed power of the United States, did not happen. The army got a late start on its way to Utah, not setting out from Fort Leavenworth until mid-July. The force's commander, William Harney, and its cavalry unit ended up staying behind, ordered instead to suppress the fighting between pro- and anti-slavery factions in Kansas. As the army neared the Utah Territory later that fall, guerrilla attacks by the Mormon militia slowed its advance. The early onset of winter halted its invasion. The lull allowed backchannel negotiations to begin. By June 1858, a resolution to the conflict emerged. The United States Army entered Salt Lake City and new territorial officials were installed, while Brigham Young and other leaders of the rebellion received pardons from President Buchanan.[64]

With one civil war averted, another erupted on the Plains in the late 1850s. Towns in western Missouri became the gathering points from which proponents and opponents of slavery jumped into the fray in neighboring Kansas. While Kansas bled, matters remained more peaceful to the north along the Platte River. For the moment, only words, some-times heated, were exchanged between emigrants holding opposing views about slavery.[65]

The diversion of the United States Army, first to face down Mormons breaking away from American authority and then to fight seceding Southern states, relieved some of the pressures on Plains Indians. With the onset of the "War Between the States," the army of the United States greatly reduced its presence on the Plains. That, however, brought only a temporary and in-complete reprieve for Plains Indians. After the Civil War, the United States Army returned with larger numbers, with more firepower, and with a mis-sion to wage uncivil war against Plains Indians.

As a geological process, erosion describes what happened to Chimney Rock across the eons. Erosion also serves as a metaphor to depict what happened around Chimney Rock across two decades in the mid-nineteenth century. Although various observers claimed to have witnessed the diminution of the rock's chimney, the changes wrought by wind and water were almost imper-ceptible in the short run of human lifetimes. Not so, the shifts of relations between emigrants and Indians, which eroded much more quickly.[66]

In many respects, the ascendance of cooperation and the avoidance of violence on the overland trail follows the lessons learned in later versions of *The Oregon Trail* and in earlier chapters of this alternative history. Along the overland trails, Indians and Americans suspended suspicions enough to en-gage in peaceful exchanges. Trades didn't build lasting trust, but the transfers of goods and information permitted travelers to proceed on and produced at least some benefits for Indian inhabitants.

That was what both Indians and emigrants wanted. Or what Indians and emigrant men wanted. White women on the overland trails often longed to go back home, a rift inside wagons not figured into *The Oregon Trail.* Perhaps, the next edition of the game could allow female characters the choice of not playing? Of course, while that option would reflect the prefer-ence that many women on the overland trails entertained in their diaries, it would rewrite history. The decision about staying or going was almost never theirs to make.

Nor have computer players learned about the divide between Mormons and Gentiles, especially those from Missouri and Illinois, the places from which Latter-day Saints had recently been expelled. Here, too, adversaries sometimes overcame their difference. For the most part, they stuck to op-posite sides of the Platte River, the better to stay out of each other's way and keep the peace that generally prevailed on their adjacent trails. Utah, however, proved only a fleeting refuge for Mormon emigrants.

Goodwill between Indians and Americans on the overland trail was also fragile. Neither forgot prior experiences and preexisting prejudices. As evidenced by encounters on the way to and from Chimney Rock, comity was again conditional. When numbers on the trail shifted and when the American nation-state stepped up its interventions, armed conflicts battered the traces of past peace on the Plains. Compared to the geological process that eroded Chimney Rock, the peace between emigrants and Indians and the corrosion of concord on the Platte River portions of the overland trails flickered in the slightest blip.

For Plains Indians who lived through the tumultuous decades of the 1840s and 1850s when so many Americans passed through their territories, the worst was still to come. As Thomas Twiss, an Indian agent for the United States, informed an assembly of Lakota, Cheyenne, and Arapaho headmen in September 1859, the time when Americans merely crossed the Plains was coming to an end. Soon, "white men" would be "settling in every part of your country," building houses, planting corn, and raising "herds of cattle where once you had plenty of buffalo." During the 1860s and 1870s, what for Indians was a gloomy prediction largely came to pass. The process of American settlement and Indian eviction unfolded unevenly on the grasslands of the North American interior, with the next chapter of this alternative history beginning with that end of independence for Plains Indians. Its focus is on Dodge City, Kansas, a place four hundred miles south of Chimney Rock, whose frontier origins conjure anything but amity.[67]

6

Dodge City

Don't Shoot First

GETTING PEOPLE TO VISIT DODGE City and stay has long been a problem for the town's boosters. The idea of Dodge as somewhere to "get the hell out of" took hold early in its existence. Shortly after the town's founding in 1872, a joke circulated about a railroad passenger on a westbound train in Kansas. Queried by the conductor about where he was headed, the traveler replied, "Hell." The conductor's response: "That's 65 cents and get off at Dodge." A decade later, Dodge's reputation inspired another piece of dark humor: Turned away from heaven for having lived a sinful life, a dead man found himself rejected by the devil as well. That left him with a "sorrowful heart" to contemplate a worse fate: "Will I have to go back to Dodge for eternity?" he asked.[1]

Dodge City rose to fame and infamy when cattle trails terminated there in the mid-1870s. Its heyday—when longhorns from Texas were driven by cowboys to Dodge City and from there shipped by rail to the East—was short-lived. For around ten years, Dodge thrived as one of the destinations for what historian Donald Worcester declared "the greatest migration of livestock in human history." Ever since, Dodge has lived off and at times tried to live down its renown as the wooliest and wickedest of "cow-towns." Initially resistant to retelling tales that exalted Dodge's rampant lawlessness and violence, the town's chamber of commerce eventually embraced the tourist dollars that historical reconstructions and re-enactments brought. In 2009, the Ford County Development Corporation unveiled a new marketing campaign that invited visitors to "GET THE HECK OUT OF into DODGE!" From the Boot Hill Museum (located on the site of the old graveyard and featuring a reconstructed Old West street and stores), to the giant longhorn statue, to the lifesize bronzes of legendary lawman Wyatt Earp and his TV counterpart James Arness (garbed as Marshal Matt Dillon from *Gunsmoke*), to the Famous Gunfighters Wax Museum (oddly sharing a building with the Kansas Teachers Hall of Fame), the downtown tourist draws remain fixated on the years when murder and mayhem supposedly reigned in Dodge. On the edge of town, the Boot Hill Casino opened in 2009, it too seeking to cash in on Dodge City's sinful reputation.[2]

Making a profitable virtue out of historical vices made sense, for no site has been more closely associated with the American West at its wildest than Dodge City. First in the pages of newspapers and dime novels and later on movie and television screens, Dodge City became synonymous with the "Wild West." More than the evocation of a mythic time and place, Dodge has served as a stand-in for all sites where disorder trumps law and violence runs amok. Vietnam in the 1960s, drug war–torn inner cities in the 1970s and 1980s, and Afghanistan and Iraq in the first decades of the twenty-first century were all often likened to Dodge City. The phrase "get out of Dodge" remains a widely used expression, a sign that even as the Old West and Westerns have faded in the popular imagination, Dodge City has retained its metaphorical currency.[3]

Given all this, Dodge City would seem out of place in this alternative history. The town's birth coincided with the deadliest years of warfare between the United States and Plains Indians. Its origins traced to an unparalleled orgy of bison killing. Its brief boom, when cattle replaced buffalo as the foundation of Dodge's economy, witnessed homicides at what we would consider horrific levels.

What is the case for including Dodge City here? First, problematic as life and deaths were in Dodge City and on the trails leading to it, things were not as bad as some contemporaries claimed and as subsequent accounts made them out to be. Jokes aside, there were much worse hells in the Americanizing West and across the United States than Dodge City. That was true, too, of the lives of cowboys and of the relations between what was a multiethnic workforce. Second, and perhaps most important, the explanations for the problems that beset Dodge City were no secret. Nor were the solutions for containing violence particularly elusive. The challenge—then and now—was enforcing those controls.

Top: the logo, touting Dodge City as a place to "get the heck into," which appears on banners around downtown and has become the most recent slogan for the town's marketing campaigns. Bottom: the sign for the combined Kansas Teachers Hall of Fame and Famous Gunfighters Wax Museum. *Photos by the author*

Dodge City's beginnings lay in the conflict between Americans and Indians on the southern Plains. A fort gave birth to the town. Dodge City emerged from the shadow of Fort Dodge, thanks to the railroad, which was itself a vital weapon of the United States in its wars against Plains Indians. In Dodge's case, the railroad initially supported the slaughter of bison, an animal cleansing in the service of an ethnic cleansing.

Dodge City does have important similarities to Chimney Rock. It is situated approximately four hundred miles south, but both sites are at nearly

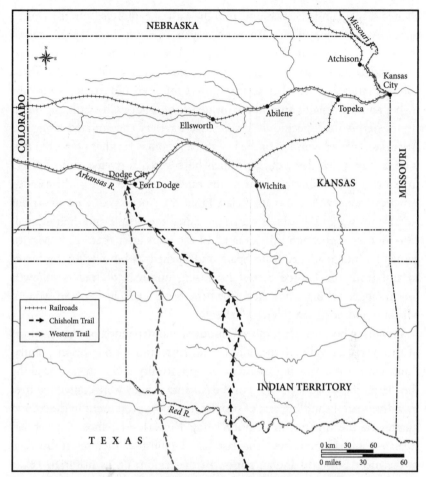

Getting the heck into and out of Dodge City, 1870s–1880s

the same longitude (Dodge is right on the 100th meridian; Chimney Rock is slightly west at 103 degrees). Both are surrounded by short grass plains where limited rainfall has hindered agriculture while nourishing herbivores. Dodge City and Chimney Rock were also both located on major east-west transportation corridors.

By the time the Platte River brought hundreds of thousands of travelers past Chimney Rock on their way to Utah, California, and Oregon in the 1840s and 1850s, the Arkansas River (on which Dodge had not yet been founded) had become an avenue on which considerable traffic moved across the Plains. Like the Platte, the Arkansas thwarted travel by boats. Wending across western Kansas, the wide, shallow, and generally sluggish waterway elicited disparaging observations from the earliest explorers from the United States. As with the Platte, American wayfarers along the Arkansas cursed the sandbars and quicksand that impeded travel on the river and next to it and condemned the sterility of the surrounding countryside. Those commentaries grew harsher as adventurers followed the Arkansas into the higher and drier plains around the future site of Dodge City. Still, the quantity of herbivores, specifically bison, that travelers encountered along the Arkansas inspired wonder. In the late 1830s, Thomas Farnham reported that it took him three days, during which he covered forty-five miles, to get from one end of a buffalo herd to the other. Farnham and profit-minded American adventurers also appreciated that the Arkansas offered a corridor suitable for wagons, while its waters sustained the people and their animals who journeyed through this "desert." In the years after 1821, when Mexico gained its independence from Spain and opened its borders to commerce to and from the United States, increasing numbers of traders followed the Arkansas, taking what they called the Santa Fe Trail between western Missouri and northern (New) Mexico.[4]

Indians, who inhabited, moved through, and depended on the resources of the Arkansas Valley (especially its immense and mobile bison population), viewed the growing traffic as an opportunity and a threat. As along the Platte, the western portions of the Arkansas Valley were contended over by a diverse and shuffling cast of peoples, the most prominent in the second quarter of the nineteenth century being Kiowas, Arapahos, Cheyennes, Apaches, and Comanches. The last had established themselves by then as the most powerful Indian nation in the region, or, as historian Pekka Hämäläinen has proposed, the most successful and expansive *empire* across a vast domain of the North American interior (a comparison not limited to other Indian groups). Like the Lakotas to the north, the Comanches were a loose confederation of bands and were relative newcomers to the Plains, having moved eastward from the Rockies (as opposed to the Lakotas, who had arrived from the other direction). The Comanches had also harnessed horse power to extend the reach of their realm, in their case from Kansas in the north through Texas in the south. Plunder enriched the Comanches at the expense of neighboring Indians and Mexicans, and captive-taking enlarged their numbers. For the Comanches and other Indians in the area, the caravans on the Santa Fe Trail presented a new and tempting target. That could take the form of trading with Santa Fe Trail wagoneers, or it could shift swiftly to raiding those who trespassed across their countries and consumed vital resources.[5]

Traders from the United States venturing to and from Santa Fe took a different view of what they considered extortionate demands or outright theft by Indians. Appealing for armed protection from the federal government, they eventually persuaded the War Department to authorize a few escorts, including one party of dragoons under the command of Nathan Boone. Such small and intermittent forays by US cavalry were more symbolic than substantial testaments to American clout, however.[6]

During and especially after the Mexican-American War, the United States Army did build and occupy forts up the Arkansas, including a rudimentary station near one of the principal fording points along the river (and near the future site of Dodge City). The post, named Fort Atkinson, aimed to better position American forces to combat Indian raiding, though military leaders insisted that the troops were there to keep the peace with Indians and between them. As a projection of American power in the region, the original fort was none too imposing. Troops stationed there nicknamed it Fort Sod, a reference to the material from which its initial structures were composed; some called it Fort Sodom, an acknowledgment that soldiers at the isolated outpost did not maintain the strictest discipline, particularly when whiskey flowed. A visitor in 1851 denigrated it as "a small insignificant military station, beneath the dignity of the United States, and at the mercy and forebearance of the Indians." Three years later, Fort Atkinson was abandoned, its sod structures leveled.[7]

The onset of the Civil War removed most of the United States Army from the Plains. With all but a handful of troops redeployed to fight in the East, the army's policing role in the West was left to territorial militias. Up the Arkansas, that opened the door for uncivil war. The most infamous incident occurred in 1864 along Sand Creek, a tributary of the Arkansas River in Colorado. There, on November 29, a volunteer cavalry under the command of John Chivington set upon an Arapaho and Cheyenne village. Ignoring the protestations of friendship by Black Kettle, the leader of the Southern Cheyenne, who waved an American flag as the cavalry advanced, Chivington ordered his troops to show no mercy. His men did not, killing and wounding hundreds of Indians, the vast majority of whom were women and children.[8]

The Civil War ended the following spring, but on the Plains, "postbellum" was a misnomer. The regular army returned to western posts and assumed a more overtly bellicose mission. Barely two months after Appomattox, Major General Grenville Dodge, writing from the headquarters for the Army's Department of the Missouri, echoed a recommendation made from the

Missouri Territory by Governor Meriwether Lewis sixty years earlier. Like Lewis, Dodge deemed it essential to keep "traders from among" the Indians. Unlike Lewis, Dodge did not believe that depriving Indians of trade goods would alone subdue them. In Dodge's view, the only effective way to deal with Indians was "to push our cavalry into the heart of their country, and force them to respect our power and to sue for peace." Even after the army had finished its bloodier business, Dodge proposed that traders and civil authorities stay on the sidelines, leaving it to military officers to handle all Indian affairs. General William T. Sherman, fresh from the scorched earth campaigns that had helped the Union win the Civil War and now charged with overseeing the army's operations in the West, agreed. Yes, the Indian wars might one day end when "all the Indian tribes are absorbed" into the population of the United States. Yet, to this endorsement of Jefferson's old hope for peace through assimilation, Sherman added an iron-fisted "or else." Some Plains Indians—Sherman singled out the Sioux and the Cheyennes— "cannot and will not settle down." And so, Sherman concluded, "they must be exterminated."[9]

What accounted for the change in the military's mandate from keeping peace and trade open on the trail to pursuing and punishing Indians far and wide and confining them on reservations? Certainly, on the southern Plains, Indian raiding surged in the 1860s. White Americans in the West, both in and out of the military, were quick to lay all blame on native adversaries. Playing from a script from prior frontiers, this generation of American Westerners dismissed Indian claims to the land and its resources. Then, they proclaimed their innocence of any wrongs done to Indians, while inveighing against the deaths and damages that Indians had caused to them. Finally, they pushed for the United States military to exact retribution. Even when there were no specific offenses to attribute to particular Indians, there was always the time-tested, one-size-fits-all rationale for why Indians must give way: the natives were "savages" who blocked civilization's advance.[10]

What the latest set of western Americans did not readily acknowledge was how the path of "progress" that had once skipped over the Plains was now settling on it. Before the Civil War, Americans had denigrated the Great Plains as a Great American Desert, a place to cross, not to colonize. That mindset made it appropriate to consign most of the area to Indians, including peoples deported from the eastern United States. Limited American demands for grasslands meant the army only had to protect emigrants from Indians and (supposedly) Indians from one another to maintain peace on and around a few trails. After the Civil War, however, several railroad lines traversed the Plains, giving the army new routes to secure. Attitudes about the fitness of the grasslands for American occupation also began to shift, spurred by the opportunities opened by the 1862 Homestead Act and the promotions of railroad corporations seeking to profit from the lands they had been granted. Increased demand for land, in turn, built pressure for wars to subjugate Indians and for a new round of removals, which added to and altered the mission of the army.[11]

Immediately after the Civil War's end, the US Army constructed a new fort on the north bank of the Arkansas near the abandoned site of Fort Atkinson. Named Fort Dodge for General Grenville Dodge and initially commanded by his nephew Major Richard Irving Dodge, the post, like its predecessor, was established to help protect trade and traffic on the Santa Fe Trail. But in keeping with its namesake's strategy, Fort Dodge was also to be a staging ground for offensives against Indians. From the fort, troops launched campaigns to combat Indians in western Kansas and to contain them within "Indian Territory" south of Kansas.[12]

Fort Dodge was not much to look at or to live in. Timber being in short supply on the Plains, structures made of wood did not entirely supplant sod houses. Neither material provided much comfort when winter temperatures plunged, summer ones peaked, and spring rains spilled the river over its banks and flooded the compound. Dietary deficiencies and sanitation problems exacerbated the diseases that spread among men in close quarters. For African American soldiers stationed at Fort Dodge, conditions were even worse. Segregated from white troops, they were relegated to sleep in a general supply area. The fort's hospital was also generally off limits to them, as it, like the officer corps, was reserved for whites only.[13]

Unappealing as Fort Dodge was to its inhabitants, it attracted an assortment of civilians catering to and cashing in on the presence and payroll of a military installation. Suppliers, some licensed, some not, congregated on the other side of the Arkansas, peddling a variety of wares, some licit, some not, to the soldiers. To put more distance between the fort and these sutlers, the post's commander encouraged merchants to relocate stores, saloons, and brothels a few miles upriver. And so was born Dodge City.

It would have remained a small town of little note, and of no exceptional ill repute, but for two key developments in the early 1870s. First, in 1871, the invention of new chemical processes for tanning buffalo hides dramatically expanded the market for those skins. Second, a year later, the arrival of the railroad brought buffalo hunters west to Dodge City and the new town's new station became the principal depot for buffalo hides shipping east.[14]

The pursuit of profits drove a buffalo-killing binge without parallel. Back at Boonesborough in 1775, the rapid depletion of the local bison population had prompted Daniel Boone to propose a bill to slow the wasting of wildlife. But the number of buffalo on the grasslands around Dodge City dwarfed those in the Kentucky Bluegrass a century earlier, and the weapons that hunters brought to the Plains could kill far more animals far more quickly than the rifles carried by Boone and his contemporaries. In the first months after the railroad's arrival, merchant Robert Wright, who had been a trader outside of Fort Dodge and was then one of the founding proprietors of Dodge City, purchased more than 200,000 hides from hunters. Soon, buffalo skulls and bones stacked ever higher by the railroad depot attested to the killing fields that the area around Dodge had become. Those piles represented only a fraction of the slaughter; for the most part, hunters left carcasses to rot on the Plains, taking only skins to sell and ship at Dodge City.[15]

The scale of the killing was unprecedented, but the spoils of the hunting conformed with prior histories. Expectations of riches brought white hunters to western Kansas, as they had once sent Daniel Boone to Kentucky and mountain men to the Rockies. Fortunes again proved elusive. On paper, the price that buffalo skins (and, to a lesser extent, meat) commanded at Dodge added up, especially for skilled hunters who could kill scores of buffalo each day. But on the Plains, it rarely worked out so well. Dangers abounded for hunters trapped by biting blizzards, trampled by sudden stampedes, and tracked down by Indians. During the winter of 1872–1873, Major Dodge counted more than a hundred buffalo hunters who had frozen to death along the Arkansas. The fort's surgeon was repeatedly pressed into service for civilian patients, performing seventy amputations on frostbitten hunters. Reflecting back years later on his experiences as a buffalo hunter in western Kansas, Frank Mayer decided that he would not do it again even for $50,000. In fact, after deducting expenses, he calculated that he had barely broken even on his two years as a hunter out of Dodge City.[16]

Also familiar was the drastic reduction of the animal population on which the livelihood of hunters depended. As at Boonesborough and at scores of places where animals were hunted and trapped for their pelts, commercial inducements quickly depleted the most valuable game in the more immediate environs of Dodge City. In early 1872, right before the railroad's arrival, William Blackmore, an English gentleman who had come to the Arkansas Valley to hunt buffalo for sport, exclaimed that for about a hundred miles south of Fort Dodge, he was never out of sight of buffalo. Just a few years later, he found "the whole country was whitened with bleached and bleaching bones." Through the terrain south of Dodge, he did not meet with buffalo until well into the Indian territory, and then only in small groups. Railroad records confirmed the observations of dwindling herds. In 1873, the first full year in which the Atchison–Topeka–Santa Fe line served Dodge City, the company's shipment of buffalo hides topped 750,000. It never again approached that tally, with the volume declining steeply in each of the next several years.[17]

The despoliation elicited all too predictable responses. Faced with a shrinking bison population, hunters tried to extend the duration of the buffalo business in western Kansas by expanding the range of their pursuits away from Dodge City. In general, that meant going further south and even venturing into Indian Territory. Predictably, too, Indians resented and resisted these incursions, which violated the integrity of the territory they had been assigned, as well as the hunting rights they had been promised. Under the terms of the 1867 Medicine Lodge Treaty, Comanches, Cheyennes, Arapahos, Kiowas, and Apaches were permitted to range north of the Indian Territory to the Arkansas River "so long as the buffalo may range thereon, in such numbers as to justify the chase." Recognizing that the slaughter perpetrated by white hunters in 1872 and 1873 threatened to prematurely close that justification, Indians stepped up their retaliations against intruders.[18]

Military officers expected the violence that unfolded. In October 1873, Major Dodge warned there would be serious consequences unless steps were taken to stop white hunters from going into the Indian Territory. But Dodge was not inclined to take any action. In part, he claimed that his force at Fort Dodge was insufficient to intervene. More important, he welcomed the extermination of the buffalo, as the slaughter served the mission of the United States Army. Plains Indians, he maintained, "could only be subdued if the herds were completely destroyed, thereby forcing the Indians to rely entirely on the government for provisions." Once the last herd was extinguished, Indians would stay on their reservations, for the Plains emptied of bison "promised nothing more than slow starvation."[19]

The problem for Plains Indians in the early 1870s was that reservations compounded slow starvation with humiliation. There, Indians suffered deprivations, both material and symbolic. The corruption and neglect of agents and the government that appointed them made matters worse. Not only had the United States failed to protect Indian hunting rights to the Arkansas, but it had also not delivered promised provisions. As General

Nelson Miles discerned, the "annual allowance of food was usually exhausted in six or seven months," which left Indians to choose between escaping and going to war or staying and enduring famine.[20]

In 1874, many Indians on the southern Plains opted for flight and fight. Dispersed bands staged scattered raids from Texas to Kansas, killing around one hundred whites that summer and fall. Residents in Dodge City grew alarmed about a possible attack; hunters abandoned the chase and sought shelter at Fort Dodge. The United States Army launched a coordinated offensive that relentlessly pursued Indians now thrown on the defensive. A series of battles diminished Indian numbers and weakened their resistance. What sealed the Indians' plight was the scarcity of buffalo, which made it impossible for them to live off the land as they formerly had. By the spring of 1875, the remnants of the resistance collapsed. Through the summer, starving Indians staggered back to surrender at Fort Sill in the Indian Territory. Seventy-five of their leaders were subsequently arrested, convicted, and sentenced to prison in Florida. Those they left behind in Indian Territory were now even more dependent on the insufficient allocations of the United States government. War had ended, but the uncivil peace that life on the agencies offered was bleak.[21]

In 1878, desperation prompted another breakout from Indian Territory. That September, a group of Cheyennes, led by Dull Knife and Little Wolf, fled north. Dull Knife, a principal chief of the Northern Cheyenne, had once been an advocate for peace with Americans, but he abandoned that stance after the Sand Creek Massacre. His band fought and remained free until 1877, when Dull Knife surrendered and was sent south to Indian Territory. There, illness, hunger, and homesickness among his people led Dull Knife to join Little Wolf and a band of followers in an attempted return to their old homelands.[22]

Initially, the editor of the *Dodge City Times* blamed "the starving and imbecile policy of Indian Agents and the Government" for forcing the suffering Cheyennes to flee. The only threat the hungry Indians heading north posed was to "the scalp of a Texas steer." But the editor's compassion and lack of concern vanished once the "renegades" moved closer to Dodge City. As news circulated of the plundering of stock and the killing of several white men and women south of Dodge, the editor's condemnations became ever more fevered. The Cheyennes, he wrote, "beat and mangled the unfortunate victims of their brutal lust." They deserved no sympathy, despite the "slush concerning the nobility of the savages that some philanthropic . . . ass in Boston or New York dishes up."[23]

The Cheyennes did not make it home. Harassed by army units from posts across the Plains, including Fort Dodge, Dull Knife and his group barely made it out of Kansas before capitulating at Fort Robinson in Nebraska. Seven of Dull Knife's followers faced charges for the acts they had committed in Kansas. The trial was to be held in Dodge City in the winter of 1879. Mobs menaced the train that brought the accused to Dodge. The editor of the *Dodge City Times* made clear that no mercy should be shown: "The grief-stricken mother who yet suffers the shame and disgrace of the Indian brute, . . . and the dead father, whose body has fed the worms and whose bones lies bleaching, cry out for vengeance, a swift, a determined, and speedy retribution." In the face of so much overt hostility, the presiding judge granted the defendants a change of venue.[24]

Indians never again threatened Dodge City (other than much later in staged re-enactments). Already in the mid-1870s, the reduction of danger from Indians relieved residents of Dodge City, but they also worried that it jeopardized the town's future. On the one hand, the confinement of Indians meant that inhabitants were safer and their property was more secure. With Indians vanquished and presumed vanishing, optimists prophesized a new era of peace and prosperity for Dodge City. But there was another hand. Absent Indians to combat, pressures to cut military expenditures prompted fears that Fort Dodge would close (and it eventually would in 1882). More immediately troubling, the decimation of bison herds, so integral to the devastation of Indians, robbed the town of the source of its initial growth and prosperity. To Robert Wright, one of the town's founders and principal merchants, Dodge City's buffalo bonanza surpassed several mining camps where he had been and where rich strikes had been made. But how would merchants like Wright, and saloonkeepers and brothel owners, maintain their businesses if they had no animals to buy and sell and no soldiers and hunters to serve? To pessimists in the mid-1870s, it appeared that Dodge, like many mining towns across the West, would bust once the natural resources that supported its boom were depleted. If not a ghost town, Dodge City seemed likely to become a dot on the map of no historical, or alternative historical, notoriety.[25]

Created in 1980, a bronze sculpture of a Texas longhorn now sits in the center of Dodge City at the intersection of Second Avenue and Wyatt Earp Boulevard. As the accompanying plaque relates, longhorns "gave Dodge City its place in history as 'Queen of the Cowtowns.'" The monument

El Capitan, a lifesize statue of a Texas longhorn (though one with exceptionally long horns) welcomes visitors to Dodge City and commemorates its heritage as a destination for cattle from Texas. *Photo by the author*

commemorates the period from 1875 to 1886 when "over 4 million head were driven up the trail to the Santa Fe railhead in Dodge City." Those millions, the plaque could have added, rescued the town from historical obscurity, coming along just as the near extermination of bison deprived Dodge of its founding rationale. Ecologically, one herbivore replaced another on the Plains; economically, the cattle trails from Texas lifted Dodge above other cowtowns in Kansas, though its reign as queen lasted only a few years. In addition to cattle, the trails brought cowboys to Dodge. The era when cowboys drove longhorns from Texas to Kansas and then romped in Dodge City was also brief. But the work of cowboys on the trail and their play in the town have cast a very long historical shadow. That has made it hard to see the evidence of people getting along, at least getting along better than they did elsewhere.[26]

Admittedly, getting along better than elsewhere was a low bar in post-bellum America. Things could hardly be worse than what was happening to American Indians across the Great Plains in the years after the Civil War. As General William T. Sherman told Kansans who came to see him on a rail tour that took him (along with President Rutherford B. Hayes) through Dodge City in 1879, the Indians were gone, and he did not "care where they are gone to." The crowd laughed. Sherman's joke and the audience's response revealed how much white settlers on the Plains reveled in the destruction of Indians, applauding wars, no matter how uncivil, waged against native peoples and peace, no matter how callous, imposed upon them. Not that relations between peoples (and "races") looked much rosier away from the Plains and east of the latest Americanizing West. As white Westerners who wanted Indians gone pointed out, their Eastern counterparts expressed sympathy for the plight of Indians only after native peoples had largely vanished from their midst, having been banished from their homelands on that side of the continent. Their removal from the Southern states, Thomas Hart Benton correctly discerned, "made room for the spread of slaves." True, the Civil War had ended the legal enslavement of African Americans, and, in its immediate aftermath, the passage of several constitutional amendments had extended some legal protections to freedpeople. But, across the now former Confederate States of America, terrorist campaigns undermined the rights of the recently emancipated and "redeemed" white supremacist regimes.[27]

No wonder that many African Americans in those states looked elsewhere, with Kansas a particular beacon of hope. Symbolically, Kansas held special appeal, as its "bleeding" in the 1850s anticipated the great struggle for emancipation to come. In the words of a freedman from Louisiana, Kansas was sacred because its soil was "washed by the blood of humanitarians for the cause of black freedom." Substantively, the 1862 Homestead Act, which offered 160 acres of land to settlers and carried no overt racial restrictions, also beckoned African Americans to the Kansas plains. Pulled by that opportunity and pushed by terrorist violence, approximately 20,000 freedpeople, the majority of whom hailed from Kentucky, Tennessee, Mississippi, and Louisiana, moved to Kansas to homestead. By decade's end, one group had settled Nicodemus, which was located 130 miles north of Dodge City. Around that newly established, nearly all-Black town, these "Exodusters," as the African Americans who settled Nicodemus and other parts of Kansas were called, began to farm.[28]

That Exodusters settled so far west on the Plains reflected how biases against farming the "Great American Desert" were dimming in the 1870s. Around Nicodemus, African American pioneers pushed agriculture to the one hundredth meridian, a longitudinal marker that has come to be seen as a fault line for farming. Beyond it, average yearly rainfall falls below the twenty-inch minimum required to grow a crop of corn absent irrigation. But the first forays of Black and white farmers into central and western Kansas coincided with several wet years in which annual precipitation considerably eclipsed the twenty-inch benchmark. That watery bonanza gave Exodusters and other homesteaders reason to believe in claims that "rain would follow the plow." Their faith bolstered by "science" that made agriculture the instigator for permanent (and positive) climate change, Exodusters took up lands at the longitude of Dodge City.[29]

Dodge City, however, saw no influx of Exodusters (and no rush of farmers) in the 1870s. Instead, its efflorescence as a cowtown owed to enduring prejudices against farming there and to the needs of the Atchison, Topeka, and Santa Fe Railroad to establish a new depot for cattle coming up from Texas, which lay beyond the pale of American agriculture. Over the course of the 1870s, a series of towns in central Kansas had served that purpose, only to lose their status to the advance of agriculture and to the demands of farmers for quarantines against tick-infested Texas longhorns. For Dodge City, the demise of cowtowns where south-north cattle trails had previously met east-west rail lines came just in time, as its bison-based economy was fast approaching extinction. Beginning in 1875 when the Atchison, Topeka, and Santa Fe opened a stockyard and taking off in 1876 when 250,000 longhorns accompanied by more than one thousand herders descended on Dodge, the town gained a second life as the end of the trail for Texas cattle and Texas cowboys.[30]

In its new incarnation, Dodge City's hellish reputation scared some people, including freedpeople, away. Not jokingly, an Illinois newspaper in 1878 declared that "without question, Dodge City is the worst place of its size on this earth." Only a small number of African Americans took up residence, and then usually not for long. The 1880 census recorded just 42 "Negro" or "Mulatto" inhabitants of Dodge. These individuals represented 3.3 percent of the town's population. They generally held the lower-paying jobs available to them. Best paid were several Black cooks in Dodge's hotels and saloons. Less well compensated were porters, dishwashers, and waiters. Some worked in stables. Others were listed generically as laborers, typically paid about $1.25 per day. For African American women, domestic service was the most common occupation recorded in the census, with earnings falling between $1.50 to $3.00 per week plus room and board. The prevailing wages afforded a fragile subsistence, and the positions provided little chance for advancement. Five years later, the occupational profile looked roughly the same for Dodge's Black population, which had grown to 68. But only two names appeared in the registers for 1880 and 1885, the vast majority of earlier inhabitants having lived only briefly in Dodge before moving on.[31]

Insofar as persistence often correlated with prosperity in frontier towns like Dodge, the failure of African American inhabitants to remain indicated the opposite—which put them in good company. Transience was common in Dodge during its heyday as a cowtown. That was especially true for young, single men, who made up a significant portion of Dodge City's early residents, both white and Black.[32]

Transience compounded by tragedy characterized the lives of many of the young, single women who worked in Dodge as prostitutes. Exactly how many "sporting women" there were in town was hard to pin down. Dodge's detractors inflated the total, with one Kansas newspaper insisting in 1878 that "every house is a brothel." An only slightly more conservative estimate that year put the number of prostitutes at 120, which would have amounted to more than one-half of all the adult females in the town's population. By contrast, prostitutes nearly disappeared from official registers. The 1880 census included only seven "sporting women," with perhaps forty to fifty other sex workers covering their tracks by being listed under other occupations. Transience also interfered with any accurate counting. Demand for prostitutes was much higher during the months when cowboys were in town than the rest of the year. Because of that seasonality, many women shuttled between Dodge and brothels elsewhere. On paper, at least, prostitutes earned several times more than women in other jobs. But that was before the added expenses of their business siphoned off income. Pimps, madams, and doctors took substantial cuts for their services, as did the bribes, fees, and fines exacted by law enforcement officers and municipal authorities. Sexually transmitted diseases and physical abuse took a different kind of toll, with the result that most prostitutes got out of the trade with no savings, if they got out alive. And Black prostitutes generally fared worse than their white counterparts, earning less and enjoying fewer protections from violent customers and predatory associates.[33]

Still, for recently emancipated African American men and women, there were many, many worse places of its size or any size than Dodge City. To freedpeople, geographic mobility was not so much a mark of their failure as of their freedom. After all, the ability to move as one pleased had been denied to the enslaved. What's more, going to and getting out of Dodge separated them from fellow former slaves who remained in the South and who found their movements restricted anew by the enactment of "Black Codes."[34]

Staying in Dodge City was hard for freedpeople, as was living there, but neither was as hard as staying and living in the former Confederacy. Although their occupations and opportunities in Kansas cowtowns were limited in practice, legal discriminations fell considerably away. In the late 1870s and early 1880s in Dodge, Black children attended school with whites, while Black men voted in elections, served on interracial juries, and testified in trials against white defendants. From those courts, African American men and women convicted of crimes received sentences akin to whites found guilty of the same offenses and were jailed alongside white prisoners. The extralegal punishments of those who trespassed racial boundaries in their intimate relations also relaxed. In 1879, Dodge witnessed a marriage between a "colored male cook" and a "white female." According to a local newspaper report, the officiant united "the African and the American without the least apparent reluctance." Such indifference was not the norm. At the conclusion of the ceremony, "a large crowd of 'stiffs' . . . shower[ed]" the newlyweds with rotten eggs. But the "African" husband and "American" wife, like a few other unmarried interracial couples in Dodge, escaped the lynchings suffered by merely accused Black transgressors in the postbellum South.[35]

The circumstances of African Americans in Dodge were even better, relatively speaking, for those who came just to play and not to stay. During Dodge's run as "Queen of the Cowtowns," the annual influx of cowboys doubled the city's population each summer and multiplied manyfold the number of African Americans in the town. Over the course of the high season, well over a thousand cowboys came to Dodge, of whom around two to three hundred were Black men. Having spent three months or more driving longhorns up from Texas, cowboys—white, Black, and Hispanic (who also made up a substantial portion of herding crews)—arrived eager to carouse. Businesses in Dodge readily abetted the spending splurges of visitors. At least in the cowtown's early years, enterprisers did not segregate their lodgings, stores, saloons, dance halls, gambling establishments, and brothels (the last four often connected to one another, if not housed in the same establishment) when separating cowboys of different complexions from their wages.[36]

More remarkable and unexpected, cowboy teams on the trail eschewed segregation, blended ways, and dampened interethnic hostilities. Back in Texas, where the trail to Dodge began, relations between the peoples who comprised herding teams augured the opposite. There, many of the traditions of cattle-driving culture had migrated from Mexico (and before that from Spain). Cowboy ways on the trail to Kansas showed those origins in a vocabulary largely derived from Spanish, and in technologies and techniques whose lineages traced to Mexico and Iberia. Tejanos had played a vital role in the development of cattle-raising culture in Texas, and their Mexican American progeny remained a significant presence among Kansas-bound cowboy teams. Before the Civil War in east Texas, ranch work generally fell to African American slaves. Driving herds to New Orleans offered experiences that they and their offspring brought to the trails to Kansas after the war. A number of Indians, whose horsemanship was unrivaled, also joined the cowboy workforce on the ways north from Texas. The largest contingent of Texas-based drovers were white Americans, many of whom had roots in the Old South and in cattle culture there. In common across these ethnic lines, most cowboys were young and single. But past animosities overshadowed any commonalities of age and marital status. In Texas, before and after the Civil War, white Americans imposed their supremacy, deploying violence to keep Indians, Mexican Americans, and African Americans in a subordinated place. For their part, non-white peoples bitterly resented those who had conquered, enslaved, and oppressed them. Now thrown together for months at a time on the trail to Kansas, multiethnic cowboy crews appeared to combine the most combustible of mixes: young, single men with histories of virulent and violent antagonisms. And yet, on those drives, cowboys rarely turned their guns on one another.[37]

Several factors contributed to the low level of gun violence among cowboys on the trail. Some cowboys, like Teddy Abbott, kept their guns close at hand and regarded them as essential for self-protection. "I always carried a gun because it was the only way I knew how to fight," remembered Abbott. Fist fighting, he dismissed as "nigger stuff," to which "a white man wouldn't stoop." But Abbott was in the minority among cowboys on the trail. One reason drovers did not shoot each other or themselves more often was that guns were not always at the ready. The six-shooters we associate with cowboy gunplay were expensive. The preferred model, which Colt introduced in 1873 and which was nicknamed the "Peacemaker," cost fifty dollars, a price beyond the means of most cowboys. Besides, on the trail, many opted to make peace by letting fists, not firearms, settle fights, which, contrary to Abbott's view, held no racialized taint. No doubt, cowpunchers found it easier to stick to punching one another because prohibitions on alcohol on the trail kept heated emotions, and lethal guns, under control.[38]

More than not killing one another, multiethnic cattle-driving crews managed to mostly get along on their multi-month journeys to Kansas. They had to, in spite of the biases they held. Moving longhorns ten to fifteen miles per day, day after day with no days off, over tough terrain in harsh conditions, was in turn monotonous, arduous, and dangerous. On the trail, the exhausting workday stretched from before sunup to after sundown, and even longer, with less sleep, for night-watch shifts were also part of the regimen. Although older "wishtories" made cowboys the paragons of American individualism, successful drives depended on effective teamwork. It required at least eight men to move a thousand head of cattle; with some of the larger herds, teams numbered twenty or more men. Crews of any size needed to coordinate efforts to keep cattle together and each other alive. Shared hardships and shared tasks bred solidarities among cattle-herding teams, which cut against the animosities that men brought to the trail.[39]

In addition to individualism, American mythology once wishfully coupled cowboying and independence. But like hunters and trappers and prospectors, other frontier occupations that gave rise to similar lore, the structure of the cattle-driving economy conspired against cowboys securing much property and, thus, achieving an essential foundation for independence. During the nineteenth century, American ideas about personal independence also demanded that men (and the status was available only to men) work for themselves. To labor for wages, as cowboys did, was by definition to be dependent, a condition to which women, children, and the enslaved were consigned, but adult men aspired to escape. That cow*boys* earned low wages for seasonal employment limited their economic mobility and precluded almost all of them from becoming cattle*men* (those who owned the cattle). Instead of becoming proprietors of livestock and ranches, experienced cowboys could reasonably hope only to become trail bosses, a position that paid about fifty dollars per month. The compensation of their subordinates averaged only about thirty dollars per month, or a dollar a day, plus "chuck." That put their wages on par with laborers in Dodge City. After being paid in Dodge and quickly blowing through their wages there, cowboys faced a prolonged period of unemployment. Most headed back to Texas, where they scratched out a spare existence doing ranch work. As Karl Marx's son-in-law Edward Aveling observed after a tour of the United States in the 1880s, "the life of the 'free' cowboy is as much that of a slave as is the life of his Eastern brother, the Massachusetts mill-hand." The Marxist perspective overstated the unfreedom of the cowboy, but the life of cattle herders was a long way from the ideal of independence. Which is why the majority of drovers were young, single men, why only about one-third of Kansas-bound herders returned for a second journey, and why on average cowboys lasted only seven years in the saddle before seeking a home off the range.[40]

As a rule, non-white cowboys got the worst of it. They often found themselves wrangling horses and riding at the rear of herds, where the dust particularly choked and the smell especially offended. Blacks "were usually called on to the hardest work around an outfit," admitted a white drover named John Hendrix. These added burdens and dangers included "taking the first pitch out of the rough horses," testing water when a trailing herd came to a swollen stream, battling a fighting bull or steer, and enduring a double night shift in inclement weather. "These Negroes knew their place," Hendrix noted, and they "stay[ed] in it." Relegated to the lower rungs of the cowboy hierarchy and pay scale, African American, Mexican American, and Native American herders had few opportunities to advance. They had almost no chance to become trail bosses, it being unthinkable in the 1870s and 1880s for cattlemen to give non-white men control over their property and authority over white cowboys. The few Mexican American and African American exceptions who rose in the ranks, like their non-white brethren to their rear, did not escape the vicious slurs and brutal assaults by which white men displayed their prejudices and asserted their supremacy. "Greasers" and "chili-eaters" were the gentler insults hurled at Mexican American cowboys; "nigger" plus a first name was how white cowboys often addressed their African American peers.[41]

Relative to white Americans, the opportunities afforded African Americans (and other non-white people) in, around, and on the way to Dodge were significantly circumscribed. Yet, compared to the prospects, discriminations, segregations, and violence they had endured, Dodge City and the trail to it looked much better than the worse hells they had known.

In 1968, Robert Dykstra published *The Cattle Towns* and fired a "shot heard round the world" (of Western historians)—although the book's revolutionary claim was about shots not fired. Examining the records of Kansas

View of Dodge City in 1882 looking north from the Arkansas River. Featured on the map are sites that herald the town's bid to show off its middle-class respectability. Absent from the map is the "Boot Hill" cemetery, as well as any of the many brothels and the fifteen to twenty saloons for which Dodge City was much better known. *Courtesy of Kansas Historical Society*

cattle depots, Dykstra contended that gunfights, which Western lore made synonymous with Dodge City, were very rare there. Shootings—and killings—were also much less common than Westerns and Western histories had long presumed. Between 1870 and 1885, by Dykstra's reckoning, the five largest cowtowns, including Dodge City, averaged only 1.5 adult homicides per year. For Dodge, his sampling took in the period from 1876 to 1885, with a tally of 15 killings for that ten-year span, which also averaged 1.5 homicides per year. Those numbers meant that Dodge and its sibling cities had gotten an unfair rap, for the evidence showed them to be not nearly as murderous as myth and metaphor have made them out to be. In the wake of its publication, Dykstra's book prompted a closer look at the enforcement of law and the incidence of disorder in Dodge City, as well as a broader exploration of the causes and patterns of violence across the American West. Fifty-plus years later, it is clear from a voluminous and contentious scholarship that Dodge was no peaceful haven during its cowtown heyday. But it is also now established that the worst years of lethal interpersonal violence preceded Dodge City's emergence as a depot for cattle and a carousing spot for cowboys. In fact, measured by the chances of being killed by another person, there were far more deadly places in the American West in the decades after the Civil War than Dodge City during its reign as queen of the cowtowns. That Dodge was not as safe as it might have been, or as dangerous as it has been made out to be, pointed to the efficacy and limits of fee-based law enforcement and controls on guns.[42]

The killings that made Dodge City notorious started early in the town's existence, years before, in fact, it saw any longhorns or cowboys. The first recorded homicide in Dodge coincided with its founding in the summer of 1872. The victim was a man known as Black Jack, who was an African American, though at least in this instance his racial identity was not marked by the n-word preceding his first name. His killer was a gambler called Denver, who shot Jack in front of one of Dodge's saloons. Denver was not prosecuted, and, years later, he expressed no remorse. To the contrary, he joked that he had shot his victim "in the top of the head just to see him kick."[43]

It was a distressing precedent, and soon to be repeated. Shortly after Black Jack's murder, an unknown assailant gunned down another Black man. Within a year of the first homicide, a third African American, William Taylor, was shot dead after trying to prevent a group of drunken men from stealing his wagon. Again, the perpetrators treated the crime as a source of humor, one of them relating that "the best joke was that after killing the nig we took his hat and put it on the mule that was [also] killed."[44]

Over the first twelve months of its existence, several more homicides occurred in and around Dodge. A total of at least eighteen have been documented for the period from August 1872 to July 1873. Although the exact tally remains uncertain, the final resting place of the dead was settled. They were buried, some with their boots still on, but often without a coffin (owing to the high price of lumber on the Plains), in a new cemetery established on a hill just north of the town's main thoroughfare. Their killers, like Black Jack's, escaped prosecution. And the bison hunters, railroad employees, and transient laborers who gambled and partied in Dodge's saloons and brothels evinced little concern about the murders and murderers in their midst. According to one witness to three shootings in November 1872, the victims were "thrown into the streets, while the dance went merrily on."[45]

The particulars of each homicide varied, but the general situation in Dodge predicted high levels of lethal, interpersonal violence. The elements that correlated with similar surges in homicides elsewhere were all in place in Dodge. As the murders of at least three African Americans in Dodge's first year indicated, race, or, more specifically in these cases, what today would qualify as "hate crimes," sparked lethal violence in the postbellum American West. In those days, it was merely the prerogatives of white supremacy lashing out. In addition to ethnic triggers, the town's population fit perfectly the demographic profile that scholars have found typified the wildest parts of the West (and the world). In its infancy, Dodge City's population tilted disproportionately toward unmarried and unmoored men. In early 1873, men outnumbered women nearly seven to one in Dodge, with many more males drifting in and out of town. Among residents and transients, younger men predominated. The average age of the populace in Dodge in the first years of settlement was under thirty.[46]

A host of cultural factors furthered the likelihood of violence. Topping that list was the premium so many men in Dodge put on preserving their honor, and how quick they were to take offense against insults, real and imagined. Add the pressures that high-stakes gambling generated and the inhibitions that alcohol removed, and eruptions seemed inevitable. The absence of effective enforcement of nonviolent order, as attested by the lack of prosecutions of killers, removed another key restraining ingredient. Finally, the fact that gamblers generally carried their guns made them deadly.[47]

In its first year, Dodge City lived down to predictions, but by the time it had morphed into a cowtown, it was nowhere close to the killing field it had been. William Taylor's murder helped set Dodge on a less violent path, even as it nearly provoked a much larger splattering of blood. Taylor had been a servant to Colonel Richard Dodge, and his murder incensed the colonel and the African American soldiers whom he commanded at the post. Some of these troops talked of retribution, with rumors spreading that the soldiers intended to attack the town and burn it down. Responding to the perceived threat, around forty white bison hunters congregated outside the fort. The leader of the hunters threatened to kill Colonel Dodge and other white officers at Fort Dodge and then "take the damn Negroes down to the Arkansas River and drown them." Cooler heads prevailed, averting for the moment a battle between an army of African American soldiers and an armed force of white hunters. That no subsequent incident brought civilians and soldiers to the edge of combat owed to changes in town. Dodge City's principal merchants regarded the murder of Taylor and the battle that almost followed as "the last straw." Convinced that the town's prospects and their personal prosperity depended on curbing violence, they contracted a number of men to impose some order.[48]

Exactly whom they hired is not known, other than William L. "Bully" Brooks. Previously a stage driver and buffalo hunter and always a gambler,

Brooks had killed several men, had engaged in multiple gunfights, and had committed an assortment of other crimes. He had also served a stint as city marshal in another Kansas town, and that experience apparently qualified him to clean up Dodge. In his new position in Dodge City in which he lasted less than a year, Brooks lived up to his nickname, bullying those who crossed him and adding to the census at Boot Hill.[49]

Once Dodge City was legally incorporated in 1875, its elected mayor and city council replaced privately hired guns with an official policing force. The most celebrated of these officers, Wyatt Earp, served parts of four years as an assistant city marshal, earning a degree of fame, and some fortune, for his exploits in Dodge City. Like Brooks, Earp had a checkered past. Before arriving in Dodge in 1876, he had briefly been a lawman in Wichita, a Kansas cowtown with similar challenges to keeping the peace. Briefly was generally all that Earp ever stayed in one place or at one job. Moving on was the only constant in a life that had seen him shift from state to state and from jobs in various saloons, gambling halls, and brothels. Work in those enterprises continued when he arrived in Kansas, where he added bison hunter and then what he called "lawing" to his resume. As a lawman in Wichita and then in Dodge, Earp, like Brooks before him and like several of his colleagues in Dodge, kept his hands in the vice businesses that he now policed.[50]

If sensationalized contemporary reports and cinematically inspired retrospective depictions are to be believed, Earp and fellow Dodge City lawmen engaged in constant gunfights. Yet between 1876 and 1879, the years in which Earp was employed in Dodge City, the municipality saw only seven shooting deaths. For all the hysteria then and hype later, gunfights were rare during Dodge's reign as the principal cattle town. Duels, so commonplace in Westerns, were even rarer. Indeed, while gunfire caused the vast majority of homicides, gunfights, which involved an exchange of shots, did not. By Robert Dykstra's estimation, which covered homicides across five cattle towns including Dodge, less than a third of those fatally wounded returned fire. "A good share of them," concluded Dysktra, "were apparently not even armed."[51]

One reason gunfights were uncommon was that Earp and other lawmen strove to avoid them. Rather than shooting their guns, they preferred to use them to slam the heavy barrel into the head of a miscreant. Done effectively, and Earp was particularly efficient at it, "buffaloing" delivered a knockout blow that temporarily pacified the drunk and disorderly. Hauled off to jail, the buffaloed awakened hours later, often hungover and presumably concussed.[52]

The economics of policing incentivized lawmen to make more arrests. In Dodge City (and lots of other places around the United States), marshals and their deputies augmented modest salaries by collecting fees for services. From the perspective of elected officials, this fee-based system had a distinct advantage: it reduced the need to raise general taxes. In the late 1870s, salaries for police accounted for around 40 percent of Dodge City's budget. It would have been a higher percentage had fees not supplemented salaries for law enforcement officers. For those engaged in "lawing," each arrest brought a $2.50 stipend. That money added up, especially during the busiest times of year, when Dodge City lawmen cumulatively made around three hundred arrests in a "good" month. Reformers around the nation decried the corruption that this fee-based system invited. It certainly did in Dodge, where the fees for arrests earned by Earp and his associates eclipsed their salaries. What's more, the official ledgers did not account for the money that Earp and others pocketed as partners in the very vice businesses most subject to fines, or for the bribes they took from the operators of those enterprises.[53]

Nonetheless, for all its flaws, the system did discourage lawmen from shooting first and asking questions later. Dead men, after all, could not be arrested, and they paid no fines. As Earp recollected to his biographer Stuart Lake, "there were some killings in personal quarrels" in Dodge City in 1876, "but none by peace officers."[54]

More than the pursuit of fees, which indirectly suppressed only police shootings, the enactment of local weapon control ordinances directly addressed and reduced all shootings. The state of Kansas had on its books an 1868 statute that prohibited vagrants, intoxicated persons, and former Confederate soldiers from carrying a pistol, bowie-knife, dirk, or other deadly weapon, with violators subject to a $100 fine and three months in prison. In 1874, the commissioners of Ford County, where Dodge City was located and became the county seat, implemented a law similar to the state one.

The following year, the Dodge City Council established its own municipal code in which it broadened the categories of prohibited weapon carriers. In anticipation of the influx of cowboys the next summer, Dodge's government adopted the rules in place in already operating Kansas cattle towns. Specifically, Section Seven of Ordinance Four held "that no person shall in the city of Dodge City carry concealed about his or her person any pistol, Bowie knife, slingshot, or other dangerous or deadly weapon except United States, state, county, township, or city officers." In 1876, the city council expanded the ban to encompass the carrying of weapons, "concealed or otherwise." The measures required visitors to Dodge to turn in their weapons upon arrival at check racks to be provided at corrals, hotels, stores, saloons, and gambling places. It also ordered proprietors of those establishments not to return weapons to intoxicated persons. As a public reminder, a sign posted on an abandoned well-head at the center of Dodge City proclaimed: "THE CARRYING OF FIRE ARMS strictly PROHIBITED."[55]

The controls appeared to have an immediate impact. Compared to the dozens of homicides that Dodge City experienced in its first years, the number fell dramatically after the enactment of the weapon-control measures. Even as more than a thousand cowboys swarmed into Dodge City in the summer of 1876, Earp recalled only "some killings." Casting doubt on Earp's memory, Dykstra's review of local newspapers turned up no reported murders that year. The next year, with even more cowboys in town, he also found zero homicides recorded within the city's limits.[56]

In 1878, the number of homicides jumped to five. The increase was still far below prior levels, but it elicited concerns about inadequate administration of the no-carry law. Already in March 1878, before any of the killings in town that year, the *Ford County Globe* critiqued the lack of enforcement of the weapon bans. Under the headline "The Festive Revolver," the newspaper warned that "some of the 'boys' in direct violation of City Ordinances carry firearms without being called to account for the same." That they did so openly, the *Globe*'s editor claimed, indicated that they were a "friend of the marshal or policeman."[57]

Although the *Globe* blamed bad men and corrupt lawmen, the problems with enforcement reflected wider ambivalences in the community. During the second half of the 1870s, the mayor and council members backed the ban in principle; in practice, they were divided about how stringent enforcement should be. Officials feared that cracking down too harshly on carrying cowboys would chase customers from the saloons, gambling halls, and brothels on which the town government depended for a substantial portion of its revenues. The owners of "respectable" enterprises were also of two minds. On the one hand, they had pressed for measures to curb shootings to protect their prospects and Dodge's. On the other hand, they, too, did not want to lose the business that cattlemen, cowboys, and gamblers did in their stores and hotels.[58]

Tensions along these lines persisted through Dodge City's cowtown era. An impromptu compromise emerged, which involved unevenly enforcing the ordinances in different parts of town. On the north side of Dodge,

The sign at the intersection of Front and Second Street in Dodge City that reminded visitors that carrying firearms was not allowed in the city. In practice, the prohibition was unevenly enforced, especially on the south side of what was called the "Deadline." *Courtesy of the Kansas Historical Society*

greater decorum reigned, and lawmen more zealously disarmed those who carried in defiance of the city-wide ban. But south of what locals called the "Deadline," where vice businesses clustered, lax enforcement ruled. Here, on what was literally the wrong side of the tracks—the Deadline began at the Atchison, Topeka, and Santa Fe rail line and extended to the Arkansas River—police generally looked the other way when drunken cowboys blew off steam by harmlessly firing their guns in the air. "They wanted our trade," discerned Teddy Abbott, which "was how us cowboys got away with a lot of such stunts."[59]

It was harder to let it go when those cowboys or gamblers shot one another. Even then, Dodge City courts administered criminal referrals with a light touch that bore scant relation to the lore of severe frontier justice. Prosecutors proffered lesser charges, and magistrates and jurors gave wide latitude to self-defense claims in order to exonerate shooters.[60]

Not so, however, when the gunfire struck a bystander or a lawman. Those incidents prompted calls for more diligent disarming of men (and women, meaning prostitutes) everywhere in Dodge. Such was the case in April 1878, when, barely a month after the *Ford County Globe* inveighed against the failures of marshals and policemen, Marshal Ed Masterson was killed by a drunken cowboy. The killer, Jack Wagner, had relinquished one of his weapons, but had concealed a second, with which he shot Masterson in the abdomen at close range. Mortally wounded, Masterson managed to shoot and kill Wagner before collapsing.[61]

Masterson's murder put Dodge City in the national spotlight again for all the wrong reasons. Widely circulated accounts of Masterson's death reinforced Dodge City's reputation as unsafe and unsavory. The episode exemplified the dangers that constabularies in Dodge faced when dealing with unpredictable, inebriated, and armed men.

The glare cast by this fatal incident obscured the more mundane realities of policing in Dodge during its cowtown years. Jack Wagner's presence in Dodge in April showed that cowboys came to Dodge year-round, but summer and to a lesser extent autumn were when most drives to Kansas ended and when the waves of rowdy visitors crested. The rest of the year, Dodge generally quieted down—so much so that city officials assigned idle lawmen to tasks well outside the job descriptions of gunfighting idols. Rounding up stray animals, repairing sidewalks, inspecting chimneys, and cleaning manure from the streets occupied lawmen during the off-season. Even Wyatt Earp. But not happily and not for too long. Instead, come fall, he resigned his position in Dodge and followed cowboys south to Texas or venturing west to New Mexico. In those destinations, he dealt faro and gambled himself, as he had done on the side in Dodge. The difference was that during the off-season, lawing was what he did on the side, as when he was hired to track down a gang of train robbers in Texas one winter. Each spring, at least through 1879, he returned to his gig in Dodge City.[62]

In September 1879, Earp quit Dodge again. This time, he ventured to the Arizona Territory, joining several of his brothers in the mining boom town of Tombstone. And this time, he did not come back to Dodge City the following spring. He remained instead in Tombstone, where in October 1881, he engaged in what became the most famous of Western gunfights. Far more than his stints in Dodge, the shootout near the OK Corral and the shootings that followed it made Wyatt Earp a controversial legend in his own time.[63]

Earp did return briefly to Dodge City in 1883. He came back at the request of an old friend, Luke Short. The rivalry between Short's saloon, the Long Branch, and a competitor's establishment had morphed into a political contest fought out in the municipal election of April 1883. Short's candidate lost, and the winners soon sought to claim their spoils. The new mayor, backed by a slight majority of the city council, passed several reform measures, including ones aimed at curbing gambling and prostitution. Directly targeting Short, he ordered the city marshal to arrest three female singers at the Long Branch, who were alleged to be prostitutes. Resisting the incursion into his saloon, Short exchanged gunfire with the police officer who came to make the arrests. No one was struck, but Short and five of his associates were arrested and ordered to leave town by May 1. They did, but the battle was not done. Both sides stoked the conflict by seeding stories that once more put a national spotlight on Dodge's turbulence. Short also invited old confederates like Earp (and Ed Masterson's more famous brother, "Bat") to lend their celebrity and their gunfighting skills to his struggle. Earp arrived on May 31, 1883, and his presence and Masterson's made what was tabbed "the Dodge City War" even more the fodder for national news coverage.[64]

Back in Dodge, Earp announced he was prepared to fight, but he would be "better pleased" if Short's return were without bloodshed. City council members dangled the possibility of a temporary reprieve for Short, a compromise that Earp rejected. On June 3, Short rejoined Earp in Dodge City, and, together with a number of well-armed accomplices, they appeared ready to make good on Earp's willingness to fight. "Everything is quiet," reported the *Chicago Tribune*, "but the air seems heavy with an impending calamity."[65]

Expectations about a repeat of a bloody gunfight along the lines of the OK Corral did not materialize. Within two weeks of Earp's arrival in Dodge City, matters resolved peacefully. Short regained his place at the Long Branch saloon, and, below the Deadline, gamblers and prostitutes again serviced the demands of that year's visiting cowboys. The Dodge City War, so full of sound and fury, destroyed no property and shed no blood. Dodge once again did not fulfill calamitous predictions.[66]

Even so, change was in the air. In 1880, an election in Kansas approved amending the state's constitution to outlaw the manufacture, sale, and consumption of alcohol. Tellingly, the cause of prohibition secured only one-fifth of the vote in Ford County, and Dodge City leaders ignored the ban.

Yet, even in Dodge, advocates for going dry were growing more vocal. In a victory for the cause of temperance, an 1882 municipal ordinance banned alcohol in the city jail and forbade police from drinking on duty. It also barred law enforcement officials from working on the side for private businesses, including for saloons, gambling halls, and brothels. That obviously was not how Earp understood lawing, and it removed any incentive he had to remain in Dodge City. Luke Short, too, sensed the turning of the political and moral climate. In November 1883, a few months after winning his battle to stay in Dodge, Short sold his interest in the Long Branch and left town.[67]

As long as large numbers of cattle and cowboys continued to come from Texas to Dodge City, economic interests reined in anti-vice campaigns. Through the first half of the 1880s, keeping cattlemen and cowboys happy and keeping them spending in town trumped efforts to curb their enthusiasms. Revenue from saloons, brothels, and gambling halls and an added tax on prostitutes and professional gamblers remained too important to the city budget to really go to war against those enterprises and enterprisers.[68]

But Dodge City's days at the end of the trail from Texas closed soon enough. The drives in 1886 marked the last time that herds of longhorns and hordes of cowboys descended on Dodge. Its eleven-year reign as queen of the Cowtowns was longer than that of any of its predecessors. But like earlier established cowtowns in Kansas, Dodge City fell victim to the encroachments of farmers and to their demands for quarantines against longhorns. Unlike those predecessors, Dodge City did not abdicate its crown to an ascendant rival to its west in Kansas. Rather, broader changes in the Western cattle industry and the building of new railroad lines across the Great Plains shifted the destination of drives away from Kansas and dethroned Dodge.[69]

The only homicide in Dodge City in 1886 occurred on April 15. It was, by Dykstra's count, the thirty-sixth violent death in Dodge since its founding fifteen years before. As with so many of those homicides since the cattle drives to Dodge began in 1876, the killing took place south of the Deadline. Because this shooting took place on the wrong side of the tracks, because it grew out of a long-standing feud, and because both men were armed when the incident transpired, the jury acquitted the defendant. That was in keeping with the way such cases were handled in Dodge City during its heyday at the end of cattle trails from Texas.[70]

Historians continue to deliberate their verdict about homicides in Dodge City. While Robert Dykstra credited the lawmakers and lawmen of Kansas cattle towns for successfully limiting lethal violence, many historians remain unpersuaded. Critics contended that Dykstra undercounted homicides by leaving out killings that took place outside the city limits. When included, these killings in the near vicinity of Dodge added as many as eighteen homicides to the town's tally. Others questioned the value of raw numbers and average annual rates, when what mattered were per capita figures. Only by rendering homicide counts in Dodge City on the basis of how many per 100,000 inhabitants would its historical statistics conform with how modern crime rates are kept and be properly compared with data collected in other places at other times. Converted, Dodge City's numbers no longer look very good. Its average of 1.5 homicides per year multiplies nearly a hundredfold when calculated on the basis used by the Federal Bureau of Investigation for its "Uniform Crime Reports." The numbers look even worse in years when homicides spiked. Consider 1878, the year in which murders reached their highest point during Dodge's cowtown reign. That year's five homicides roughly equate to 500 per 100,000. By contrast, no metropolitan statistical area in the United States today comes anywhere close to those rates. For 2018, according to the Uniform Crime Reports, Pine Bluff, Arkansas, ranked as the "murder and nonnegligent manslaughter" capital of the United States. Its homicide rate was just over 22 per 100,000.[71]

Dykstra has not conceded his case for Dodge. How useful, he asked, is the per 100,000 conversion in Kansas cattle towns where the population was small, the census of inhabitants excluded the flood of transients, and a single homicide completely altered the picture (especially when the change was from zero in one year to one the next)? Dykstra also returned to the scene of the crimes, publishing a new book in 2017 that recounted the birth of the myth of the Wild West in Dodge City and re-counted the number of homicides. Their new tally of 36 for the period from 1872 to 1886 upped the annual rate to 2.4 per year. But half of those homicides happened in the last six months of 1872 and first six months of 1873. Only 18 occurred during Dodge's days as a cowtown. That translated to just 1.64 per year.[72]

Inspired in part by Dykstra's work, historians dug into crime records, counting homicides and calculating rates for sites across the nation and the West. Compared to Northeastern cities and Midwestern farm towns, inhabitants and visitors to Dodge City and many other places in the post– Civil War West were ten or more times more likely to be murdered. Yet, compared to Western "peers," Dodge does not fare so poorly. As the table compiles, Dodge City's rate and ranking varies considerably. Depending on whether one uses Dykstra's count and resulting rate of 50+ per 100,000 persons or higher tallies, which raise the rate above 150 per 100,000 inhabitants,

Dodge City moves up or down these rankings. But even using the higher estimate, Dodge City trails a number of sites whose homicide files have been excavated and tabulated.[73]

Ranking of Selected Homicide Rates in the Old West[74]

Location, Date	Homicide Rate per 100,000 Persons
Arizona, 1870	577
Cheyenne County, NE, 1867–1876	260
Wyoming, 1870	167
Los Angeles, CA, 1847–1870	158
Dodge City (and sibling cities), KS, 1876–1885	155
Nebraska Panhandle, 1877–1886	114
New Mexico, 1870	93
Texas, 1865–1868	68
Dodge City, KS, 1876–1886	50+
Lincoln County, NE, 1876–1877	41

For this alternative history, the conclusion about homicides across the West and the inclusion of Dodge City in this book rest on those missing murders. Absent a system that discouraged police shootings and disarmed at least some possible shooters, homicides in Dodge City might well have continued on the course set during the settlement's lethal first twelve months. That would have vaulted Dodge City to the top of this negative ranking. Instead, the acts of lawmakers and the actions of lawmen kept things from being worse. Of course, they might have been better had the carrying of firearms been truly strictly prohibited on both sides of the Deadline. Dodge would still not have been a place where everyone got along, but a few more would have gotten out alive.

Does Dodge City really offer any lessons in concord? Not if we believe what contemporaries said about the place, or what generations of stories about the Wild West have put on pages and screens. Separating facts from fictions reduces the carnage, but it still leaves us with a history overflowing with examples of people fighting one another—and too often killing one another. Nothing in Dodge City's early history as an outcrop of a military installation and an outpost for bison hunters signaled comity. Indian-white relations started off on the wrong foot and went downhill as treaties were violated and bison were extinguished. In 1878, after Indians on the southern Plains appeared vanquished, the editor of the *Dodge City Times* expressed empathy for the plight of fleeing Cheyenne. But that flicker of compassion lasted barely a week. Thereafter, he joined a chorus in Dodge City that mocked the misguided sympathies of Easterners and called for the extermination of Indians.

By 1878, Dodge City had completed its transition to cowtown, the era in which its sins and shootings became national news. But while vice and violence dominated (and still dominate) tales about the queen of Cowtowns and the cattle trails to it, this alternative history calls attention to relations between cowboys of different complexions that defied prior patterns, to opportunities for African Americans that surpassed what they had known, and to homicides that did not happen. True, Dodge City was not a haven of intercultural amity and racial equality. Such places exist only in our current "wishtories." On the trail from Texas to Kansas, white supremacism was too deeply entrenched to be upended. Its harshest features, however, were suspended when multiethnic cowboy crews teamed up to get cattle to Dodge City. Ditto in Dodge, where African American visitors and inhabitants found more freedom and greater opportunity than was available to them in Texas or other parts of the former Confederacy.

Accounting for missing murders moves us into controversial territory. But Robert Dykstra's count, even when adjusted upward, invites explanations for why homicide rates fell in Dodge City after its tumultuous first twelve months and why its tumultuous heyday was not as murderous as some other sites in the American West or as Western lore made those years out to be. A correlation, if not a causation, points to the impact that fee-based law enforcement and bans on carrying firearms had on the incidence of shootings and killings within town. It is also worth pointing out what was not said in Dodge City. Municipal authorities did not consult with constitutional experts when they decided that the carrying of firearms should be strictly prohibited. Nor did concerns about Second Amendment rights govern how diligently lawmen disarmed visitors who carried weapons openly or concealed. Instead, what determined where weapon controls applied was geography, and what determined their limited enforcement was economics.

As yet, tourists to Dodge City do not learn this alternative history. Dodge City's chief attraction, the Boot Hill Museum, leans heavily on the lore. In summer, that means re-enacted gunfights. Year round, the museum's orientation film, narrated by one of the cast members of the long-running television series *Gunsmoke,* delivers the legend as older "wishtories" once did. That includes a scene in which a tough-looking cowboy enters a saloon, his six-shooter prominently displayed. In ones that follow, the wild town gets tamed by tougher lawmen like Wyatt Earp, who were so effective and efficient as gunfighters that soon they had "nothing left to shoot but tin cans."[75]

An alternative orientation would have the cowboy checking his gun before entering the saloon. Or being buffaloed instead of gunned down in a duel. An African American would be included in the scene. And Dodge City might seem a place to get the heck into.

Conclusion

———◆◆◆———

IN 2010, A NEW WESTERN, *Red Dead Redemption*, generated rave reviews and record sales. According to the aggregator Megacritic.com, *Red Dead Redemption* scored a 95 (out of 100) rating. Normally staid reviewers rolled out seldom-used superlatives. The *New York Times* hailed it as a "tour de force," a gush the essayist had never previously employed in more than a thousand articles for the newspaper. Numerous critics reached for cinematic, literary, and artistic comparisons. Likening it to "the po-mo Westerns of Clint Eastwood and Cormac McCarthy," the reviewer for *Rolling Stone* marveled at how the production "brings the myth of the American West to life just to deconstruct it and does the same for the whole concept of redemption itself." The *New Yorker* critic raved about "the finest dawns and dusks in all of moving pictures," adding that painter "Albert Bierstadt couldn't make morning light look this good." It was not just critics who loved *Red Dead Redemption*; it also defied conventional wisdom about the declining commercial prospects of Westerns. "Everyone assured us the Wild West was dead and of no interest to people anymore," admitted one of *Red Dead Redemption*'s creators. Yet in the first three days after its release, *Red Dead Redemption* grossed $725 million ($85 million more than the year's biggest blockbuster, *Avengers: Infinity War*, took in at the box office during its opening weekend).[1]

In 2018, the creators of *Red Dead Redemption* followed up by releasing a prequel, *Red Dead Redemption II*. Once more, critics swooned. The

New York Times praised its "desire to be both grand and granular," to tell "individual stories against the backdrop of national and cultural identity, deconstructing the genres while advancing the form."[2]

The *Red Dead Redemption*s are not movies or television programs; they are computer games in which players script their own Westerns. In the parlance of gamers, the imagined West that players enter is an "open world." In the original *Redemption*, which is set in 1911, the premise has its fictional protagonist, a rogue turned rancher named John Marston, blackmailed by Pinkertons into tracking down his old gang. Eliminating them wins Marston amnesty and the player the game. The prequel turns back the clock to 1899 and casts the player as Arthur Morgan, the right-hand man to the leader of the outlaw band with which Marston rode (and now rides again). Like Marston, Morgan wrestles between abiding old loyalties and seizing new opportunities to rectify past wrongs. Marston's and Morgan's choices are literally in the player's hand. The player directs the trails they follow and the actions they take. For Morgan, it can lead to a Dodge City–like cattle town called Valentine. For both, it can turn their lives around, bringing atonement and peace. Or not. More often, players (at least the ones I've watched) seem content to forgo their avatars' shot at redemption. Instead,

The images and iconography in *Red Dead Redemption* and *Red Dead Redemption II* borrowed from classic depictions of the West in Westerns, and characters struck familiar poses. One of the sites featured in *Red Dead Redemption II*, the town of Valentine, is supposedly based on Dodge City, Kansas. *Courtesy of Rockstar Games*

they load Marston and Morgan up with an array of weapons, proceed to splatter plenty of graphically red blood, before ending up dead.[3]

This would seem to offer few lessons about what Marston and Morgan can teach us about peace and friendship. In the parlance of this book, *Red Dead Redemption* and *Red Dead Redemption II* do not meet the tests of alternative history or alternate history (or, for that matter, history). Nothing in those open worlds actually happened in our world, which disqualifies their inclusion in an alternative history. Nor are any of the people or settings "real," divorcing what subsequently transpires in the Red Dead Redemptions from alternate history. The verisimilitude to older "wishtories" is more apparent. The scenery in the games conjures landscapes in scores of classic Westerns, and the characters come out of central casting. But bloodshed in those older Westerns was ultimately redemptive; violence ushered the victory of "civilization" over "savagery" and of "justice" over "lawlessness." By contrast, the gunplay in *Red Dead Redemption* and *Red Dead Redemption II* manifest no triumphal destinies. For many players, nihilism trumps nobility in the bloody sprees into which the games often devolve. In that regard, as several critics noted, the *Red Dead Redemption*s took their cues from the so-called anti-Westerns of the late 1960s and 1970s, with Sam Peckinpah's *The Wild Bunch* cited as the most obvious forerunner for the random and rampant violence.[4]

These open world games inhabit a world apart from more recent "wishtories" exemplified by Disney's *Pocahontas* and the bicentennial commemorations of the Lewis and Clark expedition. Those fantasies dispatch disputes and celebrate cross-cultural concord. In terms of computer games, their closer kin are the later editions of *The Oregon Trail*, which also reward players for peaceful dealings with the Indians they encounter.

Still, we should not dismiss the redeeming features of *Red Dead Redemption* and *Red Dead Redemption II*. If most players choose to go out in a blaze of gore, some follow an alternative road. Players can choose not to shoot first. Sometimes that does not work out. Sometimes those spared turn on Marston and Morgan. Sometimes other bad guys do Marston and Morgan in. Sometimes the agents of the state—sheriffs, soldiers, and bounty hunters—give them no quarter and exacerbate violence. But sometimes acts of compassion and exchanges of goods and gifts create bonds. Unexpected alliances emerge, though these can easily unravel—all in all, not unlike what happened at Chillicothe, Apple Creek, Fort Clatsop, Chimney Rock, and Dodge City.

The 1987 publication of Patricia Nelson Limerick's *The Legacy of Conquest: The Unbroken Past of the American West* heralded the dawning of the "New Western History." Synthesizing several decades of then-recent scholarship, Limerick's book capsized the progressive presumptions on which Westerns and Western histories had once floated. In this book and other writings, Limerick dismissed the construct of "frontier" as outmoded and ethnocentric and did away with the divide that cleaved the West after the supposed closing of the frontier from its earlier history. In place of long-time shibboleths, she argued for a history in which conquest and its legacy were the defining experiences of the region across its colonialist past and present.[5]

Thirty-plus years after the appearance of *The Legacy of Conquest*, the New Western History has settled into middle age. In academic circles, it has become the old orthodoxy. Through the lenses of conquest, empire, ethnic cleansing, genocide, and settler colonialism, a generation of historical scholarship has exposed the destructive forces and eliminationist impulses that channeled the westward expansion of the United States and sculpted the West as it is today.[6]

The episodes featured in this book do not unseat that history. Nor do they sit apart from it. Conquest and colonialism shaped the histories of Chillicothe, Apple Creek, Fort Clatsop, Chimney Rock, and Dodge City, as they did the rest of what became the West(s) of the United States. But for a time, geopolitical and intercultural currents constrained the exclusive occupation of these places by Americans under the uncontested rule of the United States. For varying durations—some better remembered, some mostly misremembered, and some almost entirely erased—those alternative relations presented an adjacent face of the American frontier.

Alternatives were in play at the village of Chillicothe on the Little Miami River when Daniel Boone was taken there in 1778. At the time, the United States existed as a declaration, but words on parchment did not make facts on ground. The establishment of Boonesborough and several other stations in Kentucky coincided with the outbreak of the American Revolution, and, in line with the Declaration of Independence's notable phrase, Boone and the white men who accompanied him moved across the Appalachians in pursuit of happiness. But in their case, happiness, which equated with private ownership of land, had nothing to do with expanding the territory of the United States. For Kentucky's first white settlers, familial and local concerns mattered most. Their tenuous bonds to would-be proprietors, to Virginia, to the United States, and to the British Empire fluctuated, depending on which of these entities appeared ready to guarantee their land titles and protect them from Indians.

The same calculus held among Ohio Valley Indians. They, too, subordinated national and imperial loyalties to village interests and were divided about how best to defend their countries. Some attempted to steer clear of the war between white men, either by maintaining neutrality or by moving away. Some carried out small-scale raids to harass Kentuckians and confine them to their forts. Some turned to the British to support larger campaigns that might evict the intruders. And then there was the audacious bid to reset relations with Americans in Kentucky that Blackfish and Chillicothe Shawnees attempted in 1778. By sparing Boone and the saltmakers, adopting the majority of the captives, and preparing to incorporate the people of Boonesborough into their village, an alternative to continuing combat opened.

The reset did not take. A couple of adoptees embraced their new situation. Most resisted their incorporation into Shawnee families. Boone was ambivalent, but he, too, rejected the temptations of life in Chillicothe. Gambit scuttled, Shawnees never again invited Americans in large numbers to live among them as one people in the Ohio Country. Instead, both Indians and Americans in the Ohio Valley attached their fates to outside forces. With the British Empire and the United States behind them, the war-making capacities of rival inhabitants grew. A dark and bloody ground got darker and bloodier. Because numbers were on their side and the British Empire proved a feckless ally, Americans "covered" their dead with reinforcements far more easily than the Indians did. By the mid-1790s, both sides of the Ohio River were firmly in American hands, the United States had won its First West, and Chillicothe, at least the one on the Little Miami River, vanished.

The Shawnees lost all at Chillicothe, but all was not lost for the Shawnees. Their traditions of migrations once more enabled their perseverance, with refugees from the First American West establishing new villages in Spanish Louisiana. Daniel Boone and hundreds of other Americans, having lost their lands in Kentucky, joined the Shawnees on the west side of the Mississippi River. The reunion of exiles portended a renewal of warfare. That did not happen during the 1790s and the first years of the nineteenth century. Relocated Shawnees and Americans lived not as one people, but they cohabited peaceably nearby one another. Especially around Apple Creek, the Shawnees not only persevered, they prospered.

The agendas of recent "Truth and Reconciliation Commissions" hold that to reset relations, an essential first step is to uncover and acknowledge historic wrongs. Only when crimes against humanity are properly recorded and remembered can peoples and nations get past them and move toward rapprochements. No such commission gathered in Spanish Louisiana. There was no recognition of what we would now call an ethnic cleansing of the Shawnees (and other Indians) from the Ohio Country, no reckoning for their lands and lives lost. Instead, the reset rested on Daniel Boone's contrary wisdom that sometimes peace depended on forgetting what happened in war.

Before dismantling our Truth and Reconciliation apparatus, we should remember that getting along in Spanish Louisiana required more than letting bygones be bygones. For recent "cruelest enemies" to live serenely alongside one another, a host of other factors had to fall into place. Absent the presence of a shared enemy, the weakness of the colonial regime, and their limited and balanced numbers, Shawnees and Americans probably would not have overcome their differences. That became clear when each of these factors fell away. As the threat posed by the Osages ebbed, as the United States supplanted Spanish (and French) rule and fortified its position in a new West across the Mississippi, and as Americans (both free and enslaved) flooded into what became the state of Missouri, the ability to forget no longer protected the peace between Ohio Valley transplants or the property of Indians around Apple Creek. In fact, Americans in Missouri then took lands away from Shawnees (and Delawares). The result in the 1820s and 1830s was another round of ethnic cleansings.

That William Clark oversaw these deportations bared just how fragile were the foundations on which amicable relations between Americans and Indians stood. Clark came of age in Kentucky when it was still a dark and bloody ground and served in the United States Army in its campaigns to displace Ohio Indians in the 1790s. Those experiences were crucial in securing his commission as co-captain of the Corps of Discovery. On the expedition, Clark and Lewis remembered what had happened in earlier wars with Indians, as evidenced by brash talk and bellicose displays in their encounters with Sioux Indians early in the journey and by the suspicions they maintained about the thievery of Indian men and the lechery of Indian women. But the further they traveled, the more they understood that diplomacy, not militancy, was critical to the Corps of Discovery's peaceful passage through scores of Indian countries and to the Pacific Ocean.

The Corps of Discovery's sojourn at Fort Clatsop on the Oregon coast is well remembered for several incidents that gestured toward amity and equality across racial and gender lines. But while the votes of Sacagawea and York about the siting of the fort and Sacagawea's accepted request to view a beached whale provide feel-good fodder for "wishtories," the fuller story of the winter at Fort Clatsop was characterized, figuratively and literally, by wet blankets. Clark, Lewis, and the members of the Corps of Discovery were not the best guests or hosts. They never mastered the intricacies of native cultures and politics, nor the etiquettes of diplomacy with Indians, so their commerce with neighboring Indians was rarely cordial, even when sex was involved. Still, Lewis and Clark were sufficiently diplomatic that relations with Indians remained peaceful, though precariously so.

Upon their return from the expedition, Lewis and Clark assumed new offices that made them responsible for establishing a *Pax Americana*, across a territory claimed by the United States that now reached to the Rocky Mountains. Clark's tenure as the chief intermediary for the United States with Indians west of the Mississippi River stretched across more than thirty years. Early on, he used the threat of stopping trade to coerce the Osages into land cessions. Other treaties soon followed that strengthened the power of the United States in its new West. Yet Clark stood up to the demographic tide of Americans and to the demands that Shawnees and Delawares surrender their lands around Apple Creek. Or at least he did until Missouri voters, most of whom had no memory of happier times living alongside Indians, threw Clark out of the governor's office in 1820. Thereafter, Clark bent his dealings with Indians to the will of a white man's democracy, which resulted in the expulsion of the Shawnees and Delawares and the erasure of even their traces from around Apple Creek.

Human hands cannot erase Chimney Rock (though geological processes have eroded it). Thanks to the second and subsequent editions of the computer game *The Oregon Trail*, the records of peaceful exchanges between emigrating Americans and Indians on the major overland thoroughfare that ran past Chimney Rock have not been erased from popular accounts either. Millions of players know that Indians assisted overland travelers during the 1840s and 1850s and can assist them in the game's journey as well. As is usual in "wishtories," players who successfully pass Chimney Rock and survive all the way to Oregon presumably live happily ever after. Not so for the peoples who inhabited the country around Chimney Rock. Gamers, though, do not learn how conflicts among emigrants roiled caravans, why intercultural amity on the trail eroded, and what unhappy outcomes awaited Indians on the Great Plains.

We can identify factors that built up and broke down alternative relations on the overland trail. From the start of migrations across the Plains in the 1840s, tensions between Americans and Indians abounded. But as long as caravans were just passing through, as long as their numbers were limited, and as long as the United States military was mostly absent, Americans and Indians put aside their mistrusts to trade with one another. Stresses increased, as did conflicts, after the discovery of gold in California, which multiplied the numbers of Americans on the trail and increased the presence of the United States military on the Plains. The final breakdown of peaceful intercourse occurred after the Civil War. That is when Americans started to settle in numbers on the Plains, including even beyond the one hundredth meridian. It is also when the United States unleashed its army and its bureaucracy, both with lethal consequences for Plains Indians.

Dodge City makes an unlikely culminating chapter to this alternative history. Its founding climaxed a century of conquest by the United States. Transformed into a cowtown, Dodge City became notorious for its vice and violence. Its name still stands in for anarchic places seething with red-hot hatreds and stained by the blood of too many dead.

Yet, closer and comparative perspective offers Dodge City a measure of redemption. Racial animosities, at least as directed at African Americans, were less pronounced in Dodge City, and on the cattle drives to it, than they were in other parts of the American West and the United States. In Dodge and on the trail, Blacks lived better and Black lives mattered more than in the Southern states from which most cowboys hailed. In most of the years that Dodge City reigned as a cowtown, it was also less deadly than several other places in the post–Civil War American West, including ones with similar demographic profiles.

And the lessons of that for us? From Dodge, the most obvious would be that incentivizing police not to shoot first and disarming men before they drank and gambled saved lives. Enforcement, however, was too uneven to fully redeem Dodge City, or to make it an indisputable laboratory for lawmakers and lawmen today.

Alas, that is the case for the instructions from across this alternative history. Much as we might wish for a historical "how to" guide for how we can overcome our differences, the past is not so prescriptive. Lacking the freedom of alternate history, we cannot swap out one fact or switch off one factor. Nor can we will into existence different outcomes or isolate one true cause. The episodes chronicled and dissected in *Peace and Friendship* do not yield lessons that are readily applied anywhere and anytime.

There is much we can learn from examples of unstable common ground, but the directions from this alternative history are controversial, contradictory, and, contingent. In Dodge City, the actions by agents of the state reduced violence. The opposite occurred elsewhere. At Chillicothe, Apple Creek, and Chimney Rock, the interventions of nations and empires upset local containments and upped the levels of violence. And nowhere in this alternative history can we find a record of continuous concord. Even as foes forgot, or at least put aside, past enmities, differences were not permanently overcome. The legacy of broken concord on American frontiers from the Ohio Valley to the Pacific Coast and through the first century of the history of the United States underscores instead how ephemeral were understandings between peoples and across cultures.

No doubt, the collapses frustrate those seeking a sure, straight path to lasting peace and friendship. Seeing the demise of alternative relations only as dead ends, however, is too dark a view. From this alternative history, we should not shortchange the existence—and in some cases the persistence—of hospitable, harmonious, and inclusive cohabitations, even if these did give way. So, too, should we remember the imperfect arrangements that forestalled violence for a while. Commemorating compromises that were compromised means accepting that the legacies of concord are not all we might wish for. But better broken concord than no concord. And better to continue to seek out places and periods where people once (and not just once upon a time) overcame differences, for there lies our road to redemption.

NOTES

Introduction

1. William Clark, December 12, 1805, in Gary Moulton, ed., *The Journals of the Lewis and Clark Expedition*, https://lewisandclarkjournals.unl.edu/item/lc.jrn.1805-12-12#lc.jrn.1805-12-12.02.

2. Francis Paul Prucha, *Indian Peace Medals in American History* (Lincoln: University of Nebraska Press, 1976), 16–24.

3. Patricia Nelson Limerick, *The Legacy of Conquest: The Unbroken Past of the American West* (New York: W. W. Norton, 2006), made "conquest" and not "frontier" *the* keyword of Western American history. I review the shifting interpretations of the history of the American frontier and West in "Frontiers, Borderlands, Wests," in *American History Now*, ed. Eric Foner and Lisa McGirr (Philadelphia: Temple University Press, 2011), 263–286.

4. Patrick Wolfe, "Settler Colonialism and the Elimination of the Native," *Journal of Genocide Studies* 8 (December 2006): 387–409. For influential overviews of settler colonial theory and applications of it to American frontier histories, see Lorenzo Veracini, *Settler Colonialism: A Theoretical Overview* (London: Palgrave Macmillan, 2010); Veracini, *The Settler Colonial Present* (London: Palgrave Macmillan, 2015); Jeffrey Ostler and Nancy Shoemaker, "Settler Colonialism in Early American History: An Introduction," *William and Mary Quarterly*, 3rd ser., 76 (July 2019): 361–368; Patrick Wolfe, "Land, Labor, and Difference: Elementary Structures of Race," *American Historical Review* 106 (June 2001): 866–905; Michael Adas, "Settler Colony to Global Hegemon: Integrating the Exceptionalist Narrative of the American Experience into World History," *American*

Historical Review 105 (December 2001): 1692–1720; James Belich, *Replenishing the Earth: The Settler Revolution and the Rise of the Anglo World, 1789–1839* (Oxford: Oxford University Press, 2009); Margaret D. Jacobs, *White Mother to a Dark Race: Settler Colonialism, Maternalism, and the Removal of Indigenous Children in the American West and Australia* (Lincoln: University of Nebraska Press, 2003); Walter L. Hixon, *American Settler Colonialism: A History* (New York: Springer Nature, 2013); Kelly Lytle Hernández, *City of Inmates: Conquest, Rebellion, and the Rise of Human Caging in Los Angeles, 1771–1965* (Chapel Hill: University of North Carolina Press, 2017). For examples of how the construct of ethnic cleansing has been applied to North American history, see John Mack Faragher, *A Great and Noble Scheme: The Tragic Story of the Expulsion of the French Acadians from Their American Homeland* (New York: W. W. Norton, 2005); Gary Clayton Anderson, *Ethnic Cleansing and the Indian: The Crime That Should Haunt America* (Norman: University of Oklahoma Press, 2014); Christopher D. Haveman, *Rivers of Sand: Creek Indian Emigration, Relocation, and Ethnic Cleansing in the American South* (Lincoln: University of Nebraska Press, 2016); Claudio Saunt, *Unworthy Republic: The Dispossession of Native Americans and the Road to Indian Territory* (New York: W. W. Norton, 2020). On genocides against Indians in the United States, see Benjamin Madley, *An American Genocide: The United States and the California Indian Catastrophe, 1846–1873* (New Haven, CT: Yale University Press, 2016); Jeffrey Ostler, *Surviving Genocide: Native Nations and the United States from the American Revolution to Bleeding Kansas* (New Haven, CT: Yale University Press, 2019).

5. Martin Cruz Smith, *The Indians Won* (New York: Belmont Books, 1982); Douglas C. Jones, *The Court-Martial of George Armstrong Custer* (New York: HarperCollins, 1996); Peter Meech, *Billy the Kid: A Novel* (Boulder, CO: Sentient Publications, 2020).

6. The website for "Uchronia: The Alternate History List" (http://www.uchronia.net/) provides a bibliography of titles in this genre. Many of the books and short stories listed on the Uchronia website involve time traveling, though these alternate history fictions remain distinct from the extensive genre of science fictions that transport Westerns into space. For an analysis of that genre, see Carl Abbott, *Frontiers Past and Future: Science Fiction and the American West* (Lawrence: University Press of Kansas, 2006).

7. For examples of counterfactual speculations by academic historians, see Niall Ferguson, ed., *Virtual History* (New York: Basic Books, 1999); Robert Cowley, ed., *What Ifs? of American History: Eminent Historians Imagine What Might Have Been* (New York: Penguin, 2003).

8. Adam Gopnik, "Uncivil Wars," *New Yorker*, https://www.newyorker.com/magazine/2020/02/10/did-lincoln-really-matter (quotation); Edward H. Carr, *What Is History?* (New York: Penguin Books, 1961), quotation on 127; Edward P. Thompson, "The Poverty of Theory or an Orrery of Errors," in *The Poverty of Theory and Other Essays* (London: Merlin Press, 1978), quotation on 108.

9. For Grammarist distinction between "alternate" and "alternative," see http://grammarist.com/usage/alternate-alternative/.

10. "Alternative Wests" is the theme of a special issue of the *Pacific Historical Review* 86 (February 2017): 4–152. Like my vision of an alternative history of the American frontier, the contributors to this issue of the *Pacific Historical Review* rethink manifest destiny by considering alternatives to United States expansionism that happened (as opposed to ones that require counterfactuals to set in motion). An even more recent application is Dean Itsuji Saranillo, *Unsustainable Empire: Alternative Histories of Hawai'i Statehood* (Durham, NC: Duke University Press, 2018). In thinking about how the sites in this book have been marked or unmarked, forgotten or misremembered, I am indebted to Ari Kelman, *A Misplaced Massacre: Struggling over the Memory of Sand Creek* (Cambridge, MA: Harvard University Press, 2013). My understanding of reconciliations has been influenced by Sherry L. Smith, "Reconciliation and Restitution in the American West," *Western Historical Quarterly* 41 (Spring 2010): 4–25.

11. Viewed this way, the debt my project owes to new and newer Western histories becomes apparent. Most obvious is the influence of Richard White, *The Middle Ground: Indians, Empires, and Republics in the Great Lakes Region, 1650–1815* (New York: Cambridge University Press, 1991). For an informative consideration of the impact of White's book, see Philip J. Deloria, "What Is the Middle Ground, Anyway?," *William and Mary Quarterly*, 3rd. series, 63 (January 2006): 15–22. As Deloria discusses, in the wake of White's book, scholars went in search of other middle grounds. Following White, historians found (or claimed to find) similar intercultural compositions in other places at other times. Rather than a landscape dominated by Europeans, the "middle grounding" of early American history emphasized the power that native peoples exercised and their ability to negotiate the forms that colonialism took. As good examples of studies in the vein, see Eric Hinderaker, *Elusive Empires: Constructing Colonialism in the Ohio Valley, 1673–1800* (New York: Cambridge University Press, 1997); and Andrew Cayton and Fredrika Teute, eds., *Contact Points: American Frontiers from the Mohawk Valley to the Mississippi, 1750–1830* (Chapel Hill: University of North Carolina Press, 1998). The geopolitical foundation for middle grounds, Jeremy Adelman and I posited, most often emerged in the interior of the continent, where the claims of European empires overlapped. In these "borderlands" during the eighteenth century, Indians successfully played imperial rivals off against one another, which allowed them to negotiate more favorable terms of trade and sustain more inclusive frontiers. See Jeremy Adelman and Stephen Aron, "From Borderlands to Borders: Empires, Nation-States, and the Peoples in Between in North American History," *American Historical Review* 104 (June 1999): 814–841; and Stephen Aron, *American Confluence: The Missouri Frontier from Borderland to Border State* (Bloomington: Indiana University Press, 2006). More recently, White's book has prompted

scholars to invert older formulations that presume European dominance from the onset of colonization. These studies have instead affirmed the existence and persistence of "native grounds," zones where Europeans remained subordinated to Indians and where Indians dictated the rules and Europeans were the ones who had to accommodate. Excellent examples of this "turn" in the literature include Kathleen DuVal, *The Native Ground: Indians and Colonists in the Heart of the Continent* (Philadelphia: University of Pennsylvania Press, 2006); Julianna Barr, *Peace Came in the Form of a Woman: Indians and Spaniards in the Texas Borderlands* (Chapel Hill: University of North Carolina Press, 2007); Brian Delay, *War of a Thousand Deserts: Indian Raids and the U.S.-Mexican War* (New Haven, CT: Yale University Press, 2008); Pekka Hämäläinen, *The Comanche Empire* (New Haven, CT: Yale University Press, 2008); Claudio Saunt, *West of the Revolution: An Uncommon History of 1776* (New York: W. W. Norton, 2014); Michael A. McDonnell, *Masters of Empire: Great Lakes Indians and the Making of America* (New York: Farrar, Straus & Giroux, 2015); Susan Sleeper-Smith, *Indigenous Prosperity and American Conquest: Indian Women of the Ohio River Valley, 1690–1792* (Chapel Hill: University of North Carolina Press, 2018); Jacob F. Lee, *Masters of the Middle Waters: Indian Nations and Colonial Ambitions along the Mississippi* (Cambridge, MA: Harvard University Press, 2019). Enormously influential as well, on newer Western histories and on this alternative history, is Anne Hyde, *Empires, Nations, and Families: A New History of the North American West, 1800–1860* (Lincoln: University of Nebraska Press, 2011). In Hyde's account, the interests of the first two elements of her title (empires and nations) remain subordinated to those of the third (families) for most of the period under study.

12. The recognition that "common ground" was found *and lost* distinguishes my alternative history from studies that suggest historians have overstated the extent of violence in the history of the American West. For two important books with very different in approaches but with a shared emphasis on deflating exaggerated conceptions about the ubiquity of Western violence, see Terry L. Anderson and Peter J. Hill, *The Not So Wild, Wild West: Property Rights on the Frontier* (Stanford, CA: Stanford University Press, 2004); Robert R. Dykstra, *The Cattle Towns* (New York: Knopf, 1971). My understanding of the often attenuated and abbreviated moments of concord also separates this alternative history from more whiggish accounts that offer a "things are getting better" take on intercultural discord (and violence). Particularly influential (and exemplary of this approach) are Steven Pinker's recent books. See his *The Better Angels of Our Nature: Why Violence Has Declined* (New York: Penguin, 2011); and *Enlightenment Now: The Case for Reason, Science, and Humanism* (New York: Penguin, 2018).

13. For the 2008 Sears advertising campaign, see https://www.ethos3.com/2008/12/the-sears-wishtory-campaign-great-storytelling/, and for Vanessa

Hudgens's "American wishtory," see https://www.youtube.com/watch?v= KWiLw_O3UWA. I have examined the relationship between "wishtories" and histories of the American West, particularly as they relate to the interpretation of Western American art, in "Wishtory and History: An Illustrated Tour," in *Unlocking the History of the Americas,* ed. Duane King (Tulsa: Gilcrease Museum, 2016): 10–25; and "From Romance to Convergence," in *The Art of the West: Selected Works from the Autry Museum,* ed. Amy Scott (Norman: University of Oklahoma Press, 2018), vii–xii.

Chapter 1

1. On Tecumseh's birthplace, see John Sugden, *Tecumseh: A Life* (New York: Henry Holt, 2013), 20–23. For the location of Chillicothe on the Little Miami, as well as other Shawnee villages in Ohio, including relocated versions of Chillicothe, see Helen H. Tanner, *Atlas of Great Lakes Indian History* (Chicago: University of Chicago Press, 1987), 80.

2. In addition to serving as the president of the Greene County Historical Society, William Albert Galloway also authored *Old Chillicothe: Shawnee and Pioneer History* (Xenia, OH: Buckeye Press, 1934). Photographs of several of the historical signs and monuments appear in the book opposite pages 70 and 120. The site also has markers about Simon Kenton's captivity, Tecumseh's life, and the Bullskin Trail. For more on the campaigns to erect the markers and preserve them, see the following items that are collected in the "Old Town" folder, Greene County Local History and Genealogy Room, Xenia Library: "Roadside Park Plan May Save Old Town Historical Markers," May 4, 1950; "Historians Fight to Preserve Famous Old Town Markers," April 27, 1950; "Oldtown's Past Rich in History and Adventure, Its Present Uneventful," *Journal Herald,* June 27, 1977; "Old Town Monuments," Xenia *Daily Gazette,* April 13, 2011; and in the "Old Chillicothe" folder, Greene County Local History and Genealogy Room, Xenia Library, see the "Nomination Form for National Register of Historic Places Inventory," April 21, 1975.

3. William Galloway spent considerable time among Shawnees, who had been removed to Oklahoma. His book, *Old Chillicothe,* draws extensively on his interviews with the Indians, and thus offers their side of the history of the Ohio town in ways that the markers and monuments do not.

4. Colin Calloway, "'We Have Always Been the Frontier': The American Revolution in Shawnee Country," *American Indian Quarterly* 16 (1992): quotation on 39.

5. On the history of the Shawnees and the particular roles traditionally assigned to these five divisions (the spellings of which vary in different accounts) in this and the following paragraphs, see Vernon Kinietz and Erminie W. Voegelin, eds., "Shawnese Traditions: C. C. Trowbridge's Account," Occasional Contributions from the Museum of Anthropology of the University of Michigan 9 (June 1939), passim; Thomas Wildcat Alford, *Civilization and the Story of the Absentee Shawnees, as Told to*

Florence Drake (Norman: University of Oklahoma Press, 1936), 44; James Howard, *Shawnee!: The Ceremonialism of a Native American Tribe and Its Cultural Background* (Athens: Ohio University Press, 1981); Charles Callender, "Shawnee," in *Handbook of North American Indians: Northeast*, ed. William C. Sturtevant and Bruce Trigger, Vol. 15 (Washington, DC: Smithsonian Institution, 1978), 622–635; Calloway, " 'We Have Always Been the Frontier,' " 39–52; Stephen Warren, *The Worlds the Shawnees Made: Migration and Violence in Early America* (Chapel Hill: University of North Carolina Press, 2014), 27–179; Sami Lakomäki, *Gathering Together: The Shawnee People through Diaspora and Nationhood, 1600–1870* (New Haven, CT: Yale University Press, 2014), 13–71.

6. David Hackett Fischer, *Albion's Fatal Seed: Four British Folkways in America* (Oxford: Oxford University Press, 1989), 605–782; Patrick Spero, *Frontier Country: The Politics of War in Early Pennsylvania* (Philadelphia: University of Pennsylvania Press, 2016), 34–48; Mariann Wokeck, *Trade in Strangers: The Beginnings of Mass Migration to North America* (University Park: Pennsylvania State University Press, 1999), 37–58.

7. On Boone's boyhood and most other parts of his biography, historians go back to the interviews collected by Lyman C. Draper during the nineteenth century. Draper's own biography of Boone was never completed, but has now been published as Lyman C. Draper, *The Life of Daniel Boone*, ed. Ted Franklin Belue (Mechanicsburg: Stackpole Books, 1998). For Boone's ancestry and early years in Pennsylvania, see 101–123. Recent biographies that add valuable details to Draper's account of Boone's early years include John Mack Faragher, *Daniel Boone: The Life and Legend of an American Pioneer* (New York: Henry Holt, 1992), 9–39; Robert Morgan, *Boone: A Biography* (Chapel Hill, NC: Algonquin Books, 2007), 1–21; Meredith Mason Brown, *Frontiersman: Daniel Boone and the Making of America* (Baton Rouge: Louisiana State University Press, 2013), 3–11. In addition to writing a definitive biography of Daniel Boone, John Mack Faragher has digitized the research notes for that volume, for which all future researchers on Daniel Boone, myself included, are in his debt. See Andrew Offenburger, comp., "Digitizing *Daniel Boone*: The Research Notes of John Mack Faragher," https://sourcenotes.miamioh.edu/daniel-boone/.

8. On the emergence of hunting by white men in the cis-Appalachian backcountry and the cross-cultural borrowings that enabled the expansion of hunting, see Terry G. Jordan and Matti Kaups, *The American Backwoods Frontier: An Ethnic and Ecological Interpretation* (Baltimore: Johns Hopkins University Press, 1989), 211–232; Ted Franklin Belue, *The Long Hunt: Death of the Buffalo East of the Mississippi* (Mechanicsburg, PA: Stackpole Books, 1996), 55–67; Stephen Aron, *How the West Was Lost: The Transformation of Kentucky from Daniel Boone to Henry Clay* (Baltimore: Johns Hopkins University Press, 1996), 21–27; Andrea L. Smalley, *Wild by Nature: North American Animals Confront Colonization* (Baltimore: Johns Hopkins University Press, 2017), 158–171.

9. Calvin Martin, *Keepers of the Game: Indian-Animal Relationships and the Fur Trade* (Athens: University of Georgia Press, 2008), 113–149; Aron, *How the West Was Lost*, 24–25.

10. Michael N. McConnell, *A Country Between: The Upper Ohio Valley and Its Peoples, 1724–1774* (Lincoln: University of Nebraska Press, 1992), 5–20, 107–112; Elizabeth Mancke, "The Ohio Country and Indigenous Geopolitics in Early Modern North America, circa 1500–1760," *Ohio Valley History* 18 (Spring 2018): 19–23; Warren, *The Worlds the Shawnees Made*, 180–207; Lakomäki, *Gathering Together*, 42–71; Richard White, *The Middle Ground: Indians, Empires, and Republics in the Great Lakes Region, 1650–1815* (New York: Cambridge University Press, 1991), 186–222.

11. On the migrations of the Boones, his life in North Carolina, and his first trans-Appalachian long hunts as discussed in this and the next two paragraphs, see Faragher, *Daniel Boone*, 40–87; Brown, *Frontiersman*, 12–53; Morgan, *Boone*, 25–87.

12. John D. Shane interview with Daniel Bryan, c. 1844, Draper Mss. 22C14(1); Daniel Bryan to Lyman C. Draper, February 27, 1843, Draper Mss. 22C5.

13. Draper, *The Life of Daniel Boone*, 215–219; John Bakeless, *Daniel Boone: Master of the Wilderness* (Mechanicsburg, PA: Stackpole Books, 1939), 51–52.

14. John D. Shane interview with Daniel Boone Bryan, Draper Mss., State Historical Society of Wisconsin, Madison, 22C14; Lyman C. Draper interview with Nathan and Olive Boone, 6S46–52.

15. John D. Shane interview with Daniel Boone Bryan, Draper Mss. 22C14 (quotation). Fifteen years after the meeting between Boone and Emery, John Filson appended an account of it to his book on *The Discovery, Settlement, and Present State of Kentucke*. The appendix, "The Adventures of Col. Daniel Boon; containing a Narrative of the Wars of Kentucke," made Filson's book an international bestseller, and it made Boone a legend in his own time. While Boone endorsed the accuracy of the narrative, Filson's version altered or deleted several key details of the encounter. Readers of Filson's book, for example, did not learn the name of Will Emery. Of his capture in December 1769, Filson's Boone recalled only that he and Stuart had been treated "with common savage usage" and "plundered of what we had." See John Filson, *The Discovery, Settlement, and Present State of Kentucke (1784): An Online Electronic Text Edition*, ed. Paul Royster, 41, DigitalCommons@University, Nebraska-Lincoln.

16. Archibald Henderson, "The Creative Forces in Westward Expansion," *American Historical Review* 20 (October 1914): 100.

17. Boone's bold bid to preemptively settle and gain title to land in Kentucky followed on a conception of property rights that historian Richard Maxwell Brown described as the "homestead ethic." See Richard Maxwell Brown, "Backcountry Rebellions and the Homestead Ethic in America,

1740–1799," in *Tradition, Conflict, and Modernization: Perspectives on the American Revolution*, ed. Richard Maxwell Brown and Don E. Fehrenbacher (New York: Elsevier Science, 1977), 73–99.

18. *Virginia Gazette*, January 14, 1773, quoted in Rob Harper, *Unsettling the West: Violence and State Building in the Ohio Valley* (Philadelphia: University of Pennsylvania Press, 2018), 48; Joseph Doddridge, *Notes on the Settlement and Indian Wars of the Western Parts of Virginia and Pennsylvania from 1763 to 1783* (Pittsburgh: University of Pennsylvania Press, 1912), 85.

19. Draper, *The Life of Daniel Boone*, 283–290; James William Hagy, "The First Attempt to Settle Kentucky: Boone in Virginia," *Filson Club History Quarterly* 44 (1970): 229–230.

20. James McAfee Journal, 1773, Draper Mss. 4CC1–12; Virginius C. Hall, ed., "Journal of Isaac Hite, 1773," *Bulletin of the Historical and Philosophical Society of Ohio* 12 (October 1954): 262–281; Neal O. Hammon, "Captain Harrod's Company, 1774: A Reappraisal," *Register of the Kentucky Historical Society* 72 (July 1974): 224–242.

21. William Stewart Lester, *The Transylvania Colony* (Spencer, IN: Samuel R. Guard, 1935); Nancy O'Malley, *Boonesborough Unearthed* (Lexington: University Press of Kentucky, 2019), 7–12.

22. Louisa Company Articles of Agreement, Draper Mss. 1CC2; "Proposals for the Encouragement of settling the Lands purchased by Richard Henderson & Co. on the Branches of the Mississippi River from the Cherokee tribe of Indians, December 25, 1774," in *The Colonia; Records of North Carolina*, ed. William L. Saunders, 25 vols. (Raleigh: University of North Carolina Press, 1886–1905), 9:1129–1131; "Deposition of James Robinson, April 16, 1777," in *Calendar of Virginia State Papers and Other Manuscripts*, ed. William P. Palmer (Richmond: R. F. Walker, 1875–1893), 1:285–287; "Treaty of Watauga," in *Boonesborough: Its Founding, Pioneer Struggles, Indian Experiences, Transylvania Days, and Revolutionary Annals*, ed. George W. Ranck (London: Forgotten Books, 2018), 151–156.

23. John Floyd to William Preston, April 21, 1775, in Neal O. Hammon and James R. Harris, "'In a dangerous situation': Letters of Col. John Floyd, 1774–1783," *Register of the Kentucky Historical Society* 83 (Summer 1985): quotation on 210; Washington quoted in Lester, *The Transylvania Colony*, 41. For the proclamations by the governors of North Carolina and Virginia against the Transylvania Colony, see "A Proclamation by Governor Martin Against Richard Henderson and the Transylvania Purchase, February 10, 1775," in Saunders, *The Colonial Records of North Carolina*, 9:1124; "Proclamation of Lord Dunmore Against 'Richard Henderson and His Abettors,' March 21, 1775," in Ranck, *Boonesborough*, 181–182.

24. "Oconestoto to the Delegates in Convention, June 24, 1775," in *Revolutionary Virginia: The Road to Independence*, ed. William J. Van Schreevan, 7 vols. (Charlottesville: University Press of Virginia, 1973–1983), quotation on 3:219. See also "Judge Richard Henderson's Journal of a

Trip to 'Cantuckey' and of Events at Boonesborough in 1775," in Ranck, *Boonesborough*, 177; Daniel Boone to Richard Henderson, April 1, 1775, Draper Mss. 17CC166–167; Lewis H. Kirkpatrick, ed., "The Journal of William Calk, Kentucky Pioneer," *Mississippi Valley Historical Review* 7 (March 1921): 369; "Statement of Felix Walker, 1826, when 91 Years of Age," in "A Partial List of Those at Fort Boonesborough," comp. Katherine Phelps, *Register of the Kentucky Historical Society* 23 (May 1925): 148–149.

25. Kirkpatrick, ed., "The Journal of William Calk," 367; "Letter of Judge Henderson (June 12, 1775) to Proprietors Remaining in North Carolina," in Ranck, *Boonesborough*, 184; James Rood Robertson, ed., *Petitions of the Early Inhabitants of Kentucky to the General Assembly of Virginia, 1769–1792* (Louisville: University of Kentucky Press, 1914), 48–52, Harper, *Unsettling the West*, 67–94.

26. Lyman C. Draper interview with Delinda Boone Craig, November 8–9, 1866, Draper Mss. 30C48–49 (quotation); Lyman C. Draper interview with Nathan and Olive Van Bibber Boone, October 25–November 9, 1851, Draper Mss. 6S96–101; Lyman C. Draper interview with Morgan and Elizabeth Boone Bryan, November 25, 1851, Draper Mss. 6S301–302; Matthew Pearl, *The Taking of Jemima Boone: Colonial Settlers, Tribal Nations, and the Kidnap That Shaped America* (New York: HarperCollins, 2021).

27. Harper, *Unsettling the West*, 87; Gregory Evans Dowd, *A Spirited Resistance: The North American Indian Struggle for Unity, 1745–1815* (Baltimore: Johns Hopkins University Press, 1992), 65–89.

28. "Col. John Bowman to Gen. Edward Hand, December 12, 1777," in *Frontier Defense on the Upper Ohio, 1777–1778*, ed. Reuben G. Thwaites and Louise P. Kellogg (Madison: Wisconsin Historical Society, 1912), 181–183; R. S. Cotterrill, *History of Pioneer Kentucky* (Cincinnati: Johnson & Hardin, 1917), 111–118. Morgan, *Boone*, 219; Brown, *Frontiersman*, 118–120.

29. Cornstalk quoted in Colin G. Calloway, *The American Revolution in Indian Country: Crisis and Diversity in Native American Communities* (New York: Cambridge University Press, 1995), 164; "General Edward Hand to Jasper Yeates, December 24, 1777," in Thwaites and Kellogg, eds., *Frontier Defense on the Upper Ohio*, quotation on 188; Harper, *Unsettling the West*, 100–105.

30. Aron, *How the West Was Lost*, 59–70.

31. O'Malley, *Boonesborough Unearthed*, 27.

32. For Boone's recollections of his capture and reintroduction to Will Emery as recounted by his son, see Lyman C. Draper interview with Nathan and Olive Boone, Draper Mss. 6S106–107.

33. "Guy Johnson to Lord George Germain, March 12, 1778," in *Documents of the American Revolution, 1770–1783*, ed. K. G. Davies, 21 vols. (Shannon: Irish University Press, 1972–1981), 15:68; "Gov. Henry Hamilton to Sir Guy Carleton, April 25, 1778," in Thwaites and Kellogg, eds., *Frontier Defense on the Upper Ohio*, 283.

34. Boone's speech quoted in Lyman C. Draper interview with Joseph Jackson, Draper Mss. 11C62(8); Deposition of Ansel Goodman, October 29, 1832, Draper Mss. 11C28.
35. Draper with Joseph Jackson, Draper Mss. 11C62. Boone was provided with a running translation of the Indians' speeches by Pompey, a former Virginia slave who had lived among the Shawnees for some time and often served as an interpreter.
36. Statement of Boone Hays, 1846, Draper Mss. 23C36(3–4); Draper with Joseph Jackson, Draper Mss. 11C62(9); Draper interview with Nathan and Olive Boone, Draper Mss., 6S109–110.
37. Orley E. Brown, ed., *The Captivity of Jonathan Alder and His Life with the Indians* (Akron: University of Akron Press, 2010), quotation on 14.
38. Brown, *Frontiersman*, quotation on 134.
39. "Gov. Henry Hamilton to Sir Guy Carleton, April 25, 1778," in Thwaites and Kellogg, eds., *Frontier Defense on the Upper Ohio*, 283. For details of the salt-makers' travails, see Ted Franklin Belue, "Terror in the Canelands: The Fate of Daniel Boone's Salt Boilers," *Filson Club History Quarterly* 68 (January 1994): 3–34; William Dodd Brown, ed., "The Capture of Daniel Boone's Saltmakers: Fresh Perspectives from Primary Sources," *Register of the Kentucky Historical Society* 83 (Winter 1985): 1–18.
40. "Gov. Henry Hamilton to Sir Guy Carleton, April 25, 1778," in Thwaites and Kellogg, eds., *Frontier Defense on the Upper Ohio*, quotation on 283.
41. Filson, *The Discovery, Settlement, and Present State of Kentucke*, quotations on 77. See also the description of Chillicothe by John Bowman in 1779 in "Bowman's Journal Expedition against Chillicothe, May–June 1779," *Ohio History Journal* 19 (October 1910): 453. For a consideration of how cultural borrowing made Indian villages look more like pioneer stations, see Larry L. Nelson, "Cultural Mediation, Cultural Exchange, and the Invention of the Ohio Frontier," *Ohio History Journal* 105 (Winter–Spring 1996): 86–87.
42. Mancke, "The Ohio Country and Indigenous Geopolitics in Early Modern North America," 19–23.
43. Harper, *Unsettling the West*, quotation on 12; Harold B. Gill Jr. and George M. Curtis III, eds., *A Man Apart: The Journal of Nicholas Cresswell, 1774–1781* (Lanham, MD: Lexington Books, 2009), 77–78; Robert Englebert, "Colonial Encounters and the Changing Contours of Ethnicity: Pierre-Louis de Lorimier at the Edges of Empire," *Ohio Valley History* 18 (Spring 2018): 54–58; Linda Clark Nash, ed., *The Journals of Pierre-Louis de Lorimier, 1777–1795* (Montreal: Baraka Books, 2012), 75–79; Eugene F. Bliss, ed., *Diary of David Zeisberger a Moravian Missionary among the Indians of Ohio*, 2 vols. (St. Clair Shores: Scholarly Press, 1972), 1:125; Galloway, *Old Chillicothe*, 44–45; McConnell, *A Country Between*, 210–220.
44. Franklin B. Dexter, ed., *Diary of David McClure: Doctor of Divinity, 1748–1820* (New York: Knickerbocker Press, 1899), quotation on 85;

John W. Jordan, ed., "Journal of James Kenny, 1761–1763," *Pennsylvania Magazine of History and Biography* 37 (1913): 22; Paul A. W. Wallace, ed., *Thirty Thousand Miles with John Heckewelder* (Pittsburgh: University of Pittsburgh Press, 1958), 41, 44; David Jones, *A Journal of Two Visits Made to Some Nations of Indians on the West Side of the River Ohio in the Years 1772 and 1773* (Burlington, NJ: Isaac Collins, 1774), 56; McConnell, *A Country Between*, 219.

45.   Draper, *The Life of Daniel Boone*, quotation on 477–478; John C. Boone to Lyman C. Draper, November 20, 1890, Draper Mss. 16C132, State Historical Society of Wisconsin, Madison (quotation). When Lyman Draper wrote up his version of this episode, he cleaned up the grandson's quotation. After Boone "blistered his hands" from working the axe, he complained that Blackfish was "making a slave of me," for "in Kentucky I had servants to do such work." Draper, *The Life of Daniel Boone*, quotation on 477. On women's labor and power among the Shawnees, see Kinietz and Voegelin, eds., "Shawnese Traditions," 33–34; Susan Sleeper-Smith, *Indigenous Prosperity and American Conquest: Indian Women of the Ohio River Valley, 1690–1792* (Chapel Hill: University of North Carolina Press, 2018).

46.   Kinietz and Voegelin, eds., "Shawnese Traditions," 12–13; Dowd, *A Spirited Resistance*, 1–22.

47.   Lyman C. Draper interview with Nathan and Olive Van Bibber Boone, Draper Mss. 6S117–119; Morgan, *Boone*, 248–249.

48.   Deposition of Ansel Goodman, Draper Mss. 11C28 (quotation); Chester Raymond Young, ed., *Westward into Kentucky: The Narrative of Daniel Trabue* (Lexington: University Press of Kentucky, 1981), 57; John Dabney Shane interview with Daniel Boone Bryan, 1844, Draper Mss. 22C14(12); Neal O. Hammon, ed., *My Father, Daniel Boone: The Draper Interviews with Nathan Boone* (Lexington: University Press of Kentucky, 1999), 60.

49.   Chester Raymond Young, ed., *Westward into Kentucky: The Narrative of Daniel Trabue* (Lexington: University Press of Kentucky, 1981), quotation on 57; Shane with Daniel Boone Bryan, Draper Mss. 22C14(12); Lyman C. Draper interview with Josiah Collins, Draper Mss. 12CC74–75.

50.   "Deposition of William Hancock, July 17, 1778," in *Frontier Advance on the Upper Ohio, 1778–1779*, ed. Louise P. Kellogg (Madison: State Historical Society of Wisconsin, 1916), 114.

51.   Young, ed., *Westward into Kentucky*, 57; "Deposition of Stephen Hancock," in "History in Circuit Court Records," ed. Charles Staples, *Register of the Kentucky Historical Society* 32 (January 1934): 8; "John Bowman to George Rogers Clark, October 14, 1778," in *George Rogers Clark Papers, 1771–1781*, ed. John Alton James (Springfield: Trustees of the Illinois State Historical Library, 1912), 69–70.

52.   O'Malley, *Boonesborough Unearthed*, 31–34.

53.   Ibid., 32–33.

54. Young, *Westward into Kentucky*, 57; Lyman C. Draper with Josiah Collins, Draper Mss. 1274–1275; John Dabney Shane interview with John Gass, Draper Mss. 11CC12; Morgan, *Boone*, 257.

55. Young, ed., *Westward into Kentucky*, 58–59; John Dabney Shane interview with Nathaniel Hart Jr., Draper Mss. 17CC198; John Dabney Shane interview with Jesse Daniel, Draper Mss. 11CC94.

56. Brown, *Frontiersman*, 152–153.

57. Young, ed., *Westward into Kentucky*, quotations on 58.

58. Thomas D. Clark, ed., *The Voice of the Frontier: John Bradford's Notes on Kentucky* (Lexington: University Press of Kentucky, 1993), 17–20; O'Malley, *Boonesborough Unearthed*, 33–35.

59. Young, ed., *Westward into Kentucky*, quotations on 63.

60. Ibid., 63; Major Jonathan E. Fields, "The Curious Court-Martial of Daniel Boone," *Army Lawyer* 46 (January 2016): 65–73.

61. Kenton quoted in John James to Lyman C. Draper, November 12, 1835, Draper Mss. 11C76; Young, ed., *Westward into Kentucky*, 64.

62. John Dabney Shane interview with Daniel Boone Bryan, 1844, Draper Mss. 22C14(12) (quotation).

63. Filson, *The Discovery, Settlement, and Present State of Kentucke*, quotation on 54.

64. Draper, *The Life of Daniel Boone*, quotation on 521; Faragher, *Daniel Boone*, quotation on 170; Morgan, *Boone*, quotation on 240.

65. The fullest discussion of disaffection in revolutionary Kentucky can be found in Patricia Watlington, "Discontent in Frontier Kentucky," *Register of the Kentucky Historical Society* 65 (April 1967): 77–93; and Watlington, *The Partisan Spirit: Kentucky Politics, 1779–1792* (Chapel Hill: University of North Carolina Press, 2012), 31–34.

66. "John Floyd to William Martin, May 19, 1776," in "'In a Dangerous Situation': Letters of Col. John Floyd, 1774–1783," ed. Neal O. Hammon and James R. Harris, *Register of the Kentucky Historical Society* 83 (Summer 1985): 214 (quotation).

67. See Harper, *Unsettling the West*, for a thorough explanation of the ways in which states and empires transformed frontier conflicts.

68. John James Audubon, *Ornithological Biography . . . Interspersed with Delineations of American Scenery and Manners* (Philadelphia: Judah Dobson, 1831), quotation on 504–505; Draper Mss. 9B101, 3B42; 12C39. For an example of how the killing of a family member resulted in blinding hatred of Indians and a life spent killing Indians, see the case of Tom Quick, as excavated in Patrick Griffin, *American Leviathan: Empire, Nation, and Revolutionary Frontier* (New York: Farrar, Straus & Giroux, 2007), 3–17. More than any other topic, the association between Daniel Boone and the Indians goes to the heart of the enigma of Boone's character. In the nineteenth century, an emphasis on the "bad blood" between Daniel Boone and treacherous Indian adversaries answered doubts about the frontiersman's devotion to the cause of civilization.

The reputation of Boone came to rest on his Indian-killing laurels. In the hagiographic tradition of popular fiction and epic biography, the slaughter of Indians ennobled Boone as the agent of European civilization. On the ways in which biographers and mythmakers have viewed Boone's relations with Indians, see Richard Slotkin, *Regeneration through Violence: The Mythology of the American Frontier, 1600–1860* (Middletown, CT: Wesleyan University Press, 1973), 288–265; Faragher, *Daniel Boone*, 320–351; Michael A. Lofaro, "The Many Lives of Daniel Boone," *Register of the Kentucky Historical Society* 102 (October 2004): 488–511.

69. William Smith, *An Historical Account of the Expedition against the Ohio Indians in the Year 1764* (Philadelphia: W. Bradford, 1765), quotations on 27, 29; Interview with Charles Tucker, June 26–27, 1868, Draper Mss. 23S172–177; Col. Henry Bouquet to Gen. Thomas Gage, November 15, 1764, in "Bouquet Papers," *Michigan Pioneer Collections* 19 (1892): 281; John Slover, "The Narrative of John Slover," in *A Collection of Some of the Most Interesting Narratives of Indian Warfare in the West*, ed. Samuel L. Metcalf (New York: William G. Hunt, 1977), 58.

70. Cornstalk quoted in Calloway, *The American Revolution in Indian Country*, 165.

71. James Axtell, "The White Indians of Colonial America," *William and Mary Quarterly*, 3rd. ser., 32 (January 1975): 58; Matthew C. Ward, "Redeeming the Captives: Pennsylvania Captives among the Ohio Indians, 1755–1765," *Pennsylvania Magazine of History and Biography* 125 (July 2001): 164–166; Daniel E. Crowe, "James Smith among the Indians: Cultural Captives on the Early American Frontier, 1755–1812," *Filson Club History Quarterly* 73 (1999): 117–138.

72. Statement of Joseph Jackson, April 1844, Draper Mss. 11C62(11), 11C63; Leonard Bliss to Lyman Draper, December 18, 1850, Draper Mss. 24C119(1); Draper's Notes to interview with Ezekiel Lewis, Draper Mss. 30J80; Brown, *Frontiersman*, 194–195.

73. Belue, *Terror in the Canelands*, 3–34; Draper, *The Life of Daniel Boone*, 480–484.

74. Morgan, *Boone*, quotation on 249.

75. Eligah Bryan to Lyman C. Draper, May 12, 1885, Draper Mss. 4C33(3–4) (quotation).

76. "Bowman's Expedition against Chillicothe, May–June 1779," *Ohio Archaeological and Historical Publications* 19 (1910): 446–459; "Bowman's Campaign of 1779," *Ohio Archaeological and Historical Publications* 22 (1913): 502–519; Draper Mss. 5D1–20, 49J90.

77. Galloway, *Old Chillicothe*, 14, 43, 49 67–68; James Alton James, ed., *George Rogers Clark Papers, 1771–1781* (Springfield, IL, 1912), cxxix–cxli, 451–453, 476–484; Galloway, *Old Chillicothe*, 67–68; John H. Moore, "A Captive of the Shawnees, 1779–1784," *West Virginia History* 23 (1962): 291; J. Martin West, ed., *Clark's Shawnee Campaign of 1780: Contemporary Accounts*

(Springfield, OH: Clark County Historical Society, 1975); Tanner, ed., *Atlas of Great Lakes Indian History*, 71–73, 82–87.

78. "Col. William Christian to Gov. Benjamin Harrison, September 28, 1782," in *Calendar of Virginia State Papers and Other Manuscripts*, ed. William P. Palmer et al., 11 vols. (Richmond: R. F. Walker, 1875–1893), 3:331; Colin Calloway, *The Shawnees and the War for America* (New York: Penguin Books, 2007), 67–84. The fortunes of Shawnees who migrated to Spanish Louisiana are taken up in Chapter 3.

79. Quotations in Calloway, *The American Revolution in Indian Country*, 173, 174.

80. G. Glenn Clift, ed., "The District of Kentucky, 1783–1787, as Pictured by Harry Innes in a Letter to John Brown," *Register of the Kentucky Historical Society* 54 (October 1956): 369; Harry Innes (Danville) to Major General Knox, July 7, 1790, Harry Innes Papers, Library of Congress, Washington, DC; Colin G. Calloway, *The Shawnees and the War for America* (New York: Penguin Books, 2007), 85–108; Colin G. Calloway, *The Indian World of George Washington: The First President, the First Americans, and the Birth of the Nation* (New York: Penguin Books, 2018), 378–450.

81. Daniel R. Gresmer, "'Bettering Our Circumstances': Settler Colonialism in Ohio during the 1780s," *Ohio History* 124 (Spring 2017): 22–40; John Bowes, *Land Too Good for Indians: Northern Indian Removal* (Norman: University of Oklahoma Press, 2016), 23–32; Andrew R. L. Cayton, "'Noble Actors' upon the 'Theatre of Honour': Power and Civility in the Treaty of Greenville," in *Contact Points: American Frontiers from the Mohawk Valley to the Mississippi, 1750–1830*, ed. Andrew R. L. Cayton and Fredrika J. Teute (Chapel Hill: University of North Carolina Press, 1998), 235–269.

82. Hammon, ed., *My Father, Daniel Boone*, quotation on 60.

83. John D. Shane interview with Joshua McQueen, Draper Mss., quotation on 13CC21; "Journal of the House of Delegates of the Transylvania Colony," in Ranck, *Boonesborough*, 206; Aron, *How the West Was Lost*, 53–57; Belue, *The Long Hunt*, 97–134.

84. For Boone's certificate, see "The Certificate Book of the Virginia Land Commission, 1779–1780," *Register of the Kentucky Historical Society* 21 (1923): 82. For the workings of land laws in Kentucky, see Aron, *How the West Was Lost*, 58–81.

85. Daniel Boone, Receipt, December 24, 1781, Miscellaneous Manuscripts Collection, Library of Congress, Washington, DC; Daniel Boone Deed, July 20, 1786, Samuel Wilson Collection, Special Collections, Margaret I. King Library, University of Kentucky; Thomas Marshall, Account Book, 1782–1783, Thomas Marshall Papers, Filson Historical Society, Louisville, Kentucky; Deposition of Daniel Boone, March 18, 1799, Draper Mss. 15C25(12); Joan E. Brookes-Smith, ed., *Master Index Virginia Surveys and Grants, 1774–1791* (Frankfort: Kentucky Historical Society 1976), 17, 88; Joan E. Brookes-Smith, ed., *Index for Old Kentucky*

Surveys and Grants (Frankfort: Kentucky Historical Society, 1975), 14; Willard Rouse Jillson, "The Land Surveys of Daniel Boone," *Register of the Kentucky Historical Society* 44 (April 1946): 86–100; Willard R. Jillson, ed., *With Compass and Chain: A Brief Narration of the Activities of Col. Daniel Boone as a Land Surveyor in Kentucky* (Frankfort: Kentucky Historical Society, 1954); Neal O. Hammon and James Russell Harris, "Daniel Boone the Surveyor: Old Images and New Realities," *Register of the Kentucky Historical Society* 102 (October 2004): 534–566; Neal O. Hammon and James Russell Harris, "Daniel Boone the Businessman: Revising the Myth of Failure," *Register of the Kentucky Historical Society* 112 (Winter 2014): 5–50.

86.   For a sampling of judgments against Boone, see Bourbon County Court, Order Book A, 1786–1793, 133, 139, 161, 243 (Microfilm at Margaret I. King Library); Michael L. Cook, ed., *Virginia Supreme Court District of Kentucky: Order Books, 1783–1792* (Evansville, IN: Cook Publications, 1988), 108, 110, 130, 187, 215, 218, 242, 255, 259, 274, 300, 347, 410, 417, 525.

Chapter 2

1.   https://shsmo.org/manuscripts/ramsay/ramsay_cape_girardeau.html; Louis Houck, ed., *The Spanish Regime in Missouri*, 2 vols. (Chicago: Lakeside Press, 1909), 1:213–214, 220.

2.   Quotation from https://mostateparks.com/park/trail-tears-state-park. For a complete list of historical markers and their locations by county in Missouri (as of October 5, 2018), see https://www.hmdb.org/results. asp?State=Missouri. On Indian removals from east of the Mississippi River, see Claudio Saunt, *Unworthy Republic: The Dispossession of Native Americans and the Road to Indian Territory* (New York: W. W. Norton, 2020); Stuart Banner, *How the Indians Lost Their Land: Law and Power on the Frontier* (Cambridge, MA: Harvard University Press, 2005), 191–227.

3.   For an excellent overview of the establishment and development of Upper Louisiana under French and Spanish rule, see William E. Foley, *The Genesis of Missouri: From Wilderness Outpost to Statehood* (Columbia: University of Missouri Press, 1989).

4.   Ysabel Sandoval, trans., "The Beginning of Spanish Missouri: Instructions, D'Ulloa to Rui, 1767," *Missouri Historical Society Collections* 3 (April 1908): quotations on 145, 152, 159; Gilbert C. Din, "Captain Francisco Ríu y Morales and the Beginnings of Spanish Rule in Missouri," *Missouri Historical Review* 94 (January 2000): 121–145; Jacob F. Lee, *Masters of the Middle Waters: Indian Nations and Colonial Ambitions along the Mississippi* (Cambridge, MA: Harvard University Press, 2019), 161–163.

5.   Stuart Banner, *Legal Systems in Conflict: Property and Sovereignty in Missouri, 1750–1860* (Norman: University of Oklahoma Press, 2000), quotation on 17; Robert R. Archibald, "From 'La Louisiane' to 'Luisiana': The Imposition of Spanish Administration in the Upper Mississippi Valley," *Gateway Heritage* 11 (Summer 1990): 26–33.

6. Sandoval, "The Beginning of Spanish Missouri: Instructions, D'Ulloa to Rui, 1767," quotations on 160; "Secret Instructions of Ulloa to Captain Rui, Dated January 7, 1767," in *The Spanish Regime in Missouri: A Collection of Papers and Documents Relating to Upper Louisiana Principally within the Present Limits of Missouri during the Dominion of Spain, From the Archives of the Indies at Seville*, ed. Louis Houck, 2 vols. (Chicago: R. R. Donnelley & Sons, 1909), quotation on 1:26; Abraham P. Nasatir, *Borderland in Retreat: From Spanish Louisiana to the Far Southwest* (Albuquerque: University of New Mexico Press, 1976), 9.

7. Foley, *The Genesis of Missouri*, 39; Carl H. Chapman, "The Indomitable Osage in Spanish Illinois (Upper Louisiana) 1763–1804," in *The Spanish in the Mississippi Valley, 1762–1804*, ed. John Francis McDermott (Urbana: University of Illinois Press, 1974), 287–308; "Report of Indian Traders, Given Passports by Don Francisco Cruzat, Dated November 28, 1777," in Houck, *The Spanish Regime in Missouri*, 1:139; Willard H. Rollings, *The Osage: An Ethnohistorical Study of Hegemony on the Prairie-Plains* (Columbia: University of Missouri Press, 1992), 137; Tai S. Edwards, *Osage Women and Empire: Gender and Power* (Lawrence: University Press of Kansas, 2018), 38–60.

8. Document No. 88, Petition by the inhabitants of Ste. Genevieve, July 3, 1779, in A. Lloyd Collins, comp., "Ste. Genevieve Archives: Translated from the Original French Language into English," Unpublished typescripts at Western Historical Manuscripts Collection, State Historical Society of Missouri, Columbia (quotation); "Letter of Governor Miro to Don Joseph Galvez, 1782," in Houck, *The Spanish Regime in Missouri*, quotation on 1:209; Cruzat to Miró, August 23, 1784, in "Spain in the Mississippi Valley, 1765–1794: Part II: Post War Decade, 1782–1791," *Annual Report of the American Historical Association for the Year 1945*, ed. Lawrence Kinnaird, Vol. III (Washington, DC: American Historical Association, 1946), quotation on 117; Abraham P. Nasatir, *Borderland in Retreat: From Spanish Louisiana to the Far Southwest* (Albuquerque: University of New Mexico Press, 1976), 35–66; John Bowes, *Land Too Good for Indians: Northern Indian Removal* (Norman: University of Oklahoma Press, 2017), 91–93.

9. Robert Englebert, "Colonial Encounters and the Changing Contours of Ethnicity: Pierre-Louis de Lorimier at the Edges of Empire," *Ohio Valley History* 18 (Spring 2018): 45–69.

10. "Official Letters of Louis Lorimier, 1787–1793," in Houck, *The Spanish Regime in Missouri*, quotation on 2:50–51; Linda Clark Nash, ed., *The Journals of Pierre-Louis de Lorimier, 1777–1795* (Montreal: Baraka Books, 2012), 76–77, 83–84, 105; "Letter of Instructions: Carondelet to Howard," *Missouri Historical Society Collections* 3 (January 1908): 86; Tanis C. Thorne, *The Many Hands of My Relations: French and Indians on the Lower Missouri* (Columbia: University of Missouri Press, 1996), 90–96; Carl J. Ekberg and William E. Foley, eds., *An Account of Upper Louisiana by Nicholas de Finiels* (Columbia: University of Missouri Press, 1989), 34–35, 41, 49; Walter

A. Schroeder, *Opening the Ozarks: A Historical Geography of Missouri's Ste. Genevieve District, 1760–1830* (Columbia: University of Missouri Press, 2002), 70, 373; Daniel H. Usner Jr., "An American Indian Gateway: Some Thoughts on the Migration and Settlement of Eastern Indians around Early St. Louis," *Gateway Heritage* 11 (Winter 1990–91): 42–51; Lynn Morrow, "Trader William Gilliss and Delaware Migration in Southern Missouri," *Missouri Historical Review* 75 (January 1981): 148–150.

11. *Missouri Guide*, 35–37, 524–25; Sami Lakomäki, *Gathering Together: The Shawnee People through Diaspora and Nationhood, 1600–1870* (New Haven, CT: Yale University Press, 2014), 171–172; Stephen Warren, *The Shawnees and Their Neighbors, 1795–1870* (Urbana: University of Illinois Press, 2005), 75–76.

12. Rollings, *The Osage*, 186; "Official Letters of Louis Lorimier, 1787–1793," in Houck, *The Spanish Regime in Missouri*, 2:51.

13. Ruby Matson Robins, ed., "The Missouri Reader: Americans in the Valley," pt. 1, *Missouri Historical Review* 45 (April 1951): 280–282; "Letter of Colonel George Morgan to Don Diego de Garoqui," in Houck, *The Spanish Regime in Missouri*, 1:286–309.

14. Jefferson quoted in Gilbert C. Din, "Spain's Immigration Policy in Louisiana and the American Penetration, 1792–1803," *Southwestern Historical Quarterly* 76 (January 1973): 255.

15. "Protest of Governor Miró against Grant to Col. George Morgan, Dated 1789," in Houck, *The Spanish Regime in Missouri*, quotations on 1:276–277; Gilbert C. Din, "The Immigration Policy of Governor Esteban Miró in Spanish Louisiana," *Southwestern Historical Quarterly* 73 (October 1969): 155–175; C. Richard Arena, "Land Settlement Policies and Practices in Spanish Louisiana," in McDermott, *The Spanish in the Mississippi Valley*, 51–60.

16. "Letter of Carondelet in Regard to the Formation of American Settlements on the Mississippi Below New Madrid, 1793," in Houck, *The Spanish Regime in Missouri*, 1:413; "Carondelet Reports on Danger of an American Settlement at the Ecores a Margo, 1793," in ibid., 2, 15–20.

17. Lynn Morrow, "New Madrid and Its Hinterland: 1783–1826," *Bulletin of the Missouri Historical Society* 36 (July 1980): 241–250.

18. "Official Letters to Louis Lorimier, 1787–1793," in Houck, *The Spanish Regime in Missouri*, quotation on 2:52; Nash, ed., *The Journals of Pierre-Louis de Lorimier*, 106–107; "Perez to Miro, November 8, 1791," in Nasatir, ed., *Before Lewis and Clark*, 1:149–150; "Trudeau to Carondelet, July 25, 1792," in ibid., 1:156–157; "Trudeau to Carondelet, March 2, 1793," in ibid., 1:167–169; "Trudeau to Carondelet, April 10, 1793," in ibid., 1:171–173; "Trudeau to Carondelet, July 13, 1793," in ibid., 1:185–186.

19. "A Fort among the Troublesome Osages–1795," in Houck, *The Spanish Regime in Missouri*, quotation on 2:104; Nash, ed., *The Journals of Pierre-Louis de Lorimier*, 142–145, 156–157; Ekberg, *Colonial Ste. Genevieve*, 101;

Gilbert C. Din and A. P. Nasatir, *The Imperial Osages: Spanish-Indian Diplomacy in the Mississippi Valley* (Norman: University of Oklahoma Press, 1983), 217–254; Lee, *Masters of the Middle Waters*, 179–185.

20. Jay Gitlin, *The Bourgeois Frontier: French Towns, French Traders, and American Expansion* (New Haven, CT: Yale University Press, 2010), 13–46; Patricia Cleary, *The World, the Flesh, and the Devil: A History of Colonial St. Louis* (Columbia: University of Missouri Press, 2011), 36–131; William E. Foley and David C. Rice, *The First Chouteaus: River Barons of Early St. Louis* (Urbana: University of Illinois Press, 1983), 45–54.

21. "Dealing of Americans with the Indians, 1795," from General Archives of the Indies. Seville. Department of Santo Domingo, Louisiana and Florida, Case 87; Drawer 1; Bundle 22 (Typescript in Papers from Spain, Missouri Historical Society, St. Louis), quotation on 16.

22. "Trudeau's Report Concerning the Settlements of the Spanish Illinois Country, 1798," in Houck, *The Spanish Regime in Missouri*, 2:255; see also "Expedition under Don Carlos Howard to Upper Louisiana, 1796," in ibid., 2:127; "Fear of English Invasion of Upper Louisiana, . . . 1800," in ibid., 2:285, 290.

23. "Trudeau's Report Concerning the Settlements of the Spanish Illinois Country, 1798," in Houck, *The Spanish Regime in Missouri*, quotation on 2:255.

24. Alan Taylor, *The Civil War of 1812: American Citizens, British Subjects, Irish Rebels, and Indian Allies* (New York: Random House, 2010), 49–68.

25. "Trudeau's Report Concerning the Settlements of the Spanish Illinois Country, 1798," in Houck, *The Spanish Regime in Missouri*, 2:256; Pierre Charles de Hault Delassus Deluzieres, *An Official Account of the Situation, Soil, Produce, &c. of That Part of Louisiana Which Lies Between the Mouth of the Missouri and New Madrid, or L'Anse a La Graise, and on the West Side of the Mississippi* (Lexington, KY: J. Bradford, 1796), 3–6.

26. Schroeder, *Opening the Ozarks*, quotation on 99.

27. George P. Garrison, ed., "A Memorandum of M. Austin's Journey from the Lead Mines in the Country of Wythe in the State of Virginia to the Lead Mines in the Province of Louisiana West of the Mississippi, 1796–1797," *American Historical Review* 5 (April 1900): quotation on 542. On Moses Austin, see David B. Gracy II, "Moses Austin and the Development of the Missouri Lead Industry," *Gateway Heritage* 1 (Spring 1981): 45; James Alexander Gardner, *Lead King: Moses Austin* (St. Louis: Sunrise, 1980).

28. Neal O. Hammon, ed., *My Father, Daniel Boone: The Draper Interviews with Nathan Boone* (Lexington: Kentucky University Press, 1999), 107–108. On the migration of the Boone family, see Ben L. Emmons, Letter [1926?], Western Historical Manuscripts Collection, C995, vol. 1, #16; John K. Hulston, "Daniel Boone's Sons in Missouri," *Missouri Historical Review* 47 (July 1947): 361–364; Hazel Atterbury Spraker, *The Boone Family: A Genealogical History of the Descendants of George and Mary Boone Who*

Came to America in 1717 (1922; repr. Baltimore: Genealogical Publishing Company, 1974), 127; Douglas Hurt, *Nathan Boone and the American Frontier* (Columbia: University of Missouri Press, 1998), 23–29; John Mack Faragher, *Daniel Boone: The Life and Legend of an American Pioneer* (New York: Henry Holt, 1992), 274–285.

29. Lyman C. Draper interview with Nathan and Olive Van Bibber Boone, October 25–November 9, 1851, Draper Mss. 6S222–224; Lawrence Elliott, *The Long Hunter: A New Life of Daniel Boone* (New York: Reader's Digest Press, 1976), 188; Faragher, *Daniel Boone*, 279; Meredith Mason Brown, *Frontiersman: Daniel Boone and the Making of America* (Baton Rouge: Louisiana State University Press, 2008), 229–230.

30. Draper interview with Nathan and Olive Van Bibber Boone, Draper Mss. 6S222–225; Faragher, *Daniel Boone*, 285–287.

31. Interview with Mrs. Elizabeth McCourtney, June 3–4, 1868, Draper Mss. 24S200–202; Interview with James Long, c. 1868, Draper Mss. 24S164–165; Interview with Elizabeth Musick, May 1868, Draper Mss. 22S168–170; Lakomäki, *Gathering Together*, 171; Stephen Warren, *The Shawnees and Their Neighbors, 1795–1870* (Urbana: University of Illinois Press, 2009), 78; Robert Morgan, *Boone: A Biography* (Chapel Hill, NC: Algonquin Books, 2007), 248.

32. John C. Boone to Lyman C. Draper, November 20, 1890, Draper Mss. 16C132, State Historical Society of Wisconsin, Madison (quotation); Interview with Nathan and Olive Van Bibber Boone, October 25–November 9, 1851, Draper Mss. 6S228; Elijah Bryan to Lyman C. Draper, October 23, 1884, Draper Mss. 4C34; Interview with Delinda Boone Craig, November 8–9, 1866, Draper Mss. 30C66–67; John Mack Faragher, "'More Motley Than Mackinac': From Ethnic Mixing to Ethnic Cleansing on the Frontier of the Lower Missouri, 1783–1833," in *Contact Points: American Frontiers from the Mohawk Valley to the Mississippi, 1750–1830*, ed. Andrew R. L. Cayton and Fredrika Teute (Chapel Hill: University of North Carolina Press, 1998), 309–313; Stephen Aron, "The Legacy of Daniel Boone: Three Generations of Boones and the History of Indian-White Relations," *Register of the Kentucky Historical Society* 95 (Summer 1997): 225–230.

33. Lyman C. Draper interview with Joseph McCormick, March 16, 1871, Draper Mss. 30C110–113 (quotations).

34. Ekberg and Foley, eds., *An Account of Upper Louisiana*, quotation on 52; Russell L. Gerlach, "Population Origins in Rural Missouri," *Missouri Historical Review* 71 (October 1976): 13; Schroeder, *Opening the Ozarks*, 10; James R. Shortridge, "The Expansion of the Settlement Frontier in Missouri," *Missouri Historical Review* 75 (October 1980): 67; Conevery Bolton Valencius, *The Health of the Country: How American Settlers Understood Themselves and Their Land* (New York: Basic Books, 2002).

35. Ekberg and Foley, eds., *An Account of Upper Louisiana*, 50, 55, 65; M. Perrin du Lac, *Travels through the Two Louisianas, and among the Savage Nations*

of the Missouri; Also, in the United States along the Ohio, and the Adjacent Provinces, in 1801, 1802, & 1803 (London: R. Phillips, 1807), 44. For similar considerations of creole ways and contrasts with American customs, see Volney, *View of the Climate and Soil of the United States of America*, 337–347; Georges-Victor Collot, *A Journey in North America, Containing a Survey of the Countries Watered by the Mississippi, Ohio, Missouri, and Other Affluing Rivers; With Exact Observations on the Course and Soundings of These Rivers; And on the Towns, Villages, Hamlets and Farms of that Part of the New-World; Followed by Philosophical, Political, Military and Commercial Remarks and a Projected Line of Frontiers and General Limits*, 2 vols. (Paris: A. Bertrand, 1826), 1:233, 248, 277.

36. Carl J. Ekberg, *French Roots in the Illinois Country: The Mississippi Frontier in Colonial Times* (Urbana: University of Illinois Press, 1998), 138–170; Ekberg, *Francois Vallé and His World: Upper Louisiana Before Lewis and Clark* (Columbia: University of Missouri Press, 2002), 158–202; Ekberg, *Stealing Indian Women: Native Slavery in the Illinois Country* (Urbana: University of Illinois Press, 2007), 9–94; Cécile Vidal, "From Incorporation to Exclusion: Indians, Europeans, and Americans in the Mississippi Valley from 1699–1830," in *Empires of the Imagination: Transatlantic Histories of the Louisiana Purchase*, ed. Peter J. Kastor and François Weil (Charlottesville: University of Virginia Press, 2009), 64.

37. Dick Steward, "'With the Scepter of a Tyrant': John Smith T and the Mineral Wars," *Gateway Heritage* 14 (Fall 1993): 28–29; Ekberg and Foley, eds., *An Account of Upper Louisiana*, 124; George P. Garrison, ed., "A Memorandum of M. Austin's Journey from the Lead Mines in the Country of Wythe in the State of Virginia to the Lead Mines in the Province of Louisiana West of the Mississippi, 1796–1797," *American Historical Review* 5 (April 1900): 519.

38. "Trudeau's Report Concerning the Settlements of the Spanish Illinois Country, 1798," in Houck, *The Spanish Regime in Missouri*, quotation on 2:256.

39. Meredith Mason Brown, *Frontiersman: Daniel Boone and the Making of America* (Baton Rouge: Louisiana State University Press, 2008), quotation on 134.

40. David B. Gracy II, *Moses Austin: His Life* (San Antonio: Trinity University Press, 1987), quotation on 115; James F. Keefe and Lynn Morrow, eds., *The White River Chronicles of S. C. Turnbo: Man and Wildlife on the Ozarks Frontier* (Fayetteville: University of Arkansas Press, 1994), 1–13; Lynn Morrow, "New Madrid and Its Hinterland," 241–242; Morrow, "Trader William Gilliss," 147–151; Usner, "An American Indian Gateway," 42–51; Stephen Aron, "The Legacy of Daniel Boone: Three Generations of Boones and the History of Indian-White Relations," *Register of the Kentucky Historical Society* 95 (Summer 1997): 225–230.

41. Nash, ed., *The Journals of Pierre-Louis de Lorimier*, 95–197.

42. Joseph Jackson quoted in Lakomäki, *Gathering Together*, 169.

43. Nash, ed., *The Journals of Pierre-Louis de Lorimier*, quotations on 109, 190; Ekberg and Foley, eds., *An Account of Upper Louisiana*, 90, 98; Zenon Trudeau to Baron Carondelet, March 12, 1795, in Nasatir, ed., *Before Lewis and Clark*, 1:317–319; "Trudeau's Report Concerning the Settlements of the Spanish Illinois Country, 1798," in Houck, *The Spanish Regime in Missouri*, 2:251; Thorne, *The Many Hands of My Relations*, 105; Rollings, *The Osage*, 191.

44. Thomas Jefferson to Robert Livingston, April 18, 1802, in Paul Leicester Ford, ed., *The Writings of Thomas Jefferson*, 10 vols. (New York: G. P. Putnam's Sons, 1892–1899), quotation on 8:144.

45. How the United States came to acquire peacefully the Louisiana Territory is concisely recounted in Walter Nugent, *Habits of Empire: A History of American Expansion* (New York: Vintage Books, 2008), 41–72, a book that contrasts this acquisition with the bloodier conquests that characterized much of the westward expansion of the United States.

46. Ames quoted in Richard White, "The Louisiana Purchase and the Fictions of Empire," in Kastor and Weil, eds., *Empires of the Imagination*, 38. The greater fiction at the time and in the textbook treatment of the Louisiana Purchase is the erasure of the Indian presence and perspectives. When these are included, the accounting of the costs of the Louisiana Purchase becomes much more expensive in both blood and treasure, a point powerfully detailed in Robert Lee, "Accounting for Conquest: The Price of the Louisiana Purchase of Indian Country," *Journal of American History* 103 (March 2017): 921–942.

47. Meriwether Lewis, November 23, 1803, in Gary E. Moulton, ed., *The Journals of the Lewis and Clark Expedition*, https://lewisandclarkjournals. unl.edu/item/lc.jrn.1803-11-23#lc.jrn.1803-11-23.01.

48. Ibid.

49. Thomas Jefferson, "Instructions to Meriwether Lewis," June 20, 1803, https://founders.archives.gov/documents/Jefferson/01-40-02-0136-0005 (quotation); James Ronda, *Lewis and Clark among the Indians* (Lincoln, NE: Bison Books, 1984), 1–16; William E. Foley, "The Lewis and Clark Expedition's Silent Partners: The Chouteau Brothers of St. Louis," *Missouri Historical Review* 77 (January 1983): 131–146.

50. William E. Foley, *A History of Missouri*, Vol. 1, *1673–1820* (Columbia: University of Missouri Press, 1971), quotation on 72.

51. J. Stille to Nathaniel Leonard, July 5, 1804, Army Papers, Missouri Historical Society, St. Louis (quotation); William Clark, May 31, 1804, in Moulton, ed., *The Journals of the Lewis and Clark Expedition*, https://lewisandclarkjournals.unl.edu/item/lc.jrn.1804-05-31#lc. jrn.1804-05-31.01.

52. Donald Jackson, *Thomas Jefferson and the Stony Mountains: Exploring the West from Monticello* (Urbana: University of Illinois Press, 1981), 34; Bernard Sheehan, *Seeds of Extinction: Jeffersonian Philanthropy and the*

American Indian (Chapel Hill: University of North Carolina Press, 1973), 245–250; Anthony F. C. Wallace, *Jefferson and the Indians: The Tragic Fate of the First Americans* (Cambridge, MA: Harvard University Press, 1999), 224, 248–257.

53. Amos Stoddard to H. Dearborn, June 3, 1804, in "Papers of Captain Amos Stoddard," in *Missouri Historical Society Glimpses of the Past* 2 (May–September 1935): 103–105.

54. Dorothy Penn, ed., "The Missouri Reader: The French in the Valley," pt. 2, *Missouri Historical Review* 40 (January 1946): 274–275; Amos Stoddard to H. Dearborn, June 3, 1804, in "Papers of Captain Amos Stoddard," in *Missouri Historical Society Glimpses of the Past* 2 (May–September 1935): 105–106; Ruby Matson Robins, ed., "The Missouri Reader: Americans in the Valley," pt. 1, *Missouri Historical Review* 45 (October 1950): 2–5; Russel L. Gerlach, *Settlement Patterns in Missouri: A Study of Population Origins with a Wall Map* (Columbia: University of Missouri Press, 1986), 15.

55. Hammon, ed., *My Father, Daniel Boone*, 122–123; R. Douglas Hurt, *Nathan Boone and the American Frontier* (Columbia: University of Missouri, 1998), 34–40; Rollings, *The Osage*, 184.

56. Schroeder, *Opening the Ozarks*, 375–377.

57. Ekberg and Foley, eds., *An Account of Upper Louisiana*, quotation on 34–35; Document No. 79, Manuel Gayoso de Lemos to chiefs and considered men of Shawnee Nation in the Illinois territory, May 17, 1799, in Collins, comp., "Ste. Genevieve Archives"; Perrin du Lac, *Travels through the Two Louisianas*, 45–46; Amos Stoddard, *Sketches, Historical and Descriptive, of Louisiana* (Philadelphia: Matthew Carey, 1812), 210, 215; Keefe and Morrow, eds., *The White River Chronicles of S. C. Turnbo*, 7; Schroeder, *Opening the Ozarks*, 374–375. On the emergence of syncretic cultural elements in eighteenth-century Pennsylvania, see Faragher, *Daniel Boone*, 17–23; Terry G. Jordan and Matti Kaups, *The American Backwoods Frontier: An Ethnic and Ecological Interpretation* (Baltimore: Johns Hopkins University Press, 1989). For the furthering of this process of cultural borrowings between Indians and Anglo-Americans in the Ohio Valley, see Stephen Aron, "Pigs and Hunters: 'Rights in the Woods' on the Trans-Appalachian Frontier," in *Contact Points: American Frontiers from the Mohawk Valley to the Mississippi, 1750–1830*, ed. Andrew R. L. Cayton and Fredrika J. Teute (Chapel Hill: University of North Carolina Press, 1998), 175–204; Aron, *How the West Was Lost*, 1–57, 102–123. And for the fruition of these developments in the confluence region, see Faragher, "'More Motley Than Mackinaw,'" 304–326.

58. Duncan C. Wilkie, "Archaeological Reconnaissance Survey of the Apple Creek Drainage: Perry and Cape Girardeau Counties, Missouri," Report prepared for the Historic Preservation Program, Division of Parks and Historic Preservation, Missouri Department of Natural Resources (Jefferson City: Missouri Department of Natural Resources, 1984), 153–154.

59. Stoddard, *Sketches, Historical and Descriptive of Louisiana*, quotation on 215.

60. Schroeder, *Opening the Ozarks*, 375–377.

61. Meriwether Lewis, November 25, 1803, in Moulton, ed., *The Journals of the Lewis and Clark Expedition*, https://lewisandclarkjournals.unl.edu/item/lc.jrn.1803-11-25 (quotation); Stoddard, *Sketches, Historical and Descriptive of Louisiana*, 215.

Chapter 3

1. William Clark, November 24, 1805, quotations in Gary Moulton, ed., *The Journals of the Lewis and Clark Expedition*, https://lewisandclarkjournals.unl.edu/item/lc.jrn.1805-11-24.

2. Ibid.

3. On past and recent commemorations of the Lewis and Clark expedition, see the essays in Kris Fresonke and Mark Spence, eds., *Lewis and Clark: Legacies, Memories, and New Perspectives* (Berkeley: University of California Press, 2004), 155–282. I have also examined the changing ways in which the Lewis and Clark expedition has been remembered through various anniversaries in "The Afterlives of Lewis and Clark," *Southern California Quarterly* 87 (Spring 2005): 27–46; and "The 'We' in West," *Western Historical Quarterly* 49 (Spring 2018): 1–15.

4. In addition to "the vote," the other incident from the winter at Fort Clatsop that figured prominently in bicentennial productions was the excursion in early January 1806 to see a beached whale. As Lewis reported, "the Indian woman" (referring to Sacagawea) "was very importunate to be permitted to go," having "traveled a long way to see the great waters, and that now that monstrous fish was also to be seen," the captains "indulged" her. Not much to go on, but from that spare account, bicentennial productions spun "wishtories" about female empowerment and inclusivity. See Meriwether Lewis, January 6, 1806, in Moulton, ed., *The Journals of the Lewis and Clark Expedition*, https://lewisandclarkjournals.unl.edu/item/lc.jrn.1806-01-06 (quotation).

5. The President to Meriwether Lewis, January 22, 1804, in Clarence E. Carter, ed., *The Territorial Papers of the United States*, Vol. 13, *The Territory of Louisiana-Missouri, 1803–1806* (Washington, DC: United States National Archives and Records, 1948), quotations on 15.

6. Thomas Jefferson to Robert Patterson, March 2, 1803, in Donald Jackson, ed., *The Letters of the Lewis and Clark Expedition with Related Documents, 1783–1854*, 2 vols. (Urbana: University of Illinois Press, 1978), quotation on 1:21.

7. John Logan Allen, "Imagining the West: The View from Monticello," in *Thomas Jefferson and the Changing West*, ed. James P. Ronda (Albuquerque: University of New Mexico Press, 1997), 3–23; James P. Ronda, *Finding the West: Explorations with Lewis and Clark* (Albuquerque: University of New Mexico Press, 2001), 12; William Clark,

January 21, 1804, in Moulton, ed., *The Journals of the Lewis and Clark Expedition*, https://lewisandclarkjournals.unl.edu/item/lc.jrn.1804-01-21-1.

8. Appendix A in Moulton, ed., *The Journals of the Lewis and Clark Expedition*, https://lewisandclarkjournals.unl.edu/item/lc.jrn.v02.appendix.a, provides excellent capsule biographies of the members of the Corps and of their recruitment.

9. William Clark, January 10, 1804, in ibid., https://lewisandclarkjournals.unl.edu/item/lc.jrn.1804-01-10#lc.jrn.1804-01-10.01; Meriwether Lewis to Thomas Jefferson, December 19, 1803 and December 28, 1803, in Jackson, ed., *The Letters of Lewis and Clark Expedition*, 1:145–147, 148–156; James Ronda, *Lewis and Clark among the Indians* (Lincoln: University of Nebraska Press, 1984), 1–16; William E. Foley, "The Lewis and Clark Expedition's Silent Partners: The Chouteau Brothers of St. Louis," *Missouri Historical Review* 77 (January 1983): 131–146.

10. On the role and importance of peace medals in this diplomacy, see Francis Paul Prucha, *Peace and Friendship: Indian Peace Medals in American History* (Madison: State Historical Society of Wisconsin, 1971); Paul R. Cutright, "Lewis and Clark Indian Peace Medals," *Bulletin of the Missouri Historical Society* 24 (January 1968): 160–167.

11. William Clark, August 3, 1804, in Moulton, ed., *The Journals of the Lewis and Clark Expedition*, https://lewisandclarkjournals.unl.edu/item/lc.jrn.1804-08-03 (quotations).

12. On the encounter with the Lakotas, see James Ronda, *Lewis and Clark among the Indians* (Lincoln: University of Nebraska Press, 1984), 27–41; Jeffrey Ostler, *The Plains Sioux and U.S. Colonialism from Lewis and Clark to Wounded Knee* (Cambridge: Cambridge University Press, 2004), 18–21; Pekka Hämäläinen, *Lakota America: A New History of Indigenous Power* (New Haven, CT: Yale University Press, 2019), 127–143.

13. See the entries for September 26, 1804, by William Clark, John Ordway, Patrick Gass, and Joseph Whitehouse, in Moulton, ed., *The Journals of the Lewis and Clark Expedition*, https://lewisandclarkjournals.unl.edu/item/lc.jrn.1804-09-26.

14. See the entries for September 27, 1804, by William Clark (quotation), John Ordway, Patrick Gass, and Joseph Whitehouse, in ibid., https://lewisandclarkjournals.unl.edu/item/lc.jrn.1804-09-27#lc.jrn.1804-09-27.04; and for September 28, 1804, by the same men, in ibid., https://lewisandclarkjournals.unl.edu/item/lc.jrn.1804-09-28.

15. William Clark, Estimate of the Eastern Indians, Part 2, Winter 1804–1805, in ibid., https://lewisandclarkjournals.unl.edu/item/lc.jrn.1804-1805.winter.part2#lc.jrn.1804-1805.winter.part1.01 (quotations).

16. Peter Onuf, "'We Shall All Be Americans': Thomas Jefferson and the Indians," *Indiana Magazine of History* 95 (June 1999): 103–141; Robert M. Owens, "Jeffersonian Benevolence on the Ground: The Indian Land Cession Treaties of William Henry Harrison," *Journal of the Early Republic* 22 (Fall 2002): 405–435; Anthony F. C. Wallace, *Jefferson and the*

Indians: The Tragic Fate of the First Americans (Cambridge, MA: Harvard University Press, 1999).

17.   For an incisive exploration of Lakota politics and how little Lewis and Clark understood about it, see Hämäläinen, *Lakota America*, 118–163.

18.   William Clark, October 15, 1804, in Moulton, ed., *The Journals of the Lewis and Clark Expedition*, https://lewisandclarkjournals.unl.edu/item/ lc.jrn.1804-10-15 (quotation). See also Ronda, *Lewis and Clark among the Indians*, 36–37, 62–64, 106–107, 208–210, 232–233; William R. Swagerty, *The Indianization of Lewis and Clark*, 2 vols. (Norman: University of Oklahoma Press, 2012), 2:557–617.

19.   Carolyn Gilman, *Lewis and Clark: Across the Divide* (Washington, DC: Smithsonian, 2003), 111–133.

20.   Carolyn Gilman, "A World of Women," *Gateway Heritage* 24 (Fall 2003– Winter 2004): quotation on 46; for a Nez Perce version of the Lewis and Clark expedition, including details about William Clark's reputed offspring, see "William Clark's Nez Perce Son: A Tsoopnitpeloo Legend as Told by Otis Halfmoon of the Nez Perce Tribe," *Discovering Lewis and Clark: A Legacy Website*, http://www.lewis-clark.org/index.htm.

21.   Ronda, *Lewis and Clark among the Indians*, quotation on 64.

22.   Annie H. Abel, ed., *Tabeau's Narrative of Loisel's Expedition to the Upper Missouri* (Norman: University of Oklahoma Press, 1939), quotation on 197.

23.   In coming to this conclusion, I follow Ronda, *Lewis and Clark among the Indians*, 67–112 and *passim*.

24.   Elizabeth Fenn, *Encounters at the Heart of the World: A History of the Mandan People* (New York: Macmillan, 2014), 205–228.

25.   William Clark, Part 2: Estimate of the Eastern Indians, Winter 1804–1805, in Moulton, ed., *The Journals of the Lewis and Clark Expedition*, https:// lewisandclarkjournals.unl.edu/item/lc.jrn.1804-1805.winter.part2#lc. jrn.1804-1805.winter.part1.01 (quotation); Fenn, *Encounters at the Heart of the World*, 208–213.

26.   Virginia Scharff, *Twenty Thousand Roads: Women, Movement, and the West* (Berkeley: University of California Press, 2003), 11–33; Thomas P. Slaughter, *Exploring Lewis and Clark: Reflections on Men and Wilderness* (New York: Random House, 2003), 86–113; Laura McCall, "Sacagawea: A Historical Enigma," in *Ordinary Women, Extraordinary Lives: Women in American History*, ed. Kriste Lindenmeyer (Wilmington, DE: SR Books, 2000), 39–54; Angela Cavender Wilson, "A New Encounter: The Native Oral Tradition of Lewis and Clark," in *Lewis and Clark: Journey to Another America*, ed. Alan Taylor (Ann Arbor: University of Michigan Press, 2003), 196–197, 208–210; Larry E. Morris, *The Fate of the Corps: What Became of the Lewis and Clark Explorers after the Expedition* (New Haven, CT: Yale University Press, 2004), 106–117, 210–213.

27.   Meriwether Lewis, July 28, 1805, in Moulton, ed., *The Journals of the Lewis and Clark Expedition*, https://lewisandclarkjournals.unl.edu/ item/lc.jrn.1805-07-28#lc.jrn.1805-07-28.01 (quotation); William Clark,

December 29, 1805, in ibid., https://lewisandclarkjournals.unl.edu/
item/lc.jrn.1805-12-29#lc.jrn.1805-12-29.01; William Clark, undated
Winter 1804–1805, in ibid., https://lewisandclarkjournals.unl.edu/item/
lc.jrn.1804-1805.winter.part5#lc.jrn.1804-1805.winter.part5.03. For an
incisive assessment of the blind spots displayed by Lewis and Clark and
other members of the Corps of Discovery when it came to their views of
Sacagawea, Indian women, and white women in the United States, see
Gilman, *Lewis and Clark*, 111–133.

28. Meriwether Lewis, August 17, 1805 ("really affecting"), in Moulton, ed.,
The Journals of the Lewis and Clark Expedition, https://lewisandclarkjourn
als.unl.edu/item/lc.jrn.1805-08-17#lc.jrn.1805-08-17.01; William Clark,
October 13, 1805 ("The Wife"), in ibid., https://lewisandclarkjournals.unl.
edu/item/lc.jrn.1805-10-13#lc.jrn.1805-10-13.01.

29. John Ordway, March 22, 1806, in ibid., https://lewisandclarkjournals.unl.
edu/item/lc.jrn.1806-03-22#lc.jrn.1806-03-22.03 (quotation).

30. Elliott Coues, ed., *New Light on the Early History of the Greater
Northwest: The Manuscript Journals of Alexander Henry the Younger
and of David Thompson*, 2 vols. (1897; reprint, London: Forgotten
Books, 1965), 1:349–350; Candace S. Greene and Russell Thornton,
eds., *The Year the Stars Fell: Lakota Winter Counts at the Smithsonian*
(Lincoln: University of Nebraska Press, 2007), 133–141; Colin G. Calloway,
One Vast Winter Count: The Native American West before Lewis and Clark
(Lincoln: University of Nebraska Press, 2003), 428–430.

31. Clark quoted in Jay H. Buckley, *William Clark: Indian Diplomat*
(Norman: University of Oklahoma Press, 2008), 112.

32. William Clark, November 7, 1805, in Moulton, ed., *The Journals of the
Lewis and Clark Expedition*, https://lewisandclarkjournals.unl.edu/item/
lc.jrn.1805-11-16#lc.jrn.1805-11-16.05 (quotation).

33. William Clark, March 12, 1806, in ibid., https://lewisandclarkjourn
als.unl.edu/item/lc.jrn.1806-03-12#lc.jrn.1806-03-12.03 (quotation);
Swagerty, *The Indianization of Lewis and Clark*, 1:191–218, 261–314. For
the log of miles traveled, see William Clark, undated, Winter 1805–1806,
Part 1: Estimated Distances from Fort Mandan to the Pacific Coast, in
Moulton, ed., *The Journals of the Lewis and Clark Expedition*, https://
lewisandclarkjournals.unl.edu/item/lc.jrn.1805-1806.winter.part1#lc.
jrn.1805-1806.winter.part1.01.

34. Meriwether Lewis, July 13, 1805, in ibid., https://lewisandclarkjournals.
unl.edu/item/lc.jrn.1804-1805.winter.part2#lc.jrn.1804-1805.winter.part1.01
(quotation); Meriwether Lewis, February 24, 1806, in ibid., https://lewisa
ndclarkjournals.unl.edu/item/lc.jrn.1806-02-24#lc.jrn.1806-02-24.01
(quotation); William Clark, November 22, 1805, ibid., https://lewisandcl
arkjournals.unl.edu/item/lc.jrn.1805-11-22#lc.jrn.1805-11-22.03 (quotation);
Swagerty, *The Indianization of Lewis and Clark*, 1:261–343; ibid., 2:345–484;
Albert Furtwangler, *Acts of Discovery: Visions of America in the Lewis and
Clark Journals* (Urbana: University of Illinois Press, 1999), 91–109.

35. William Clark, December 7, 1805, in Moulton, ed., *The Journals of the Lewis and Clark Expedition*, https://lewisandclarkjournals.unl.edu/item/ lc.jrn.1805-12-07#lc.jrn.1805-12-07.02 (quotation).

36. Patrick Gass, May 7, 1806, in ibid., https://lewisandclarkjournals.unl.edu/ item/lc.jrn.1806-05-07#lc.jrn.1806-05-07.04 (quotation); Swagerty, *The Indianization of Lewis and Clark*, quotation on 2:425.

37. Patrick Gass, March 20, 1806, in Moulton, ed., *The Journals of the Lewis and Clark Expedition*, https://lewisandclarkjournals.unl.edu/item/ lc.jrn.1806-03-20#lc.jrn.1806-03-20.04 (quotation). Gass estimated 131 elk killed; Joseph Whitehouse tallied 155. They agreed on the number of deer.

38. William Clark, November 23, 1805, in Moulton, ed., *The Journals of the Lewis and Clark Expedition*, https://lewisandclarkjournals.unl.edu/item/ lc.jrn.1805-11-23 (quotation); William Clark, December 9, 1805, in ibid., https://lewisandclarkjournals.unl.edu/item/lc.jrn.1805-12-09.

39. William Clark, December 10, 1805, in ibid., https://lewisandclarkjournals. unl.edu/item/lc.jrn.1805-12-10 (quotation).

40. William Clark, December 12, 1805, in ibid., https://lewisandclarkjourn als.unl.edu/item/lc.jrn.1805-12-12#lc.jrn.1805-12-12.03; William Clark, December 20, 1805, in ibid., https://lewisandclarkjournals.unl.edu/item/ lc.jrn.1805-12-20.

41. William Clark, December 24, 1805, in ibid., https://lewisandclarkjournals. unl.edu/item/lc.jrn.1805-12-24 (quotation).

42. Meriwether Lewis, January 6, 1806, in ibid., https://lewisandclarkjourn als.unl.edu/item/lc.jrn.1806-01-06 (quotation). Although Lewis and Clark stridently condemned the sexual relations of coastal Indians, the captains were more generous in their broader assessment of gender roles. "In common with other savage nations they make their women perform every species of domestic drudgery," wrote Lewis, "but in almost every species of this drudgery the men also participate." Moreover, "notwithstanding the survile manner in which they treat their women they pay much more rispect to their judgment and oppinions in many rispects than most indian nations; their women are permitted to speak freely before them, and sometimes appear to command with a tone of authority; they generally consult them in their traffic and act in conformity to their opinions." Meriwether Lewis, January 6, 1806, ibid.

43. Meriwether Lewis, January 4, 1806, in ibid., https://lewisandclarkjourn als.unl.edu/item/lc.jrn.1806-01-04#lc.jrn.1806-01-04.01 (quotations); William Clark, December 30, 1805, in ibid., https://lewisandclarkjourn als.unl.edu/item/lc.jrn.1805-12-30; Meriwether Lewis, February 20, 1806, in ibid., https://lewisandclarkjournals.unl.edu/item/lc.jrn.1806-02-20#lc. jrn.1806-02-20.03.

44. Meriwether Lewis, January 1, 1806, in ibid., https://lewisandclarkjournals. unl.edu/item/lc.jrn.1806-01-01 (quotations).

45. Meriwether Lewis, February 28, 1806, in ibid., https://lewisandclarkjourn als.unl.edu/item/lc.jrn.1806-02-28 (quotation, italics added). Both Lewis

and Clark used the same verb ("suffer") to describe Indian overnight guests on March 17–18, 1806, in ibid., https://lewisandclarkjournals.unl.edu/item/lc.jrn.1806-03-18; Meriwether Lewis, February 24, 1806, and Joseph Whitehouse, February 24, 1806, in ibid., https://lewisandclarkjournals.unl.edu/item/lc.jrn.1806-02-24.

46. William Clark, December 29, 1805, in ibid., https://lewisandclarkjournals.unl.edu/item/lc.jrn.1805-12-29#lc.jrn.1805-12-29.01 (quotation).

47. Carolyn Gilman, *Lewis and Clark: Across the Divide* (Washington, DC: Smithsonian, 2003), 246–247; Ronda, *Lewis and Clark among the Indians*, 208–210; Swagerty, *The Indianization of Lewis and Clark*, 2:596–606.

48. Meriwether Lewis, March 15, 1806, in Moulton, ed., *The Journals of the Lewis and Clark Expedition*, https://lewisandclarkjournals.unl.edu/item/lc.jrn.1806-03-15#lc.jrn.1806-03-15.04 (quotation); Meriwether Lewis, March 17, 1806, in ibid., https://lewisandclarkjournals.unl.edu/item/lc.jrn.1806-03-17.

49. William Clark, November 21, 1805, in ibid., https://lewisandclarkjournals.unl.edu/item/lc.jrn.1805-11-21#lc.jrn.1805-11-21.01.

50. Meriwether Lewis, March 17, 1806, in ibid., https://lewisandclarkjournals.unl.edu/item/lc.jrn.1806-03-17#lc.jrn.1806-03-17.05 (quotations).

51. Meriwether Lewis, March 17, 1806, in ibid., https://lewisandclarkjournals.unl.edu/item/lc.jrn.1806-03-17#lc.jrn.1806-03-17.05 (quotations).

52. Meriwether Lewis, March 17, 1806, in ibid., https://lewisandclarkjournals.unl.edu/item/lc.jrn.1806-03-17#lc.jrn.1806-03-17.05; Meriwether Lewis, February 12, 1806, in ibid., https://lewisandclarkjournals.unl.edu/item/lc.jrn.1806-02-12#lc.jrn.1806-02-12.03.

53. John Ordway, March 18, 1806, in ibid., https://lewisandclarkjournals.unl.edu/item/lc.jrn.1806-03-18#lc.jrn.1806-03-18.03 (quotations).

54. William Clark, March 19, 1806, in ibid., https://lewisandclarkjournals.unl.edu/item/lc.jrn.1806-03-19 (quotations); William Clark, March 23, 1806, in ibid., https://lewisandclarkjournals.unl.edu/item/lc.jrn.1806-03-23.

55. Meriwether Lewis, March 19, 1806, in ibid., https://lewisandclarkjournals.unl.edu/item/lc.jrn.1806-03-20 (quotation).

56. Clark included this quotation in his journal entry of November 30, 1805. Lewis did the same in his of January 9, 1806, in ibid., https://lewisandclarkjournals.unl.edu/item/lc.jrn.1805-11-30#lc.jrn.1805-11-30.03 and https://lewisandclarkjournals.unl.edu/item/lc.jrn.1806-01-09#lc.jrn.1806-01-09.01.

57. Ronda, *Lewis and Clark among the Indians*, 202–203.

58. Meriwether Lewis, January 4, 1806, in Moulton, ed., *The Journals of the Lewis and Clark Expedition*, https://lewisandclarkjournals.unl.edu/item/lc.jrn.1806-01-04#lc.jrn.1806-01-04.01 (quotation).

59. Ronda, *Lewis and Clark among the Indians*, 182–184, 191–192, 208–210; Swagerty, *The Indianization of Lewis and Clark*, 2:588.

60. Meriwether Lewis, February 20, 1806, in Moulton, ed., *The Journals of the Lewis and Clark Expedition*, https://lewisandclarkjournals.unl.edu/item/lc.jrn.1806-02-20#lc.jrn.1806-02-20.03 (quotations).

Chapter 4

1. Jefferson quoted in Betty Houchin Winfield, "Public Perception of the Expedition," in *Lewis and Clark: Journey to Another America*, ed. Alan Taylor (St. Louis: Missouri Historical Society Press, 2003), 187. A report on the reception given Lewis and Clark upon their return to St. Louis appeared in the Frankfort, Kentucky, newspaper *The Western World* on October 11, 1806, and is reprinted in James P. Ronda, ed., *Voyages of Discovery: Essays on the Lewis and Clark Expedition* (Helena: Montana Historical Society Press, 1998), 203–205.

2. Meriwether Lewis, April 11, 1806, in Gary E. Moulton, ed., *Journals of the Lewis and Clark Expedition*, https://lewisandclarkjournals.unl.edu/item/lc.jrn.1806-04-11#lc.jrn.1806-04-11.01 (quotation).

3. William Clark, May 17, 1806, in Moulton, ed., *Journals of the Lewis and Clark Expedition*, https://lewisandclarkjournals.unl.edu/item/lc.jrn.1806-05-17#lc.jrn.1806-05-17.02 ("icy barrier"); Meriwether Lewis, June 8, 1806, in ibid., https://lewisandclarkjournals.unl.edu/item/lc.jrn.1806-06-08#lc.jrn.1806-06-08.01 ("As we have not time").

4. Meriwether Lewis, July 27, 1806, in ibid,, https://lewisandclarkjournals.unl.edu/item/lc.jrn.1806-07-27#lc.jrn.1806-07-27.01.

5. William Clark, August 30, 1806, in ibid., https://lewisandclarkjournals.unl.edu/item/lc.jrn.1806-08-30#lc.jrn.1806-08-30.03 (quotation); Larry E. Morris, *The Fate of the Corps: What Became of the Lewis and Clark Explorers after the Expedition* (New Haven, CT: Yale University Press, 2004), 5–22.

6. For the captains' assessment of their success in finding the best route, see William Clark, February 14, 1806, in Moulton, ed., *Journals of the Lewis and Clark Expedition*, https://lewisandclarkjournals.unl.edu/item/lc.jrn.1806-02-14#lc.jrn.1806-02-14.02.

7. James R. Bentley, ed., "Two Letters of Meriwether Lewis to Major William Preston," *Filson Club History Quarterly* 44 (April 1970): quotation on 172.

8. Stephen Aron, *American Confluence: The Missouri Frontier from Borderland to Border State* (Bloomington: Indiana University Press, 2006), 115–127.

9. "Frederick Bates to Richard Bates, May 31, 1807," in *Life and Papers of Frederick Bates*, ed. Thomas Maitland Marshall, 2 vols. (St. Louis: Missouri Historical Society, 1926): quotation on 1:137–138.

10. Patricia Tyson Stroud, *Bitterroot: The Life and Death of Meriwether Lewis* (Philadelphia: University of Pennsylvania Press, 2018), 196–215.

11. Meriwether Lewis, "Observations and reflections on the present and future state of Upper Louisiana, in relation to the government of the Indian nations inhabiting that country, and the trade and intercourse with the same," [August 1807], in *Letters of the Lewis and Clark Expedition with Related Documents, 1783–1854*, ed. Donald Jackson, 2 vols. (Urbana: University of Illinois Press, 1978), quotation on 700 (italics in original).

12. Ibid., quotation on 714.

13. Ibid., quotations on 704.

14. On Lewis's lack of understanding of local politics in Upper Louisiana and the reception he received upon his return to the territory, see Richard Dillon, *Meriwether Lewis: A Biography* (New York: Coward-McCann, 1965), 288–300.

15. Meriwether Lewis's Receipt Book, Meriwether Lewis Collection, Missouri Historical Society, St. Louis.

16. On the influence of the Chouteaus, see William E. Foley and C. David Rice, *The First Chouteaus: River Barons of Early St. Louis* (Champaign and Urbana: University of Illinois Press, 1983), 87–104.

17. William E. Foley, "James A. Wilkinson: Territorial Governor," *Bulletin of the Missouri Historical Society* 25 (1968): 3–17; Andro Linklater, *An Artist in Treason: The Extraordinary Double Life of General James Wilkinson, Commander in Chief of the U.S. Army and Agent 13 in the Spanish Secret Service* (New York: Walker Books, 2009), 218–246; Jay Gitlin, *The Bourgeois Frontier: French Towns, French Traders & American Expansion* (New Haven, CT: Yale University Press, 2010), 47–67; Stuart Banner, *Legal Systems in Conflict: Property and Sovereignty in Missouri, 1750–1860* (Norman: University of Oklahoma Press, 2000), 90–98.

18. "Frederic Bates to Richard Bates, March 24, 1808," in *The Life and Papers of Frederic Bates*, ed. Thomas Maitland Marshall, 2 vols. (St. Louis: Missouri Historical Society, 1926), 1:316–317; "Lewis to Dearborn, July 1, 1808," in *The Territorial Papers of the United States, Vol. 15, The Territory of Louisiana-Missouri, 1815–1821*, ed. Clarence E. Carter (Washington, DC: Department of State, 1951, 14:196–203.

19. Jefferson quoted in J. Frederick Fausz, "Becoming 'a Nation of Quakers': The Removal of the Osage Indians from Missouri," *Gateway Heritage* 21 (Summer 2000): 32.

20. Christian Schultz, *Travels on an Inland Voyage through the States of New York, Pennsylvania, Virginia, Ohio, Kentucky, and Tennessee, and through the Territories of Indiana, Louisiana, Mississippi, and New Orleans; Performed in the Years 1807 and 1808; Including a Tour of Nearly Six Thousand Miles*, 2 vols. (New York: Isaac Riley, 1810), 2:94; Stoddard, *Sketches, Historical and Descriptive, of Louisiana*, 215; "Frederic Bates to Meriwether Lewis, April 28, 1807," in Marshall, *The Life and Papers of Frederic Bates*, 1:105; Daniel H. Usner Jr., "An American Indian Gateway: Some Thoughts on the Migration and Settlement of Eastern Indians around Early St. Louis," *Gateway Heritage* 11 (Winter 1990–1991): 43.

21. "Frederic Bates to Richard Bates, March 24, 1808," in Marshall, *The Life and Papers of Frederic Bates*, 1:316–317; "Lewis to Dearborn, July 1, 1808," in Carter, *Territorial Papers*, 14:196–203.

22. Kate L. Gregg, ed., *Westward with Dragoons: The Journal of William Clark on His Expedition to Establish Fort Osage, August 25 to September 22, 1808* (Fulton, MO: Ovid Bell Press, 1937), quotation on 58; Neal O. Hammon, ed., *My Father, Daniel Boone: The Draper Interviews with*

Nathan Boone (Lexington: University Press of Kentucky, 1999), quotation on 126; Tai S. Edwards, *Osage Women and Empire: Gender and Power* (Lawrence: University Press of Kansas, 2018), 61–92.

23. "William Clark to Henry Dearborn, September 23, 1808," in Carter, *Territorial Papers*, 14:224–228; Gregg, ed., *Westward with Dragoons*, quotation on 41. The full text of Clark's 1808 treaty with the Osages is printed on pages 64–68.

24. "Governor Lewis to Pierre Chouteau, October 3, 1808," in Carter, *Territorial Papers*, 14:229; Governor Meriwether Lewis to President Thomas Jefferson, December 15, 1808, in McCarter & English Indian Claim Cases, Box 18, Folder 4, Exhibit 144 (quotations); Rollings, *The Osage*, 227–229.

25. Fausz, "Becoming a Nation of Quakers," 37.

26. Meriwether Lewis to President Thomas Jefferson, December 15, 1808, in McCarter & English Indian Claim Cases, Box 18, Folder 4, Exhibit 144 (quotations); Meriwether Lewis to Thomas Jefferson, December 15, 1808, Thomas Jefferson Papers, National Archives, Founders Online (quotations).

27. "Governor Lewis to Pierre Chouteau, October 3, 1808," in Carter, *Territorial Papers*, 14:229; William Clark, "Part 2: Estimate of Eastern Indians," Winter 1804–1805, in Moulton, *Journals of the Lewis & Clark Expedition*, https://lewisandclarkjournals.unl.edu/item/lc.jrn.1804-1805.win ter.part2#lc.jrn.1804-1805.winter.part1.01; Meriwether Lewis to President Thomas Jefferson, December 15, 1808, in McCarter & English Indian Claim Cases, Box 18, Folder 4, Exhibit 144; Rollings, *The Osages*, 227–229.

28. Stoddard, *Sketches, Historical and Descriptive of Louisiana*, 215; Brooks Blevins, *A History of the Ozarks*, Vol. 1, *The Old Ozarks* (Champaign and Urbana: University of Illinois Press, 2018), 33, Schroeder, *Opening the Ozarks*, 375–376, 391, 394, 396.

29. "Louis Lorimier to Acting Governor Browne, February 19, 1807," in Carter, *Territorial Papers*, 14:112; "Petition of Louis Lorimier in the name and behalf of the Shawnee and Delaware Indians, settled within the Territory of Louisiana," August 16, 1806, Indian Collections, Missouri Historical Society, St. Louis.

30. Meriwether Lewis, "A Proclamation," in Marshall, *The Life and Papers of Frederic Bates*, 1:337–340; Schroeder, *Opening the Ozarks*, 167–173; Aron, *American Confluence*, 144–145.

31. "Proclamation by Governor Lewis, April 6, 1809," in Carter, *Territorial Papers*, 14:261 (quotations).

32. "Frederick Bates to Richard Bates, July 14, 1809," in Marshall, *The Life and Papers of Frederick Bates*, 2: 68 (quotation).

33. Stroud, *Bitterroot*, 248–285.

34. For careful siftings of evidence and presentation of differing views about Lewis's death, see John D. W. Guice, ed., *By His Own Hand? The Mysterious Death of Meriwether Lewis* (Norman: University of Oklahoma Press, 2006); Morris, *The Fate of the Corps*, 54–74, 203–209. For a taste of the more conspiratorial speculations and accusations, see Paul Schrag and Xaviant

Haze, *The Suppressed History of America: The Murder of Meriwether Lewis and the Mysterious Discoveries of the Lewis and Clark Expedition* (Rochester, VT: Bear, 2011), in which the authors claim a powerful cabal orchestrated Lewis's assassination to keep him from revealing the evidence that the explorers had found of ancient visitors to the Americas. These records, the authors allege, later vanished when Smithsonian executive John Wesley Powell and his colleagues decided that, for humanity's good, they had best systematically destroy the proof about the European origins of American Indians.

35.   William Clark to Toussaint Charboneau, August 20, 1806, in William Clark Papers, Missouri Historical Society, St. Louis (quotation). Although one might expect a love affair between Clark and Sacagawea to be featured in bicentennial productions about the Lewis and Clark expedition, the better example comes from the sesquicentennial, principally in the 1955 feature film *The Far Horizons*. In the film, Clark, played by Charlton Heston, and Sacagawea, with Donna Reed cast in the role, have a romantic sub-plot. In 2011, *Time* magazine listed *The Far Horizons* as one of the ten most historically misleading films. See Frances Romero, "The Far Horizons," *Time*, January 25, 2011, http://entertainm ent.time.com/2011/01/26/top-10-historically-misleading-films/slide/the-far-horizons-1955/.

36.   Jay H. Buckley, *William Clark: Indian Diplomat* (Norman: University of Oklahoma Press, 2008), xiii–xvi, 113.

37.   "William Clark to James Madison, April 10, 1811," and "William Eustis to William Clark," in Carter, *Territorial Papers*, 14:452 (quotations).

38.   Julia Hancock Clark quoted in Landon Y. Jones Jr., "The Council That Changed the West: William Clark at Portage des Sioux," *Gateway Heritage* 24 (Fall 2003–Winter 2004): 89.

39.   "William Clark to the Secretary of War, August 20, 1814," in Carter, *Territorial Papers*, 14:786 (quotation).

40.   *Missouri Gazette*, May 28, 1814.

41.   Clark quoted in Robert Lee, "The Boon's Lick Land Rush and the Coming of the Missouri Crisis," in *A Fire Bell in the Past: The Missouri Crisis at 200*, Vol. 1, *Western Slavery, National Impasse*, ed. Jeff Pasley and John Craig Hammond (Columbia: University of Missouri Press, 2021), 86.

42.   Robert L. Fisher, "The Treaties of Portage des Sioux," *Mississippi Valley Historical Review* 19 (March 1933): 495–508.

43.   "A Proclamation by Governor Clark," March 9, 1815, in Carter, *Territorial Papers*, quotation on 41; Lee, "The Boon's Lick Land Rush and the Coming of the Missouri Crisis," 77–112.

44.   "Talks," in *American State Papers. Class II. Indian Affairs*, 2 vols. (Washington, DC: Gales and Seaton, 1834), 2:11 (quotations); Sami Lakomäki, *Gathering Together: The Shawnee People through Diaspora and Nationhood, 1600–1870* (New Haven, CT: Yale University Press, 2014), 176–178. The theft of Shawnee property and improvements as part of the

pressure put on Indians to give up their lands and as an additional reward to usurping settlers exemplifies what Michael Witgen has called "the political economy of plunder." See Michael Witgen, *Seeing Red: Indigenous Land, American Expansion, and the Political Economy of Plunder in North America* (Chapel Hill: University of North Carolina Press, 2021).

45. "Copies of Proclamations issued by the Governor of Missouri Territory, December 4, 1815," in Carter, *Territorial Papers*, 15:192.

46. "Governor Clark to the President, January 22, 1816," in Carter, *Territorial Papers*, 15:105.

47. "Resolutions of the Territorial Assembly, January 22, 1816: To the Honourable the Senate and House of Representatives of the United States of America in Congress," in Carter, *Territorial Papers*, 15:106–107; "Resolutions of the Territorial Assembly, January 24, 1817," in ibid., quotation on 235.

48. Copy of letter from Mr. Welch, Baptist Missionary to Corresponding Secretary, June 20, 1818, Robert McClure Snyder Jr. Papers, Western Historical Manuscripts Collections, Missouri State Historical Society, C3524, Folder 62.

49. "John G. Heath to Frederic Bates, January 14, 1816," in Marshall, *The Life and Papers of Frederic Bates*, 2:297.

50. Rufus Babcock, ed., *Forty Years of Pioneer Life: Memoir of John Mason Peck D.D.* (Carbondale: Southern Illinois University Press, 1965), quotation on 146; Justus Post to John Post, November 20, 1816, Justus Post Papers, Missouri Historical Society, St. Louis (quotation); William Clark, "A Report of the Names and probable Number of the Tribes of Indians in the Missouri Territory, the Amount of Annuities paid them, the Amount of Expences of provisions issued to them at the Distribution of their Annuities and on every other occasion of the Amount of Presents other than provisions which ought to be distributed among them," November 4, 1816, Indian Collections, Missouri Historical Society, St. Louis; "The State of the Indians of Missouri Territory from Information 1817," Western Historical Manuscripts Collections, C1628, State Historical Society of Missouri, Columbia.

51. "Alexander McNair to Josiah Meigs, January 27, 1816," in Carter, *Territorial Papers*, 15:112; *Missouri Gazette*, March 2, 1816.

52. Perry McCandless, "Alexander McNair (1775–1826)," in *Dictionary of Missouri Biography*, ed. Lawrence O. Christensen, William E. Foley, Gary R. Kremer, and Kenneth H. Winn (Columbia: University of Missouri Press, 1999), 538–540.

53. Jerome O. Steffen, *William Clark: Jeffersonian Man on The Frontier* (Norman: University of Oklahoma Press, 1977), 125.

54. William E. Foley, "After the Applause: William Clark's Failed 1820 Gubernatorial Campaign," *Gateway Heritage* 24 (Fall 2003–Winter 2004): quotations on 143; Peter J. Kastor, *William Clark's World: Describing America in an Age of Unknowns* (New Haven, CT: Yale University Press, 2011), 195–201.

55. Rev. Jedidiah Morse, *A Report to the Secretary of War of the United States on Indian Affairs, Comprising a Narrative of a Tour Performed in the Summer of 1820, under a Commission from the President of the United States, for the Purpose of Ascertaining, for the Use of the Government the Actual State of the Indian Tribes in Our Country* (New Haven, CT: S. Converse, 1822), 366; "Statement Showing the Names and Numbers of the Different Tribes of Indians Now Remaining within the Limits of the Several States and Territories, and the Quantity of Land Claimed by Them Respectively," Department of War, Office of Indian Affairs, December 21, 1824, in McCarter & English Indian Claim Cases, Box 3, Folder 10, Mudd Library, Princeton University.

56. "Mr. Benton, . . . Communicating the Memorial of the General Assembly of the State of Missouri, on the Subject of Indians Residing within That State," May 14, 1824, 18th Cong., 1st Sess., 1824, S. Doc. 79, quotation on 1.

57. William Clark to John C. Calhoun, April 29, 1824 (quotation), in Letters Received by the Office of Indian Affairs, 1824–1881, Roll 747, St. Louis Superintendency, 1824–1851, National Archives (Copies in U.S. Superintendency of Indian Affairs, St. Louis, Records, 1824–1851, Western Historical Manuscripts Collection, C2970, State Historical Society of Missouri, Columbia).

58. "Mr. Benton, . . . Communicating the Memorial of the General Assembly of the State of Missouri," quotations on 1–3; Governor Alexander McNair, "Second Annual Message, November 4, 1822," in *The Messages and Proclamations of the Governors of the State of Missouri*, ed. Buel Leopard and Floyd C. Shoemaker (Columbia: State Historical Society of Missouri, 1922), quotation on 1:33; Governor John Miller, "First Inaugural Address, January 20, 1826," in ibid., quotation on 1:113; Governor John Miller, "Second Inaugural Address, November 18, 1828," in ibid., quotation on 1:131.

59. Timothy Flint, *Recollections of the Last Ten Years in the Valley of the Mississippi*, ed. George R. Brooks (1926; repr., Carbondale: Southern Illinois University Press, 1968), quotation on 119; Timothy Flint, *The Life and Adventures of Daniel Boone: The First Settlers of Kentucky, Interspersed with the Early Annals of the Country* (1833).

60. Thomas Hart Benton, *Thirty Years' View, or, a History of the Working of the American Government for Thirty Years, from 1820 to 1850*, 2 vols. (New York: D. Appleton, 1854–1856), quotation on 1:28; "John Scott to the Secretary of War, September 21, 1820," in Carter, *Territorial Papers*, 15:646.

61. William Clark (St. Louis) to the Secretary of War, December 8, 1823, McCarter & English Indian Claim Cases, Box 18, Folder 2, Exhibit 91 (quotations); Clark ("rest in peace") quoted in Buckley, *William Clark*, 166.

62. These treaties are printed in Charles J. Kappler, ed., *Indian Affairs: Laws and Treaties*, 7 vols. (Washington, DC: US Government Printing Office, 1904), 2: 207–209, 217–225.

63. "Treaty with the Shawnee, 1825," in Kappler, *Indian Affairs*, 2:263 (quotations). For the removal of the Delawares from Missouri, see John Bowes, *Land Too Good for Indians: Northern Indian Removal* (Norman: University of Oklahoma Press, 2016), 104–107.

64. Governor John Miller, "To the Senate," November 29, 1830, in Leopard and Shoemakers, *Messages and Proclamations*, 1:202 (quotation).

65. "Treaty with the Shawnee, 1825," in https://dc.library.okstate.edu/digital/collection/kapplers/id/26103/rec/1.

66. Flint, *Recollections of the Last Ten Years*, 119 (quotation). On the fate of *métis* in Missouri and across the Americanizing West, see Anne Hyde, *Empires, Nations, and Families: A History of the North American West, 1800–1860* (Lincoln: University of Nebraska Press, 2011), 240–256.

67. S. G. Hopkins to Major Richard Graham, August 6, 1825, Richard Graham Papers, Missouri Historical Society, St. Louis.

68. James F. Keefe and Lynn Morrow, eds., *The White River Chronicles of S. C. Turnbo: Man and Wildlife on the Ozarks Frontier* (Fayetteville: University of Arkansas Press, 1994), 1–13; George E. Lankford, "Shawnee Convergence: Immigrant Indians in the Ozarks," *Arkansas Historical Quarterly* 58 (Winter 1999): 405–411; Blevins, *A History of the Ozarks*, Vol. 1, 59–60.

69. Lakomäki, *Gathering Together*, quotation on 179; Blevins, *A History of the Ozarks*, Vol. 1, 64–65.

70. William Clark to Secretary of War, June 1, 1829, McCarter & English Indian Claim Cases, Box 24, Folder 2, Exhibit 205; Lakomäki, *Gathering Together*, 181.

71. "Treaty with the Shawnee, Etc., 1832," in Kappler, *Indian Affairs*, 370–371.

72. For an excellent account of the Cherokees' "Trail of Tears" and the road to it, see Theda Purdue and Michael D. Green, *The Cherokee Nation and the Trail of Tears* (New York: Viking Penguin, 2007). For a survey of new literature that has extended the chronology and geography of removal beyond the experience of the Cherokees, see Christina Snider, "Many Removals: Re-evaluating the Arc of Indian Dispossession," *Journal of the Early Republic* 41 (Winter 2021): 623–650.

Chapter 5

1. James Abbey, *California. A Trip across the Plains, in the Spring of 1850, Being a Daily Record of Incidents of the Trip over the Plains, the Desert, and the Mountains, Sketches of the Country, Distances from Camp to Camp, etc., and Containing Valuable Information to Emigrants, as to Where They Will Find Wood, Water, and Grass at Almost Every Step of the Journey* (Tarrytown, NY: W. Abbatt, 1933), 19; William G. Johnston, *Experiences of a Forty-Niner by William G. Johnston, a Member of the First Wagon Train to Enter California in the Memorable Year 1849* (Pittsburgh: unknown printer, 1892) 115, 114; Isaiah William Bryant, "Journal from Muscatine, Iowa, to Volcano, California, 27 May to 9 October 1853" (Nebraska State Historical

Society and Mattes Library), Digital selections transcribed by Karl
Schneider, http://prezi.com/cvprjpec7s_c/trip-across-the-plains/; James
Bennett, *Overland Journey to California: Journal of James Bennett Whose
Party Left New Harmony in 1850 and Crossed the Plains and Mountains until
the Golden West Was Reached* (London: Forgotten Books, 2018), 20; David
Morris Potter, ed., *Trail to California: The Overland Journal of Vincent
Geiger and Wakeman Bryarly* (New Haven, CT: Yale University Press,
1945), 103; Louise Barry, ed., "Overland to the Gold Fields of California
in 1852: The Journal of John Hawkins Clark, Expanded and Revised
from Notes Made during the Journey," *Kansas Historical Quarterly* 11
(August 1942): 250. For a review of travelers' reactions to Chimney Rock,
see Merrill J. Mattes, *The Great Platte River Road: The Covered Wagon
Mainline from Fort Kearny to Fort Laramie*, Nebraska State Historical
Society Publications, Vol. XXV (Lincoln: Nebraska State Historical
Society, 1969), 378–420.

2. See National Park Service, *National Historic Trails: Auto Tour Route
Interpretive Guide: Nebraska and Northeastern Colorado* (Washington,
DC: National Parks Service, 2006), esp. 58. For the Chimney Rock
National Historic Site's website, see https://www.nps.gov/nr/travel/scotts_
bluff/chimney_rock.html.

3. Kevin Wong, "The Forgotten History of 'The Oregon Trail,' as Told by
Its Creators," *Motherboard* (February 15, 2017), https://motherboard.vice.
com/en_us/article/qkx8vw/the-forgotten-history-of-the-oregon-trail-as-
told-by-its-creators. On the history and Hollywood treatment of Indians
menacing migrants on the overland trails, see Gregory F. Michno and
Susan J. Michno, *Circle the Wagons! Attacks on Wagon Trains in History and
Hollywood Films* (Jefferson, NC: McFarland, 2009).

4. Jack Yarwood, "The Making of 'The Oregon Trail': An interview with
Don Yarwitsch," *Paste* (October 22, 2015), https://www.pastemagazine.
com/articles/2015/10/the-making-of-the-oregon-trail-an-interview-with-
d.html (quotation). On the updates in the latest version, see Anna King,
"A New Spin on a Classic Video Game Gives Native Americans Better
Representation," https://www.npr.org/2021/05/12/996007048/no-bows-
and-arrows-and-no-broken-english-on-the-updated-oregon-trail.

5. Will Bagley, *Overland West: The Story of the Oregon and California
Trails*, Vol. I: *So Rugged and Mountainous: Blazing the Trails to Oregon
and California, 1812–1848* (Norman: University of Oklahoma Press,
2010), quotations on 85, 86, see also 3–15; Sarah Keyes, "Beyond the
Plains: Migration to the Pacific and the Reconfiguration of America,
1820s–1900s" (PhD diss., University of Southern California, 2012), 4–6.

6. Stephen Aron, *American Confluence: Missouri Frontier from Borderland to
Border State* (Bloomington: Indiana University Press, 2006), 229–233.

7. Governor John Miller, "Third Biennial Address," November 20, 1832,
in Buel Leopard and Floyd C. Shoemaker, eds., *The Messages and
Proclamations of the Governors of the State of Missouri* (Columbia: State

Historical Society of Missouri, 1922), 1:170; Dorothy Neuhoff, "The Platte Purchase," 310–311, 318–319, 340–341, in McCarter & English Indian Claim Cases, Mudd Library, Princeton University, Box 7, Folder 2, Exhibit 519; Bert Anson, "Variations of the Indian Conflict: The Effect of the Emigrant Indian Removal Policy, 1830–1854," *Missouri Historical Review* 59 (October 1964): 81–82.

8. R. David Edmunds, "Potawatomis in the Platte Country: An Indian Removal Incomplete," *Missouri Historical Review* 68 (1974): 375–384.

9. Stephen C. LeSueur, *The 1838 Mormon War in Missouri* (Columbia: University of Missouri Press, 1987), 8–142; R. J. Robertson Jr., "The Mormon Experience in Missouri, 1830–1839," *Missouri Historical Review* 68 (1973–1974): 280–298, 393–415; Sally Denton, *American Massacre: The Tragedy at Mountain Meadows, September 1857* (New York: Vintage, 2003), 39–40.

10. LeSueur, *The 1838 Mormon War in Missouri*, 143–244; Clark V. Johnson, "The Missouri Redress Petitions: A Reappraisal of Mormon Persecutions in Missouri," *Brigham Young University Studies* 26 (1986): 31–44.

11. W. Darrell Overdyke, ed., "A Southern Family on the Missouri Frontier: Letters from Independence, 1843–1855," *Journal of Southern History* 17 (May 1951): 216–218; Eugene T. Wells, "The Growth of Independence, Missouri 1827–1850," *Bulletin of the Missouri Historical Society* 16 (October 1959): 33–46; A. Theodore Brown, *Frontier Community: Kansas City to 1870* (Columbia: University of Missouri Press, 1963), 53–59.

12. Francis Parkman, *The Oregon Trail*, ed. A. B. Guthrie Jr. (Boston: Ginn, 1910), quotations on 14, 15, 16.

13. Eva Emery Dye, ed., "Boone Family Reminiscences as Told to Mrs. Dye," *Oregon Historical Quarterly* 42 (September 1941): 221; Interview with Mary Ann Boone, December 7, 1907, Francis Whittemore Cragin Notebooks, Early Far West Notebooks, Typescript in Western Americana Room Denver Public Library, 10:21–22; Interview with Mrs. Ben Spencer, September 25, 1903, Francis Whittemore Cragin Notebooks, 20:11. For a brief sketch of the life of Albert Gallatin Boone, see Nicholas P. Hardeman, "Albert Gallatin Boone," in *The Mountain Men and the Fur Trade of the Far West*, ed. Leroy R. Hafen, 10 vols. (Glendale, CA: Arthur H. Clark, 1965–1972), 8:31–47. For Albert Boone's career as a trader in western Missouri, see his letters and account books in the Warfield Collection, William Andrews Clark Library, Los Angeles, and in the Sublette Papers, Missouri Historical Society, St. Louis. Albert's journeys and his business not only required that he negotiate cultural borders, but that he also cross an international boundary. Trapping and trading in what was still northern Mexico, Albert facilitated his dealings by converting to Catholicism. In Spanish Louisiana, previous generations of Boones had made similar professions, but these were nothing more than conversions of convenience—required to obtain land grants, hold civil offices, and get married. By contrast, Albert's

spiritual convictions were sincere, and he remained a Catholic long after the United States had completed its takeover of northern Mexico. See Interview with Mary B. Spencer, September 22, 1903, Francis Whittemore Cragin Notebooks, 20:3–4.

14. Otis B. Spencer, "A Sketch of the Boone-Bent Families," *Westport Historical Quarterly* 8 (March 1973): 99–105; David C. Beyreis, *Blood in the Borderlands: Conflict, Kinship, and the Bent Family, 1821–1920* (Lincoln: University of Nebraska Press, 2020), 97; Hardeman, "Albert Gallatin Boone," 31–47.

15. Hardeman, "Albert Gallatin Boone," 42.

16. Elijah Bristow, "For Oregon!" *Springfield Illinois Journal* 11 (November 1847), http://historymatters.gmu.edu/d/6231/ (quotation).

17. Thomas Richards Jr., *Breakaway Americas: Contested Sovereignty and Contingent Destiny in the Era of U.S. Expansion* (Baltimore: Johns Hopkins University Press, 2019), 182–213.

18. John D. Unruh Jr., *The Plains Across: The Overland Emigrants and the Trans-Mississippi West, 1840–1860* (Urbana: University of Illinois Press, 1979), 119.

19. Ibid., 28–61; Michael L. Tate, *Indians and Emigrants: Encounters on the Overland Trails* (Norman: University of Oklahoma Press, 2006), 3–19.

20. Classic studies of American views about the "Great American Desert" include Walter Prescott Webb, *The Great Plains* (Boston: Ginn, 1931); Henry Nash Smith, *Virgin Land: The American West as Symbol and Myth* (Cambridge, MA: Harvard University Press, 1950); Eugene Hollon, *The Great American Desert* (New York: Oxford University Press, 1969); Patricia Nelson Limerick, *Desert Passages: Encounters with the American Deserts* (Albuquerque: University of New Mexico Press, 1985).

21. Parkman, *The Oregon Trail*, quotations on 39, 56; National Park Service, *National Historic Trails*, quotation on 2 ("too thick"); Clarence B. Bagley, "Crossing the Plains," *Washington Historical Quarterly* 13 (July 1922): quotation on 171.

22. Parkman, *The Overland Trail*, quotations on 26, 54, 52; Tate, *Indians and Emigrants*, 9.

23. Barry, ed., "Overland to the Gold Fields in 1852," 234; Unruh, *The Plains Across*, 167–173; Tate, *Indians and Emigrants*, 33, 40.

24. *Daily Missouri Republican*, September 9, 1847.

25. Richardson quoted in Unruh, *The Plains Across*, 175; Barry, ed., "Overland to the Gold Fields in 1852," 239. Some emigrants, it should be noted, saw no Indians at all during their first weeks on the trail and occasionally for even longer. For examples of emigrants having no contact, see Unruh, *The Plains Across*, 179. On the prevalence of horse and stock theft on the trail, the tendency to blame Indians, and examples in which white men were the true perpetrators, see Matthew Luckett, *Never Caught Twice: Horse Stealing in Western Nebraska, 1850–1890* (Lincoln: University of Nebraska Press, 2021), 27–64.

26.   Unruh, *The Plains Across*, 185. Remarkably thorough as Unruh's scouring
of emigrant accounts and other records was, some killings may have
escaped being recorded in any extant source. Still, Unruh's findings
have been generally confirmed by other studies based on different
samples and sometimes a more specific regional or chronological
focus. See Glenda Riley, *Women and Indians on the Frontier, 1825–1915*
(Albuquerque: University of New Mexico Press, 1984), 155; Robert L.
Munkres, "The Plains Indian Threat on the Oregon Trail before 1860,"
Annals of Wyoming 40 (October 1968): 193–194; Christopher G. Clark,
"The Myth of Indian Aggression in Early Nebraska," *Platte Valley Review* 14
(Spring 1986): 26–34.

27.   Alonzo Delano, *Life on the Plains and among the Diggings; Being Scenes and
Adventures of an Overland Journey to California: with Particular Incidents
of the Route, Mistakes and Sufferings of the Emigrants, the Indian Tribes,
the Present and Future of the Great West* (Auburn, NY: Miller, Orton &
Mulligan 1857), quotation on 65; Tate, *Indians and Emigrants*, 151; Unruh,
The Plains Across, 412.

28.   Unruh, *The Plains Across*, 124; Keyes, "Beyond the Plains," 161–201.

29.   Parkman, *The Oregon Trail*, quotations on 38–39. Historians have
confirmed Parkman's estimation about the state of residence from which
emigrants resided. See, for example, John Mack Faragher, *Women and
Men on the Overland Trail* (New Haven, CT: Yale University Press, 1979),
189, where in the sample set, Missouri accounted for 23.5% of "previous
residence of emigrant families," topping the list. It was followed closely by
Illinois at 22.6%.

30.   Parkman, *The Oregon Trail*, 39.

31.   Denton, *American Massacre*, 85 ("Pukes"); Unruh, *The Plains Across*, 302;
Unruh, *The Plains Across*, 18–19, 302, 334–335.

32.   Barry, ed., "Overland to the Gold Fields in 1852," quotations on 246, 252.

33.   Harriet Scott Palmer quoted in Bagley, *Overland West*, 166; Abbey,
California, quotation on May 25, 1850, https://www.loc.gov/item/33009
652/; George F. Weisel, ed., "Dodson's Death: Diary of John F. Dodson,"
Montana: The Magazine of Western History 3 (Spring 1953): 27; Unruh, *The
Plains Across*, 164–166; Tate, *Indians and Emigrants*, 58, 96–99.

34.   Robert Lewis, ed., "The Diary of James Madison Coon and Nancy Iness
(Miller) Coon on the Oregon Trail from Mercer County, Illinois to
Clackamas County, Oregon in 1847," quotation on June 27, 1847, http://www.
rootsweb.com/~orbenton/COONDIAR.htm (accessed on March 1, 2016);
Riley, *Women and Indians on the Frontier, 1825–1915*, 170–173.

35.   Crockett quoted in Bagley, *Overland West*, 219; Helen Carpenter, "A Trip
across the Plains in an Ox Wagon, 1857," in *Ho for California!: Women's
Overland Diaries from the Huntington Library*, ed. Sandra L. Myres (San
Marino, CA: Huntington Library Press, 1980), quotation on 114. On
the contrasts between men's and women's expectations and experiences
on the trail, see Lillian Schlissel, *Women's Diaries of the Westward Journey*

(New York: Schocken Books, 1987), 13–16; Faragher, *Women and Men on the Overland Trail,* 16–39, 66–87, 110–143; Julie Roy Jeffrey, *Frontier Women: The Trans-Mississippi West, 1840–1880* (New York: Hill & Wang, 1979; revised edition, 1998), 35–64.

36. Unruh, *The Plains Across,* 119, 185.

37. Malcolm J. Rohrbough, *Days of Gold: The California Gold Rush and the American Nation* (Berkeley: University of California Press, 1997), quotations on 2, 1.

38. Unruh, *The Plains Across,* 120. The overland trails remained the favored route for emigrants to California from the Mississippi Valley, Upper South, and Midwest of the United States. Tens of thousands more people came to California in these same years from the East Coast and Gulf Coast of the United States, as well as from Europe, South America, Asia, and Australia. Most of these, however, came by sea.

39. Rohrbough, *Days of Gold,* quotation on 62; Mattes, *The Great Platte River Road,* 178; Unruh, *The Plains Across,* 119–122, 385.

40. Calculations about average travel time are compiled in Unruh, *The Plains Across,* 403.

41. Mattes, *The Great Platte River Road,* 62, estimates that in 1849 women made up only 2 percent of California-bound overland travelers. On negotiations within families, see Rohrbough, *Days of Gold,* 32–54. For a particularly poignant set of letters back and forth between a gold-seeking husband and the wife he left behind, see J. S. Holliday, *The World Rushed In: The California Gold Rush Experience* (Norman: University of Oklahoma Press, 1981).

42. Susan Lee Johnson, *Roaring Camp: The Social World of the California Gold Rush* (New York: W. W. Norton, 2000), 100–103, 114–121.

43. Elliott West, *The Contested Plains: Indians, Goldseekers, and the Rush to Colorado* (Lawrence: University Press of Kansas, 1998), 230.

44. Bennett, *Overland Journey to California,* quotation on 19; Tate, *Indians and Emigrants,* 105–106, 155.

45. Tate, *Indians and Emigrants,* 122–127; Andrew Isenberg, *The Destruction of the Bison: An Environmental History, 1750–1920* (New York: Cambridge University Press, 2000), 119–122.

46. Pekka Hämäläinen, *Lakota America: A New History of Indigenous Power* (New Haven, CT: Yale University Press, 2019), quotation on 214.

47. Matthew C. Field, *Prairie and Mountain Sketches,* ed. Kate L. Gregg and John Francis McDermott (Norman: University of Oklahoma Press, 1957), quotation on 30.

48. Jeffrey Ostler, *The Plains Sioux and U.S. Colonialism from Lewis and Clark to Wounded Knee* (New York: Cambridge University Press, 2004), 32–37.

49. John Tyler, "First Annual Message," December 7, 1841, https://millercen ter.org/the-presidency/presidential-speeches/december-7-1841-first-annual-message (quotation).

50. Stephen W. Kearny, "Report of a Summer Campaign to the Rocky Mountains &c. in 1845," Typescript at Kansas Historical Society, https://www.kshs.org/index.php?url=km/items/view/210397, quotations on 11, 9; Parkman, *The Oregon Trail*, 183–184; Unruh, *The Plains Across*, 205; Bagley, *Overland West*, 230–231.

51. "Treaty of Fort Laramie with Sioux, etc., 1851," in *Indian Affairs: Laws and Treaties*, ed. Charles J. Kappler, 7 vols. (Washington, DC: Government Printing Office, 1904), 2:594; Hämäläinen, *Lakota America*, 215–222; Ostler, *The Plains Sioux and U.S. Colonialisms from Lewis and Clark to Wounded Knee*, 36–37.

52. Fitzpatrick quoted in Robert M. Utley, *Frontiersmen in Blue: The United States Army and the Indian, 1848–1865* (New York: Macmillan, 1967), 55.

53. "Treaty of Fort Laramie with Sioux, etc., 1851," in Kappler, *Indian Affairs*, 2:595.

54. Michael L. Tate, *The Frontier Army in the Settlement of the West* (Norman: University of Oklahoma Press, 1999), 29–51; Robert M. Utley, *The Indian Frontier of the American West, 1846–1890* (Albuquerque: University of New Mexico Press, 1984), 37–47, 60–63.

55. Ostler, *The Plains Sioux and U.S. Colonialism from Lewis and Clark to Wounded Knee*, quotation on 40; Tate, *Indians and Emigrants*, 219–220; Unruh, *The Plains Across*, 214–215.

56. P. Richard Metcalf, "Grattan Massacre," in *The New Encyclopedia of the American West*, ed. Howard R. Lamar (New Haven, CT: Yale University Press, 1998), quotation on 446 ("authorized to arrest"); Unruh, *The Plains Across*, quotation on 215 ("lurk in the vicinity"); R. Eli Paul, *Blue Water Creek and the First Sioux War, 1854–1856* (Norman: University of Oklahoma Press, 2004).

57. Susan Bordeaux Bettelyoun and Josephine Waggoner, *With My Own Eyes: A Lakota Woman Tells Her People's History*, ed. Emily Levine (Lincoln: Bison Books, 1998), quotations on 53–54.

58. Keyes, "Beyond the Plains," 202–239.

59. "Instructions to General W. S. Harney," June 29, 1857, in *The Utah Expedition, 1857–1858: A Documentary Account of the United States Military Movement under Colonel Albert Sydney Johnston, and the Resistance by Brigham Young and the Mormon Nauvoo Legion*, ed. LeRoy R. Hafen and Ann W. Hafen (Glendale, CA: A. H. Clark, 1982), 30–34; William P. MacKinnon, ed., *At Sword's Point: Part I: A Documentary History of the Utah War to 1858* (Norman: University of Oklahoma Press, 2008), 151–184; Denton, *American Massacre*, 126.

60. "Proclamation of Governor Young," in Hafen and Hafen, *A Documentary Account of the United States Military Movement under Colonel Albert Sydney Johnston*, 63–65; MacKinnon, ed., *At Sword's Point*, 223–256.

61. David L. Bigler and Will Bagley, eds., *Innocent Blood: Essential Narratives of the Mountain Meadows Massacre* (Norman, OK: Arthur H. Clark, 2008), 31–55, 93–164; Denton, *American Massacre*, 171–189.

62. The coincidence in the date became the title of Leonard Griffiths, *The First 9/11 in America: September 11, 1857: Mountain Meadows Massacre* (Meadville, PA: Christian Faith, 2020). For excellent accounts of the episode, see Will Bagley, *Blood of the Prophets: Brigham Young and the Massacre at Mountain Meadows* (Norman: University of Oklahoma Press, 2002); Ronald W. Walker, Richard E. Turley Jr., and Glenn M. Leonard, *Massacre at Mountain Meadows: An American Tragedy* (New York: Oxford University Press, 2008).

63. Brent M. Rogers, *Unpopular Sovereignty: Mormons and the Federal Management of Early Utah Territory* (Lincoln: University of Nebraska Press, 2017). For an interpretation that stresses the shared fanaticism of the Mormons who perpetrated the Mountain Meadows Massacre and the Methodists who were the victims, and the ways in which this cast the larger conflict as a "holy war," see Sarah Barringer Gordon and Jan Shipps, "Fatal Convergence in the Kingdom of God: The Mountain Meadows Massacre in American History," *Journal of the Early Republic* 37 (Summer 2017), 307–347;

64. Hafen and Hafen, eds., *The Utah Expedition, 1857–1858*, 138–177, 263–293; William P. MacKinnon, ed., *At Sword's Point, Part 2: A Documentary History of the Utah War, 1858–1859* (Norman: University of Oklahoma Press, 2016), 187–243, 347–381, 505–554.

65. Keyes, "Beyond the Plains," 65–109.

66. An 1895 measurement by the United States Geological Survey fixed the summit of Chimney Rock at 4,242 feet above sea level. An 1865 survey put the elevation at 4,225, a loss of 17 feet over 70 years. Mattes, *The Great Platte River Road*, 379–380.

67. Thomas S. Twiss, United States Indian Agency of the Upper Platte, September 18, 1859, "Report of the Commissioner of Indian Affairs," Ex. Doc. 35, 36th Congress, 1st Session, Senate, quotation on 7.

Chapter 6

1. Craig Miner, *West of Wichita: Settling the High Plains of Kansas, 1865–1890* (Lawrence: University Press of Kansas, 1986); 26 ("That's 65 cents"); *Dodge City Times*, May 13, 1886 ("sorrowful heart").

2. Donald Worcester, "Chisholm Trail," in *The New Handbook of Texas*, ed. Ron Tyler et al., 6 vols. (Austin: Texas State Historical Association, 1966), 2:89. On the evolution of attitudes in Dodge City about its history (and the marketing of it), see Kevin Britz and Roger L. Nichols, *Tombstone, Deadwood, and Dodge City: Recreating the Frontier West* (Norman: University of Oklahoma Press, 2018). On more recent reinventions and marketing campaigns, see Michael B. Husband, Judith A. Heberling, and William Hunter, *Reimagining Dodge. . . : A Heritage Tourism Master Plan for Dodge City and Ford County, Kansas* (Report by Heberling Associates, 2009).

3. On the continuing prevalence of Dodge City in myth and as metaphor, see Robert R. Dykstra and Jo Ann Manfra, *Dodge City and the Birth of the Wild West* (Lawrence: University Press of Kansas, 2017), 1–5; Stewart L. Udall, Robert R. Dykstra, Michael A. Bellesiles, Paula Mitchell Marks, and Gregory H. Nobles, "How the West Got Wild: American Media and Frontier Violence: A Roundtable," *Western Historical Quarterly* 31 (Autumn 2000): 377–395; Richard Slotkin, *Gunfighter Nation: The Myth of the Frontier in Twentieth-Century America* (New York: Atheneum, 1992), esp. 286–292, 494–496, 522–525, 591–613.

4. Christopher Knowlton, *Cattle Kingdom: The Hidden History of the Cowboy West* (New York: Mariner Books, 2017), 5; on the exploration of the Arkansas and disparaging reviews of the river and its environs, see Dan Flores, "A Very Different Story: Exploring the Southwest from Monticello with the Freeman and Custis Expedition of 1806," *Montana: The Magazine of Western History* 50 (March 2000): 2–17; Jared Orsi, *Citizen Explorer: The Life of Zebulon Pike* (New York: Oxford University Press, 2014), 127–174; William H. Goetzmann, *Exploration and Empire: The Explorer and the Scientist in the Winning of the American West* (New York: Knopf, 1966), 48–53, 59–62; Andrew C. Isenberg, *The Destruction of the Bison* (New York: Cambridge University Press, 2000), 21.

5. Pekka Hämäläinen, *The Comanche Empire* (New Haven, CT: Yale University Press, 2008); Pekka Hämäläinen, *Lakota America: A New History of Indigenous Power* (New Haven, CT: Yale University Press, 2019); Brian Delay, *War of a Thousand Deserts: Indian Raids and the U.S.-Mexican War* (New Haven, CT: Yale University Press, 2008); Elliott West, *The Contested Plains: Indians, Goldseekers, and the Rush to Colorado* (Lawrence: University Press of Kansas, 1998); David Dary, *The Santa Fe Trail: Its History, Legends, and Lore* (New York: Knopf, 2000).

6. R. Douglas Hurt, *Nathan Boone and the American Frontier* (Columbia: University of Missouri, 1998), 140–171; Louis Pelzer, *Marches of the Dragoons in the Mississippi Valley: An Account of Marches and Activities of the First Regiment United States Dragoons in the Mississippi Valley between the Years 1833 and 1850* (Iowa City: State Historical Society of Iowa, 1917), 97–107.

7. Odie B. Faulk, *Dodge City: The Most Western Town of All* (New York: Oxford University Press, 1977), quotation on 18.

8. Ari Kelman, *A Misplaced Massacre: Struggling over the Memory of Sand Creek* (Cambridge, MA: Harvard University Press, 2013); Robert M. Utley, *Frontiersmen in Blue: The United States Army and the Indian, 1848–1861* (New York: Macmillan, 1967), 281–297.

9. Major Gen. G. M. Dodge to Maj. Gen. John Pope, June 17, 1865, *War of the Rebellion*, Serial 102, quotation on 912, https://ehistory.osu.edu/books/official-records/102/0912; W. T. Sherman to John Sherman, August 9, 1867, and December 30, 1866, in *The Sherman Letters: Correspondence*

between General and Senator Sherman from 1837 to 1891, ed. Rachel Sherman Thorndike (New York: Charles Scribner's Sons, 1894), quotations on 293, 287.

10. For the rationales for removal that resulted in the expulsion of Indians east of the Mississippi by the end of the 1830s and continued to justify later dispossessions of Indians from lands west of the Mississippi after the Civil War, see Claudio Saunt, *Unworthy Republic: The Dispossession of Native Americans and the Road to Indian Territory* (New York: W. W. Norton, 2020). On the persistence of "injured innocents" as a trope offered by white American Westerners, see Patricia Nelson Limerick, *The Legacy of Conquest: The Unbroken Past of the American West* (New York: W. W. Norton, 1987), 35–54.

11. Robert M. Utley, *The Indian Frontier of the American West, 1846–1890* (Albuquerque: University of New Mexico Press, 1984), 99–127; Utley, *Frontier Regulars: The United States Army and the Indian, 1866–1891* (New York: Macmillan, 1973), 147–167; Richard White, *Railroaded: The Transcontinentals and the Making of Modern America* (New York: W. W. Norton, 2011), 59–62, 455–456, 465–466, 489–491.

12. David Kay Strate, *Sentinel to the Cimarron: The Frontier Experience of Fort Dodge, Kansas* (Dodge City, KS: Cultural Arts & Heritage Center, 1970); Robert W. Frazier, *Forts of the West: Military Forts and Presidios and Posts Commonly Called Forts West of the Mississippi River to 1898* (Norman: University of Oklahoma Press, 1965), 52–53.

13. William B. Shillingberg, *Dodge City: The Early Years, 1872–1886* (Norman: University of Oklahoma Press, 2009), 31–50. For more general examinations of the place of African Americans in the frontier army after the Civil War, see William H. Leckie and Shirley A. Leckie, *The Buffalo Soldiers: A Narrative of the Black Cavalry in the West*, rev. ed. (Norman: University of Oklahoma Press, 2003); Kevin Adams, *Class and Race in the Frontier Army: Military Life in the West, 1870–1890* (Norman: University of Oklahoma Press, 2009), 164–183.

14. Dykstra and Manfra, *Dodge City and the Birth of the Wild West*, 10–11; Shillingberg, *Dodge City*, 73–76.

15. Robert M. Wright, *Dodge City: The Cowboy Capital and the Great Southwest in the Days of the Wild Indian, the Buffalo, the Cowboy, Dance Halls, Gambling Halls, and Bad Men* (Wichita, KS: Wichita Eagle Press, 1913), 69–85, 138–139; Rex W. Strickland, ed., "The Recollections of W. S. Glenn, Buffalo Hunter," *Panhandle-Plains Historical Review* 22 (1949): 25–31; C. Robert Haywood, *The Merchant Prince of Dodge City: The Life and Times of Robert M. Wright* (Norman: University of Oklahoma Press, 1988), 37–54; Tom Clavin, *Dodge City: Wyatt Earp, Bat Masterson, and the Wickedest Town in the American West* (New York: St. Martin's Press, 2017), 44; Dykstra and Manfra, *Dodge City and the Birth of the Wild West*, 58–61.

16. Samuel Carter III, *Cowboy Capital of the World: The Saga of Dodge City* (New York: Doubleday, 1973), 24; Frank H. Mayer and Charles B. Roth,

The Buffalo Harvest (Denver: Sage Books, 1958), 64; Henry H. Raymond, "Diary of a Dodge City Buffalo Hunter, 1872–1873," ed. Joseph W. Snell, *Kansas History Quarterly* 31 (Winter 1965): 350–351.

17. Blackmore quoted in Shillingberg, *Dodge City*, 77; Wright, *Dodge City, the Cowboy Capital*, 75, 158; Richard Irving Dodge, *The Plains of the Great West and Their Inhabitants; Being a Description of the Plains, Game, Indians, &c. of the Great American Desert* (New York: G. Putnam's Sons, 1877), 119–147; Faulk, *Dodge City*, 22–47; Isenberg, *The Destruction of the Bison*, 121–143, 155–163.

18. Charles J. Kappler, ed., *Indian Affairs: Laws and Treaties*, Vol. II: *Treaties* (Washington, DC: Government Printing Office, 1904), quotation on 980; Olive K. Dixon, *Life of "Billy" Dixon: Plainsman, Scout, and Pioneer* (Dallas: P. L. Turner, 1927), 111; Faulk, *Dodge City*, 37–38.

19. Dodge quoted in Shillingberg, *Dodge City*, 117; and Carter, *Cowboy Capital of the World*, 32.

20. Nelson A. Miles, *Personal Recollections and Observations of General Nelson A. Miles* (Chicago: Werner, 1896), quotation on 157.

21. Shillingberg, *Dodge City*, 115–152; S. C. Gwynne, *Empire of the Summer Moon: Quanah Parker and the Rise and Fall of the Comanches, the Most Powerful Indian Tribe in American History* (New York: Scribner, 2010), 274–287; Utley, *Frontier Regulars*, 225–241.

22. Jerome A. Greene, *January Moon: The Northern Cheyenne Breakout from Fort Robinson, 1878–1879* (Norman: University of Oklahoma Press, 2020); Miner, *West of Wichita*, 109–118; Mari Sandoz, *Cheyenne Autumn* (Lincoln, NE: Bison Books, 1992, orig. 1953).

23. *Dodge City Times*, September 28, 1878 ("the starving and imbecile"); ibid., September 14, 1878 ("the scalp"); ibid., November 2, 1878 ("beat and mangled").

24. *Dodge City Times*, "The Gentle Savage," February 22, 1879 (quotations). Before being granted a change of venue, Northern Cheyenne prisoners were held in the Dodge City Jail, where Sheriff Bat Masterson provided four of them with ledgers. The art the prisoners produced in these ledgers offers considerable insight into their historical experiences. This ledger art is collected and examined in Denise Low and Ramon Powers, *Northern Cheyenne Ledger Art by Fort Robinson Breakout Survivors* (Lincoln: University of Nebraska Press, 2020).

25. Wright, *Dodge City, the Cowboy Capital*, 138.

26. On the creation of the statue and its placement in Dodge City, see Kathy Bell, "El Capitan Arrives," *Dodge City Daily Globe*, November 1, 2016, 6. General studies of longhorns, cowboys, and the trail to Dodge on which this section draws include J. Frank Dobie, *The Longhorns* (Boston: Little, Brown, 1950); David Dary, *Cowboy Culture: A Saga of Five Centuries* (New York: Alfred A. Knopf, 1981); Joe B. Frantz and Julian Ernest Choate Jr., *The American Cowboy: The Myth and the Reality* (Norman: University of Oklahoma Press, 1955); Richard W. Slatta, *Cowboys of the Americas* (New Haven, CT: Yale University Press, 1990).

27. Sherman quoted in Richard White, *The Republic for Which It Stands: The United States during Reconstruction and the Gilded Age, 1865–1896* (New York: Oxford University Press, 2017), 431; Thomas Hart Benton, *Thirty Years' View, or, a History of the Working of the American Government for Thirty Years, from 1820 to 1850*, 2 vols. (New York: Appleton, 1854–1856), quotation on 1:28.

28. Nell I. Painter, *Exodusters: Black Migration to Kansas after Reconstruction* (New York: W. W. Norton, 1977), quotation on 159; Robert G. Athearn, *In Search of Canaan: Black Migration to Kansas, 1879–1880* (Lawrence: Regents Press of Kansas, 1978); Quintard Taylor, *In Search of the Racial Frontier: African Americans in the American West, 1528–1990* (New York: W. W. Norton, 1998), 94–102, 136–143.

29. Christopher Knowlton, *Cattle Kingdom: The Hidden History of the Cowboy West* (Boston: Mariner Books, 2017), 33–41. For average rainfall in various towns across central and western Kansas and the hopes that higher than normal precipitation inspired, see Miner, *West of Wichita*, 47–48. For examinations of the creation and dissemination of notions that "rain follows the plow" and other theories (and fantasies) about climate change in the nineteenth century, see Lawrence Culver, "Manifest Destiny and Manifest Disaster: Climate Perceptions and Realities in United States Territorial Expansion," in *American Environments: Climate— Cultures—Catastrophe*, ed. Christof Mauch and Sylvia Mayer (Heidelberg, Germany: Universitätsverlag, 2012), 19–26; Henry Nash Smith, "Rain Follows the Plow," *Huntington Library Quarterly* 1 (February 1947): 187– 188; Gary D. Libecap and Zeynep Kocabiyik Hansen, "'Rain Follows the Plow' and Dryfarming Doctrine: The Climate Information Problem and Homestead Failure in the Upper Great Plains, 1890–1925," *Journal of Economic History* 62 (2002): 86–120.

30. Stanley Vestal, *Queen of Cowtowns, Dodge City: "The Wickedest Little City in America," 1872–1886* (New York: Harper & Brothers, 1952), 86–98; Dykstra and Manfra, *Dodge City and the Birth of the Wild West*, 5; Clavin, *Dodge City*, 134.

31. Dykstra and Manfra, *Dodge City and the Birth of the Wild West*, quotation on 61; C. Robert Haywood, "'No Less a Man': Blacks in Cow Town Dodge City, 1876–1886," *Western Historical Quarterly* 19 (May 1988): 161–164; Shillingberg, *Dodge City*, 265–266.

32. C. Robert Haywood, *Victorian West: Class and Culture in Kansas Cattle Towns* (Lawrence: University Press of Kansas, 1991), 16–21; Shillingberg, *Dodge City*, 266. For a study that highlights the correlation between persistence and (relative) prosperity in frontier and rural America, see John Mack Faragher, *Sugar Creek: Life on the Illinois Prairie* (New Haven, CT: Yale University Press, 1986).

33. Kansas newspaper (Hays Sentinel) quoted in Faulk, *Dodge City*, 149; *Dodge City Times*, August 7, 1878; Haywood, *Victorian West*, 30–31, 263; Clavin, *Dodge City*, 191, 273; Knowlton, *Cattle Kingdom*, 45–47; C. Robert

Haywood, *Cowtown Lawyers: Dodge City and Its Attorneys, 1876–1886* (Norman: University of Oklahoma Press, 1988), 32–35, 79–80; Carol Leonard and Isidor Walliman, "Prostitution and Changing Morality in Frontier Cattle Towns in Kansas," *Kansas History* 2 (Spring 1979): 34–53; Anne M. Butler, *Daughters of Joy, Sisters of Misery: Prostitutes in the American West, 1865–1890* (Urbana: University of Illinois Press, 1985); Jan MacKell, *Brothels, Bordellos, and Bad Girls: Prostitution in Colorado, 1860–1930* (Albuquerque: University of New Mexico Press, 2004).

34. On the ability to move as a signature of what freedom meant to freedpeople, see Leon F. Litwack, *Been in the Storm So Long: The Aftermath of Slavery* (New York: Vintage, 1979), 292–335.

35. *Ford County Globe*, September 2, 1879 (quotations). The September 23, 1879, issue of the *Ford County Globe* carried what it called "a slanderous item" that was making the rounds, presumably about the newly wedded interracial couple. This report claimed that "the Negroes of Dodge City, shocked at the depravity of one of their race for living with a white woman, whipped and ducked the miscegenationist and would have hanged him had not the police come to his aid." See also Haywood, "'No Less a Man,'" 166–168, 181.

36. *Ford County Globe*, May 7, 1878; Andrew Isenberg, *Wyatt Earp: A Vigilante Life* (New York: Hill & Wang, 2013), 81.

37. Dary, *Cowboy Culture*, 3–43, 67–104; Terry G. Jordan, *North American Cattle-Ranching Frontiers: Origins, Diffusion, and Differentiation* (Albuquerque: University of New Mexico Press, 1993); Taylor, *In Search of the Racial Frontier*, 56–57; Terry G. Jordan, *Trails to Texas: Southern Roots of Western Cattle Ranching* (Lincoln: University of Nebraska Press, 1981); Deborah M. Liles, "Before Emancipation: Black Cowboys and the Livestock Industry," in *Black Cowboys in the American West: On the Range, On the Stage, Behind the Badge*, ed. Bruce A. Glasrud and Michael N. Searles (Norman: University of Oklahoma Press, 2016), 19–30. Estimates about the racial composition of cowboy crews vary considerably, with African Americans accounting for between one-quarter to one-seventh of the total and a roughly similar percentage for Mexicans/Mexican-Americans. See J. Marvin Hunter, ed., *The Trail Drivers of Texas* (Austin: University of Texas Press, 1985), 453; Philip J. Durham and Everett L. Jones, *The Adventures of the Negro Cowboys* (New York: Dodd, Mead, 1965), 13–19, 57–77; Faulk, *Dodge City*, 66.

38. E. C. Abbott and Helena Huntington Smith, *We Pointed Them North: Recollections of a Cowpuncher* (New York: Farrar & Rinehart, 1939), quotations on 247; Knowlton, *Cattle Kingdom*, 19–20, 53.

39. Donald Worcester, *The Chisholm Trail: High Road of the Cattle Kingdom* (Lincoln: University of Nebraska Press, 1980), 33–104; Frantz and Choate Jr., *The American Cowboy*, 35–47; Dary, *Cowboy Culture*, 190–195. For a dissection of the reality and myth of individualism among cowboys, see Don D. Walker, *Clio's Cowboys: Studies in the Historiography of the Cattle Trade* (Lincoln: University of Nebraska Press, 1981), 86–90.

40. Edward Aveling, *An American Journey* (New York: John W. Lovell, 1887), quotation on 155. The Western novelist and historian Wallace Stegner, though no Marxist, reached a similar conclusion. The cowboy, wrote Stegner, was "an overworked, under-paid hireling, almost as homeless and dispossessed as a modern crop worker." See Wallace Stegner, "Who Are the Westerners?" https://www.americanheritage.com/who-are-westerners; Lewis Atherton, *The Cattle Kings* (Bloomington: Indiana University Press, 1961), 178–181; Dary, *Cowboy Culture*, 276; Joseph A. Stout Jr., "Cowboy," in *The New Encyclopedia of the American West*, ed. Howard Lamar (New Haven, CT: Yale University Press, 1998), 265–266; James R. Wagner, "*Cowboy*: Origin and Early Use of the Term," in *The Cowboy Way*, ed. Paul H. Carlson (Lubbock: Texas Tech University Press, 2000), 11–20; *Walker, Clio's Cowboys*, 131–146.

41. Hendrix quoted in Taylor, *In Search of the Racial Frontier*, 160; Slatta, *Cowboys of the Americas*, 165–169; Arnoldo De León, "Vamos Pa' Kiansis: Tejanos in the Nineteenth-Century Cattle Drives," *Journal of South Texas* 27 (Fall 2014): 6–21.

42. Robert R. Dykstra, *The Cattle Towns* (New York: Knopf, 1968), esp. 112–148. Important studies of violence in the "Old West" in general and efforts to quantify homicide rates for particular places include Randolph Roth, Michael D. Maltz, and Douglas L. Eckberg, "Homicide Rates in the Old West," *Western Historical Quarterly* 42 (Summer 2011): 173–195; David T. Courtwright, *Violent Land: Single Men and Social Disorder from the Frontier to the Inner City* (Cambridge, MA: Harvard University Press, 2001); David Peterson del Mar, *Beaten Down: A History of Interpersonal Violence in the West* (Seattle: University of Washington Press, 2002); Eric Monkkonen, "Western Homicide: The Case of Los Angeles, 1830–1870," *Pacific Historical Review* 74 (November 2005): 603–613; Eric Monkkonen, "Homicide: Explaining America's Exceptionalism," *American Historical Review* 111 (February 2006): 76–94; Clare V. McKanna Jr., "Enclaves of Violence in Nineteenth-Century California," *Pacific Historical Review* 73 (August 2004): 391–424; Clare McKanna Jr., "Alcohol, Handguns, and Homicide in the American West: A Tale of Three Counties, 1880–1920," *Western Historical Quarterly* 26 (Winter 1995): 455–482; Clare McKanna Jr., *Homicide, Race, and Justice in the American West, 1880–1920* (Tucson: University of Arizona Press, 1997); Clare McKanna Jr., *Race and Homicide in Nineteenth-Century California* (Reno: University of Nevada Press, 2002); Roger D. McGrath, *Gunfighters, Highwaymen, and Vigilantes: Violence on the Frontier* (Berkeley: University of California Press, 1987); John Mack Faragher, *Eternity Street: Violence and Justice in Frontier Los Angeles* (New York: W. W. Norton, 2016); Robert M. Utley, *High Noon in Lincoln: Violence on the Western Frontier* (Albuquerque: University of New Mexico Press, 1987); Eric Melvin Reed, "Homicide on the Nebraska Panhandle Frontier, 1867–1901," *Western Historical Quarterly* 50 (Summer 2019): 137–160. The website

of the Criminal Justice Research Center also contains a database on "Homicide Rates in the American West," assembled by Randolph Roth, that compiles statistics from studies done across the region: https://cjrc.osu.edu/research/interdisciplinary/hvd/homicide-rates-american-west. Questions about the patterns and larger causes of violence in the American West have also generated a rich scholarship. The interpretive framework offered by Richard Maxwell Brown has been especially important in shaping historians' understandings of the larger context of struggles over the "incorporation" of the territory and its resources. See in particular his book *No Duty to Retreat: Violence and Values in American History and Society* (New York: Oxford University Press, 1992); and his essay, "Violence," in *The Oxford History of the American West*, ed. Clyde Milner II, Carol A. O'Connor, and Martha A. Sandweiss (New York: Oxford University Press, 1994), 393–425. Finally, there has been a vibrant discussion of the "myth" of the Wild West, with Richard Slotkin's work being particularly influential. See his *The Fatal Environment: The Myth of the Frontier in the Age of Industrialization, 1800–1890* (New York: Macmillan, 1985); and *Gunfighter Nation: The Myth of the Frontier in Twentieth-Century America* (New York: Macmillan, 1992). For a critique of how popular culture has exaggerated the reality of historical violence in the West, see Udall, Dykstra, Bellesiles, Marks, and Nobles, "How the West Got Wild," 277–295.

43. Wright, *Dodge City, the Cowboy Capital*, quotation on 166.
44. Shillingberg, *Dodge City*, quotation on 103, 105–106; Wright, *Dodge City, the Cowboy Capital*, 169–172; Faulk, *Dodge City*, 152.
45. Clavin, *Dodge City*, 27; Dykstra, *The Cattle Towns*, 113–115; Carter, *Cowboy Capital of the World*, 40.
46. Shillingberg, *Dodge City*, 266.
47. Shillingberg, *Dodge City*, 85; Dykstra, *The Cattle Towns*, 247–248. For a particularly valuable discussion of demographic and cultural characteristics that typified extremely violent places in the post–Civil War West and around the world, see Courtwright, *Violent Land*.
48. Vestal, *Queen of Cowtowns, Dodge City*, 31 ("take the damn"); Wright, *Dodge City, the Cowboy Capital*, 166 ("the last straw").
49. Shillingberg, *Dodge City*, 99.
50. Clavin, *Dodge City*, 130. For Earp's career as "hunter and hunted" and as jailer and jailed, see Isenberg, *Wyatt Earp*.
51. Dykstra, *The Cattle Towns*, quotation on 148. See also 144, for his table of "Cattle Town Homicides" that charts the number of murders each year from 1870 to 1885 for each of the five towns.
52. Carter, *Cowboy Capital of the World*, 68–69; Clavin, *Dodge City*, 135.
53. Courtwright, *Violent Land*, 98–99; Clavin, *Dodge City*, 129–135; Dykstra and Manfra, *Dodge City and the Birth of the Wild West*, 58. White, *The Republic for Which It Stands*, 357–360, discusses the pervasiveness of fee-based government services, including Earp and law enforcement, and

the arguments developed for and against it. See also Nicholas R. Parillo, *Against the Profit Motive: The Salary Revolution in American Government* (New Haven, CT: Yale University Press, 2013).

54. Stuart N. Lake, *Wyatt Earp: Frontier Marshal* (Boston: Houghton Mifflin, 1931), quotation on 143.

55. Vestal, *Queen of Cowtowns, Dodge City*, quotation on 96 ("that no person"); Isenberg, *Wyatt Earp*, quotation on 94 ("concealed or otherwise"); *Kansas Statutes* (1868), 378. A photograph of the sign appears in Dykstra and Manfra, *Dodge City and the Birth of the Wild West*, 132. Although the Dodge City ordinances broadened the reach of no-carry rules, the penalties ranged only from $3 to $25 for each offense, considerably less than what the state statute proposed.

56. Dykstra, *The Cattle Towns*, 144–145.

57. *Ford County Globe*, March 5, 1878 (quotations).

58. *Ford County Globe*, March 5, 1878 (quotation); Vestal, *Queen of Cowtowns, Dodge City*, 96–97, 167; Isenberg, *Wyatt Earp*, 93–94; Dykstra and Manfra, *Dodge City and the Birth of the Wild West*, 24.

59. Abbott and Smith, *We Pointed Them North*, quotation on 31; Dykstra and Manfra, *Dodge City and the Birth of the Wild West*, 65.

60. Dykstra, *The Cattle Towns*, 128–131; C. Robert Haywood, "Cowtown Courts: Dodge City Courts, 1876–1886," *Kansas History* 11 (1988): 22–34.

61. Carter, *Cowboy Capital of the World*, 70; Isenberg, *Wyatt Earp*, 93–94; Clavin, *Dodge City*, 196–200.

62. Courtwright, *Violent Land*, 98–99; Isenberg, *Wyatt Earp*, 96–97, 105; Clavin, *Dodge City*, 165.

63. Along with Dodge City and maybe Deadwood, South Dakota, Tombstone, Arizona, primarily because of the "Gunfight at the OK Corral," has come to exemplify the West at its wildest. Earp's time in Tombstone has been the subject of scores of books, films, and television shows. The scholarly literature is also voluminous. Particularly valuable among recent biographies and studies is Isenberg, *Wyatt Earp*, 128–169; and Steven Lubet, *Murder in Tombstone: The Forgotten Trial of Wyatt Earp* (New Haven, CT: Yale University Press, 2004). For a study that explores post-frontier efforts to profit from Wild West legends in these three towns, see Britz and Nichols, *Tombstone, Deadwood, and Dodge City*.

64. Jack DeMattos and Chuck Parson, *The Notorious Luke Short: Sporting Man of the Wild West* (Denton: University of North Texas Press, 2015); Dykstra and Manfra, *Dodge City and the Birth of the Wild West*, 111–112, tracks the coverage around the nation and includes a sampling of the headlines that the "Dodge City War" generated in newspapers around the nation.

65. Dykstra and Manfra, *Dodge City and the Birth of the Wild West*, quotations on 118.

66. Dykstra and Manfra, *Dodge City and the Birth of the Wild West*, 111–121; Clavin, *Dodge City*, 326–339; Shillingberg, *Dodge City*, 301–318.

67. Faulk, *Dodge City*, 181–183, 212; Shillingberg, *Dodge City*, 291; Dykstra and Manfra, *Dodge City and the Birth of the Wild West*, 88, 121, 151–155.

68. Dykstra and Manfra, *Dodge City and the Birth of the Wild West*, 58.

69. Worcester, *The Chisholm Trail*, 153–175; Carter, *Cowboy Capital of the World*, 256–259; Dykstra, *The Cattle Towns*, 293–354.

70. Dykstra and Manfra, *Dodge City and the Birth of the Wild West*, 160–161.

71. Dykstra, *The Cattle Towns*, 148. Shillingberg, *Dodge City*, claimed 18 additional homicides in the environs of Dodge City beyond those in Dykstra's count. For questions about Dykstra's undercount and what a revised figure would do to Dodge City's homicide rate per 100,000 inhabitants, see Courtwright, *Violent Land*, 96–97. For the FBI's "2018 Uniform Crime Report for Murder and Nonnegligent Manslaughter for Metropolitan Statistical Areas in the United States," see https://ucr.fbi.gov/crime-in-the-u.s/2018/crime-in-the-u.s.-2018/topic-pages/tables/table-6.

72. Dykstra and Manfra, *Dodge City and the Birth of the Wild West*, quotation on 44. For Dykstra's responses to critiques and revisions to his counts, see Robert R. Dykstra, "Quantifying the Wild West: The Problematic Statistics of Frontier Violence," *Western Historical Quarterly* 40 (Autumn 2009): 321–347; Dykstra, "Field Notes: Overdosing on Dodge City," *Western Historical Quarterly* 27 (Winter 1996): 505–514; for the revised year-by-year breakdown of homicides in Dodge City from 1872 to 1886, see Dykstra and Manfra, *Dodge City and the Birth of the Wild West*, 183–184.

73. Courtwright, *Violent Land*, 96–97.

74. Adapted from Table 2 in Reed, "Homicide on the Nebraska Panhandle Frontier," 144. See the accompanying footnote for the sources on which Reed based his tallies. I have here included only those sites for which the periodization extends to at least 1870, so as to make the higher estimate that Reed uses for Dodge City, as well as a lower one based on Dysktra's numbers.

75. For details about the Boot Hill Museum, see its website https://www.boothill.org/. Unfortunately, the museum's otherwise well-stocked gift shop does not sell copies of the orientation film, so my references to it are from the notes I took while viewing it. The quotation "nothing left to shoot but tin cans" echoes a line from Dodge's past. An item in the August 26, 1879, issue of the *Ford County Globe* reported that because "there have been only two men killed in Dodge this summer, . . . the police . . . are compelled to practice on cove oyster cans in order to keep their hands in." *Ford County Globe*, August 26, 1879.

Conclusion

1. Seth Schiesel, "Way Down Deep in the Wild, Wild West," *New York Times*, November 23, 2010, quotation, https://www.nytimes.com/2010/05/17/arts/television/17dead.html?searchResultPosition=5; Josh Dean, "Ride with the Devil," *Rolling Stone*, June 10, 2010, quotation on 48; Nicholson Baker, "Painkiller Deathstreak," *New Yorker* 86 (August 9, 2010): quotation on 59; Mike Snider, "Critics, Players Go Wild for West in Redemption," *USA Today*, May 26, 2010, 5d; Peter Suderman, "*Red Dead Redemption 2* Is True Art," *New York Times*, November 23, 2018, https://www.nytimes.com/2018/

11/23/opinion/sunday/red-dead-redemption-2-fallout-76-video-games.
html?searchResultPosition=2.

2. Suderman, "*Red Dead Redemption 2* Is True Art," quotations.

3. For a scholarly assessment of *Red Dead Redemption* and other history-
based computer games, see Dawn Spring, "Gaming History: Computer
and Video Games as Historical Scholarship," *Rethinking History* 19
(2015): 207–221.

4. On the resemblance to that era's anti-Westerns in general and to
Peckinpah's *The Wild Bunch* in particular, see Schiesel, "Way Down
Deep in the Wild, Wild West"; Louis Lalire, "Game Review: *Red Dead
Redemption*," https://www.historynet.com/wild-west-review-red-dead-red
emption.htm. On the redemptive function of violence in older frontier
tales and literature, see Richard Slotkin, *Regeneration through Violence: The
Mythology of the American Frontier, 1600–1860* (Middletown, CT: Wesleyan
University Press, 1973).

5. Patricia Nelson Limerick, *The Legacy of Conquest: The Unbroken Past of the
American West* (New York: W. W. Norton, 1987); Limerick, "What on Earth
Is the New Western History," in *Trails: Toward a New Western History*, ed.
Patricia Limerick, Clyde Milner, and Charles Rankin (Lawrence: University
Press of Kansas, 1991), 81–88; Limerick, "The Adventures of the Frontier in
the Twentieth Century," in *The Frontier in American Culture*, ed. James R.
Grossman (Berkeley: University of California Press, 1994), 66–102.

6. For a recent evaluation of Limerick's book and the reaction that followed,
see Nathalie Massip, "When Western History Tried to Reinvent
Itself: Revisionism, Controversy, and the Reception of the New Western
History," *Western Historical Quarterly* 52 (Spring 2021): 59–85.

BIBLIOGRAPHY

MANUSCRIPT COLLECTIONS

Army Papers. Missouri Historical Society, St. Louis, MO

Bourbon County Court Collection. Microfilm. Margaret I. King Library, Lexington, KY

William Clark Papers. Missouri Historical Society, St. Louis, MO

Lyman Draper Manuscript Collection. State Historical Society of Wisconsin, Madison, WI

Richard Graham Papers. Missouri Historical Society, St. Louis, MO

Indian Collections. Missouri Historical Society, St. Louis, MO

Harry Innes Papers. Library of Congress, Washington, DC

Thomas Jefferson Papers. National Archives, Washington, DC

Meriwether Lewis Collection. Missouri Historical Society, St. Louis, MO

McCarter & English Indian Claim Cases. Mudd Library, Princeton University, Princeton, NJ

Thomas Marshall Papers. Filson Historical Society, Louisville, KY

Miscellaneous Manuscripts Collection. Library of Congress, Washington, DC

Old Town Collection. Local History and Genealogy Room, Xenia Library, Xenia, OH

Justus Post Papers. Missouri Historical Society, St. Louis, MO

Typescript Collection. State Historical Society of Missouri, St. Louis, MO

Western Historical Manuscripts Collections. State Historical Society of Missouri, St. Louis, MO

Samuel Wilson Collection. Special Collections, Margaret I. King Library, University of Kentucky, Lexington, KY

PUBLISHED PRIMARY SOURCES

Abbey, James. *California. A Trip across the Plains, in the Spring of 1850, Being a Daily Record of Incidents of the Trip over the Plains, the Desert, and the Mountains, Sketches of the Country, Distances from Camp to Camp, etc., and Containing Valuable Information to Emigrants, as to Where They Will Find Wood, Water, and Grass at Almost Every Step of the Journey.* Tarrytown, NY: W. Abbatt, 1933.

Abel, Annie H., ed. *Tabeau's Narrative of Loisel's Expedition to the Upper Missouri.* Norman: University of Oklahoma Press, 1939.

Alford, Thomas Wildcat. *Civilization and the Story of the Absentee Shawnees, as Told to Florence Drake.* Norman: University of Oklahoma Press, 1936.

Aveling, Edward. *An American Journey.* New York: John W. Lovell, 1887.

Babcock, Rufus, ed. *Forty Years of Pioneer Life: Memoir of John Mason Peck D.D.* Carbondale: Southern Illinois University Press, 1965.

Bagley, Clarence B. "Crossing the Plains." *Washington Historical Quarterly* 13 (July 1922): 163–180.

Barry, Louise, ed. "Overland to the Gold Fields of California in 1852: The Journal of John Hawkins Clark, Expanded and Revised from Notes Made during the Journey." *Kansas Historical Quarterly* 11 (August 1942): 227–296.

Bell, Kathy. "El Capitan Arrives." *Dodge City Daily Globe,* November 1, 2016, 6.

Bennett, James. *Overland Journey to California: Journal of James Bennett Whose Party Left New Harmony in 1850 and Crossed the Plains and Mountains until the Golden West Was Reached.* London: Forgotten Books, 2018.

Bentley, James R., ed. "Two Letters of Meriwether Lewis to Major William Preston." *Filson Club History Quarterly* 44 (April 1970): 170–175.

Benton, Thomas Hart. "Mr. Benton, . . . Communicating the Memorial of the General Assembly of the State of Missouri, on the Subject of Indians Residing within That State," May 14, 1824, 18th Cong., 1st Sess., 1824, S. Doc. 79.

Benton, Thomas Hart. *Thirty Years' View or, a History of the Working of the American Government for Thirty Years, from 1820 to 1850.* 2 vols. New York: Appleton, 1854–1856.

Bigler, David L., and Will Bagley, eds. *Innocent Blood: Essential Narratives of the Mountain Meadows Massacre.* Norman, OK: Arthur H. Clark, 2008.

Bliss, Eugene F., ed. *Diary of David Zeisberger a Moravian Missionary among the Indians of Ohio.* 2 vols. St. Clair Shores: Scholarly Press, 1972.

Bowman, John. "Bowman's Expedition against Chillicothe, May–June 1779." *Ohio Archaeological and Historical Publications* 19 (1910): 446–459.

Bristow, Elijah. "For Oregon!" *Springfield Illinois Journal* 11 (November 1847). http://historymatters.gmu.edu/d/6231/.

Brookes-Smith, Joan E., ed. *Index for Old Kentucky Surveys and Grants.* Frankfort: Kentucky Historical Society, 1975.

Brookes-Smith, Joan E., ed. *Master Index Virginia Surveys and Grants, 1774–1791.* Frankfort: Kentucky Historical Society, 1976.

Brown, Orley E., ed. *The Captivity of Jonathan Alder and His Life with the Indians.* Akron: University of Akron Press, 2010.

Carpenter, Helen. "A Trip across the Plains in an Ox Wagon, 1857." In *Ho for California! Women's Overland Diaries from the Huntington Library*, edited by Sandra L. Myres, 93–188. San Marino: Huntington Library Press, 1980.

Carter, Clarence E., ed. *The Territorial Papers of the United States*, Vol. 13, *The Territory of Louisiana-Missouri, 1803–1806*. Washington, DC: United States National Archives and Records, 1948.

Carter, Clarence E., ed. *The Territorial Papers of the United States*, Vol. 15, *The Territory of Louisiana-Missouri, 1815–1821*. Washington, DC: Department of State, 1951.

"The Certificate Book of the Virginia Land Commission, 1779–1780." *Register of the Kentucky Historical Society* 21 (1923): 175–281.

Clift, G. Glenn, ed. "The District of Kentucky, 1783–1787, as Pictured by Harry Innes in a Letter to John Brown." *Register of the Kentucky Historical Society* 54 (October 1956): 368–372.

Collot, George-Victor. *A Journey in North America, Containing a Survey of the Countries Watered by the Mississippi, Ohio, Missouri, and Other Affluing Rivers; With Exact Observations on the Course and Soundings of These Rivers; And on the Towns, Villages, Hamlets and Farms of That Part of the New-World; Followed by Philosophical, Political, Military and Commercial Remarks and a Projected Line of Frontiers and General Limits.* 2 vols. Paris: A. Bertrand, 1826.

Cook, Michael L., ed. *Virginia Supreme Court District of Kentucky: Order Books, 1783–1792.* Evansville, IN: Cook Publications, 1988.

Coues, Elliott, ed. *New Light on the Early History of the Greater Northwest: The Manuscript Journals of Alexander Henry the Younger and of David Thompson.* 2 vols. 1897. Reprint, London: Forgotten Books, 1965.

Davies, K. G., ed. *Documents of the American Revolution, 1770–1783.* 21 vols. Shannon: Irish University Press, 1972–1981.

Delano, Alonzo. *Life on the Plains and among the Diggings; Being Scenes and Adventures of an Overland Journey to California: With Particular Incidents of the Route, Mistakes and Sufferings of the Emigrants, the Indian Tribes, the Present and Future of the Great West.* Auburn, NY: Miller, Orton & Mulligan, 1857.

Deluzieres, Pierre Charles de Hault Delassus. *An Official Account of the Situation, Soil, Produce, &c. of That Part of Louisiana Which Lies between the Mouth of the Missouri and New Madrid, or L'Anse a La Graise, and on the West Side of the Mississippi.* Lexington, KY: J. Bradford, 1796.

Dexter, Franklin B., ed. *Diary of David McClure: Doctor of Divinity, 1748–1820.* New York: Knickerbocker Press, 1899.

Doddridge, Joseph. *Notes on the Settlement and Indian Wars of the Western Parts of Virginia and Pennsylvania from 1763 to 1783.* Pittsburgh: University of Pennsylvania Press, 1912.

Dodge, Major Gen. G. M., to Maj. Gen. John Pope. June 17, 1865. War of the Rebellion, Serial 102, quotation on 912, https://ehistory.osu.edu/books/official-records/102/0912.

Dodge, Richard Irving. *The Plains of the Great West and Their Inhabitants; Being a Description of the Plains, Game, Indians, &c. of the Great American Desert.* New York: G. Putnam's Sons, 1877.

du Lac, M. Perrin. *Travels through the Two Louisianas, and among the Savage Nations of the Missouri; Also, in the United States along the Ohio, and the Adjacent Provinces, in 1801, 1802, & 1803.* London: R. Phillips, 1807.

Dye, Eva Emery, ed. "Boone Family Reminiscences as Told to Mrs. Dye." *Oregon Historical Quarterly* 42 (September 1941): 220–229.

Ekberg, Carl J., and William E. Foley, eds. *An Account of Upper Louisiana by Nicholas de Finiels.* Columbia: University of Missouri Press, 1989.

FBI. "2018 Uniform Crime Report for Murder and Nonnegligent Manslaughter for Metropolitan Statistical Areas in the United States." https://ucr.fbi.gov/crime-in-the-u.s/2018/crime-in-the-u.s.-2018/topic-pages/tables/table-6.

Field, Matthew C. *Prairie and Mountain Sketches.* Edited by Kate L. Gregg and John Francis McDermott. Norman: University of Oklahoma Press, 1957.

Filson, John. *The Discovery, Settlement, and Present State of Kentucke (1784): An Online Electronic Text Edition.* Edited by Paul Royster. DigitalCommons@ University Nebraska-Lincoln.

Flint, Timothy. *Recollections of the Last Ten Years in the Valley of the Mississippi.* Edited by George R. Brooks. 1926. Reprint, Carbondale: Southern Illinois University Press, 1968.

Ford, Paul Leicester, ed. *The Writings of Thomas Jefferson.* 10 vols. New York: G. P. Putnam's Sons, 1892–1899.

Ford County Globe. 1878–1879.

Garrison, George P., ed. "A Memorandum of M. Austin's Journey from the Lead Mines in the Country of Wythe in the State of Virginia to the Lead Mines in the Province of Louisiana West of the Mississippi, 1796–1797." *American Historical Review* 5 (April 1900): 518–523.

Gregg, Kate L., ed. *Westward with Dragoons: The Journal of William Clark on His Expedition to Establish Fort Osage, August 25 to September 22, 1808.* Fulton, MO: Ovid Bell Press, 1937.

Hafen, LeRoy R., and Ann W. Hafen, eds. *The Utah Expedition, 1857–1858: A Documentary Account of the United States Military Movement under Colonel Albert Sydney Johnston, and the Resistance by Brigham Young and the Mormon Nauvoo Legion.* Glendale: A. H. Clark, 1982.

Hammon, Neal O., ed. *My Father, Daniel Boone: The Draper Interviews with Nathan Boone.* Lexington: University Press of Kentucky, 1999.

Hammon, Neil O., and James R. Harris, eds. "'In a Dangerous Situation': Letters of Col. John Floyd, 1774–1783." *Register of the Kentucky Historical Society* 83 (Summer 1985): 202–236.

Houck, Louis, ed. *The Spanish Regime in Missouri: A Collection of Papers and Documents Relating to Upper Louisiana Principally within the Present Limits of Missouri during the Dominion of Spain, From the Archives of the Indies at Seville.* 2 vols. Chicago: R. R. Donnelley & Sons, 1909.

Jackson, Donald, ed. *Letters of the Lewis and Clark Expedition with Related Documents, 1783–1854.* 2 vols. Urbana: University of Illinois Press, 1978.

James, John Alton, ed. *George Rogers Clark Papers, 1771–1781.* Springfield: Trustees of the Illinois State Historical Library, 1912.

Jillson, Willard Rouse. "The Land Surveys of Daniel Boone." *Register of the Kentucky Historical Society* 44 (April 1946): 86–100.

Jillson, Willard Rouse. *With Compass and Chain: A Brief Narration of the Activities of Col. Daniel Boone as a Land Surveyor in Kentucky.* Frankfort: Kentucky Historical Society, 1954.

Johnston, William G. *Experiences of a Forty-Niner by William G. Johnston, a Member of the First Wagon Train to Enter California in the Memorable Year 1849.* Pittsburgh: Unknown printer, 1892.

Jones, David. *A Journal of Two Visits Made to Some Nations of Indians on the West Side of the River Ohio in the Years 1772 and 1773.* Burlington, NJ: Isaac Collins, 1774.

Jordan, John W., ed. "Journal of James Kenny, 1761–1763." *Pennsylvania Magazine of History and Biography* 37 (1913): 1–47.

Kappler, Charles J., ed. *Indian Affairs: Laws and Treaties.* 7 vols. Washington, DC: Government Printing Office, 1904.

Kappler, Charles J., ed. *Indian Affairs: Laws and Treaties*, Vol. II, *Treaties.* Washington, DC: Government Printing Office, 1904.

Kearny, Stephen W. "Report of a Summer Campaign to the Rocky Mountains &c. in 1845." Kansas Historical Society. https://www.kshs.org/index.php?url=km/items/view/210397.

Kellogg, Louise P., ed. *Frontier Advance on the Upper Ohio, 1778–1779.* Madison: State Historical Society of Wisconsin, 1916.

Kinietz, Vernon, and Erminie W. Voegelin, eds. "Shawnese Traditions: C. C. Trowbridge's Account." Occasional Contributions from the Museum of Anthropology of the University of Michigan 9 (June 1939).

Kinnaird, Lawrence, ed. "Spain in the Mississippi Valley, 1765–1794: Part II: Post War Decade, 1782–1791." In *Annual Report of the American Historical Association for the Year 1945*, Vol. III. Washington, DC: American Historical Association, 1946.

Kirkpatrick, Lewis H., ed. "The Journal of William Calk, Kentucky Pioneer." *Mississippi Valley Historical Review* 7 (March 1921): 336–377.

Leopard, Buel, and Floyd C. Shoemaker, eds. *The Messages and Proclamations of the Governors of the State of Missouri.* Columbia: State Historical Society of Missouri, 1922.

Lewis, Robert, ed. "The Diary of James Madison Coon and Nancy Iness (Miller) Coon on the Oregon Trail from Mercer County, Illinois to Clackamas County, Oregon in 1847." http://www.rootsweb.com/~orbenton/COONDIAR.htm, accessed on March 1, 2016.

Lowrie, Walter, and Walter S. Franklin, eds. *American State Papers.* Class II. Indian Affairs. 2 vols. Washington, DC: Gales and Seaton, 1834.

Marshall, Thomas Maitland, ed. *The Life and Papers of Frederic Bates.* 2 vols. St. Louis: Missouri Historical Society, 1926.

Mattes, Merrill J. *The Great Platte River Road: The Covered Wagon Mainline from Fort Kearny to Fort Laramie, Nebraska State Historical Society Publications*, Vol. XXV. Lincoln: Nebraska State Historical Society, 1969.

Metcalf, Samuel L., ed. *A Collection of Some of the Most Interesting Narratives of Indian Warfare in the West.* New York: William G. Hunt, 1977.

Miles, Nelson A. *Personal Recollections and Observations of General Nelson A. Miles.* Chicago: Werner, 1896.

Morse, Rev. Jedidiah. *A Report to the Secretary of War of the United States on Indian Affairs, Comprising a Narrative of a Tour Performed in the Summer of 1820, under a Commission from the President of the United States, for the Purpose of Ascertaining, for the Use of the Government the Actual State of the Indian Tribes in Our Country.* New Haven, CT: S. Converse, 1822.

Moulton, Gary, ed. *The Journals of the Lewis and Clark Expedition.* https://lewisandclarkjournals.unl.edu/.

Nash, Linda Clark, ed. *The Journals of Pierre-Louis de Lorimier, 1777–1795.* Montreal: Baraka Books, 2012.

National Park Service. *National Historic Trails: Auto Tour Route Interpretive Guide: Nebraska and Northeastern Colorado.* Washington, DC: National Parks Service, 2006.

Offenburger, Andrew, comp. *Digitizing Daniel Boone: The Research Notes of John Mack Faragher.* https://sourcenotes.miamioh.edu/daniel-boone/.

Palmer, William P., ed. *Calendar of Virginia State Papers and Other Manuscripts.* 11 vols. Richmond: R. F. Walker, 1875–1893.

Parkman, Francis. *The Oregon Trail.* Edited by A. B. Guthrie Jr. Boston: Ginn, 1910.

Pelzer, Louis. *Marches of the Dragoons in the Mississippi Valley: An Account of Marches and Activities of the First Regiment United States Dragoons in the Mississippi Valley between the Years 1833 and 1850.* Iowa City: State Historical Society of Iowa, 1917.

Penn, Dorothy, ed. "The Missouri Reader: The French in the Valley," pt. 2. *Missouri Historical Review* 40 (January 1946): 245–275.

Phelps, Katherine, comp. "A Partial List of Those at Fort Boonesborough." *Register of the Kentucky Historical Society* 23 (May 1925): 142–161.

Potter, David Morris, ed. *Trail to California: The Overland Journal of Vincent Geiger and Wakeman Bryarly.* New Haven, CT: Yale University Press, 1945.

Raymond, Henry H. "Diary of a Dodge City Buffalo Hunter, 1872–1873." Edited by Joseph W. Snell. *Kansas History Quarterly* 31 (Winter 1965): 345–395.

Robertson, James Rood, ed. *Petitions of the Early Inhabitants of Kentucky to the General Assembly of Virginia, 1769–1792.* Louisville: University of Kentucky Press, 1914.

Robins, Ruby Matson, ed. "The Missouri Reader: Americans in the Valley," pt. 1. *Missouri Historical Review* 45 (April 1951): 1–13.

Sandoval, Ysabel, trans. "The Beginning of Spanish Missouri: Instructions, D'Ulloa to Rui, 1767." *Missouri Historical Society Collections* 3 (April 1908): 145–169.

Saunders, William L., ed. *The Colonial Records of North Carolina.* 25 vols. Raleigh: University of North Carolina Press, 1886–1905.

Schultz, Christian. *Travels on an Inland Voyage through the States of New York, Pennsylvania, Virginia, Ohio, Kentucky, and Tennessee, and through the Territories of Indiana, Louisiana, Mississippi, and New Orleans; Performed in the Years 1807 and 1808; Including a Tour of Nearly Six Thousand Miles.* 2 vols. New York: Isaac Riley, 1810.

Smith, William. *An Historical Account of the Expedition against the Ohio Indians in the Year 1764.* Philadelphia: W. Bradford, 1765.

Spraker, Hazel Atterbury. *The Boone Family: A Genealogical History of the Descendants of George and Mary Boone Who Came to America in 1717.* 1922. Reprint, Baltimore: Genealogical Publishing Company, 1974.

Staples, Charles, ed. "History in Circuit Court Records." *Register of the Kentucky Historical Society* 32 (January 1934): 1–22.

Stoddard, Amos. "Papers of Captain Amos Stoddard." *Missouri Historical Society Glimpses of the Past* 2 (May–September 1935): 78–122.

Stoddard, Amos. *Sketches, Historical and Descriptive, of Louisiana.* Philadelphia: Matthew Carey, 1812.

Thorndike, Rachel Sherman, ed. *The Sherman Letters: Correspondence between General and Senator Sherman from 1837 to 1891.* New York: Charles Scribner's Sons, 1894.

Thwaites, Reuben G., and Louise P. Kellogg, eds. *Frontier Defense on the Upper Ohio, 1777–1778.* Madison: Wisconsin Historical Society, 1912.

"Treaty with the Shawnee, 1825." https://dc.library.okstate.edu/digital/collection/kapplers/id/26103/rec/1.

Twiss, Thomas S. United States Indian Agency of the Upper Platte, September 18, 1859, "Report of the Commissioner of Indian Affairs." Ex. Doc. 35, 36th Congress, 1st Sess., Senate.

Tyler, John. "First Annual Message." December 7, 1841. https://millercenter.org/the-presidency/presidential-speeches/december-7-1841-first-annual-message.

Van Schreevan, William J., ed. *Revolutionary Virginia: The Road to Independence.* 7 vols. Charlottesville: University Press of Virginia, 1973–1983.

Wallace, Paul A. W., ed. *Thirty Thousand Miles with John Heckewelder.* Pittsburgh: University of Pittsburgh Press, 1958.

Weisel, George F., ed. "Dodson's Death: Diary of John F. Dodson." *Montana: The Magazine of Western History* 3 (Spring 1953): 24–33.

West, J. Martin, ed. *Clark's Shawnee Campaign of 1780: Contemporary Accounts.* Springfield, OH: Clark County Historical Society, 1975.

Wright, Robert M. *Dodge City: The Cowboy Capital and the Great Southwest in the Days of the Wild Indian, the Buffalo, the Cowboy, Dance Halls, Gambling Halls, and Bad Men.* Wichita: Wichita Eagle Press, 1913.

Young, Chester Raymond, ed. *Westward into Kentucky: The Narrative of Daniel Trabue.* Lexington: University Press of Kentucky, 1981.

SECONDARY LITERATURE

Abbott, Carl. *Frontiers Past and Future: Science Fiction and the American West.* Lawrence: University Press of Kansas, 2006.

Abbott, E. C., and Helena Huntington Smith. *We Pointed Them North: Recollections of a Cowpuncher.* New York: Farrar & Rinehart, 1939.

Adams, Kevin. *Class and Race in the Frontier Army: Military Life in the West, 1870–1890*. Norman: University of Oklahoma Press, 2009.

Adas, Michael. "Settler Colony to Global Hegemon: Integrating the Exceptionalist Narrative of the American Experience into World History." *American Historical Review* 105 (December 2001): 1692–1720.

Adelman, Jeremy, and Stephen Aron. "From Borderlands to Borders: Empires, Nation-States, and the Peoples in Between in North American History." *American Historical Review* 104 (June 1999): 814–841.

Anderson, Gary Clayton. *Ethnic Cleansing and the Indian: The Crime That Should Haunt America*. Norman: University of Oklahoma Press, 2014.

Anderson, Terry L., and Peter J. Hill. *The Not So Wild, Wild West: Property Rights on the Frontier*. Stanford, CA: Stanford University Press, 2004.

Anson, Bert. "Variations of the Indian Conflict: The Effect of the Emigrant Indian Removal Policy, 1830–1854." *Missouri Historical Review* 59 (October 1964): 64–89.

Archibald, Robert R. "From 'La Louisiane' to 'Luisiana': The Imposition of Spanish Administration in the Upper Mississippi Valley." *Gateway Heritage* 11 (Summer 1990): 24–37.

Aron, Stephen. *American Confluence: The Missouri Frontier from Borderland to Border State*. Bloomington: Indiana University Press, 2006.

Aron, Stephen. *How the West Was Lost: The Transformation of Kentucky from Daniel Boone to Henry Clay*. Baltimore: Johns Hopkins University Press, 1996.

Aron, Stephen. "The Legacy of Daniel Boone: Three Generations of Boones and the History of Indian-White Relations." *Register of the Kentucky Historical Society* 95 (Summer 1997): 219–235.

Athearn, Robert G. *In Search of Canaan: Black Migration to Kansas, 1879–1880*. Lawrence: Regents Press of Kansas, 1978.

Atherton, Lewis. *The Cattle Kings*. Bloomington: Indiana University Press, 1961.

Audubon, John James. *Ornithological Biography . . . Interspersed with Delineations of American Scenery and Manners*. Philadelphia: Judah Dobson, 1831.

Axtell, James. "The White Indians of Colonial America." *William and Mary Quarterly*, 3d. ser., 32 (January 1975): 55–88.

Bagley, Will. *Blood of the Prophets: Brigham Young and the Massacre at Mountain Meadows*. Norman: University of Oklahoma Press, 2002.

Bagley, Will. *Overland West: The Story of the Oregon and California Trails*, Vol. I, *So Rugged and Mountainous: Blazing the Trails to Oregon and California, 1812–1848*. Norman: University of Oklahoma Press, 2010.

Bakeless, John. *Daniel Boone: Master of the Wilderness*. Mechanicsburg, PA: Stackpole Books, 1939.

Baker, Nicholson. "Painkiller Deathstreak." *New Yorker* 86 (August 9, 2010): 52–59.

Banner, Stuart. *How the Indians Lost Their Land: Law and Power on the Frontier*. Cambridge, MA: Harvard University Press, 2005.

Banner, Stuart. *Legal Systems in Conflict: Property and Sovereignty in Missouri, 1750–1860*. Norman: University of Oklahoma Press, 2000.

Barr, Julianna. *Peace Came in the Form of a Woman: Indians and Spaniards in the Texas Borderlands*. Chapel Hill: University of North Carolina Press, 2007.

Belich, James. *Replenishing the Earth: The Settler Revolution and the Rise of the Anglo World, 1789–1839*. Oxford: Oxford University Press, 2009.

Belue, Ted Franklin. *The Long Hunt: Death of the Buffalo East of the Mississippi*. Mechanicsburg, PA: Stackpole Books, 1996.

Belue, Ted Franklin. "Terror in the Canelands: The Fate of Daniel Boone's Salt Boilers." *Filson Club History Quarterly* 68 (January 1994): 3–34.

Bettelyoun, Susan Bordeaux, and Josephine Waggoner. *With My Own Eyes: A Lakota Woman Tells Her People's History*. Edited by Emily Levine. Lincoln: Bison Books, 1998.

Beyreis, David C. *Blood in the Borderlands: Conflict, Kinship, and the Bent Family, 1821–1920*. Lincoln: University of Nebraska Press, 2020.

Blevins, Brooks. *A History of the Ozarks*, Vol. 1, *The Old Ozarks*. Champaign and Urbana: University of Illinois Press, 2018.

Bowes, John. *Land Too Good for Indians: Northern Indian Removal*. Norman: University of Oklahoma Press, 2016.

Britz, Kevin, and Roger L. Nichols. *Tombstone, Deadwood, and Dodge City: Recreating the Frontier West*. Norman: University of Oklahoma Press, 2018.

Brown, A. Theodore. *Frontier Community: Kansas City to 1870*. Columbia: University of Missouri Press, 1963.

Brown, Meredith Mason. *Frontiersman: Daniel Boone and the Making of America*. Baton Rouge: Louisiana State University Press, 2008.

Brown, Richard Maxwell. *No Duty to Retreat: Violence and Values in American History and Society*. New York: Oxford University Press, 1992.

Brown, Richard Maxwell, and Don E. Fehrenbacher, eds. *Tradition, Conflict, and Modernization: Perspectives on the American Revolution*. New York: Elsevier Science, 1977.

Brown, William Dodd. "The Capture of Daniel Boone's Saltmakers: Fresh Perspectives from Primary Sources." *Register of the Kentucky Historical Society* 83 (Winter 1985): 1–18.

Buckley, Jay H. *William Clark: Indian Diplomat*. Norman: University of Oklahoma Press, 2008.

Butler, Anne M. *Daughters of Joy, Sisters of Misery: Prostitutes in the American West, 1865–1890*. Urbana: University of Illinois Press, 1985.

Calloway, Colin G. *The American Revolution in Indian Country: Crisis and Diversity in Native American Communities*. New York: Cambridge University Press, 1995.

Calloway, Colin G. *The Indian World of George Washington: The First President, the First Americans, and the Birth of the Nation*. New York: Penguin Books, 2018.

Calloway, Colin G. *One Vast Winter Count: The Native American West before Lewis and Clark*. Lincoln: University of Nebraska Press, 2003.

Calloway, Colin G. *The Shawnees and the War for America*. New York: Penguin Books, 2007.

Calloway, Colin G. "'We Have Always Been the Frontier': The American Revolution in Shawnee Country." *American Indian Quarterly* 16 (1992): 39–52.

Carlson, Paul H., ed. *The Cowboy Way*. Lubbock: Texas Tech University Press, 2000.

Carr, Edward H. *What Is History?* New York: Penguin Books, 1961.

Carter, Samuel, III. *Cowboy Capital of the World: The Saga of Dodge City*. New York: Doubleday, 1973.

Cayton, Andrew, and Fredrika Teute, eds. *Contact Points: American Frontiers from the Mohawk Valley to the Mississippi, 1750–1830*. Chapel Hill: University of North Carolina Press, 1998.

Christensen, Lawrence O., William E. Foley, Gary R. Kremer, and Kenneth H. Winn, eds. *Dictionary of Missouri Biography*. Columbia: University of Missouri Press, 1999.

Clark, Christopher G. "The Myth of Indian Aggression in Early Nebraska." *Platte Valley Review* 14 (Spring 1986): 26–34.

Clark, Thomas D., ed. *The Voice of the Frontier: John Bradford's Notes on Kentucky*. Lexington: University Press of Kentucky, 1993.

Clavin, Tom. *Dodge City: Wyatt Earp, Bat Masterson, and the Wickedest Town in the American West*. New York: St. Martin's Press, 2017.

Cleary, Patricia. *The World, the Flesh, and the Devil: A History of Colonial St. Louis*. Columbia: University of Missouri Press, 2011.

Cotterill, R. S. *History of Pioneer Kentucky*. Cincinnati: Johnson & Hardin, 1917.

Courtwright, David T. *Violent Land: Single Men and Social Disorder from the Frontier to the Inner City*. Cambridge, MA: Harvard University Press, 2001.

Cowley, Robert, ed. *What Ifs? of American History: Eminent Historians Imagine What Might Have Been*. New York: Penguin, 2003.

Crowe, Daniel E. "James Smith among the Indians: Cultural Captives on the Early American Frontier, 1755–1812." *Filson Club History Quarterly* 73 (1999): 117–138.

Culver, Lawrence. "Manifest Destiny and Manifest Disaster: Climate Perceptions and Realities in United States Territorial Expansion." In *American Environments: Climate—Cultures—Catastrophe*, edited by Christof Mauch and Sylvia Mayer, 7–30. Heidelberg, Germany: Universitätsverlag, 2012.

Cutright, Paul R. "Lewis and Clark Indian Peace Medals." *Bulletin of the Missouri Historical Society* 24 (January 1968): 160–167.

Dale, Edward Everett. *The Range Cattle Industry*. Norman: University of Oklahoma Press, 1960.

Dary, David. *Cowboy Culture: A Saga of Five Centuries*. New York: Alfred A. Knopf, 1981.

Dary, David. *The Santa Fe Trail: Its History, Legends, and Lore*. New York: Alfred A. Knopf, 2000.

De León, Arnoldo. "Vamos Pa' Kiansis: Tejanos in the Nineteenth-Century Cattle Drives." *Journal of South Texas* 27 (Fall 2014): 6–21.

Dean, Josh. "Ride with the Devil." *Rolling Stone*, June 10, 2010: 48.

Delay, Brian. *War of a Thousand Deserts: Indian Raids and the U.S.-Mexican War*. New Haven, CT: Yale University Press, 2008.

del Mar, David Peterson. *Beaten Down: A History of Interpersonal Violence in the West*. Seattle: University of Washington Press, 2002.

Deloria, Philip J. "What Is the Middle Ground, Anyway?" *William and Mary Quarterly*, 3rd. ser., 63 (January 2006): 15–22.

DeMattos, Jack, and Chuck Parson. *The Notorious Luke Short: Sporting Man of the Wild West*. Denton: University of North Texas Press, 2015.

Denton, Sally. *American Massacre: The Tragedy at Mountain Meadows, September 1857*. New York: Vintage, 2003.

Dillon, Richard. *Meriwether Lewis: A Biography*. New York: Coward-McCann, 1965.

Din, Gilbert C. "Captain Francisco Ríu y Morales and the Beginnings of Spanish Rule in Missouri." *Missouri Historical Review* 94 (January 2000): 121–145.

Din, Gilbert C. "The Immigration Policy of Governor Esteban Miró in Spanish Louisiana." *Southwestern Historical Quarterly* 73 (October 1969): 155–175.

Din, Gilbert C. "Spain's Immigration Policy in Louisiana and the American Penetration, 1792–1803." *Southwestern Historical Quarterly* 76 (January 1973): 255–276.

Din, Gilbert C., and A. P. Nasatir. *The Imperial Osages: Spanish-Indian Diplomacy in the Mississippi Valley*. Norman: University of Oklahoma Press, 1983.

Dixon, Olive K. *Life of "Billy" Dixon: Plainsman, Scout, and Pioneer*. Dallas: P. L. Turner, 1927.

Dobie, J. Frank. *The Longhorns*. Boston: Little, Brown, 1950.

Dowd, Gregory Evans. *A Spirited Resistance: The North American Indian Struggle for Unity, 1745–1815*. Baltimore: Johns Hopkins University Press, 1992.

Draper, Lyman C. *The Life of Daniel Boone*. Edited by Ted Franklin Belue. Mechanicsburg, PA: Stackpole Books, 1998.

Durham, Philip J., and Everett L. Jones. *The Negro Cowboys*. New York: Dodd, Mead, 1965.

DuVal, Kathleen. *The Native Ground: Indians and Colonists in the Heart of the Continent*. Philadelphia: University of Pennsylvania Press, 2006.

Dykstra, Robert R. *The Cattle Towns*. New York: Alfred A. Knopf, 1971.

Dykstra, Robert R. "Field Notes: Overdosing on Dodge City." *Western Historical Quarterly* 27 (Winter 1996): 505–514.

Dykstra, Robert R. "Quantifying the Wild West: The Problematic Statistics of Frontier Violence." *Western Historical Quarterly* 40 (Autumn 2009): 321–347.

Dykstra, Robert R., and Jo Ann Manfra. *Dodge City and the Birth of the Wild West*. Lawrence: University Press of Kansas, 2017.

Edmunds, R. David. "Potawatomis in the Platte Country: An Indian Removal Incomplete." *Missouri Historical Review* 68 (1974): 375–392.

Edwards, Tai S. *Osage Women and Empire: Gender and Power*. Lawrence: University Press of Kansas, 2018.

Ekberg, Carl J. *Francois Vallé and His World: Upper Louisiana before Lewis and Clark*. Columbia: University of Missouri Press, 2002.

Ekberg, Carl J. *French Roots in the Illinois Country: The Mississippi Frontier in Colonial Times*. Urbana: University of Illinois Press, 1998.

Ekberg, Carl J. *Stealing Indian Women: Native Slavery in the Illinois Country.* Urbana: University of Illinois Press, 2007.

Elliott, Lawrence. *The Long Hunter: A New Life of Daniel Boone.* New York: Reader's Digest Press, 1976.

Englebert, Robert. "Colonial Encounters and the Changing Contours of Ethnicity: Pierre-Louis de Lorimier at the Edges of Empire." *Ohio Valley History* 18 (Spring 2018): 45–69.

Faragher, John Mack. *Daniel Boone: The Life and Legend of an American Pioneer.* New York: Henry Holt, 1992.

Faragher, John Mack. *Eternity Street: Violence and Justice in Frontier Los Angeles.* New York: W. W. Norton, 2016.

Faragher, John Mack. *A Great and Noble Scheme: The Tragic Story of the Expulsion of the French Acadians from Their American Homeland.* New York: W. W. Norton, 2005.

Faragher, John Mack. *Sugar Creek: Life on the Illinois Prairie.* New Haven, CT: Yale University Press, 1986.

Faragher, John Mack. *Women and Men on the Overland Trail.* New Haven, CT: Yale University Press, 1979.

Faulk, Odie B. *Dodge City: The Most Western Town of All.* New York: Oxford University Press, 1977.

Fausz, Frederick. "Becoming 'a Nation of Quakers': The Removal of the Osage Indians from Missouri." *Gateway Heritage* 21 (Summer 2000): 28–39.

Fenn, Elizabeth. *Encounters at the Heart of the World: A History of the Mandan People.* New York: Macmillan, 2014.

Ferguson, Niall, ed. *Virtual History.* New York: Basic Books, 1999.

Fields, Major Jonathan E. "The Curious Court-Martial of Daniel Boone." *Army Lawyer* 46 (January 2016): 65–73.

Fischer, David Hackett. *Albion's Fatal Seed: Four British Folkways in America.* Oxford: Oxford University Press, 1989.

Fisher, Robert L. "The Treaties of Portage des Sioux." *Mississippi Valley Historical Review* 19 (March 1933): 495–508.

Flores, Dan. "A Very Different Story: Exploring the Southwest from Monticello with the Freeman and Custis Expedition of 1806." *Montana: The Magazine of Western History* 50 (March 2000): 2–17.

Foley, William E. "After the Applause: William Clark's Failed 1820 Gubernatorial Campaign." *Gateway Heritage* 24 (Fall 2003–Winter 2004): 105–111.

Foley, William E. *The Genesis of Missouri: From Wilderness Outpost to Statehood.* Columbia: University of Missouri Press, 1989.

Foley, William E. *A History of Missouri,* Vol. I, *1673–1820.* Columbia: University of Missouri Press, 1971.

Foley, William E. "James A. Wilkinson: Territorial Governor." *Bulletin of the Missouri Historical Society* 25 (1968): 3–17.

Foley, William E. "The Lewis and Clark Expedition's Silent Partners: The Chouteau Brothers of St. Louis." *Missouri Historical Review* 77 (January 1983): 131–146.

Foley, William E., and C. David Rice. *The First Chouteaus: River Barons of Early St. Louis*. Urbana: University of Illinois Press, 1983.

Frantz, Joe B., and Julian Ernest Choate Jr. *The American Cowboy*. Norman: University of Oklahoma Press, 1955.

Frazier, Robert W. *Forts of the West: Military Forts and Presidios and Posts Commonly Called Forts West of the Mississippi River to 1898*. Norman: University of Oklahoma Press, 1965.

Fresonke, Kris, and Mark Spence, eds. *Lewis and Clark: Legacies, Memories, and New Perspectives*. Berkeley: University of California Press, 2004.

Furtwangler, Albert. *Acts of Discovery: Visions of America in the Lewis and Clark Journals*. Urbana: University of Illinois Press, 1999.

Gardner, James Alexander. *Lead King: Moses Austin*. St. Louis: Sunrise, 1980.

Gerlach, Russell L. "Population Origins in Rural Missouri." *Missouri Historical Review* 71 (October 1976): 1–21.

Gerlach, Russell L. *Settlement Patterns in Missouri: A Study of Population Origins with a Wall Map*. Columbia: University of Missouri Press, 1986.

Gill, Harold B., Jr., and George M. Curtis III, eds. *A Man Apart: The Journal of Nicholas Cresswell, 1774–1781*. Lanham, MD: Lexington Books, 2009.

Gilman, Carolyn. *Lewis and Clark: Across the Divide*. Washington, DC: Smithsonian, 2003.

Gilman, Carolyn. "A World of Women." *Gateway Heritage* 24 (Fall 2003–Winter 2004): 42–47.

Gitlin, Jay. *The Bourgeois Frontier: French Towns, French Traders, and American Expansion*. New Haven, CT: Yale University Press, 2010.

Glasrud, Bruce A., and Michael N. Searles, eds. *Black Cowboys in the American West: On the Range, On the Stage, Behind the Badge*. Norman: University of Oklahoma Press, 2016.

Goetzmann, William H. *Exploration and Empire: The Explorer and the Scientist in the Winning of the American West*. New York: Alfred A. Knopf, 1966.

Gopnik, Adam. "Uncivil Wars." *New Yorker*. February 10, 2020. https://www.newyorker.com/magazine/2020/02/10/did-lincoln-really-matter.

Gordon, Sarah Barringer, and Jan Shipps. "Fatal Convergence in the Kingdom of God: The Mountain Meadows Massacre in American History." *Journal of the Early Republic* 37 (Summer 2017): 307–347.

Gracy, David B., II. "Moses Austin and the Development of the Missouri Lead Industry." *Gateway Heritage* 1 (Spring 1981): 42–48.

Gracy, David B., II. *Moses Austin: His Life*. San Antonio: Trinity University Press, 1987.

Greene, Candace S., and Russell Thornton, eds. *The Year the Stars Fell: Lakota Winter Counts at the Smithsonian*. Lincoln: University of Nebraska Press, 2007.

Greene, Jerome A. *January Moon: The Northern Cheyenne Breakout from Fort Robinson, 1878–1879*. Norman: University of Oklahoma Press, 2020.

Gresmer, Daniel R. "'Bettering Our Circumstances': Settler Colonialism in Ohio during the 1780s." *Ohio History* 124 (Spring 2017): 22–40.

Griffin, Patrick. *American Leviathan: Empire, Nation, and Revolutionary Frontier.* New York: Farrar, Straus & Giroux, 2007.

Griffiths, Leonard. *The First 9/11 in America: September 11, 1857: Mountain Meadows Massacre.* Meadville, PA: Christian Faith, 2020.

Guice, John D. W., ed. *By His Own Hand? The Mysterious Death of Meriwether Lewis.* Norman: University of Oklahoma Press, 2006.

Gwynne, S. C. *Empire of the Summer Moon: Quanah Parker and the Rise and Fall of the Comanches, the Most Powerful Indian Tribe in American History.* New York: Scribner, 2010.

Hafen, Leroy R., ed. *The Mountain Men and the Fur Trade of the Far West.* 10 vols. Glendale, CA: Arthur H. Clark, 1965–1972.

Hagy, James William. "The First Attempt to Settle Kentucky: Boone in Virginia." *Filson Club History Quarterly* 44 (1970): 227–234.

Hall, Virginius C., ed. "Journal of Isaac Hite, 1773." *Bulletin of the Historical and Philosophical Society of Ohio* 12 (October 1954): 262–281.

Hämäläinen, Pekka. *The Comanche Empire.* New Haven, CT: Yale University Press, 2008.

Hämäläinen, Pekka. *Lakota America: A New History of Indigenous Power.* New Haven, CT: Yale University Press, 2019.

Hammon, Neal O. "Captain Harrod's Company, 1774: A Reappraisal." *Register of the Kentucky Historical Society* 72 (July 1974): 224–242.

Hammon, Neal O., ed. *My Father, Daniel Boone: The Draper Interviews with Nathan Boone.* Lexington: University Press of Kentucky, 1999.

Hammon, Neal O., and James Russell Harris. "Daniel Boone the Businessman: Revising the Myth of Failure." *Register of the Kentucky Historical Society* 112 (Winter 2014): 5–50.

Harper, Rob. *Unsettling the West: Violence and State Building in the Ohio Valley.* Philadelphia: University of Pennsylvania Press, 2018.

Haveman, Christopher D. *Rivers of Sand: Creek Indian Emigration, Relocation, and Ethnic Cleansing in the American South.* Lincoln: University of Nebraska Press, 2016.

Haywood, C. Robert. *Cowtown Lawyers: Dodge City and Its Attorneys, 1876–1886.* Norman: University of Oklahoma Press, 1988.

Haywood, C. Robert. *The Merchant Prince of Dodge City: The Life and Times of Robert M. Wright.* Norman: University of Oklahoma Press, 1988.

Haywood, C. Robert. " 'No Less a Man': Blacks in Cow Town Dodge City, 1876–1886." *Western Historical Quarterly* 19 (May 1988): 161–182.

Haywood, C. Robert. *Victorian West: Class and Culture in Kansas Cattle Towns.* Lawrence: University Press of Kansas, 1991.

Henderson, Archibald. "The Creative Forces in Westward Expansion." *American Historical Review* 20 (October 1914): 86–107.

Hernández, Kelly Lytle. *City of Inmates: Conquest, Rebellion, and the Rise of Human Caging in Los Angeles, 1771–1965.* Chapel Hill: University of North Carolina Press, 2017.

Hinderaker, Eric. *Elusive Empires: Constructing Colonialism in the Ohio Valley, 1673–1800.* New York: Cambridge University Press, 1997.

Hixon, Walter L. *American Settler Colonialism: A History*. New York: Springer Nature, 2013.

Holliday, J. S. *The World Rushed In: The California Gold Rush Experience*. Norman: University of Oklahoma Press, 1981.

Hollon, Eugene. *The Great American Desert*. New York: Oxford University Press, 1969.

Houck, Louis, ed. *The Spanish Regime in Missouri*. 2 vols. Chicago: Lakeside Press, 1909.

Howard, James. *Shawnee!: The Ceremonialism of a Native American Tribe and Its Cultural Background*. Athens: Ohio University Press, 1981.

Hulston, John K. "Daniel Boone's Sons in Missouri." *Missouri Historical Review* 47 (July 1947): 361–372.

Hunter, J. Marvin, ed. *The Trail Drivers of Texas*. Austin: University of Texas Press, 1985.

Hurt, Douglas. *Nathan Boone and the American Frontier*. Columbia: University of Missouri Press, 1998.

Husband, Michael B., Judith A. Heberling, and William Hunter. *Reimagining Dodge . . . : A Heritage Tourism Master Plan for Dodge City and Ford County, Kansas*. Report by Heberling Associates, Dodge City, KS, 2009.

Hyde, Anne. *Empires, Nations, and Families: A New History of the North American West, 1800–1860*. Lincoln: University of Nebraska Press, 2011.

Isenberg, Andrew. *The Destruction of the Bison: An Environmental History, 1750–1920*. New York: Cambridge University Press, 2000.

Isenberg, Andrew. *Wyatt Earp: A Vigilante Life*. New York: Hill & Wang, 2013.

Jackson, Donald. *Thomas Jefferson and the Stony Mountains: Exploring the West from Monticello*. Urbana: University of Illinois Press, 1981.

Jacobs, Margaret D. White. *Mother to a Dark Race: Settler Colonialism, Maternalism, and the Removal of Indigenous Children in the American West and Australia*. Lincoln: University of Nebraska Press, 2003.

Jeffrey, Julie Roy. *Frontier Women: The Trans-Mississippi West, 1840–1880*. New York: Hill & Wang, 1979; revised edition, 1998.

Johnson, Clark V. "The Missouri Redress Petitions: A Reappraisal of Mormon Persecutions in Missouri." *Brigham Young University Studies* 26 (1986): 31–44.

Johnson, Susan Lee. *Roaring Camp: The Social World of the California Gold Rush*. New York: W. W. Norton, 2000.

Jones, Douglas C. *The Court-Martial of George Armstrong Custer*. New York: HarperCollins, 1996.

Jones, Landon Y., Jr. "The Council That Changed the West: William Clark at Portage des Sioux." *Gateway Heritage* 24 (Fall 2003–Winter 2004): 88–95.

Jordan, Terry G. *North American Cattle-Ranching Frontiers: Origins, Diffusion, and Differentiation*. Albuquerque: University of New Mexico Press, 1993.

Jordan, Terry G. *Trails to Texas: Southern Roots of Western Cattle Ranching*. Lincoln: University of Nebraska Press, 1981.

Jordan, Terry G., and Matti Kaups. *The American Backwoods Frontier: An Ethnic and Ecological Interpretation*. Baltimore: Johns Hopkins University Press, 1989.

Kastor, Peter J. *William Clark's World: Describing America in an Age of Unknowns.* New Haven, CT: Yale University Press, 2011.

Kastor, Peter J., and François Weil, eds. *Empires of the Imagination: Transatlantic Histories of the Louisiana Purchase.* Charlottesville: University of Virginia Press, 2009.

Keefe, James F., and Lynn Morrow, eds. *The White River Chronicles of S. C. Turnbo: Man and Wildlife on the Ozarks Frontier.* Fayetteville: University of Arkansas Press, 1994.

Kelman, Ari. *A Misplaced Massacre: Struggling over the Memory of Sand Creek.* Cambridge, MA: Harvard University Press, 2013.

Keyes, Sarah. "Beyond the Plains: Migration to the Pacific and the Reconfiguration of America, 1820s–1900s." PhD diss., University of Southern California, 2012.

King, Duane, ed. *Unlocking the History of the Americas.* Tulsa, OK: Gilcrease Museum, 2016.

Knowlton, Christopher. *Cattle Kingdom: The Hidden History of the Cowboy West.* Boston: Mariner Books, 2017.

Lake, Stuart N. *Wyatt Earp: Frontier Marshal.* Boston: Houghton Mifflin, 1931.

Lakomäki, Sami. *Gathering Together: The Shawnee People through Diaspora and Nationhood, 1600–1870.* New Haven, CT: Yale University Press, 2014.

Lalire, Louis. "Game Review: Red Dead Redemption," January 6, 2018. https://www.historynet.com/wild-west-review-red-dead-redemption.htm.

Lamar, Howard R. *Charlie Siringo's West: An Interpretive Biography.* Albuquerque: University of New Mexico Press, 2005.

Lamar, Howard R., ed. *The New Encyclopedia of the American West.* New Haven, CT: Yale University Press, 1998.

Lankford, George E. "Shawnee Convergence: Immigrant Indians in the Ozarks." *Arkansas Historical Quarterly* 58 (Winter 1999): 390–413.

Leckie, William H., and Shirley A. Leckie. *The Buffalo Soldiers: A Narrative of the Black Cavalry in the West.* Norman: University of Oklahoma Press, 2003.

Lee, Jacob F. *Masters of the Middle Waters: Indian Nations and Colonial Ambitions along the Mississippi.* Cambridge, MA: Harvard University Press, 2019.

Lee, Robert. "Accounting for Conquest: The Price of the Louisiana Purchase of Indian Country." *Journal of American History* 103 (March 2017): 921–942.

Leonard, Carol, and Isidor Walliman. "Prostitution and Changing Morality in Frontier Cattle Towns in Kansas." *Kansas History* 2 (Spring 1979): 34–53.

Lester, William Stewart. *The Transylvania Colony.* Spencer, IN: Samuel R. Guard, 1935.

LeSueur, Stephen C. *The 1838 Mormon War in Missouri.* Columbia: University of Missouri Press, 1987.

Libecap, Gary D., and Zeynep Kocabiyik Hansen. "'Rain Follows the Plow' and Dryfarming Doctrine: The Climate Information Problem and Homestead Failure in the Upper Great Plains, 1890–1925." *Journal of Economic History* 62 (2002): 86–120.

Limerick, Patricia Nelson. "The Adventures of the Frontier in the Twentieth Century." In *The Frontier in American Culture,* edited by James R. Grossman, 66–102. Berkeley: University of California Press, 1994.

Limerick, Patricia Nelson. *Desert Passages: Encounters with the American Deserts*. Albuquerque: University of New Mexico Press, 1985.

Limerick, Patricia Nelson. *The Legacy of Conquest: The Unbroken Past of the American West*. New York: W. W. Norton, 2006.

Limerick, Patricia Nelson. "What on Earth Is the New Western History." In *Trails: Toward a New Western History*, edited by Patricia Limerick, Clyde Milner, and Charles Rankin, 81–88. Lawrence: University Press of Kansas, 1991.

Linklater, Andro. *An Artist in Treason: The Extraordinary Double Life of General James Wilkinson, Commander in Chief of the U.S. Army and Agent 13 in the Spanish Secret Service*. New York: Walker Books, 2009.

Litwack, Leon F. *Been in the Storm So Long: The Aftermath of Slavery*. New York: Vintage, 1979.

Lofaro, Michael A. "The Many Lives of Daniel Boone." *Register of the Kentucky Historical Society* 102 (October 2004): 488–511.

Low, Denise, and Ramon Powers. *Northern Cheyenne Ledger Art by Fort Robinson Breakout Survivors*. Lincoln: University of Nebraska Press, 2020.

Lubet, Steven. *Murder in Tombstone: The Forgotten Trial of Wyatt Earp*. New Haven, CT: Yale University Press, 2004.

Luckett, Matthew. *Never Caught Twice: Horse Stealing in Western Nebraska, 1850–1890*. Lincoln: University of Nebraska Press, 2021.

MacKell, Jan. *Brothels, Bordellos, and Bad Girls: Prostitution in Colorado, 1860–1930*. Albuquerque: University of New Mexico Press, 2004.

MacKinnon, William P., ed. *At Sword's Point: Part 1: A Documentary History of the Utah War to 1858*. Norman: University of Oklahoma Press, 2008.

MacKinnon, William P., ed. *At Sword's Point, Part 2: A Documentary History of the Utah War, 1858–1859*. Norman: University of Oklahoma Press, 2016.

Madley, Benjamin. *An American Genocide: The United States and the California Indian Catastrophe, 1846–1873*. New Haven, CT: Yale University Press, 2016.

Mancke, Elizabeth. "The Ohio Country and Indigenous Geopolitics in Early Modern North America, circa 1500–1760." *Ohio Valley History* 18 (Spring 2018): 7–23.

Martin, Calvin. *Keepers of the Game: Indian-Animal Relationships and the Fur Trade*. Athens: University of Georgia Press, 2008.

Massip, Nathalie. "When Western History Tried to Reinvent Itself: Revisionism, Controversy, and the Reception of the New Western History." *Western Historical Quarterly* 52 (Spring 2021): 59–85.

Mayer, Frank H., and Charles B. Roth. *The Buffalo Harvest*. Denver: Sage Books, 1958.

McCall, Laura. "Sacagawea: A Historical Enigma." In *Ordinary Women, Extraordinary Lives: Women in American History*, edited by Kriste Lindenmeyer. Wilmington, DE: SR Books, 2000, 39–54.

McConnell, Michael N. *A Country Between: The Upper Ohio Valley and Its Peoples, 1724–1774*. Lincoln: University of Nebraska Press, 1992.

McDonnell, Michael A. *Masters of Empire: Great Lakes Indians and the Making of America*. New York: Farrar, Straus & Giroux, 2015.

McGrath, Roger D. *Gunfighters, Highwaymen, and Vigilantes: Violence on the Frontier*. Berkeley: University of California Press, 1987.

McKanna, Clare, Jr. "Alcohol, Handguns, and Homicide in the American West: A Tale of Three Counties, 1880–1920." *Western Historical Quarterly* 26 (Winter 1995): 455–482.

McKanna, Clare, Jr. "Enclaves of Violence in Nineteenth-Century California." *Pacific Historical Review* 73 (August 2004): 391–424.

McKanna, Clare, Jr. *Homicide, Race, and Justice in the American West, 1880–1920*. Tucson: University of Arizona Press, 1997.

McKanna, Clare, Jr. *Race and Homicide in Nineteenth-Century California*. Reno: University of Nevada Press, 2002.

Meech, Peter. *Billy the Kid: A Novel*. Boulder, CO: Sentient Publications, 2020.

Michno, Gregory F., and Susan J. Michno. *Circle the Wagons! Attacks on Wagon Trains in History and Hollywood Films*. Jefferson, NC: McFarland, 2009.

Milner, Clyde, II, Carol A. O'Connor, and Martha A. Sandweiss, eds. *The Oxford History of the American West*. New York: Oxford University Press, 1994.

Miner, Craig. *West of Wichita: Settling the High Plains of Kansas, 1865–1890*. Lawrence: University Press of Kansas, 1986.

Monkkonen, Eric. "Homicide: Explaining America's Exceptionalism." *American Historical Review* 111 (February 2006): 76–94.

Monkkonen, Eric. "Western Homicide: The Case of Los Angeles, 1830–1870." *Pacific Historical Review* 74 (November 2005): 603–618.

Moore, John H. "A Captive of the Shawnees, 1779–1784." *West Virginia History* 23 (1962): 287–296.

Morgan, Robert. *Boone: A Biography*. Chapel Hill, NC: Algonquin Books, 2007.

Morris, Larry E. *The Fate of the Corps: What Became of the Lewis and Clark Explorers after the Expedition*. New Haven, CT: Yale University Press, 2004.

Morrow, Lynn. "New Madrid and Its Hinterland: 1783–1826." *Bulletin of the Missouri Historical Society* 36 (July 1980): 241–250.

Morrow, Lynn. "Trader William Gilliss and Delaware Migration in Southern Missouri." *Missouri Historical Review* 75 (January 1981): 147–167.

Moulton, Gary. *The Lewis and Clark Expedition Day by Day*. Lincoln: University of Nebraska Press, 2018.

Munkres, Robert L. "The Plains Indian Threat on the Oregon Trail before 1860." *Annals of Wyoming* 40 (October 1968): 193–221.

Nasatir, Abraham P. *Borderland in Retreat: From Spanish Louisiana to the Far Southwest*. Albuquerque: University of New Mexico Press, 1976.

Nelson, Larry L. "Cultural Mediation, Cultural Exchange, and the Invention of the Ohio Frontier." *Ohio History Journal* 105 (Winter–Spring 1996): 72–91.

NPR. "A New Spin on a Classic Video Game Gives Native Americans Better Representation," May 12, 2021. https://www.npr.org/2021/05/12/996007048/no-bows-and-arrows-and-no-broken-english-on-the-updated-oregon-trail.

Nugent, Walter. *Habits of Empire: A History of American Expansion*. New York: Vintage Books, 2008.

O'Malley, Nancy. *Boonesborough Unearthed*. Lexington: University Press of Kentucky, 2019.

Onuf, Peter. "'We Shall All Be Americans': Thomas Jefferson and the Indians." *Indiana Magazine of History* 95 (June 1999): 103–141.

Orsi, Jared. *Citizen Explorer: The Life of Zebulon Pike*. New York: Oxford University Press, 2014.

Ostler, Jeffrey. *The Plains Sioux and U.S. Colonialism from Lewis and Clark to Wounded Knee*. Cambridge: Cambridge University Press, 2004.

Ostler, Jeffrey. *Surviving Genocide: Native Nations and the United States from the American Revolution to Bleeding Kansas*. New Haven, CT: Yale University Press, 2019.

Ostler, Jeffrey, and Nancy Shoemaker. "Settler Colonialism in Early American History: An Introduction." *William and Mary Quarterly*, 3rd ser., 76 (July 2019): 362–368.

Overdyke, W. Darrell, ed. "A Southern Family on the Missouri Frontier: Letters from Independence, 1843–1855." *Journal of Southern History* 17 (May 1951): 216–237.

Owens, Robert M. "Jeffersonian Benevolence on the Ground: The Indian Land Cession Treaties of William Henry Harrison." *Journal of the Early Republic* 22 (Fall 2002): 405–435.

Painter, Nell I. *Exodusters: Black Migration to Kansas after Reconstruction*. New York: W. W. Norton, 1977.

Parillo, Nicholas R. *Against the Profit Motive: The Salary Revolution in American Government*. New Haven, CT: Yale University Press, 2013.

Pasley, Jeff, and John Craig Hammond, eds. *A Fire Bell in the Past: The Missouri Crisis at 200*, Vol. 1, *Western Slavery, National Impasse*. Columbia: University of Missouri Press, 2021.

Paul, R. Eli. *Blue Water Creek and the First Sioux War, 1854–1856*. Norman: University of Oklahoma Press, 2004.

Pearl, Matthew. *The Taking of Jemima Boone: Colonial Settlers, Tribal Nations, and the Kidnap That Shaped America*. New York: HarperCollins, 2021.

Pinker, Steven. *The Better Angels of Our Nature: Why Violence Has Declined*. New York: Penguin, 2011.

Pinker, Steven. *Enlightenment Now: The Case for Reason, Science, and Humanism*. New York: Penguin, 2018.

Prucha, Francis Paul. *Peace and Friendship: Indian Peace Medals in American History*. Madison: State Historical Society of Wisconsin, 1971.

Purdue, Theda, and Michael D. Green. *The Cherokee Nation and the Trail of Tears*. New York: Viking Penguin, 2007.

Ranck, George W., ed. *Boonesborough: Its Founding, Pioneer Struggles, Indian Experiences, Transylvania Days, and Revolutionary Annals*. London: Forgotten Books, 2018.

Reed, Eric Melvin. "Homicide on the Nebraska Panhandle Frontier, 1867–1901." *Western Historical Quarterly* 50 (Summer 2019): 137–160.

Richards, Thomas, Jr. *Breakaway Americas: Contested Sovereignty and Contingent Destiny in the Era of U.S. Expansion*. Baltimore: Johns Hopkins University Press, 2019.

Riley, Glenda. *Women and Indians on the Frontier, 1825–1915*. Albuquerque: University of New Mexico Press, 1984.

Robertson, R. J., Jr. "The Mormon Experience in Missouri, 1830–1839." *Missouri Historical Review* 68 (1973–1974): 394–415.

Rogers, Brent M. *Unpopular Sovereignty: Mormons and the Federal Management of Early Utah Territory*. Lincoln: University of Nebraska Press, 2017.

Rohrbough, Malcolm J. *Days of Gold: The California Gold Rush and the American Nation*. Berkeley: University of California Press, 1997.

Rollings, Willard H. *The Osage: An Ethnohistorical Study of Hegemony on the Prairie-Plains*. Columbia: University of Missouri Press, 1992.

Romero, Frances. "The Far Horizons." *Time*. January 25, 2011. http://entertainm ent.time.com/2011/01/26/top-10-historically-misleading-films/slide/the-far-horizons-1955/.

Ronda, James. *Finding the West: Explorations with Lewis and Clark*. Albuquerque: University of New Mexico Press, 2001.

Ronda, James. *Lewis and Clark among the Indians*. Lincoln: University of Nebraska Press, 1984.

Ronda, James, ed. *Voyages of Discovery: Essays on the Lewis and Clark Expedition*. Helena: Montana Historical Society Press, 1998.

Roth, Randolph, Michael D. Maltz, and Douglas L. Eckberg. "Homicide Rates in the Old West." *Western Historical Quarterly* 42 (Summer 2011): 173–195.

Sachs, Honor. *Home Rule: Households, Manhood, and National Expansion on the Eighteenth-Century Kentucky Frontier*. New Haven, CT: Yale University Press, 2015.

Sandoz, Mari. *Cheyenne Autumn*. 1953. Reprint, Lincoln: Bison Books, 1992.

Saranillo, Dean Itsuji. *Unsustainable Empire: Alternative Histories of Hawai'i Statehood*. Durham, NC: Duke University Press, 2018.

Saunt, Claudio. *Unworthy Republic: The Dispossession of Native Americans and the Road to Indian Territory*. New York: W. W. Norton, 2020.

Saunt, Claudio. *West of the Revolution: An Uncommon History of 1776*. New York: W. W. Norton, 2014.

Scharff, Virginia. *Twenty Thousand Roads: Women, Movement, and the West*. Berkeley: University of California Press, 2003.

Schiesel, Seth. "Way Down Deep in the Wild, Wild West." *New York Times*, November 23, 2010. https://www.nytimes.com/2010/05/17/arts/television/17d ead.html?searchResultPosition=5.

Schlissel, Lillian. *Women's Diaries of the Westward Journey*. New York: Schocken Books, 1987.

Schrag, Paul, and Xaviant Haze. *The Suppressed History of America: The Murder of Meriwether Lewis and the Mysterious Discoveries of the Lewis and Clark Expedition*. Rochester, VT: Bear, 2011.

Schroeder, Walter A. *Opening the Ozarks: A Historical Geography of Missouri's Ste. Genevieve District, 1760–1830*. Columbia: University of Missouri Press, 2002.

Scott, Amy, ed. *The Art of the West: Selected Works from the Autry Museum.* Norman: University of Oklahoma Press, 2018.

Sheehan, Bernard. *Seeds of Extinction: Jeffersonian Philanthropy and the American Indian.* Chapel Hill: University of North Carolina Press, 1973.

Shillingberg, William B. *Dodge City: The Early Years, 1872–1886.* Norman: University of Oklahoma Press, 2009.

Shortridge, James R. "The Expansion of the Settlement Frontier in Missouri." *Missouri Historical Review* 75 (October 1980): 82–86.

Slatta, Richard W. *Cowboys of the Americas.* New Haven, CT: Yale University Press, 1990.

Slaughter, Thomas P. *Exploring Lewis and Clark: Reflections on Men and Wilderness.* New York: Random House, 2003.

Sleeper-Smith, Susan. *Indigenous Prosperity and American Conquest: Indian Women of the Ohio River Valley, 1690–1792.* Chapel Hill: University of North Carolina Press, 2018.

Slotkin, Richard. *The Fatal Environment: The Myth of the Frontier in the Age of Industrialization, 1800–1890.* New York: Macmillan, 1985.

Slotkin, Richard. *Gunfighter Nation: The Myth of the Frontier in Twentieth-Century America.* New York: Macmillan, 1992.

Slotkin, Richard. *Regeneration through Violence: The Mythology of the American Frontier, 1600–1860.* Middletown, CT: Wesleyan University Press, 1973.

Smalley, Andrea L. *Wild by Nature: North American Animals Confront Colonization.* Baltimore: Johns Hopkins University Press, 2017.

Smith, Henry Nash. "Rain Follows the Plow." *Huntington Library Quarterly* 1 (February 1947): 169–193.

Smith, Henry Nash. *Virgin Land: The American West as Symbol and Myth.* Cambridge, MA: Harvard University Press, 1950.

Smith, Martin Cruz. *The Indians Won.* New York: Belmont Books, 1982.

Smith, Sherry L. "Reconciliation and Restitution in the American West." *Western Historical Quarterly* 41 (Spring 2010): 4–25.

Snider, Christina. "Many Removals: Re-evaluating the Arc of Indian Dispossession." *Journal of the Early Republic* 41 (Winter 2021): 623–650.

Snider, Mike. "Critics, Players Go Wild for West in Redemption." *USA Today*, May 26, 2010, 5d.

Spencer, Otis B. "A Sketch of the Boone-Bent Families." *Westport Historical Quarterly* 8 (March 1973): 99–105.

Spero, Patrick. *Frontier Country: The Politics of War in Early Pennsylvania.* Philadelphia: University of Pennsylvania Press, 2016.

Spring, Dawn. "Gaming History: Computer and Video Games as Historical Scholarship." *Rethinking History* 19 (2015): 207–221.

Steffen, Jerome O. *William Clark: Jeffersonian Man on The Frontier.* Norman: University of Oklahoma Press, 1977.

Stegner, Wallace. "Who Are the Westerners?" *American Heritage* 38 (December 1987): 34–41. https://www.americanheritage.com/who-are-westerners.

Steward, Dick. "'With the Scepter of a Tyrant': John Smith T and the Mineral Wars." *Gateway Heritage* 14 (Fall 1993): 24–37.

Strate, David Kay. *Sentinel to the Cimarron: The Frontier Experience of Fort Dodge, Kansas*. Dodge City, KS: Cultural Arts & Heritage Center, 1970.

Strickland, Rex W., ed. "The Recollections of W. S. Glenn, Buffalo Hunter." *Panhandle-Plains Historical Review* 22 (1949): 15–64.

Stroud, Patricia Tyson. *Bitterroot: The Life and Death of Meriwether Lewis*. Philadelphia: University of Pennsylvania Press, 2018.

Sturtevant, William C., and Bruce Trigger, eds. *Handbook of North American Indians: Northeast*, Vol. 15. Washington, DC: Smithsonian Institution, 1978.

Suderman, Peter. "Red Dead Redemption 2 Is True Art." *New York Times*, November 23, 2018. https://www.nytimes.com/2018/11/23/opinion/sunday/red-dead-redemption-2-fallout-76-video-games.html.

Sugden, John. *Tecumseh: A Life*. New York: Henry Holt, 2013.

Swagerty, William R. *The Indianization of Lewis and Clark*. 2 vols. Norman: University of Oklahoma Press, 2012.

Tanner, Helen H. *Atlas of Great Lakes Indian History*. Chicago: University of Chicago Press, 1987.

Tate, Michael L. *The Frontier Army in the Settlement of the West*. Norman: University of Oklahoma Press, 1999.

Tate, Michael L. *Indians and Emigrants: Encounters on the Overland Trails*. Norman: University of Oklahoma Press, 2006.

Taylor, Alan. *The Civil War of 1812: American Citizens, British Subjects, Irish Rebels, & Indian Allies*. New York: Random House, 2010.

Taylor, Alan, ed. *Lewis and Clark: Journey to Another America*. St. Louis: Missouri Historical Society Press, 2003.

Taylor, Quintard. *In Search of the Racial Frontier: African Americans in the American West, 1528–1990*. New York: W. W. Norton, 1998.

Thompson, Edward P. *The Poverty of Theory and Other Essays*. London: Merlin Press, 1978.

Thorne, Tanis C. *The Many Hands of My Relations: French and Indians on the Lower Missouri*. Columbia: University of Missouri Press, 1996.

Tyler, Ron, et al., eds., *The New Handbook of Texas*. 6 vols. Austin: Texas State Historical Association, 1966.

Udall, Stewart L., Robert R. Dykstra, Michael A. Bellesiles, Paula Mitchell Marks, and Gregory H. Nobles. "How the West Got Wild: American Media and Frontier Violence: A Roundtable." *Western Historical Quarterly* 31 (Autumn 2000): 277–295.

Unruh, John D., Jr. *The Plains Across: The Overland Emigrants and the Trans-Mississippi West, 1840–1860*. Urbana: University of Illinois Press, 1979.

Usner, Daniel H., Jr. "An American Indian Gateway: Some Thoughts on the Migration and Settlement of Eastern Indians around Early St. Louis." *Gateway Heritage* 11 (Winter 1990–1991): 42–51.

Utley, Robert M. *Frontier Regulars: The United States Army and the Indian, 1866–1891*. New York: Macmillan, 1973.

Utley, Robert M. *Frontiersmen in Blue: The United States Army and the Indian, 1848–1865*. New York: Macmillan, 1967.

Utley, Robert M. *High Noon in Lincoln: Violence on the Western Frontier*. Albuquerque: University of New Mexico Press, 1987.

Utley, Robert M. *The Indian Frontier of the American West, 1846–1890*. Albuquerque: University of New Mexico Press, 1984.

Valencius, Conevery Bolton. *The Health of the Country: How American Settlers Understood Themselves and Their Land*. New York: Basic Books, 2002.

Veracini, Lorenzo. *Settler Colonialism: A Theoretical Overview*. London: Palgrave Macmillan, 2010.

Veracini, Lorenzo. *The Settler Colonial Present*. London: Palgrave Macmillan, 2015.

Vestal, Stanley. *Queen of Cowtowns, Dodge City: "The Wickedest Little City in America," 1872–1886*. New York: Harper & Brothers, 1952.

Walker, Don D. *Clio's Cowboys: Studies in the Historiography of the Cattle Trade*. Lincoln: University of Nebraska Press, 1981.

Walker, Ronald W., Richard E. Turley Jr., and Glenn M. Leonard. *Massacre at Mountain Meadows: An American Tragedy*. New York: Oxford University Press, 2008.

Wallace, Anthony F. C. *Jefferson and the Indians: The Tragic Fate of the First Americans*. Cambridge, MA: Harvard University Press, 1999.

Ward, Matthew C. "Redeeming the Captives: Pennsylvania Captives among the Ohio Indians, 1755–1765." *Pennsylvania Magazine of History and Biography* 125 (July 2001): 161–189.

Warren, Stephen. *The Shawnees and Their Neighbors, 1795–1870*. Urbana: University of Illinois Press, 2005.

Warren, Stephen. *Worlds the Shawnees Made: Migration and Violence in Early America*. Chapel Hill: University of North Carolina Press, 2014.

Watlington, Patricia. "Discontent in Frontier Kentucky." *Register of the Kentucky Historical Society* 65 (April 1967): 77–93.

Watlington, Patricia. *The Partisan Spirit: Kentucky Politics, 1779–1792*. Chapel Hill: University of North Carolina Press, 2012.

Webb, Walter Prescott. *The Great Plains*. Boston: Ginn, 1931.

Wells, Eugene T. "The Growth of Independence, Missouri 1827–1850." *Bulletin of the Missouri Historical Society* 16 (October 1959): 33–46.

West, Elliott. *The Contested Plains: Indians, Goldseekers, and the Rush to Colorado*. Lawrence: University Press of Kansas, 1998.

White, Richard. *The Middle Ground: Indians, Empires, and Republics in the Great Lakes Region, 1650–1815*. New York: Cambridge University Press, 1991.

White, Richard. *Railroaded: The Transcontinentals and the Making of Modern America*. New York: W. W. Norton, 2011.

White, Richard. *The Republic for Which It Stands: The United States during Reconstruction and the Gilded Age, 1865–1896*. New York: Oxford University Press, 2017.

Wilkie, Duncan C. *Archaeological Reconnaissance Survey of the Apple Creek Drainage: Perry and Cape Girardeau Counties, Missouri*. Report prepared for the Historic Preservation Program, Division of Parks and Historic Preservation,

Missouri Department of Natural Resources. Jefferson City: Missouri Department of Natural Resources, 1984.

Witgen, Michael. *Seeing Red: Indigenous Land, American Expansion, and the Political Economy of Plunder in North America.* Chapel Hill: University of North Carolina Press, 2021.

Wokeck, Mariann. *Trade in Strangers: The Beginnings of Mass Migration to North America.* University Park: Pennsylvania State University Press, 1999.

Wolfe, Patrick. "Land, Labor, and Difference: Elementary Structures of Race." *American Historical Review* 106 (June 2001): 866–905.

Wolfe, Patrick. "Settler Colonialism and the Elimination of the Native." *Journal of Genocide Studies* 8 (December 2006): 387–409.

Wong, Kevin. "The Forgotten History of 'The Oregon Trail,' as Told by Its Creators." *Motherboard*, February 15, 2017. https://motherboard.vice.com/en_us/article/qkx8vw/the-forgotten-history-of-the-oregon-trail-as-told-by-its-creators.

Worcester, Donald. *The Chisholm Trail: High Road of the Cattle Kingdom.* Lincoln: University of Nebraska Press, 1980.

Yarwood, Jack. "The Making of 'The Oregon Trail': An interview with Don Yarwitsch." *Paste*, October 22, 2015. https://www.pastemagazine.com/articles/2015/10/the-making-of-the-oregon-trail-an-interview-with-d.html.

INDEX

———◦◦◦———

For the benefit of digital users, indexed terms that span two pages (e.g., 52–53) may, on occasion, appear on only one of those pages.

Figures are indicated by *f* following the page number

Lewis and, 161–62, 207
Teton Sioux, 80–81
westward migration, encounters
    with, 158, 159–60
slavery
    Boone and, 39
    Clark and, 126–27
    Jefferson and, 126–27
    Missouri (Territory), in, 126–27
    removal of Indians, effect of, 181
    Upper Louisiana Territory, in, 66
smallpox, 158
Smith, John, 6–7
Smith, Joseph, 141–42, 149–50
Smith, Martin Cruz, 4–5
Smith, William, 33–35
Snake Indians, 89
Society of Friends, 13–14, 33
Southern Cheyenne Indians, 173
Spain
    Apple Creek, land grants in, 48–49
    cession of Louisiana Territory to
        France, 62–63
    Cherokee and, 47, 49
    Delaware and, 47–49
    land claims in Upper Louisiana
        Territory, 110–11
    Louisiana Purchase, reaction to, 63
    Osage and, 45–47, 50–52, 61, 70
    Shawnee and, 47–49
    Upper Louisiana Territory, Spanish
        in, 44–47, 61, 69, 70–71
    views of American settlement of
        Upper Louisiana Territory, 50,
        52–53, 54
squatters, 118, 123–24, 126, 128–
    29, 130–31
Stegner, Wallace, 258n.40
Stewart, John, 15–16
Stoddard, Amos, 65, 66, 68, 71–
    72, 109–10

Tabor, John, 133
Tarantino, Quentin, 5
Taylor, William, 189, 190

Tecumseh Motel (Xenia), 9–10, 41–42
Tecumseh (Shawnee), 9, 122, 215n.2
terminology, xiii–xiv
    American, use of term, xiv
    frontier, use of term, xiii–xiv
    translations, xiv
Teton Sioux Indians, 80–81
Thawakila clan (Shawnee), 11, 25, 37
Thompson, E.P., 5
Tombstone (Arizona), 195–96, 260n.63
tourism, 168–69, 200–1
Trabue, Daniel, 29–30
trade with Indians
    Corps of Discovery and, 151–52
    Lewis on, 173–74
    westward migration and, 151–53
Trading for Moccasins, Chimney Rock,
    Oregon Trail, 1853 (painting), 152f
Trail of Tears, 134
Trail of Tears State Park (Missouri),
    43–44, 134
Transylvania Company, 16, 18–19, 21–
    22, 32, 39–40
Treaty of Greenville (1795), 38
Treaty of San Ildefonso (1800), 62
Treaty of San Lorenzo (1795), 52
Trimble, Allen, 133
Trudeau, Zenon, 50–51, 52, 53, 54–
    55, 59
Truth and Reconciliation
    Commissions, 207
Turner, Frederick Jackson, xiii–xiv
"Twilight Zone" (television show), 6
Twiss, Thomas, 167
Tyler, John, 159

Uchronia, 212n.6
Ulloa, Antonio de, 46–47
Uniform Crime Reports, 197–98
United States Army
    bison hunting and, 177
    Civil War and, 166
    Mormons and, 163–64, 165
    postbellum West, in, 173–74, 175
    Sioux, animus toward, 173–74